CASE CLOSED

VOLUME 54

Gosho Aoyama

Case Briefing:

Subject:
Occupation:
Special Skills:
Equipment:

Jimmy Kudo, a.k.a. Conan Edogawa
High School Student/Detective
Analytical thinking and deductive reasoning, Soccer
Bow Tie Voice Transmitter, Super Sneakers,
Homing Glasses, Stretchy Suspenders

The subject is hot on the trail of a pair of suspicious men in black when he is attacked from behind and administered a strange substance which physically transforms him into a first grader. When the subject confides in the eccentric inventor Dr. Agasa, they decide to keep the subject's true identity a secret for the safety of everyone around him. Assuming the new identity of first-grader Conan Edogawa, the subject continues to assist the police force on their most baffling cases. The only problem is that most crime-solving professionals won't take a little kid's advice!

Table of Contents

CONFIDEN

CASE CLOSED

Volume 54
Shonen Sunday Edition

Story and Art by GOSHO AOYAMA

MEITANTEI CONAN Vol. 54
by Gosho AOYAMA
© 1994 Gosho AOYAMA
All rights reserved.
Original Japanese edition published by SHOGAKUKAN.
English translation rights in the United States of America, Canada,
the United Kingdom and Ireland arranged with SHOGAKUKAN.

Translation
Tetsuichiro Miyaki

Touch-up & Lettering
Freeman Wong

Cover & Graphic Design
Andrea Rice

Editor
Shaenon K. Garrity

Printed in the U.S.A.

Published by VIZ Media, LLC
P.O. Box 77010
San Francisco, CA 94107

10 9 8 7 6 5 4 3 2 1
First printing, April 2015

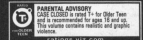

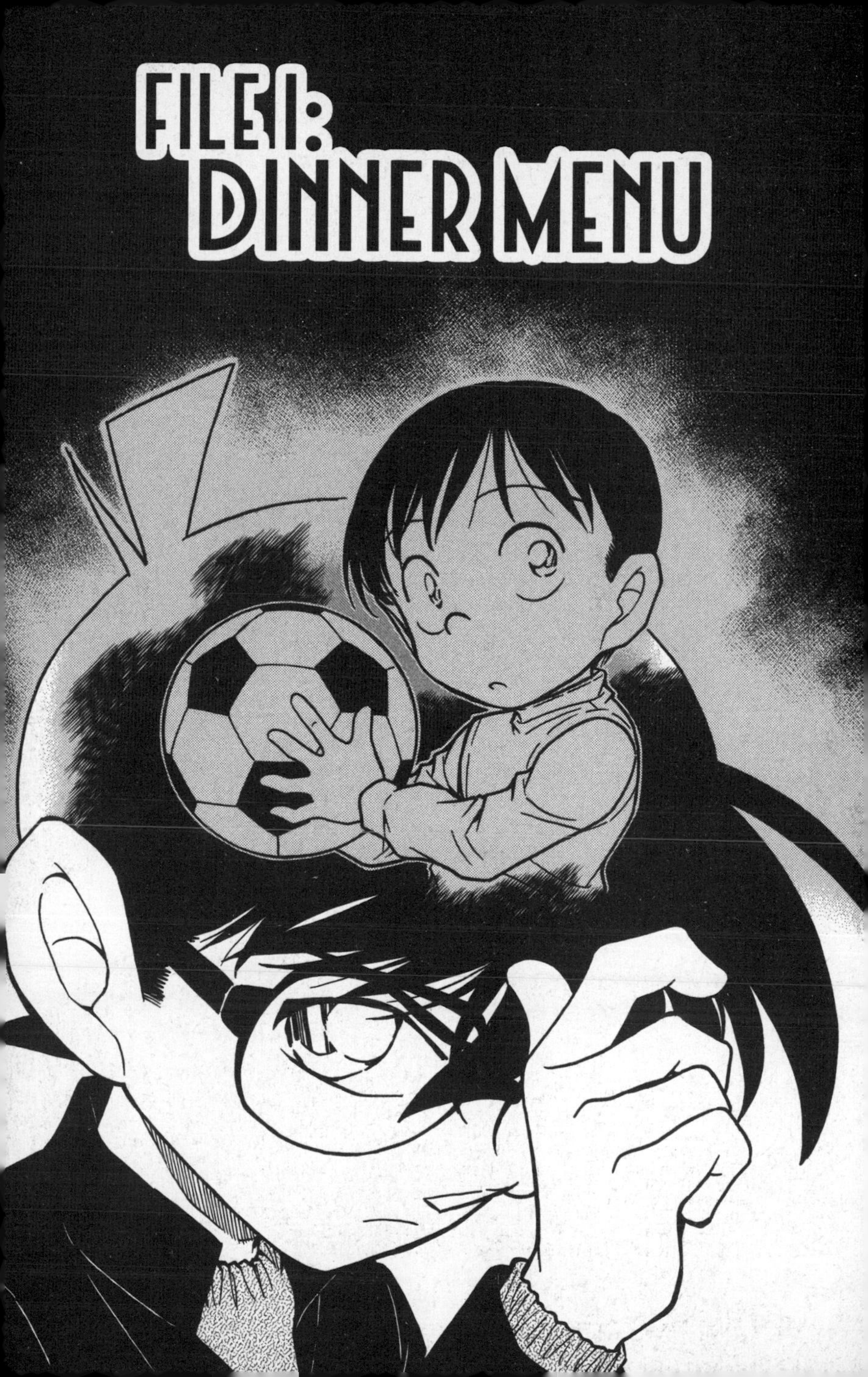
FILE 1:
DINNER MENU

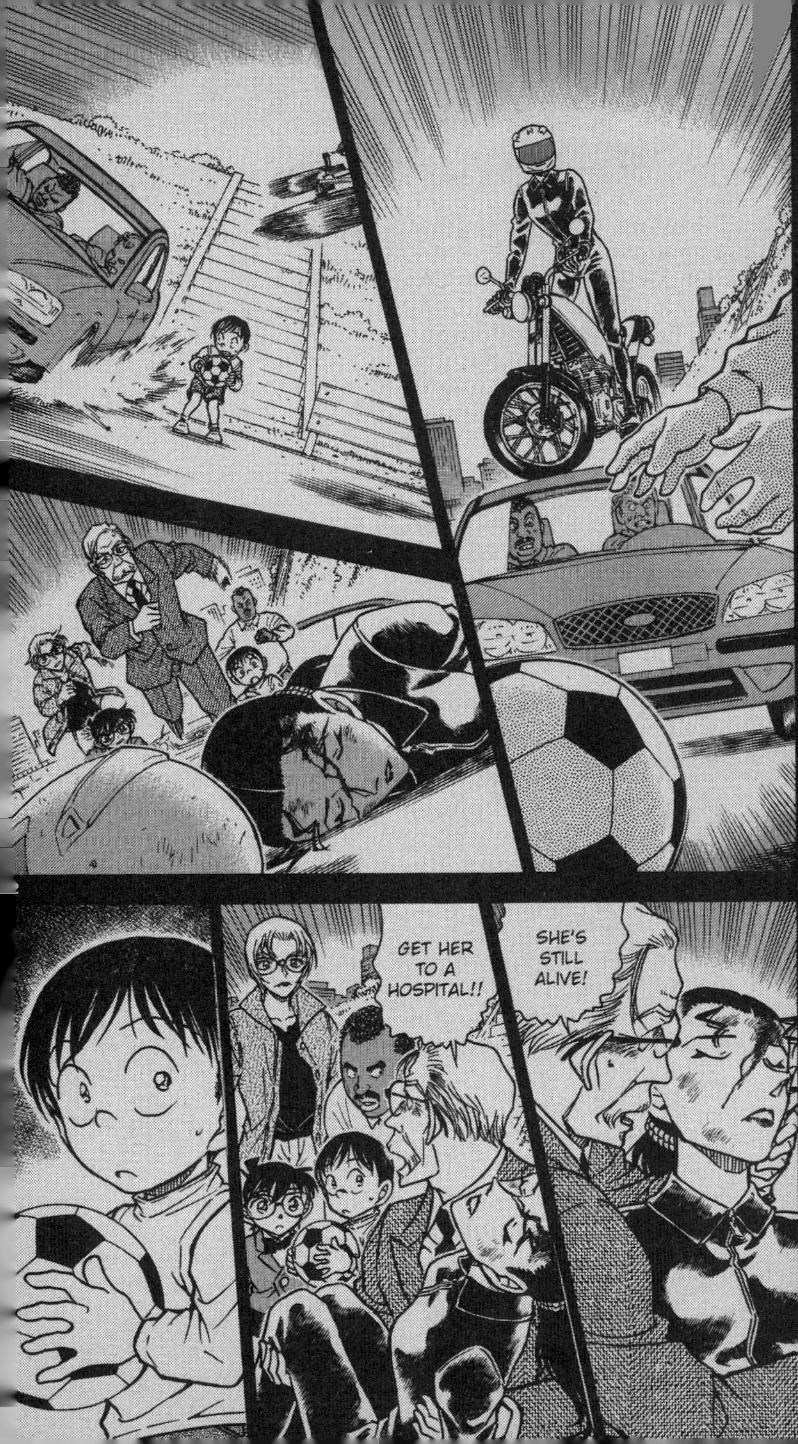
SHE'S STILL ALIVE!
GET HER TO A HOSPITAL!!

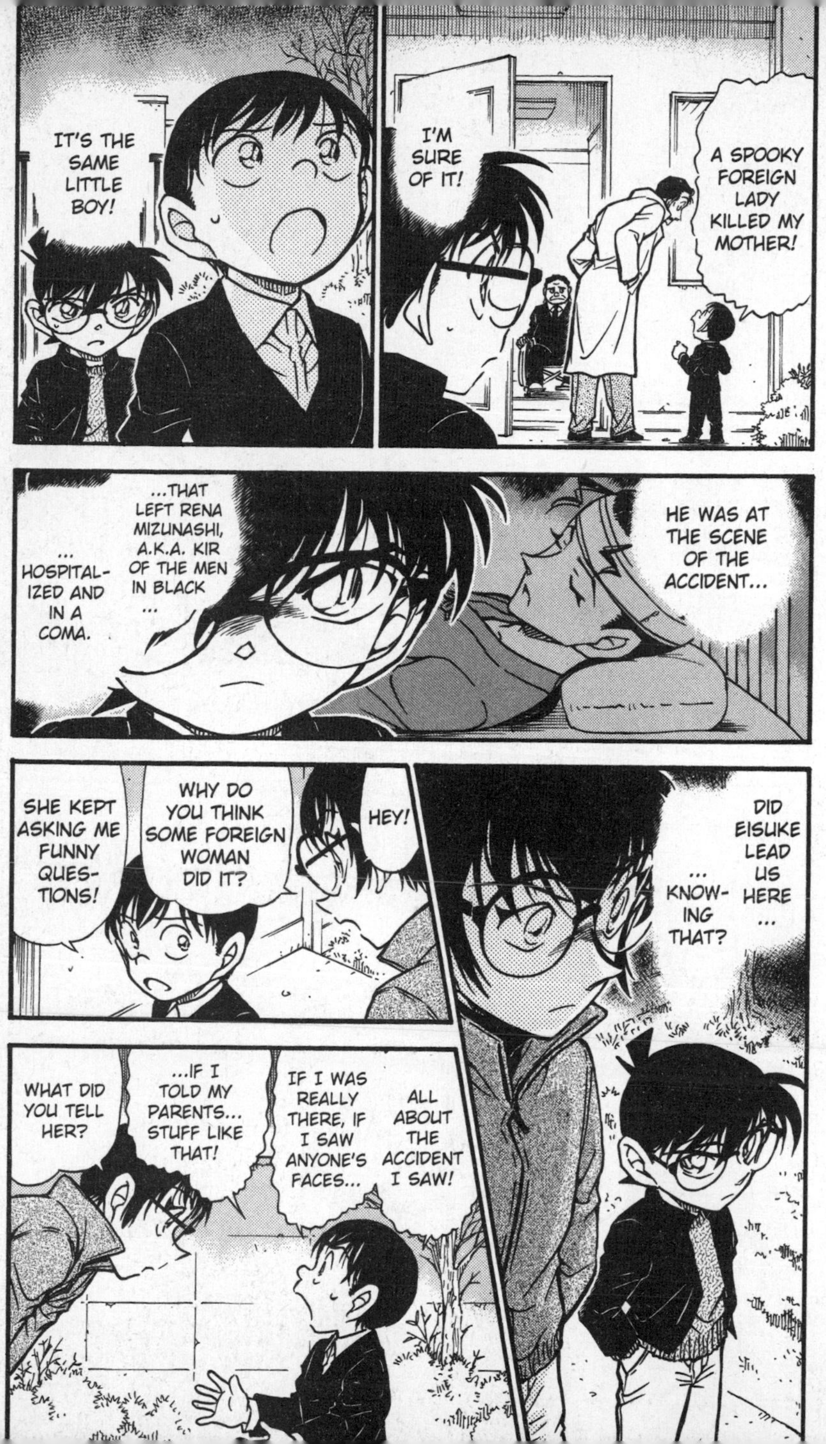
A SPOOKY FOREIGN LADY KILLED MY MOTHER!
I'M SURE OF IT!
IT'S THE SAME LITTLE BOY!
HE WAS AT THE SCENE OF THE ACCIDENT...
...THAT LEFT RENA MIZUNASHI, A.K.A. KIR OF THE MEN IN BLACK ...
... HOSPITAL-IZED AND IN A COMA.
DID EISUKE LEAD US HERE ...
... KNOW-ING THAT?
HEY!
WHY DO YOU THINK SOME FOREIGN WOMAN DID IT?
SHE KEPT ASKING ME FUNNY QUES-TIONS!
ALL ABOUT THE ACCIDENT I SAW!
IF I WAS REALLY THERE, IF I SAW ANYONE'S FACES...
...IF I TOLD MY PARENTS... STUFF LIKE THAT!
WHAT DID YOU TELL HER?

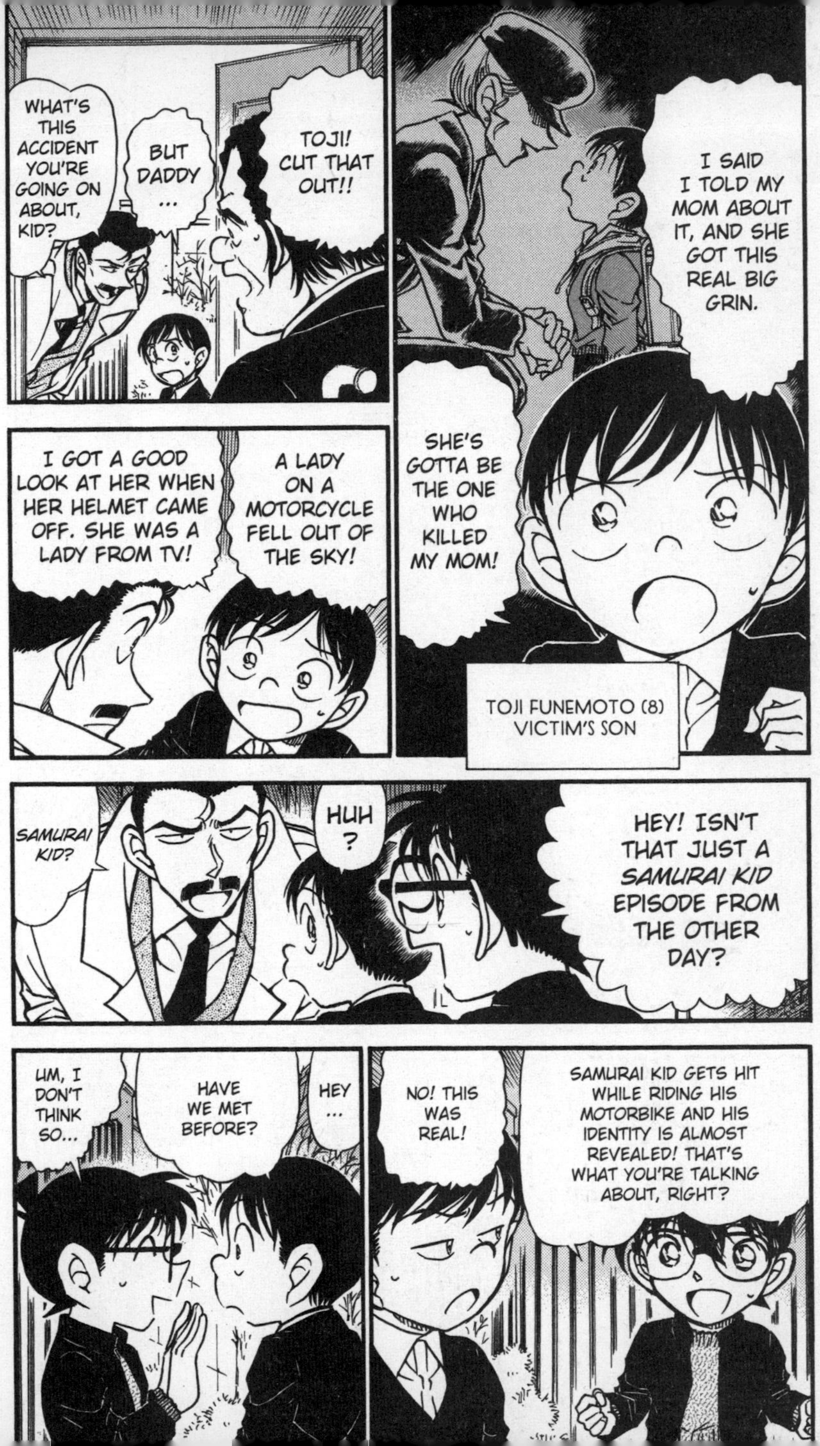
I SAID I TOLD MY MOM ABOUT IT, AND SHE GOT THIS REAL BIG GRIN.
SHE'S GOTTA BE THE ONE WHO KILLED MY MOM!
TOJI FUNEMOTO (8) VICTIM'S SON
TOJI! CUT THAT OUT!!
BUT DADDY...
WHAT'S THIS ACCIDENT YOU'RE GOING ON ABOUT, KID?
A LADY ON A MOTORCYCLE FELL OUT OF THE SKY!
I GOT A GOOD LOOK AT HER WHEN HER HELMET CAME OFF. SHE WAS A LADY FROM TV!
HEY! ISN'T THAT JUST A *SAMURAI KID* EPISODE FROM THE OTHER DAY?
HUH?
SAMURAI KID?
SAMURAI KID GETS HIT WHILE RIDING HIS MOTORBIKE AND HIS IDENTITY IS ALMOST REVEALED! THAT'S WHAT YOU'RE TALKING ABOUT, RIGHT?
NO! THIS WAS REAL!
HEY...
HAVE WE MET BEFORE?
UM, I DON'T THINK SO...

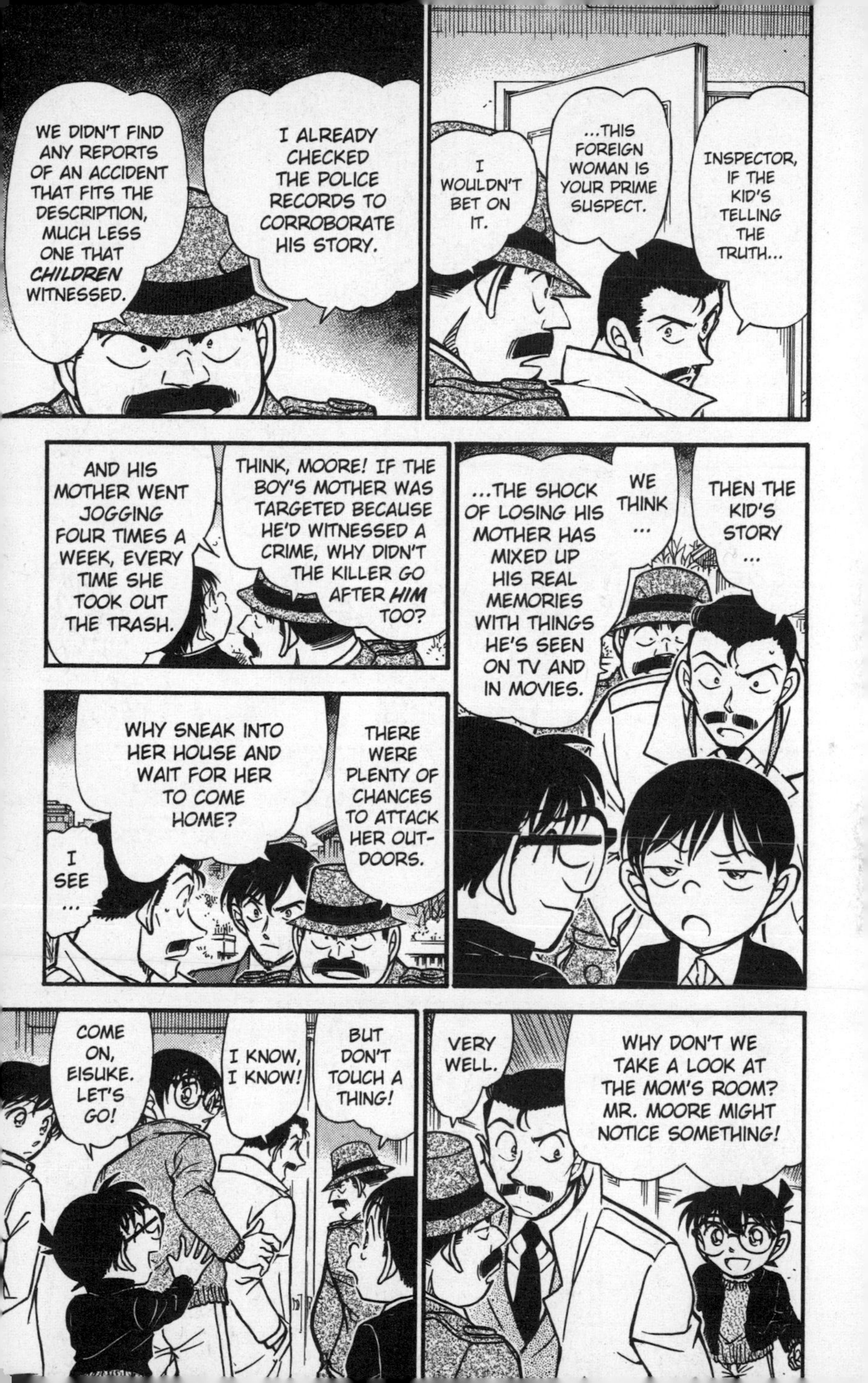
INSPECTOR, IF THE KID'S TELLING THE TRUTH...
...THIS FOREIGN WOMAN IS YOUR PRIME SUSPECT.
I WOULDN'T BET ON IT.
I ALREADY CHECKED THE POLICE RECORDS TO CORROBORATE HIS STORY.
WE DIDN'T FIND ANY REPORTS OF AN ACCIDENT THAT FITS THE DESCRIPTION, MUCH LESS ONE THAT *CHILDREN* WITNESSED.
THEN THE KID'S STORY ...
WE THINK ...
...THE SHOCK OF LOSING HIS MOTHER HAS MIXED UP HIS REAL MEMORIES WITH THINGS HE'S SEEN ON TV AND IN MOVIES.
THINK, MOORE! IF THE BOY'S MOTHER WAS TARGETED BECAUSE HE'D WITNESSED A CRIME, WHY DIDN'T THE KILLER GO AFTER *HIM* TOO?
AND HIS MOTHER WENT JOGGING FOUR TIMES A WEEK, EVERY TIME SHE TOOK OUT THE TRASH.
THERE WERE PLENTY OF CHANCES TO ATTACK HER OUT-DOORS.
WHY SNEAK INTO HER HOUSE AND WAIT FOR HER TO COME HOME?
I SEE ...
WHY DON'T WE TAKE A LOOK AT THE MOM'S ROOM? MR. MOORE MIGHT NOTICE SOMETHING!
VERY WELL.
BUT DON'T TOUCH A THING!
I KNOW, I KNOW!
COME ON, EISUKE. LET'S GO!

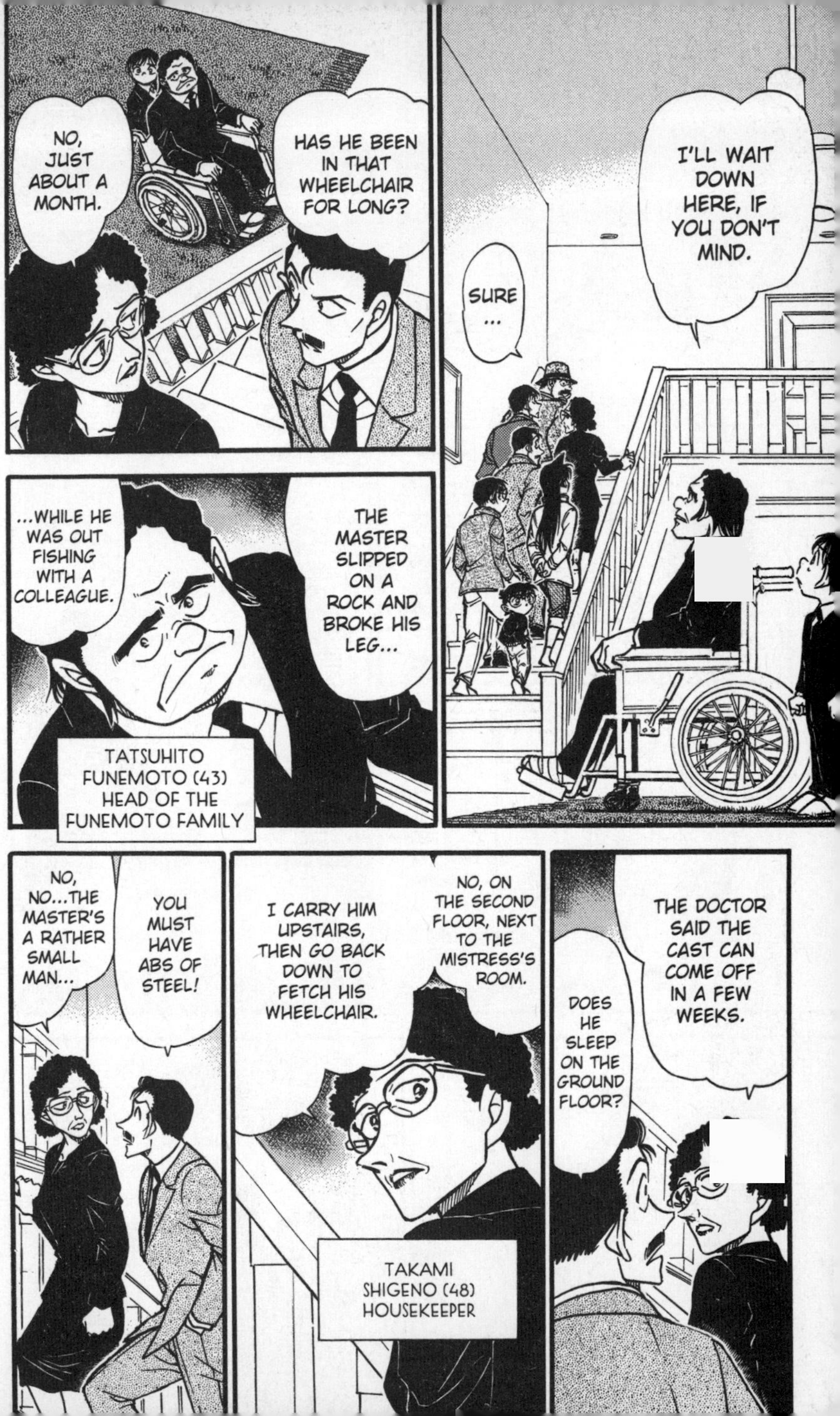
I'LL WAIT DOWN HERE, IF YOU DON'T MIND.
SURE...
HAS HE BEEN IN THAT WHEELCHAIR FOR LONG?
NO, JUST ABOUT A MONTH.
THE MASTER SLIPPED ON A ROCK AND BROKE HIS LEG...
...WHILE HE WAS OUT FISHING WITH A COLLEAGUE.
TATSUHITO FUNEMOTO (43) HEAD OF THE FUNEMOTO FAMILY
THE DOCTOR SAID THE CAST CAN COME OFF IN A FEW WEEKS.
DOES HE SLEEP ON THE GROUND FLOOR?
NO, ON THE SECOND FLOOR, NEXT TO THE MISTRESS'S ROOM.
I CARRY HIM UPSTAIRS, THEN GO BACK DOWN TO FETCH HIS WHEELCHAIR.
TAKAMI SHIGENO (48) HOUSEKEEPER
YOU MUST HAVE ABS OF STEEL!
NO, NO...THE MASTER'S A RATHER SMALL MAN...

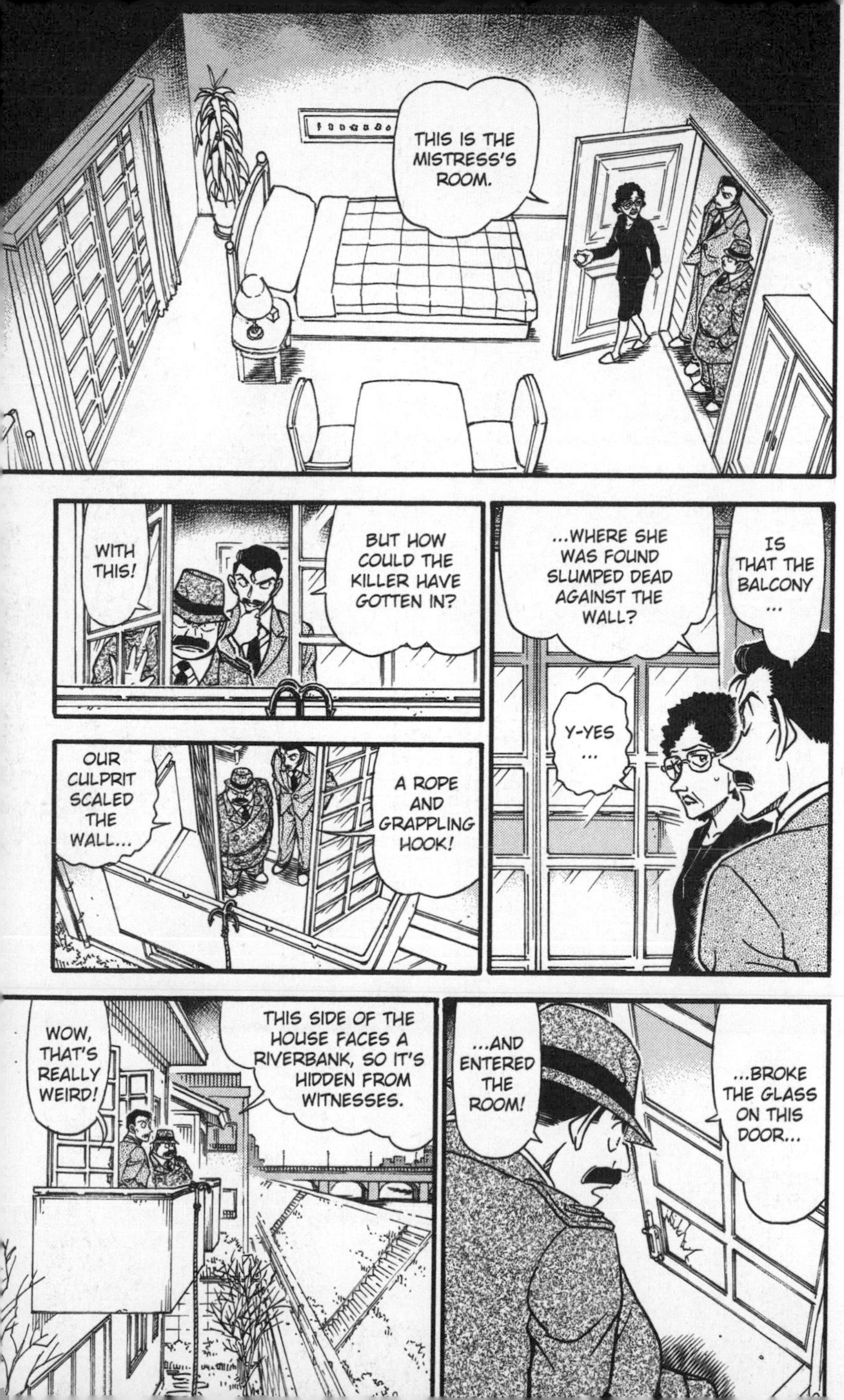
THIS IS THE MISTRESS'S ROOM.
IS THAT THE BALCONY ...
...WHERE SHE WAS FOUND SLUMPED DEAD AGAINST THE WALL?
Y-YES ...
BUT HOW COULD THE KILLER HAVE GOTTEN IN?
WITH THIS!
A ROPE AND GRAPPLING HOOK!
OUR CULPRIT SCALED THE WALL...
...BROKE THE GLASS ON THIS DOOR...
...AND ENTERED THE ROOM!
THIS SIDE OF THE HOUSE FACES A RIVERBANK, SO IT'S HIDDEN FROM WITNESSES.
WOW, THAT'S REALLY WEIRD!

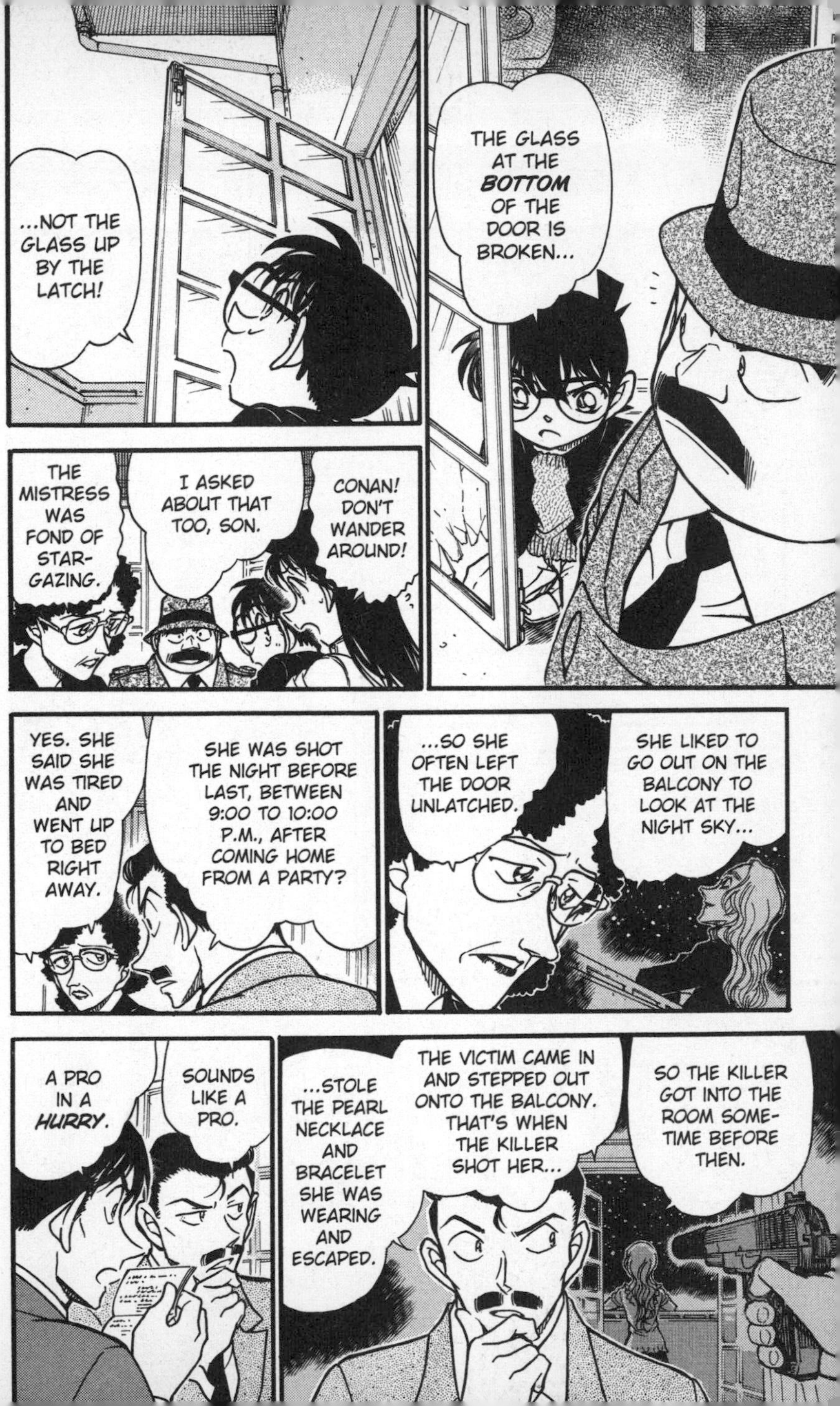
THE GLASS AT THE **BOTTOM** OF THE DOOR IS BROKEN...
...NOT THE GLASS UP BY THE LATCH!
CONAN! DON'T WANDER AROUND!
I ASKED ABOUT THAT TOO, SON.
THE MISTRESS WAS FOND OF STAR-GAZING.
SHE LIKED TO GO OUT ON THE BALCONY TO LOOK AT THE NIGHT SKY...
...SO SHE OFTEN LEFT THE DOOR UNLATCHED.
SHE WAS SHOT THE NIGHT BEFORE LAST, BETWEEN 9:00 TO 10:00 P.M., AFTER COMING HOME FROM A PARTY?
YES. SHE SAID SHE WAS TIRED AND WENT UP TO BED RIGHT AWAY.
SO THE KILLER GOT INTO THE ROOM SOME-TIME BEFORE THEN.
THE VICTIM CAME IN AND STEPPED OUT ONTO THE BALCONY. THAT'S WHEN THE KILLER SHOT HER...
...STOLE THE PEARL NECKLACE AND BRACELET SHE WAS WEARING AND ESCAPED.
SOUNDS LIKE A PRO.
A PRO IN A **HURRY**.

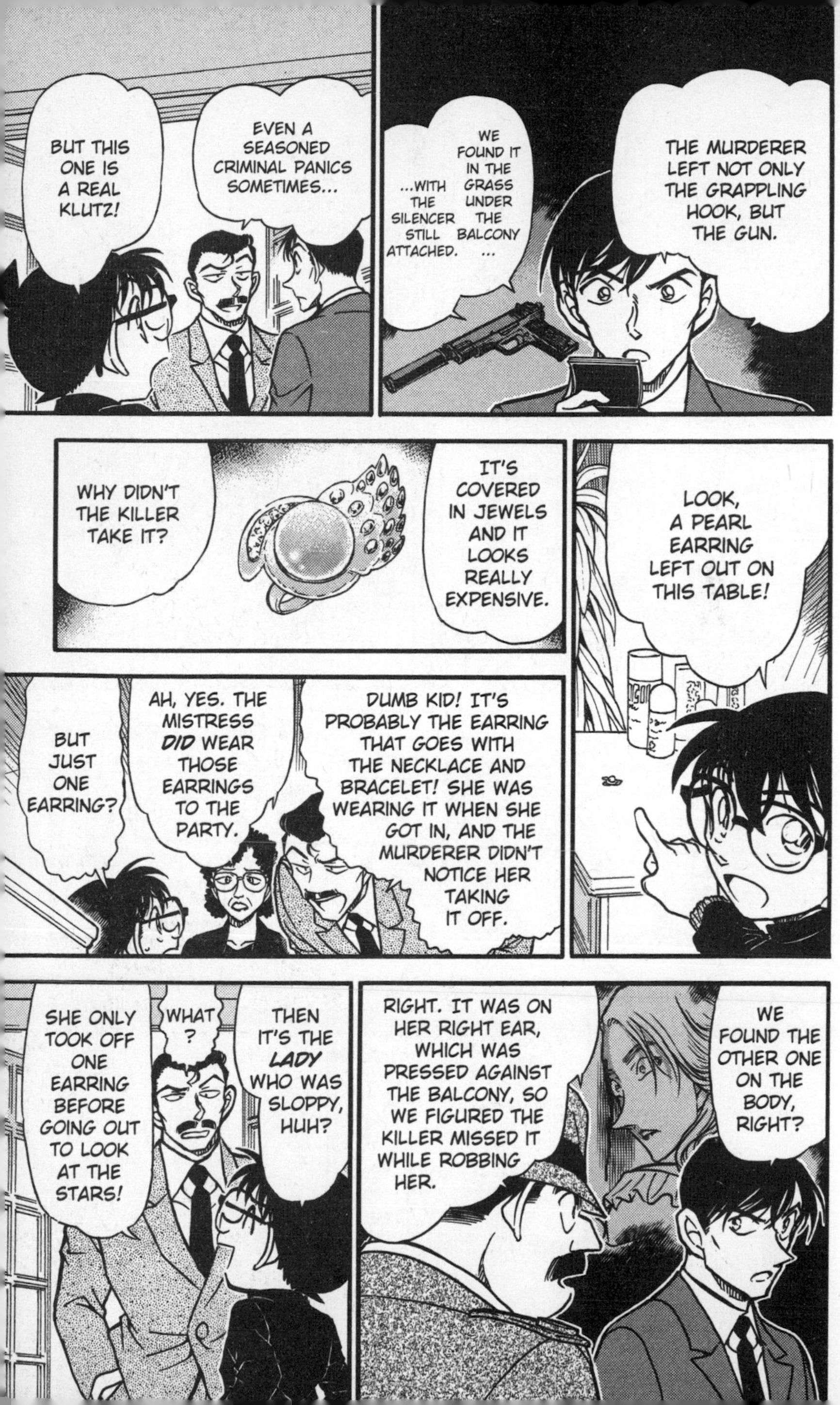
THE MURDERER LEFT NOT ONLY THE GRAPPLING HOOK, BUT THE GUN.
WE FOUND IT IN THE GRASS UNDER THE BALCONY ...
...WITH THE SILENCER STILL ATTACHED.
EVEN A SEASONED CRIMINAL PANICS SOMETIMES...
BUT THIS ONE IS A REAL KLUTZ!
LOOK, A PEARL EARRING LEFT OUT ON THIS TABLE!
IT'S COVERED IN JEWELS AND IT LOOKS REALLY EXPENSIVE.
WHY DIDN'T THE KILLER TAKE IT?
DUMB KID! IT'S PROBABLY THE EARRING THAT GOES WITH THE NECKLACE AND BRACELET! SHE WAS WEARING IT WHEN SHE GOT IN, AND THE MURDERER DIDN'T NOTICE HER TAKING IT OFF.
AH, YES. THE MISTRESS *DID* WEAR THOSE EARRINGS TO THE PARTY.
BUT JUST ONE EARRING?
WE FOUND THE OTHER ONE ON THE BODY, RIGHT?
RIGHT. IT WAS ON HER RIGHT EAR, WHICH WAS PRESSED AGAINST THE BALCONY, SO WE FIGURED THE KILLER MISSED IT WHILE ROBBING HER.
THEN IT'S THE *LADY* WHO WAS SLOPPY, HUH?
WHAT?
SHE ONLY TOOK OFF ONE EARRING BEFORE GOING OUT TO LOOK AT THE STARS!

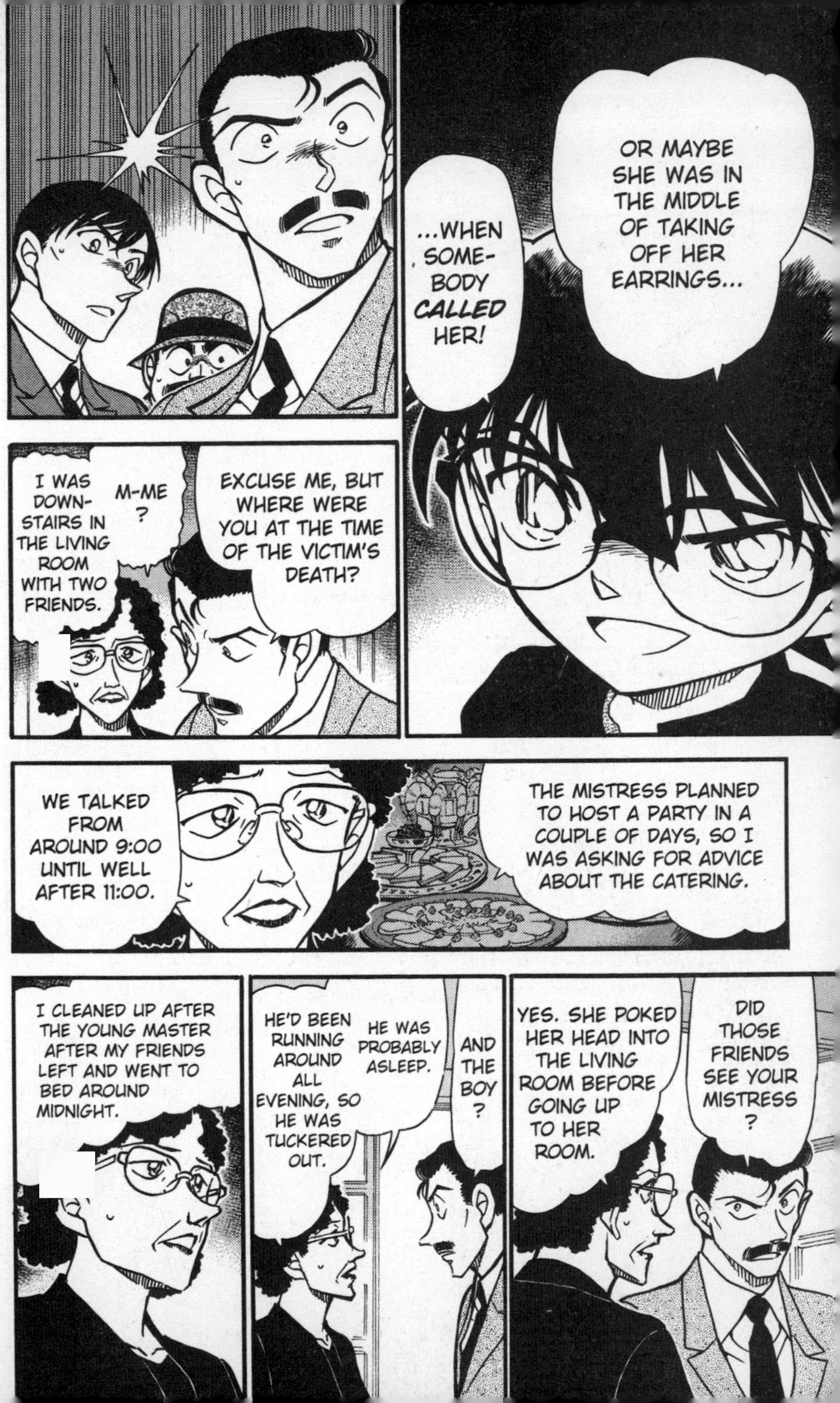
OR MAYBE SHE WAS IN THE MIDDLE OF TAKING OFF HER EARRINGS...
...WHEN SOMEBODY **CALLED** HER!
EXCUSE ME, BUT WHERE WERE YOU AT THE TIME OF THE VICTIM'S DEATH?
M-ME?
I WAS DOWNSTAIRS IN THE LIVING ROOM WITH TWO FRIENDS.
THE MISTRESS PLANNED TO HOST A PARTY IN A COUPLE OF DAYS, SO I WAS ASKING FOR ADVICE ABOUT THE CATERING.
WE TALKED FROM AROUND 9:00 UNTIL WELL AFTER 11:00.
DID THOSE FRIENDS SEE YOUR MISTRESS?
YES. SHE POKED HER HEAD INTO THE LIVING ROOM BEFORE GOING UP TO HER ROOM.
AND THE BOY?
HE WAS PROBABLY ASLEEP.
HE'D BEEN RUNNING AROUND ALL EVENING, SO HE WAS TUCKERED OUT.
I CLEANED UP AFTER THE YOUNG MASTER AFTER MY FRIENDS LEFT AND WENT TO BED AROUND MIDNIGHT.

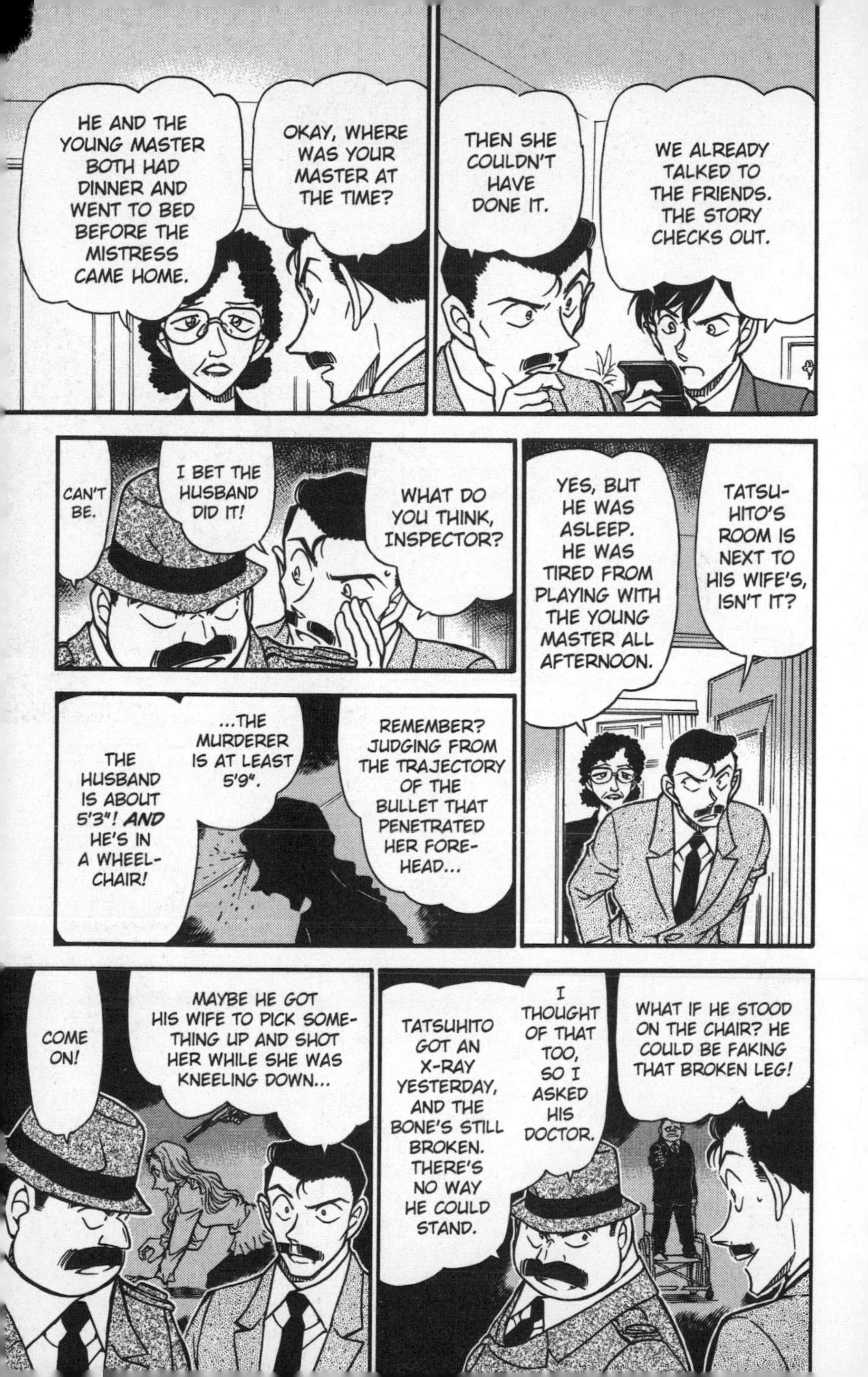
WE ALREADY TALKED TO THE FRIENDS. THE STORY CHECKS OUT.
THEN SHE COULDN'T HAVE DONE IT.
OKAY, WHERE WAS YOUR MASTER AT THE TIME?
HE AND THE YOUNG MASTER BOTH HAD DINNER AND WENT TO BED BEFORE THE MISTRESS CAME HOME.
TATSUHITO'S ROOM IS NEXT TO HIS WIFE'S, ISN'T IT?
YES, BUT HE WAS ASLEEP. HE WAS TIRED FROM PLAYING WITH THE YOUNG MASTER ALL AFTERNOON.
WHAT DO YOU THINK, INSPECTOR?
I BET THE HUSBAND DID IT!
CAN'T BE.
REMEMBER? JUDGING FROM THE TRAJECTORY OF THE BULLET THAT PENETRATED HER FOREHEAD...
...THE MURDERER IS AT LEAST 5'9".
THE HUSBAND IS ABOUT 5'3"! ***AND*** HE'S IN A WHEELCHAIR!
WHAT IF HE STOOD ON THE CHAIR? HE COULD BE FAKING THAT BROKEN LEG!
I THOUGHT OF THAT TOO, SO I ASKED HIS DOCTOR.
TATSUHITO GOT AN X-RAY YESTERDAY, AND THE BONE'S STILL BROKEN. THERE'S NO WAY HE COULD STAND.
MAYBE HE GOT HIS WIFE TO PICK SOMETHING UP AND SHOT HER WHILE SHE WAS KNEELING DOWN...
COME ON!

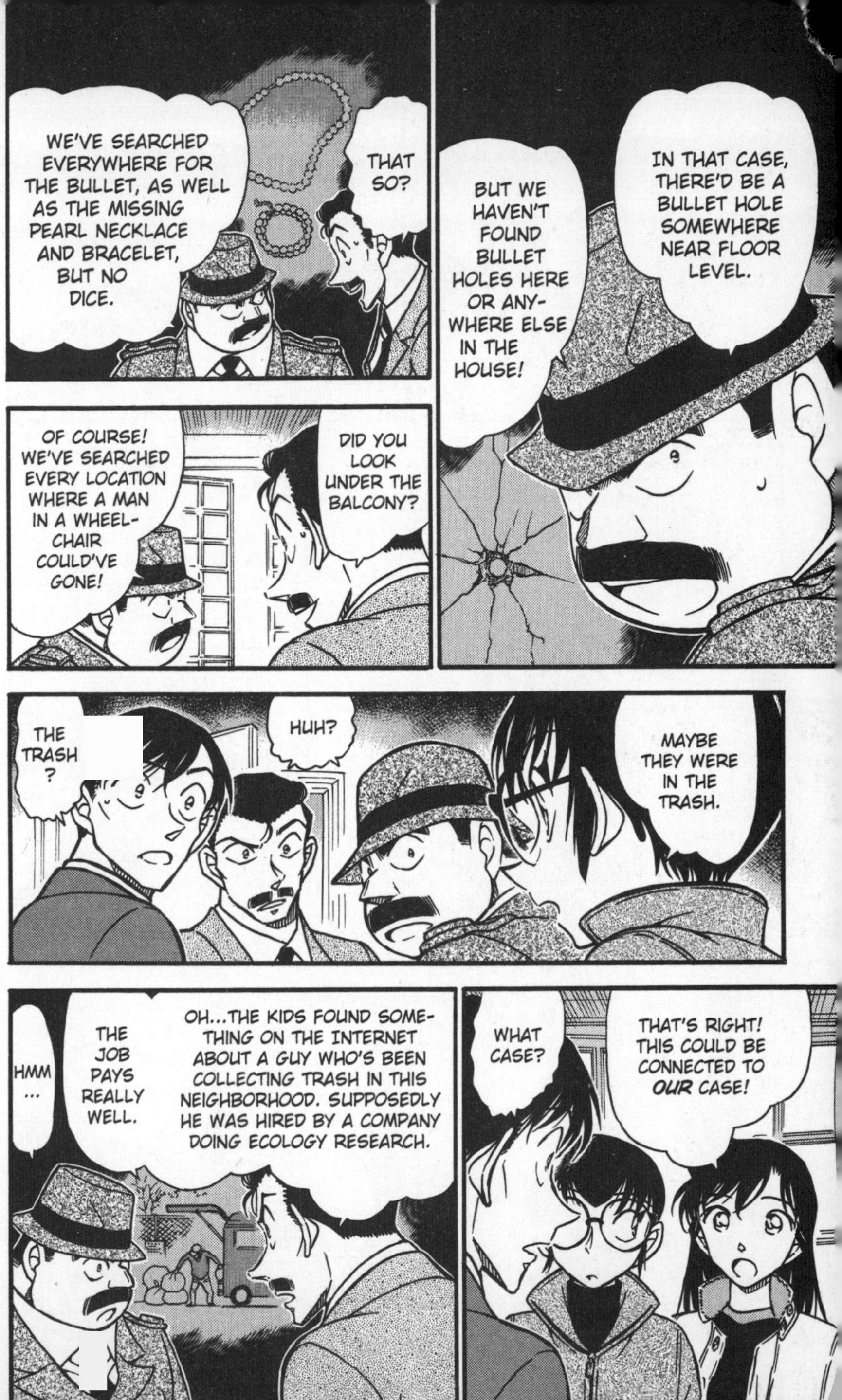
IN THAT CASE, THERE'D BE A BULLET HOLE SOMEWHERE NEAR FLOOR LEVEL.
BUT WE HAVEN'T FOUND BULLET HOLES HERE OR ANY-WHERE ELSE IN THE HOUSE!
THAT SO?
WE'VE SEARCHED EVERYWHERE FOR THE BULLET, AS WELL AS THE MISSING PEARL NECKLACE AND BRACELET, BUT NO DICE.
DID YOU LOOK UNDER THE BALCONY?
OF COURSE! WE'VE SEARCHED EVERY LOCATION WHERE A MAN IN A WHEEL-CHAIR COULD'VE GONE!
MAYBE THEY WERE IN THE TRASH.
HUH?
THE TRASH?
THAT'S RIGHT! THIS COULD BE CONNECTED TO ***OUR*** CASE!
WHAT CASE?
OH...THE KIDS FOUND SOME-THING ON THE INTERNET ABOUT A GUY WHO'S BEEN COLLECTING TRASH IN THIS NEIGHBORHOOD. SUPPOSEDLY HE WAS HIRED BY A COMPANY DOING ECOLOGY RESEARCH.
THE JOB PAYS REALLY WELL.
HMM...

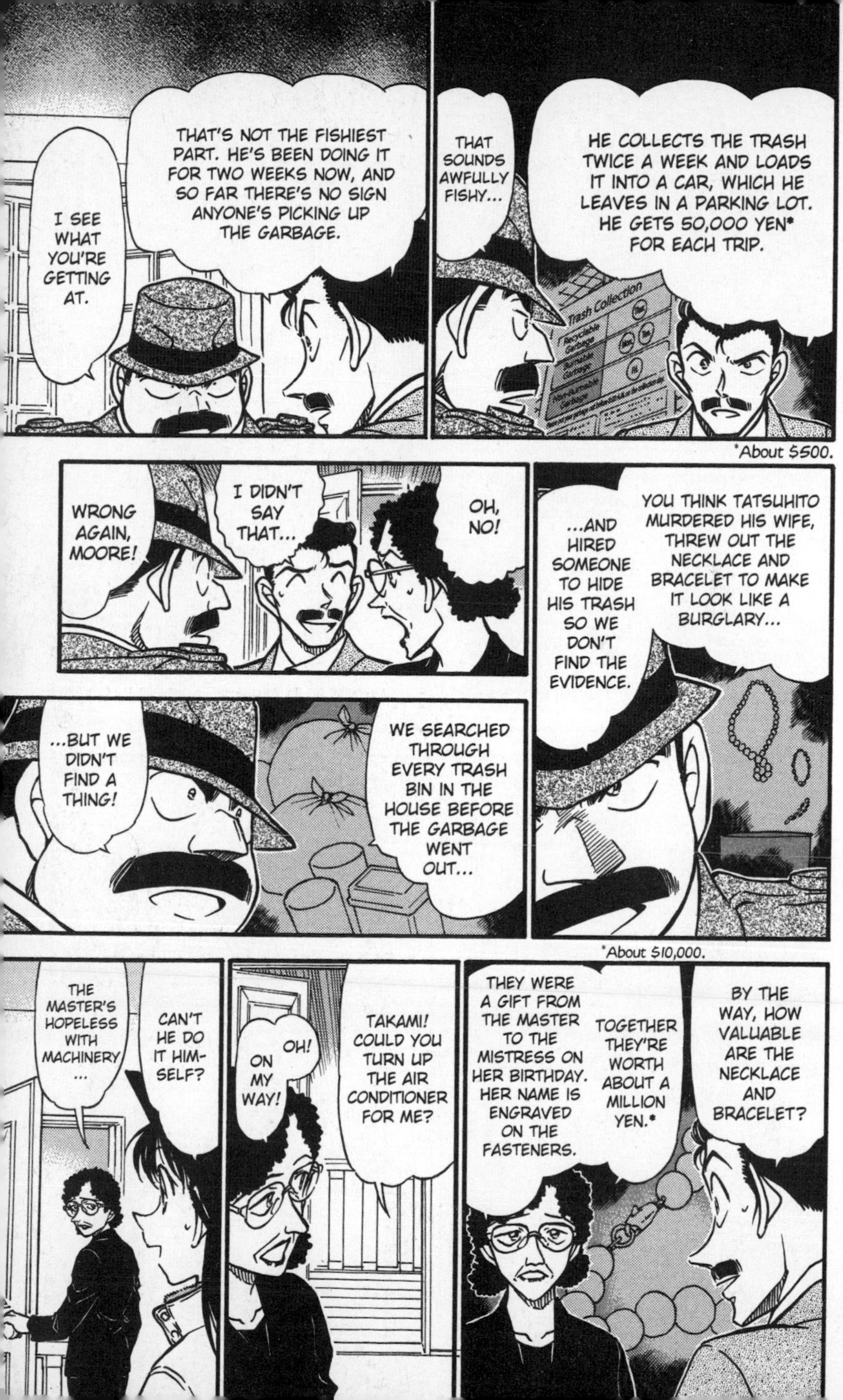
HE COLLECTS THE TRASH TWICE A WEEK AND LOADS IT INTO A CAR, WHICH HE LEAVES IN A PARKING LOT. HE GETS 50,000 YEN* FOR EACH TRIP.
Trash Collection
THAT SOUNDS AWFULLY FISHY...
THAT'S NOT THE FISHIEST PART. HE'S BEEN DOING IT FOR TWO WEEKS NOW, AND SO FAR THERE'S NO SIGN ANYONE'S PICKING UP THE GARBAGE.
I SEE WHAT YOU'RE GETTING AT.
*About $500.
YOU THINK TATSUHITO MURDERED HIS WIFE, THREW OUT THE NECKLACE AND BRACELET TO MAKE IT LOOK LIKE A BURGLARY...
...AND HIRED SOMEONE TO HIDE HIS TRASH SO WE DON'T FIND THE EVIDENCE.
OH, NO!
I DIDN'T SAY THAT...
WRONG AGAIN, MOORE!
WE SEARCHED THROUGH EVERY TRASH BIN IN THE HOUSE BEFORE THE GARBAGE WENT OUT...
...BUT WE DIDN'T FIND A THING!
*About $10,000.
BY THE WAY, HOW VALUABLE ARE THE NECKLACE AND BRACELET?
TOGETHER THEY'RE WORTH ABOUT A MILLION YEN.*
THEY WERE A GIFT FROM THE MASTER TO THE MISTRESS ON HER BIRTHDAY. HER NAME IS ENGRAVED ON THE FASTENERS.
TAKAMI! COULD YOU TURN UP THE AIR CONDITIONER FOR ME?
OH!
ON MY WAY!
CAN'T HE DO IT HIMSELF?
THE MASTER'S HOPELESS WITH MACHINERY...

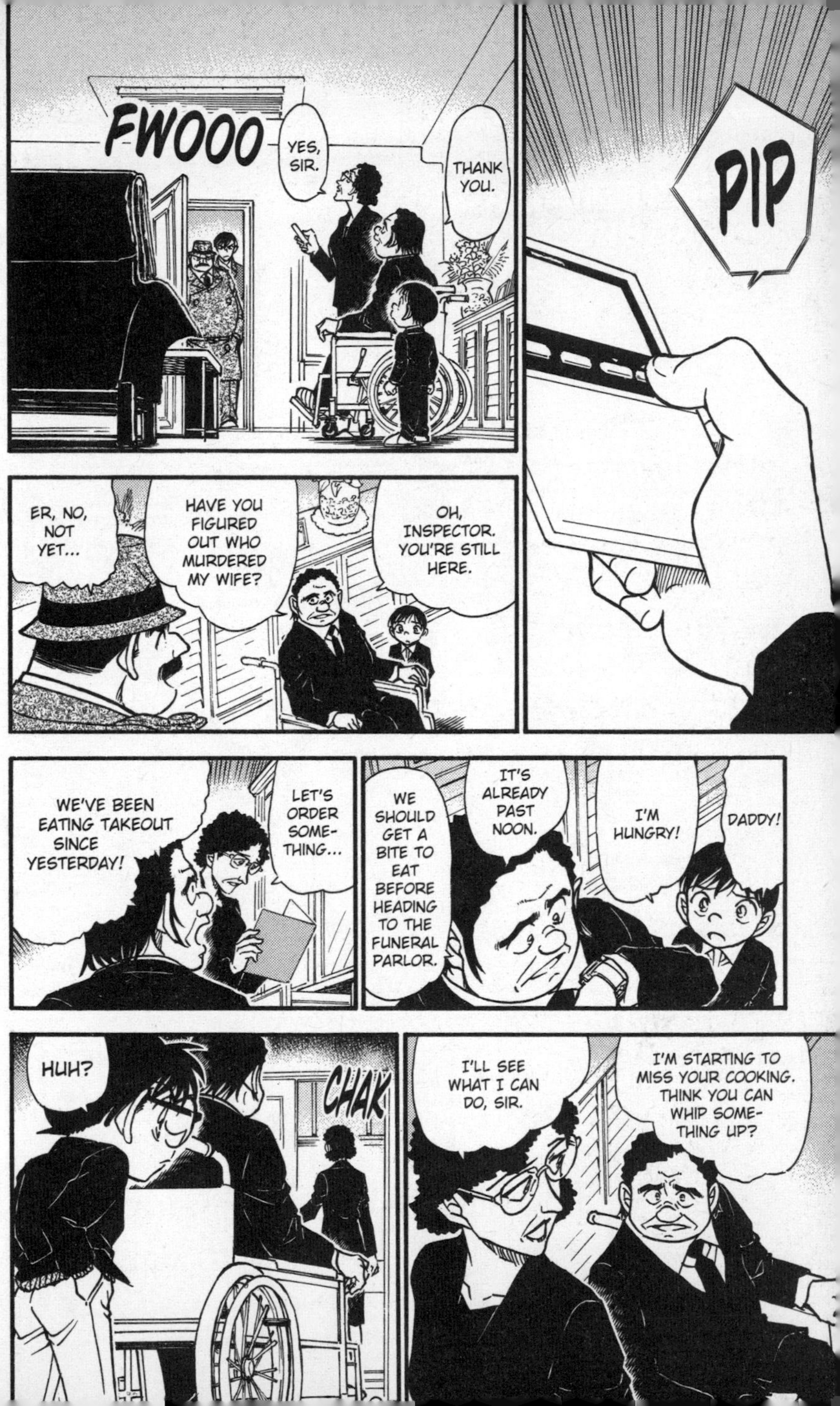
PIP
FWOOO
THANK YOU.
YES, SIR.
OH, INSPECTOR. YOU'RE STILL HERE.
HAVE YOU FIGURED OUT WHO MURDERED MY WIFE?
ER, NO, NOT YET...
DADDY!
I'M HUNGRY!
IT'S ALREADY PAST NOON.
WE SHOULD GET A BITE TO EAT BEFORE HEADING TO THE FUNERAL PARLOR.
LET'S ORDER SOME-THING...
WE'VE BEEN EATING TAKEOUT SINCE YESTERDAY!
I'M STARTING TO MISS YOUR COOKING. THINK YOU CAN WHIP SOME-THING UP?
I'LL SEE WHAT I CAN DO, SIR.
CHAK
HUH?

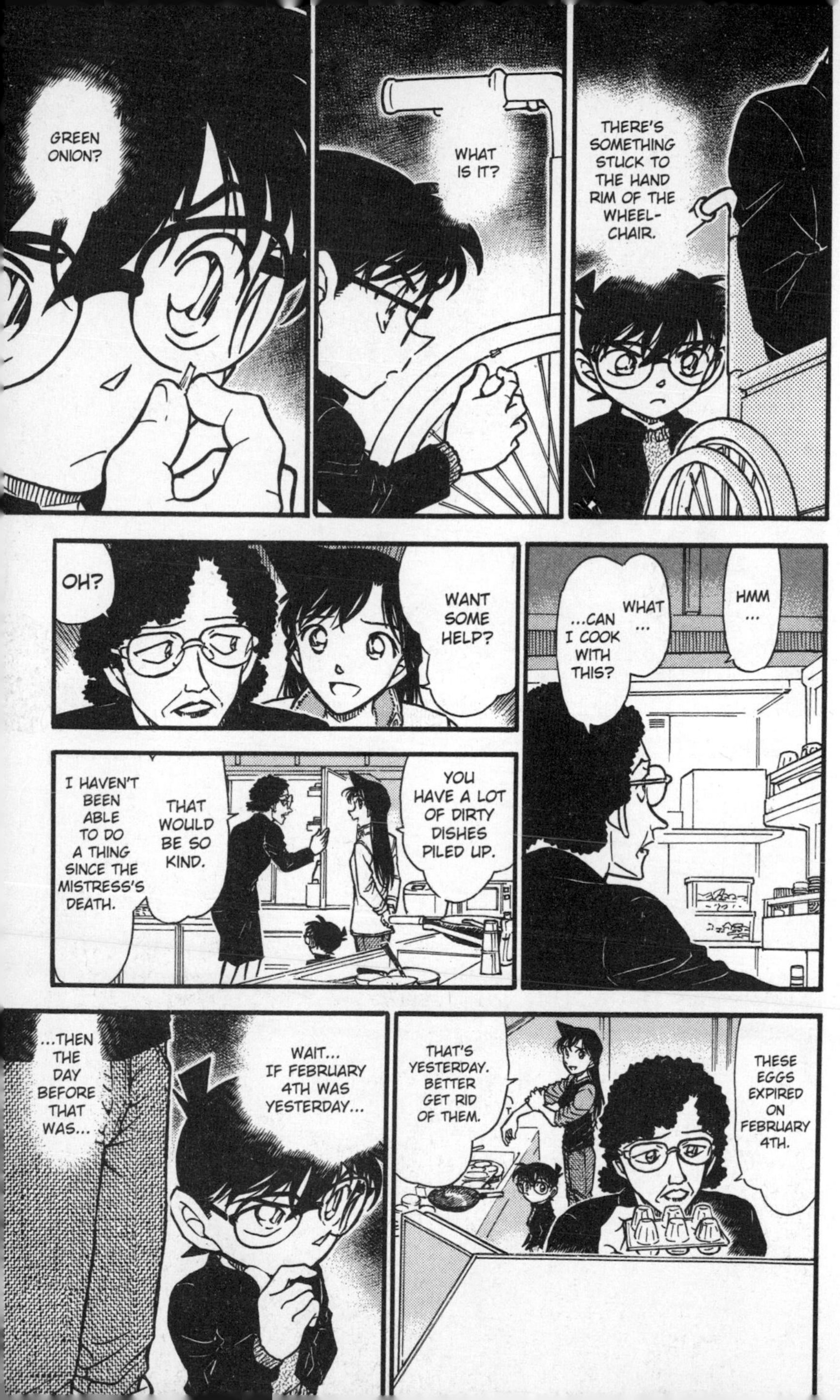
THERE'S SOMETHING STUCK TO THE HAND RIM OF THE WHEEL-CHAIR.
WHAT IS IT?
GREEN ONION?
HMM ...
WHAT ... ...CAN I COOK WITH THIS?
WANT SOME HELP?
OH?
YOU HAVE A LOT OF DIRTY DISHES PILED UP.
THAT WOULD BE SO KIND.
I HAVEN'T BEEN ABLE TO DO A THING SINCE THE MISTRESS'S DEATH.
THESE EGGS EXPIRED ON FEBRUARY 4TH.
THAT'S YESTERDAY. BETTER GET RID OF THEM.
WAIT... IF FEBRUARY 4TH WAS YESTERDAY...
...THEN THE DAY BEFORE THAT WAS...

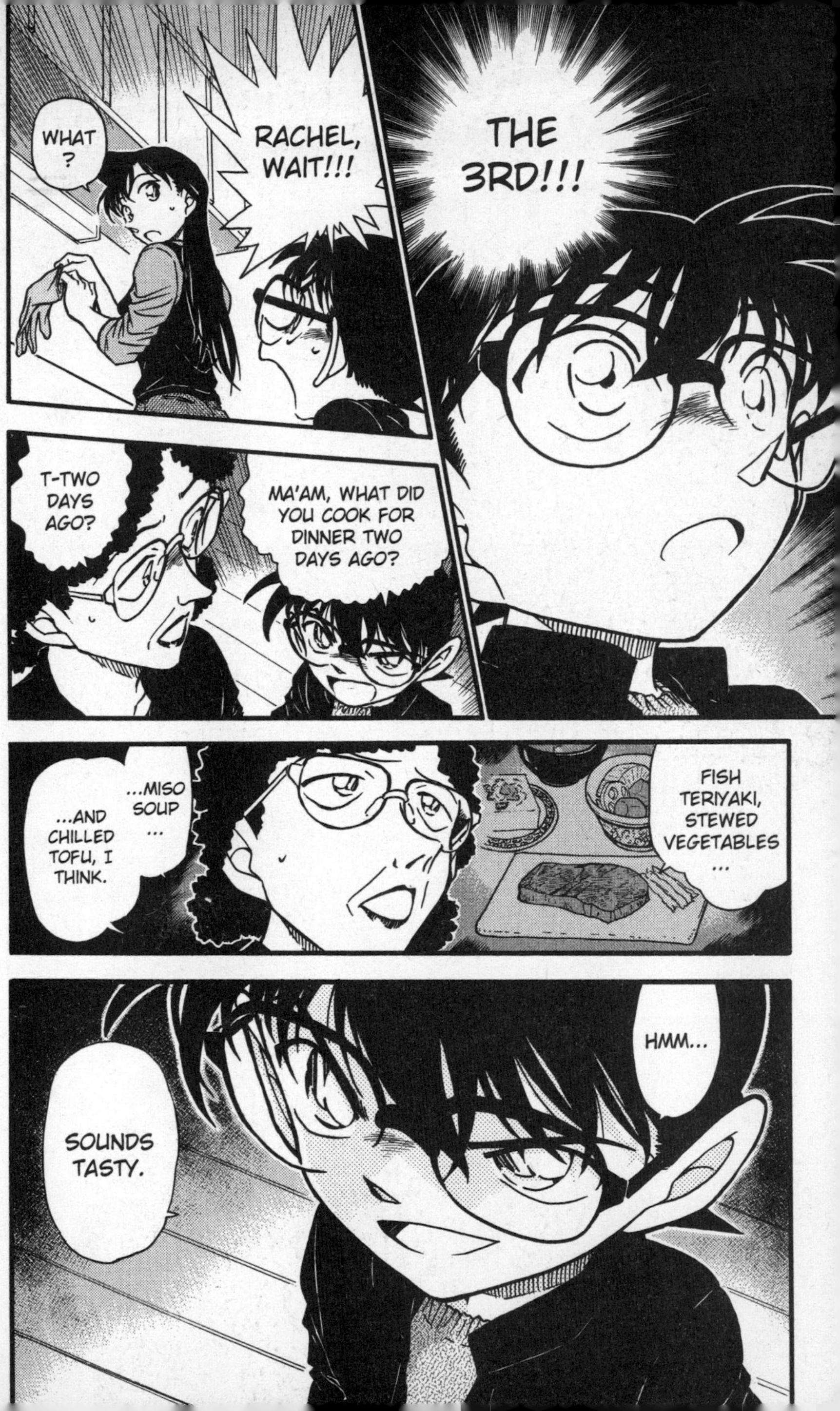
THE 3RD!!!
RACHEL, WAIT!!!
WHAT?
MA'AM, WHAT DID YOU COOK FOR DINNER TWO DAYS AGO?
T-TWO DAYS AGO?
FISH TERIYAKI, STEWED VEGETABLES...
...MISO SOUP...
...AND CHILLED TOFU, I THINK.
HMM...
SOUNDS TASTY.

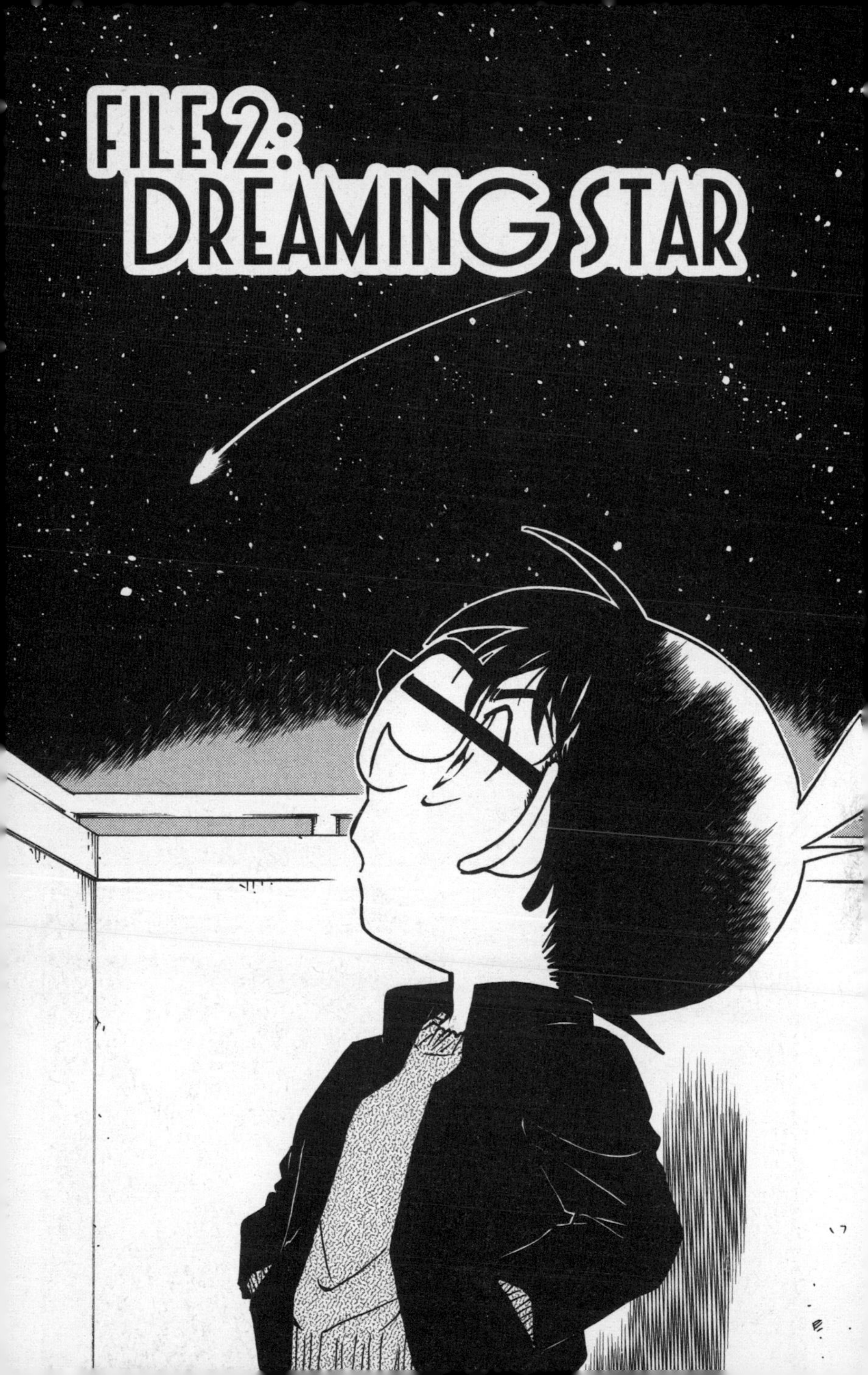
FILE 2:
DREAMING STAR

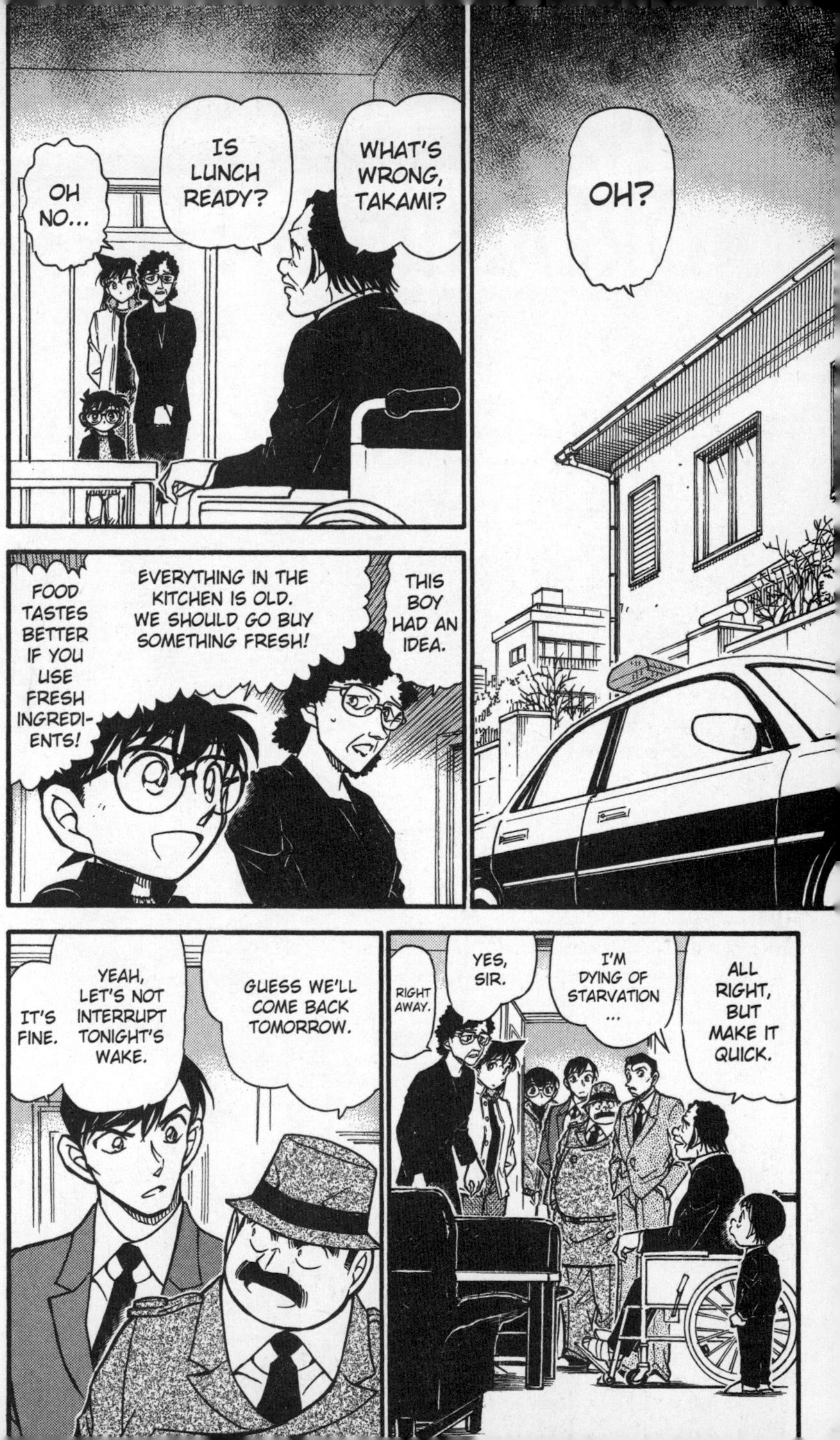
OH?
WHAT'S WRONG, TAKAMI?
IS LUNCH READY?
OH NO...
THIS BOY HAD AN IDEA.
EVERYTHING IN THE KITCHEN IS OLD. WE SHOULD GO BUY SOMETHING FRESH!
FOOD TASTES BETTER IF YOU USE FRESH INGREDI-ENTS!
ALL RIGHT, BUT MAKE IT QUICK.
I'M DYING OF STARVATION ...
YES, SIR.
RIGHT AWAY.
GUESS WE'LL COME BACK TOMORROW.
YEAH, LET'S NOT INTERRUPT TONIGHT'S WAKE.
IT'S FINE.

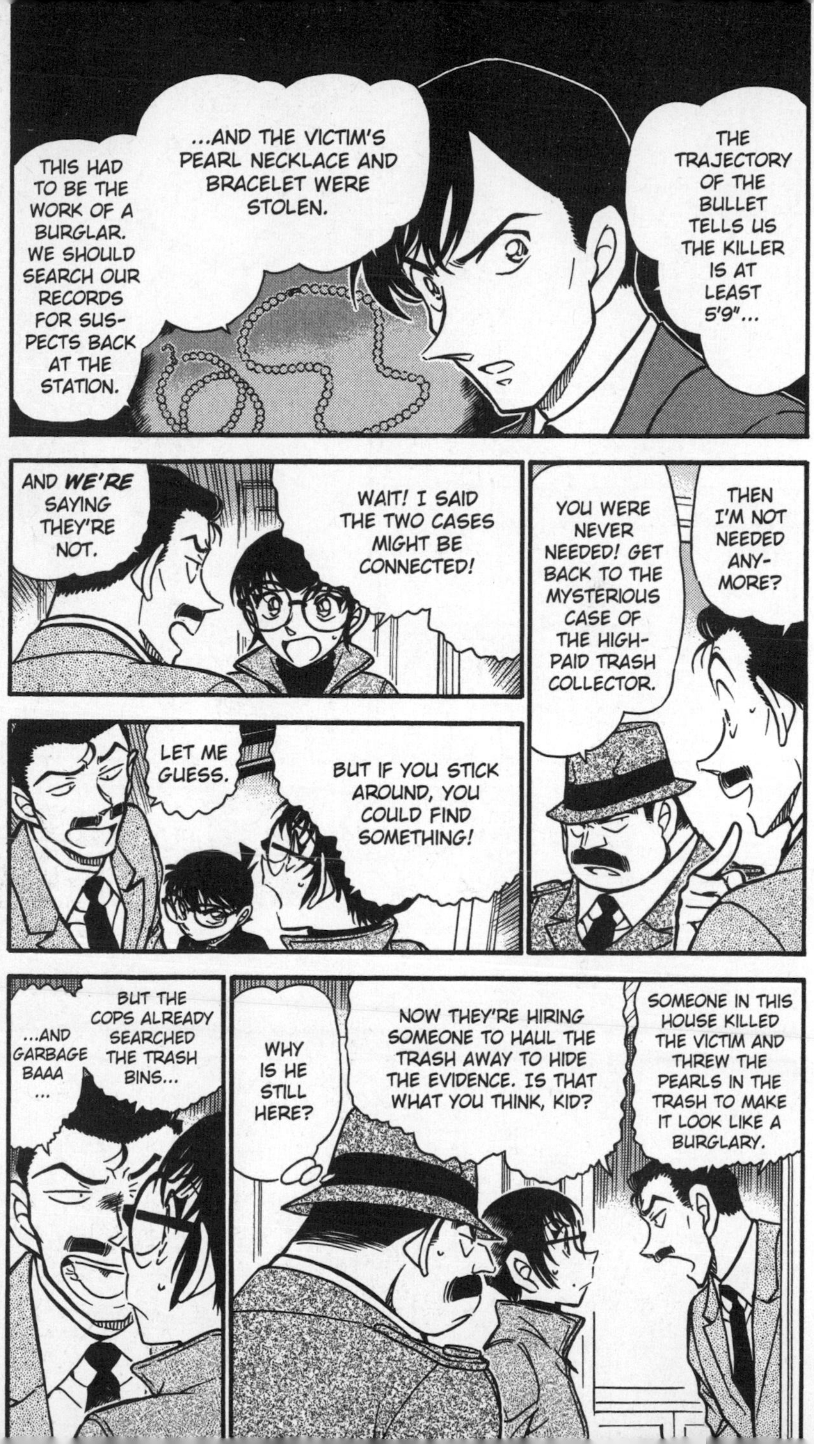
THE TRAJECTORY OF THE BULLET TELLS US THE KILLER IS AT LEAST 5'9"...
...AND THE VICTIM'S PEARL NECKLACE AND BRACELET WERE STOLEN.
THIS HAD TO BE THE WORK OF A BURGLAR. WE SHOULD SEARCH OUR RECORDS FOR SUSPECTS BACK AT THE STATION.
THEN I'M NOT NEEDED ANYMORE?
YOU WERE NEVER NEEDED! GET BACK TO THE MYSTERIOUS CASE OF THE HIGH-PAID TRASH COLLECTOR.
WAIT! I SAID THE TWO CASES MIGHT BE CONNECTED!
AND *WE'RE* SAYING THEY'RE NOT.
BUT IF YOU STICK AROUND, YOU COULD FIND SOMETHING!
LET ME GUESS.
SOMEONE IN THIS HOUSE KILLED THE VICTIM AND THREW THE PEARLS IN THE TRASH TO MAKE IT LOOK LIKE A BURGLARY.
NOW THEY'RE HIRING SOMEONE TO HAUL THE TRASH AWAY TO HIDE THE EVIDENCE. IS THAT WHAT YOU THINK, KID?
WHY IS HE STILL HERE?
BUT THE COPS ALREADY SEARCHED THE TRASH BINS...
...AND GARBAGE BAAA...

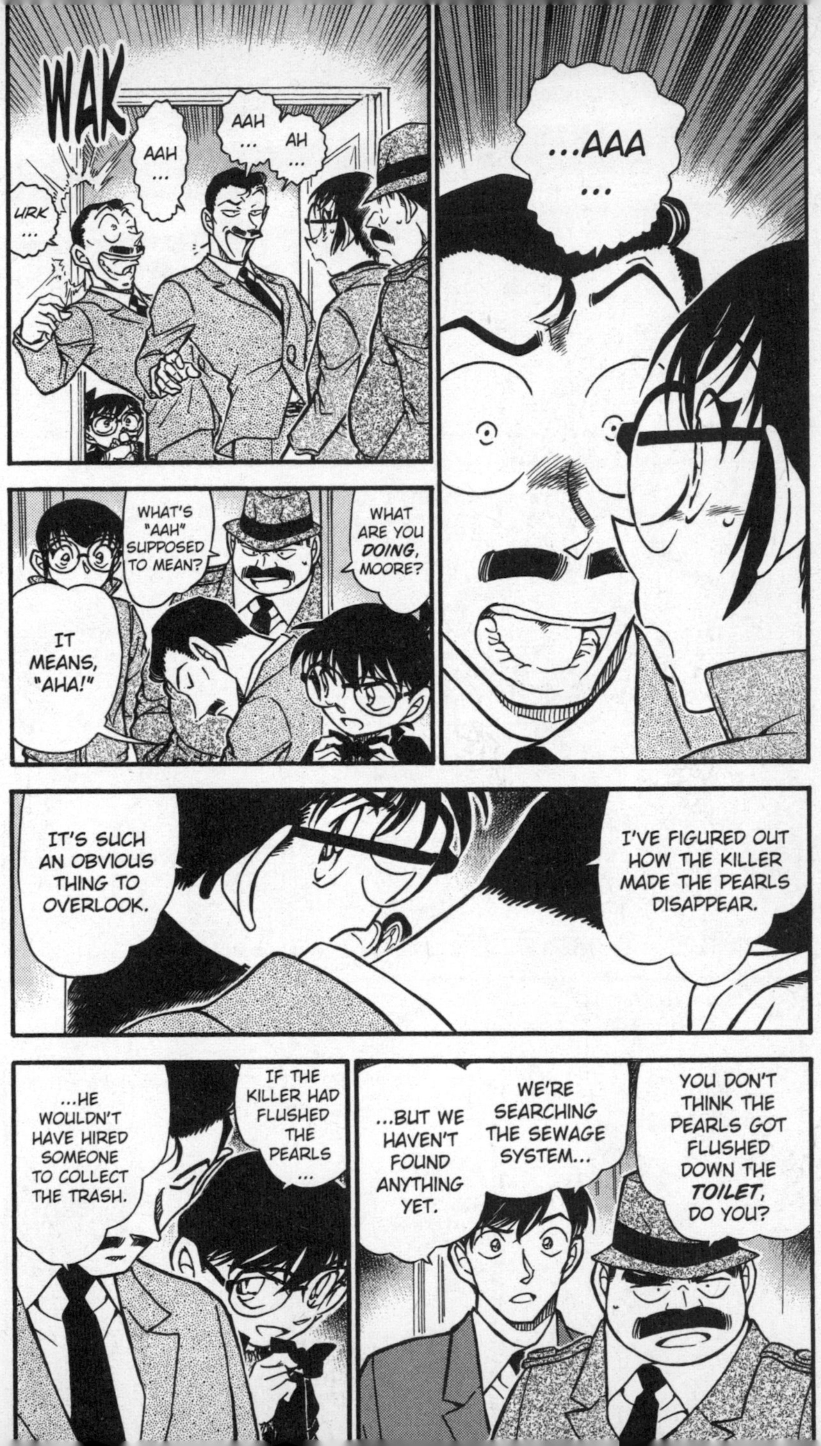
...AAA ...
AAH ... AH ...
AAH ...
WAK
URK ...
WHAT ARE YOU DOING, MOORE?
WHAT'S "AAH" SUPPOSED TO MEAN?
IT MEANS, "AHA!"
I'VE FIGURED OUT HOW THE KILLER MADE THE PEARLS DISAPPEAR.
IT'S SUCH AN OBVIOUS THING TO OVERLOOK.
YOU DON'T THINK THE PEARLS GOT FLUSHED DOWN THE TOILET, DO YOU?
WE'RE SEARCHING THE SEWAGE SYSTEM...
...BUT WE HAVEN'T FOUND ANYTHING YET.
IF THE KILLER HAD FLUSHED THE PEARLS ...
...HE WOULDN'T HAVE HIRED SOMEONE TO COLLECT THE TRASH.

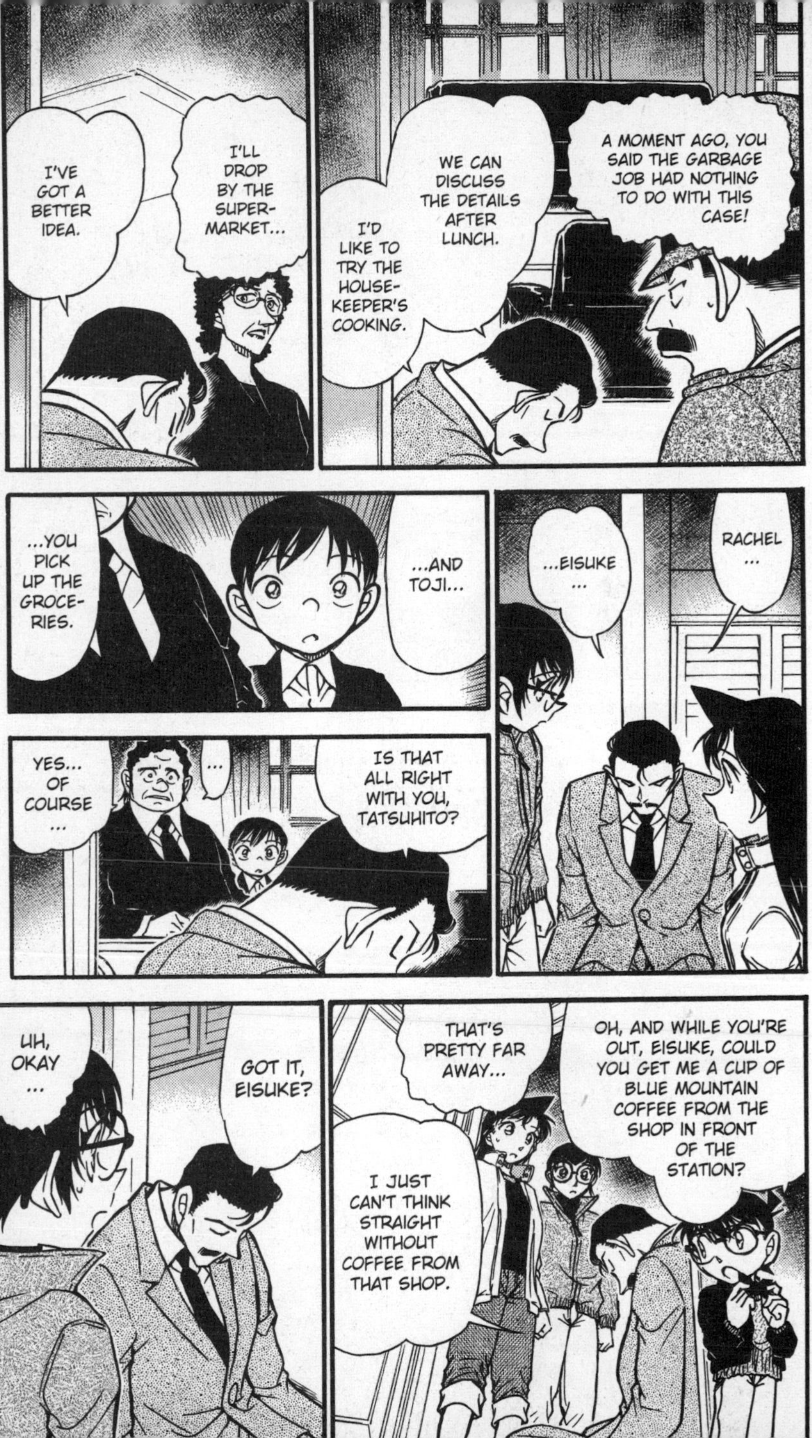
A MOMENT AGO, YOU SAID THE GARBAGE JOB HAD NOTHING TO DO WITH THIS CASE!
WE CAN DISCUSS THE DETAILS AFTER LUNCH.
I'D LIKE TO TRY THE HOUSE-KEEPER'S COOKING.
I'LL DROP BY THE SUPER-MARKET...
I'VE GOT A BETTER IDEA.
RACHEL ...
...EISUKE ...
...AND TOJI...
...YOU PICK UP THE GROCE-RIES.
IS THAT ALL RIGHT WITH YOU, TATSUHITO?
...
YES... OF COURSE ...
OH, AND WHILE YOU'RE OUT, EISUKE, COULD YOU GET ME A CUP OF BLUE MOUNTAIN COFFEE FROM THE SHOP IN FRONT OF THE STATION?
THAT'S PRETTY FAR AWAY...
I JUST CAN'T THINK STRAIGHT WITHOUT COFFEE FROM THAT SHOP.
GOT IT, EISUKE?
UH, OKAY ...

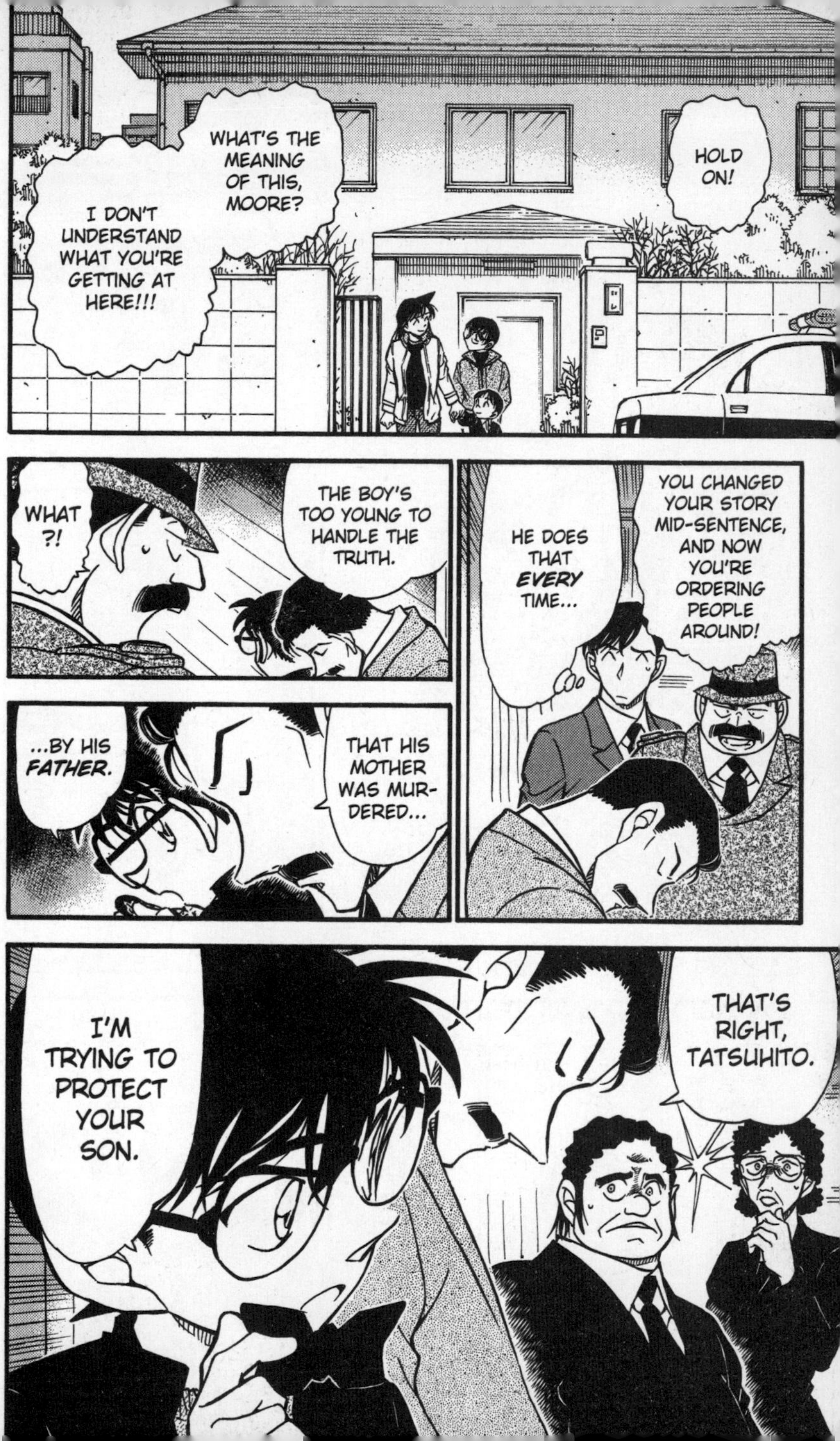
HOLD ON!
WHAT'S THE MEANING OF THIS, MOORE?
I DON'T UNDERSTAND WHAT YOU'RE GETTING AT HERE!!!
YOU CHANGED YOUR STORY MID-SENTENCE, AND NOW YOU'RE ORDERING PEOPLE AROUND!
HE DOES THAT *EVERY* TIME...
THE BOY'S TOO YOUNG TO HANDLE THE TRUTH.
WHAT?!
THAT HIS MOTHER WAS MURDERED...
...BY HIS *FATHER*.
THAT'S RIGHT, TATSUHITO.
I'M TRYING TO PROTECT YOUR SON.

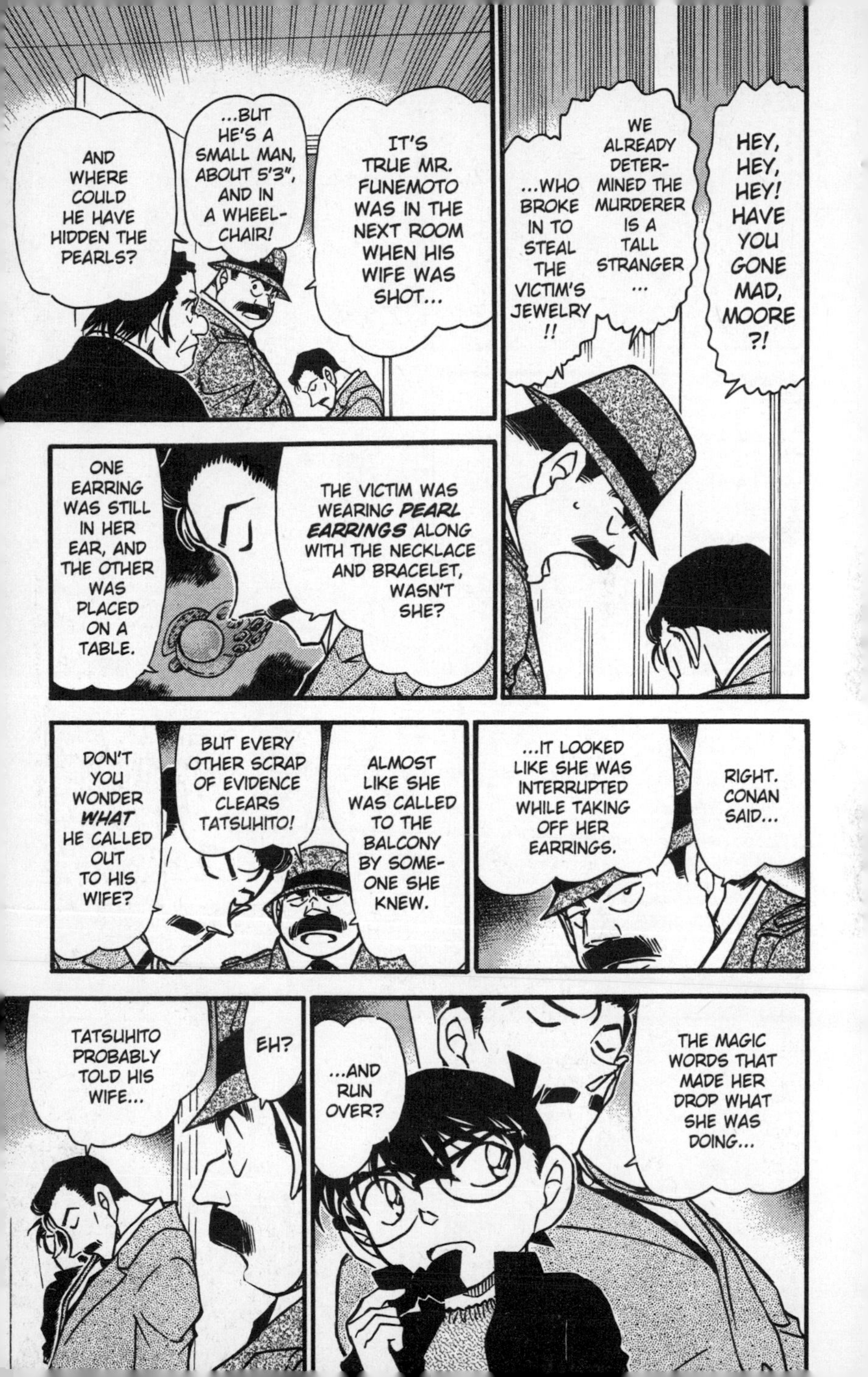
HEY, HEY, HEY! HAVE YOU GONE MAD, MOORE?!
WE ALREADY DETERMINED THE MURDERER IS A TALL STRANGER...
...WHO BROKE IN TO STEAL THE VICTIM'S JEWELRY!!
IT'S TRUE MR. FUNEMOTO WAS IN THE NEXT ROOM WHEN HIS WIFE WAS SHOT...
...BUT HE'S A SMALL MAN, ABOUT 5'3", AND IN A WHEELCHAIR!
AND WHERE COULD HE HAVE HIDDEN THE PEARLS?
THE VICTIM WAS WEARING ***PEARL EARRINGS*** ALONG WITH THE NECKLACE AND BRACELET, WASN'T SHE?
ONE EARRING WAS STILL IN HER EAR, AND THE OTHER WAS PLACED ON A TABLE.
RIGHT. CONAN SAID...
...IT LOOKED LIKE SHE WAS INTERRUPTED WHILE TAKING OFF HER EARRINGS.
ALMOST LIKE SHE WAS CALLED TO THE BALCONY BY SOMEONE SHE KNEW.
BUT EVERY OTHER SCRAP OF EVIDENCE CLEARS TATSUHITO!
DON'T YOU WONDER ***WHAT*** HE CALLED OUT TO HIS WIFE?
THE MAGIC WORDS THAT MADE HER DROP WHAT SHE WAS DOING...
...AND RUN OVER?
EH?
TATSUHITO PROBABLY TOLD HIS WIFE...

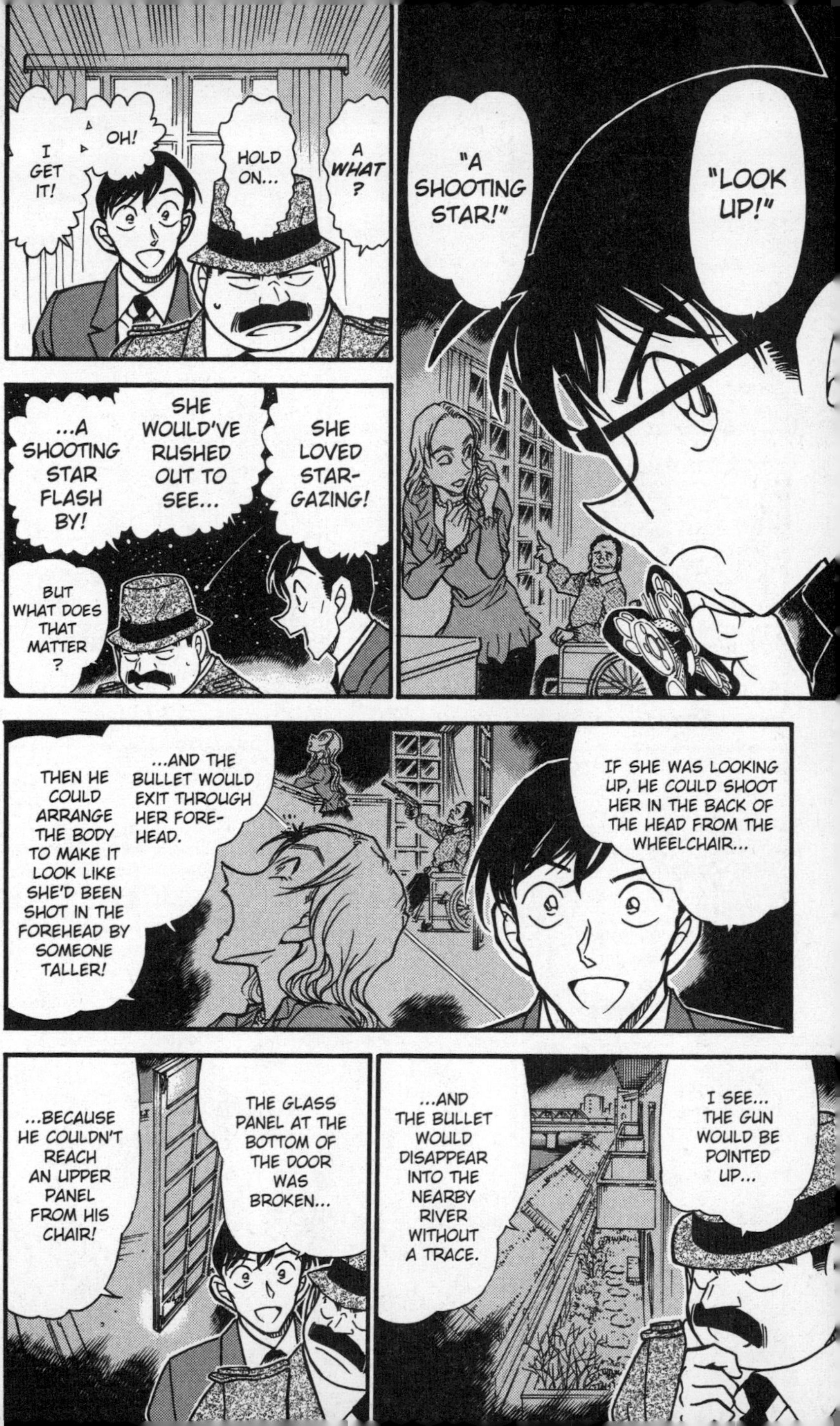
"LOOK UP!"
"A SHOOTING STAR!"
A *WHAT*?
HOLD ON...
OH!
I GET IT!
SHE LOVED STAR-GAZING!
SHE WOULD'VE RUSHED OUT TO SEE...
...A SHOOTING STAR FLASH BY!
BUT WHAT DOES THAT MATTER?
IF SHE WAS LOOKING UP, HE COULD SHOOT HER IN THE BACK OF THE HEAD FROM THE WHEELCHAIR...
...AND THE BULLET WOULD EXIT THROUGH HER FORE-HEAD.
THEN HE COULD ARRANGE THE BODY TO MAKE IT LOOK LIKE SHE'D BEEN SHOT IN THE FOREHEAD BY SOMEONE TALLER!
I SEE... THE GUN WOULD BE POINTED UP...
...AND THE BULLET WOULD DISAPPEAR INTO THE NEARBY RIVER WITHOUT A TRACE.
THE GLASS PANEL AT THE BOTTOM OF THE DOOR WAS BROKEN...
...BECAUSE HE COULDN'T REACH AN UPPER PANEL FROM HIS CHAIR!

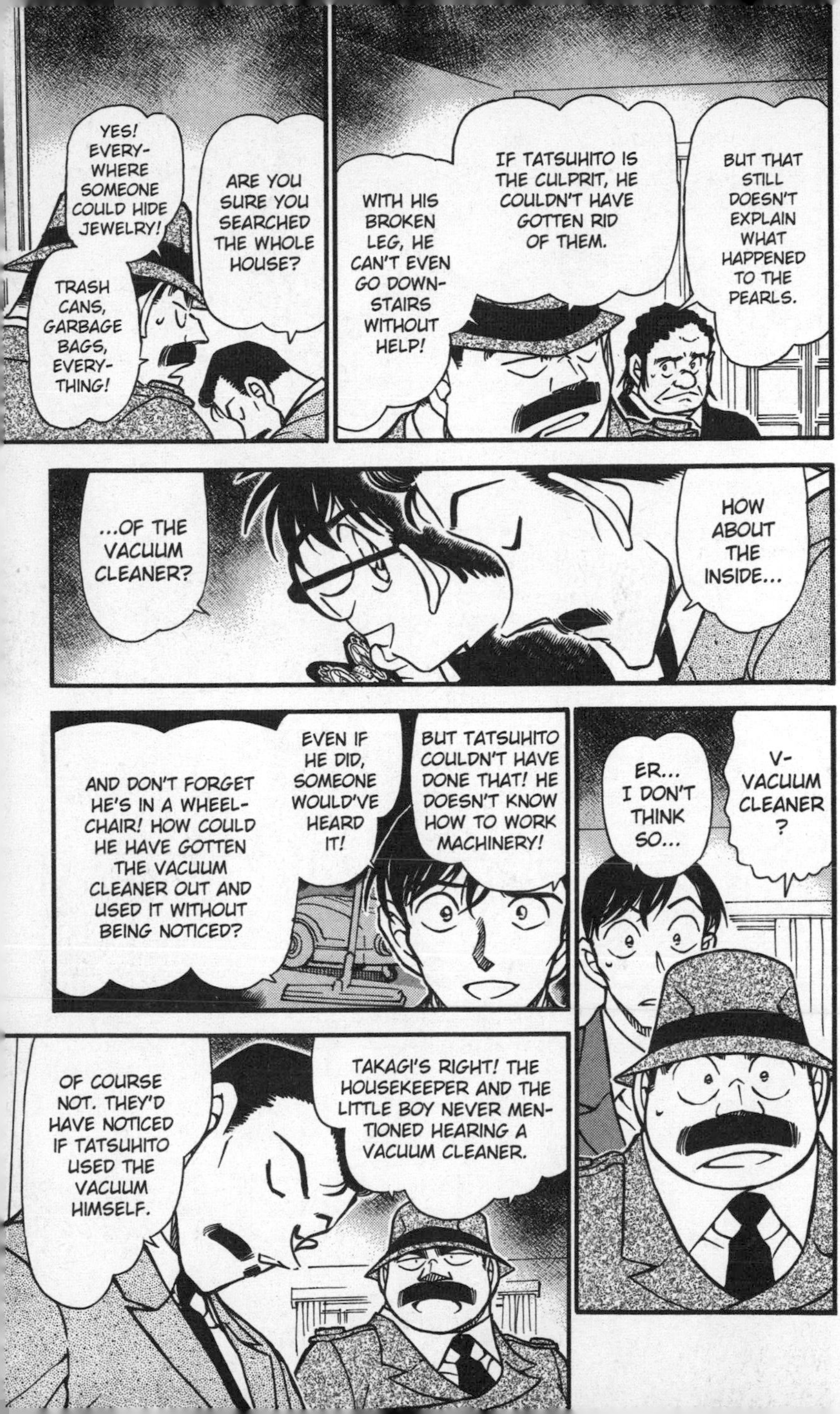
BUT THAT STILL DOESN'T EXPLAIN WHAT HAPPENED TO THE PEARLS.
IF TATSUHITO IS THE CULPRIT, HE COULDN'T HAVE GOTTEN RID OF THEM.
WITH HIS BROKEN LEG, HE CAN'T EVEN GO DOWNSTAIRS WITHOUT HELP!
ARE YOU SURE YOU SEARCHED THE WHOLE HOUSE?
YES! EVERYWHERE SOMEONE COULD HIDE JEWELRY!
TRASH CANS, GARBAGE BAGS, EVERYTHING!
HOW ABOUT THE INSIDE...
...OF THE VACUUM CLEANER?
V-VACUUM CLEANER?
ER... I DON'T THINK SO...
BUT TATSUHITO COULDN'T HAVE DONE THAT! HE DOESN'T KNOW HOW TO WORK MACHINERY!
EVEN IF HE DID, SOMEONE WOULD'VE HEARD IT!
AND DON'T FORGET HE'S IN A WHEELCHAIR! HOW COULD HE HAVE GOTTEN THE VACUUM CLEANER OUT AND USED IT WITHOUT BEING NOTICED?
TAKAGI'S RIGHT! THE HOUSEKEEPER AND THE LITTLE BOY NEVER MENTIONED HEARING A VACUUM CLEANER.
OF COURSE NOT. THEY'D HAVE NOTICED IF TATSUHITO USED THE VACUUM HIMSELF.

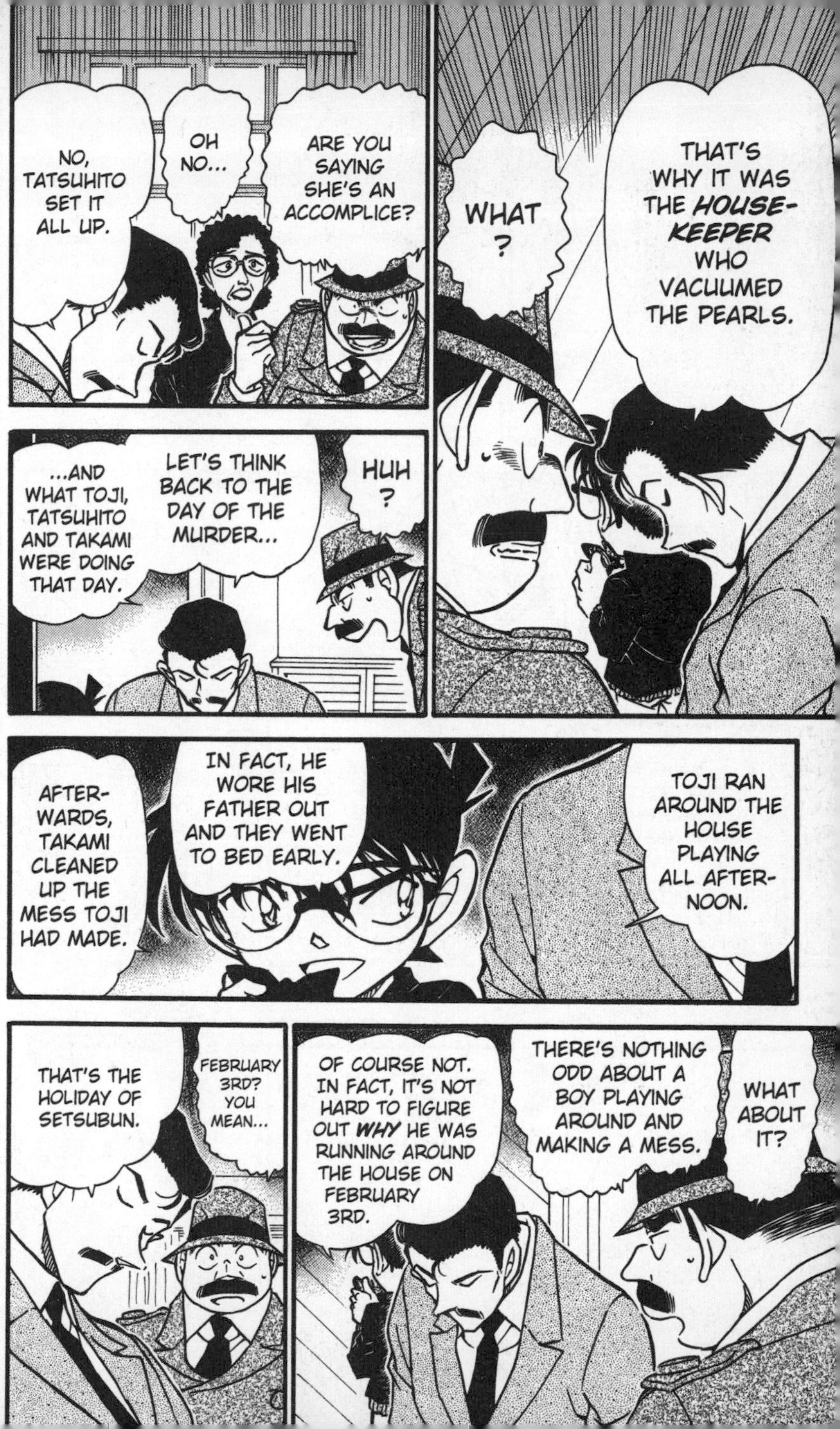
THAT'S WHY IT WAS THE ***HOUSE-KEEPER*** WHO VACUUMED THE PEARLS.
WHAT ?
ARE YOU SAYING SHE'S AN ACCOMPLICE?
OH NO...
NO, TATSUHITO SET IT ALL UP.
HUH ?
LET'S THINK BACK TO THE DAY OF THE MURDER...
...AND WHAT TOJI, TATSUHITO AND TAKAMI WERE DOING THAT DAY.
TOJI RAN AROUND THE HOUSE PLAYING ALL AFTER-NOON.
IN FACT, HE WORE HIS FATHER OUT AND THEY WENT TO BED EARLY.
AFTER-WARDS, TAKAMI CLEANED UP THE MESS TOJI HAD MADE.
WHAT ABOUT IT?
THERE'S NOTHING ODD ABOUT A BOY PLAYING AROUND AND MAKING A MESS.
OF COURSE NOT. IN FACT, IT'S NOT HARD TO FIGURE OUT ***WHY*** HE WAS RUNNING AROUND THE HOUSE ON FEBRUARY 3RD.
FEBRUARY 3RD? YOU MEAN...
THAT'S THE HOLIDAY OF SETSUBUN.

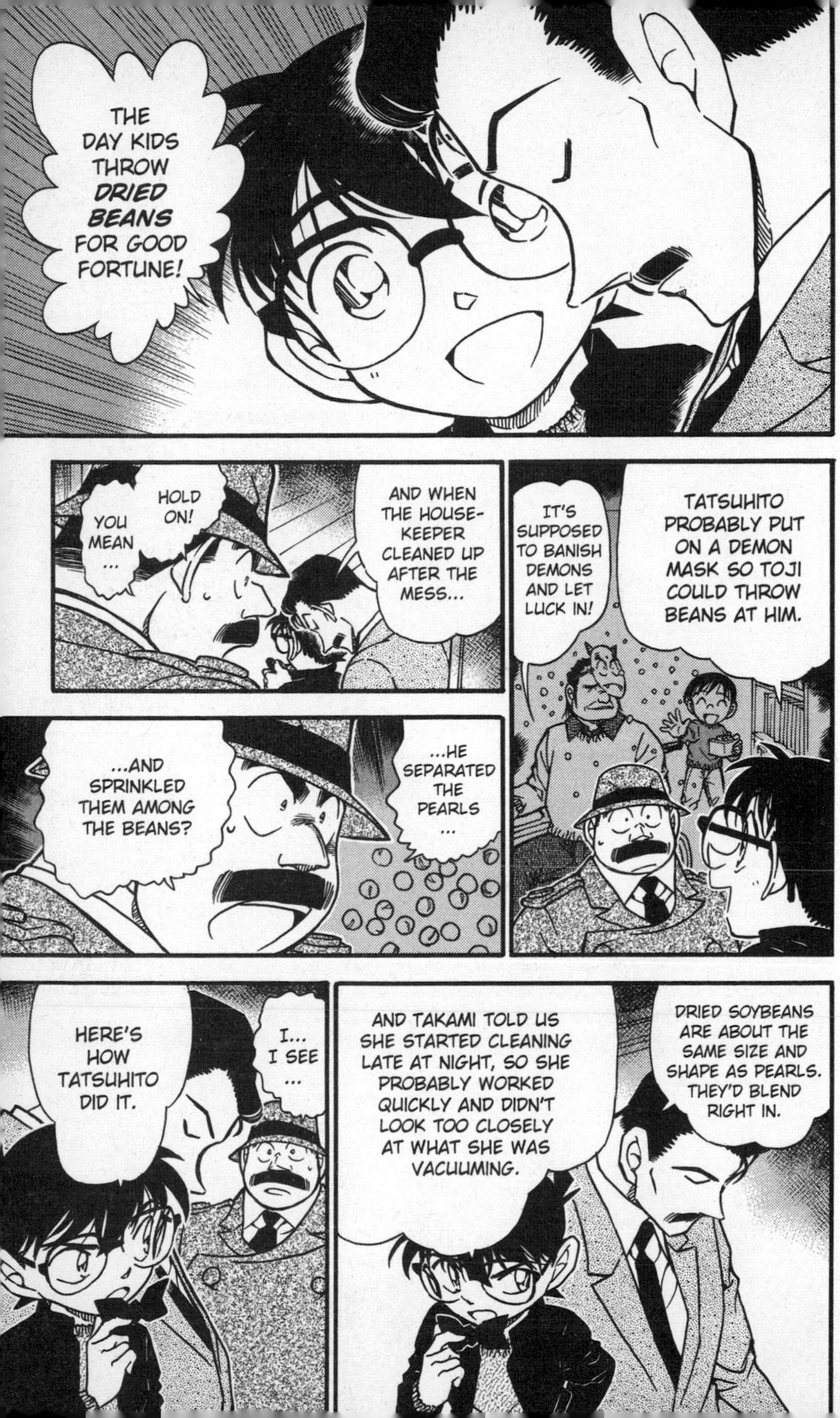
THE DAY KIDS THROW **DRIED BEANS** FOR GOOD FORTUNE!
TATSUHITO PROBABLY PUT ON A DEMON MASK SO TOJI COULD THROW BEANS AT HIM.
IT'S SUPPOSED TO BANISH DEMONS AND LET LUCK IN!
AND WHEN THE HOUSE-KEEPER CLEANED UP AFTER THE MESS...
HOLD ON!
YOU MEAN ...
...HE SEPARATED THE PEARLS ...
...AND SPRINKLED THEM AMONG THE BEANS?
DRIED SOYBEANS ARE ABOUT THE SAME SIZE AND SHAPE AS PEARLS. THEY'D BLEND RIGHT IN.
AND TAKAMI TOLD US SHE STARTED CLEANING LATE AT NIGHT, SO SHE PROBABLY WORKED QUICKLY AND DIDN'T LOOK TOO CLOSELY AT WHAT SHE WAS VACUUMING.
I... I SEE ...
HERE'S HOW TATSUHITO DID IT.

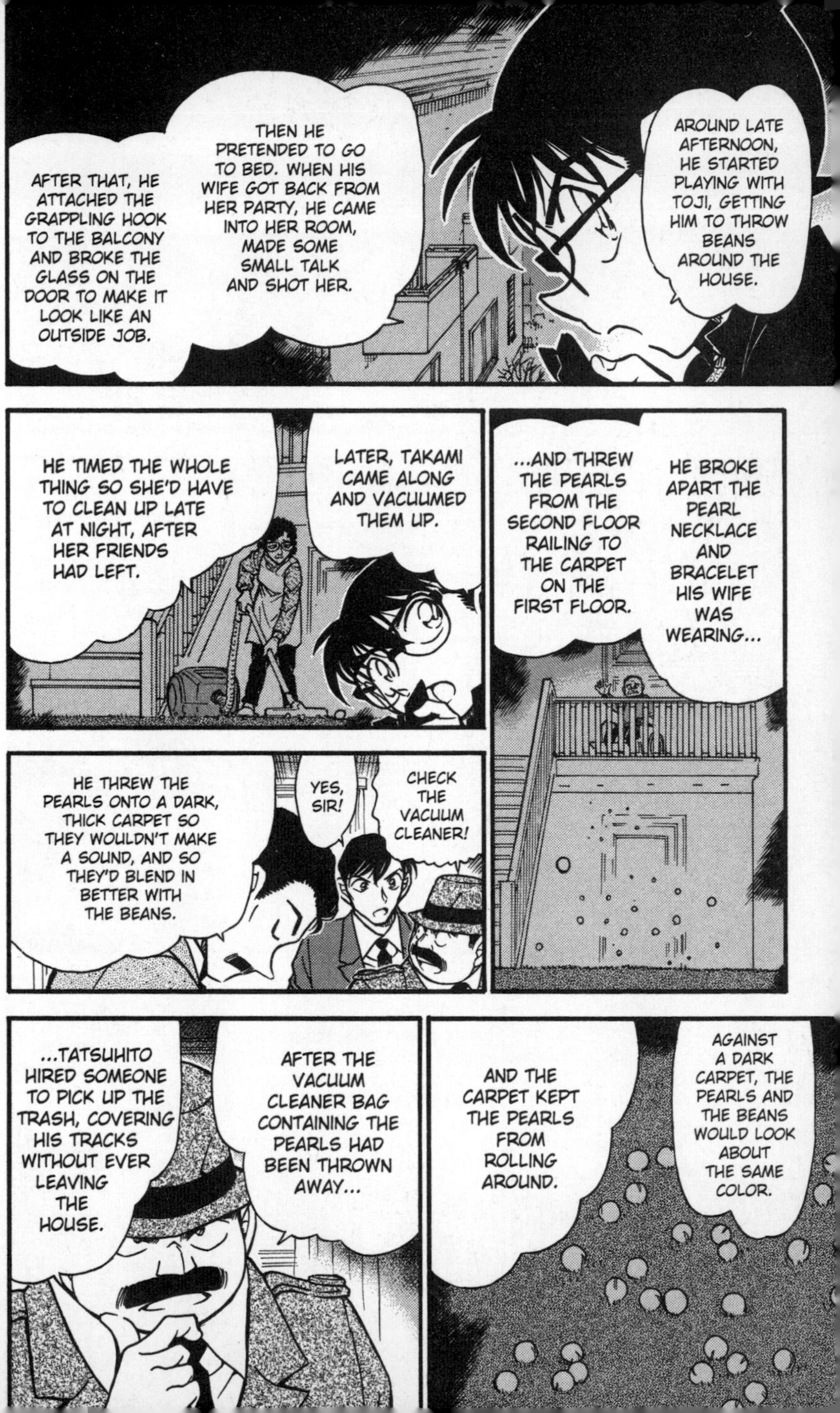
AROUND LATE AFTERNOON, HE STARTED PLAYING WITH TOJI, GETTING HIM TO THROW BEANS AROUND THE HOUSE.
THEN HE PRETENDED TO GO TO BED. WHEN HIS WIFE GOT BACK FROM HER PARTY, HE CAME INTO HER ROOM, MADE SOME SMALL TALK AND SHOT HER.
AFTER THAT, HE ATTACHED THE GRAPPLING HOOK TO THE BALCONY AND BROKE THE GLASS ON THE DOOR TO MAKE IT LOOK LIKE AN OUTSIDE JOB.
HE BROKE APART THE PEARL NECKLACE AND BRACELET HIS WIFE WAS WEARING...
...AND THREW THE PEARLS FROM THE SECOND FLOOR RAILING TO THE CARPET ON THE FIRST FLOOR.
LATER, TAKAMI CAME ALONG AND VACUUMED THEM UP.
HE TIMED THE WHOLE THING SO SHE'D HAVE TO CLEAN UP LATE AT NIGHT, AFTER HER FRIENDS HAD LEFT.
CHECK THE VACUUM CLEANER!
YES, SIR!
HE THREW THE PEARLS ONTO A DARK, THICK CARPET SO THEY WOULDN'T MAKE A SOUND, AND SO THEY'D BLEND IN BETTER WITH THE BEANS.
AGAINST A DARK CARPET, THE PEARLS AND THE BEANS WOULD LOOK ABOUT THE SAME COLOR.
AND THE CARPET KEPT THE PEARLS FROM ROLLING AROUND.
AFTER THE VACUUM CLEANER BAG CONTAINING THE PEARLS HAD BEEN THROWN AWAY...
...TATSUHITO HIRED SOMEONE TO PICK UP THE TRASH, COVERING HIS TRACKS WITHOUT EVER LEAVING THE HOUSE.

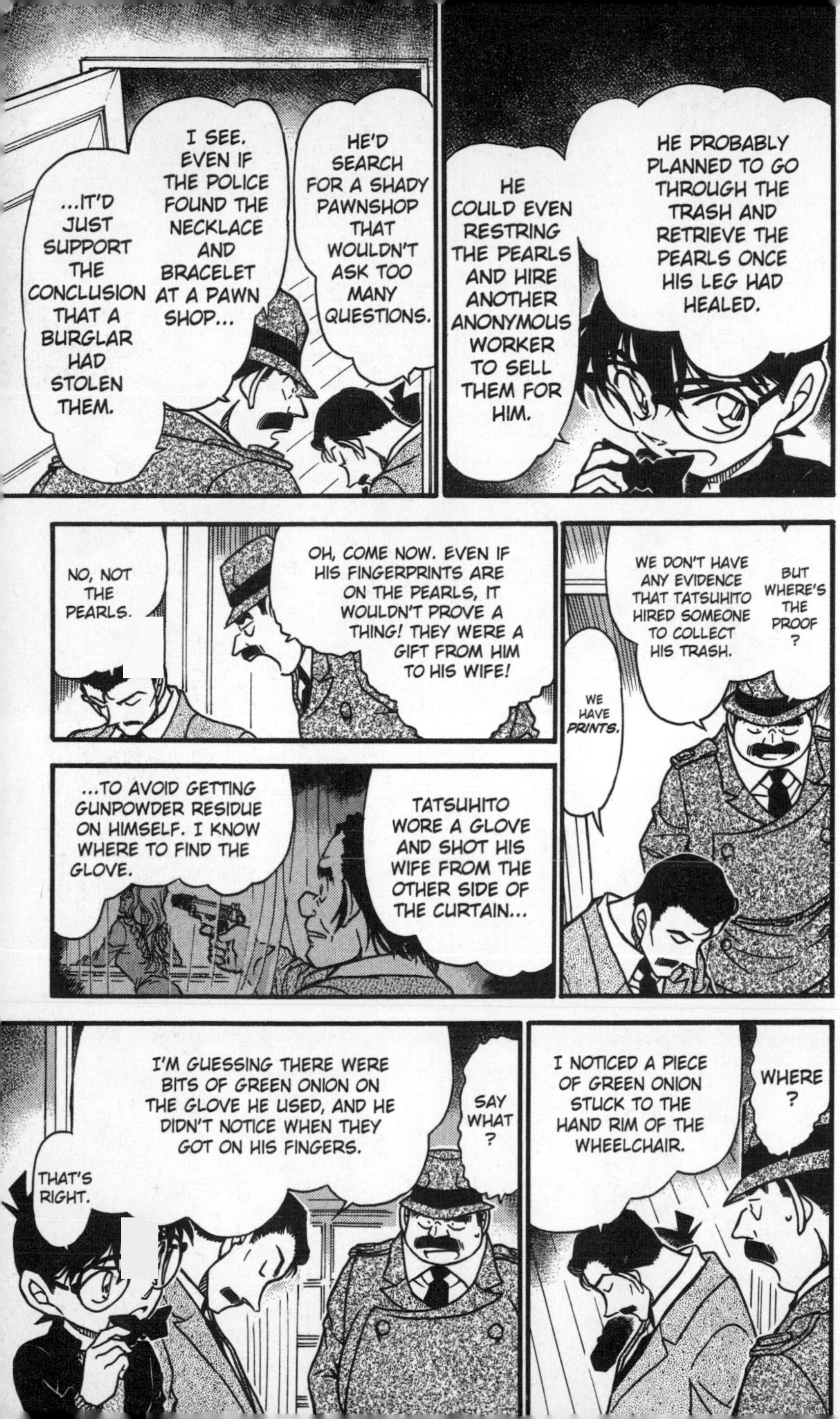
HE PROBABLY PLANNED TO GO THROUGH THE TRASH AND RETRIEVE THE PEARLS ONCE HIS LEG HAD HEALED.
HE COULD EVEN RESTRING THE PEARLS AND HIRE ANOTHER ANONYMOUS WORKER TO SELL THEM FOR HIM.
HE'D SEARCH FOR A SHADY PAWNSHOP THAT WOULDN'T ASK TOO MANY QUESTIONS.
I SEE. EVEN IF THE POLICE FOUND THE NECKLACE AND BRACELET AT A PAWN SHOP...
...IT'D JUST SUPPORT THE CONCLUSION THAT A BURGLAR HAD STOLEN THEM.
BUT WHERE'S THE PROOF?
WE DON'T HAVE ANY EVIDENCE THAT TATSUHITO HIRED SOMEONE TO COLLECT HIS TRASH.
WE HAVE *PRINTS.*
OH, COME NOW. EVEN IF HIS FINGERPRINTS ARE ON THE PEARLS, IT WOULDN'T PROVE A THING! THEY WERE A GIFT FROM HIM TO HIS WIFE!
NO, NOT THE PEARLS.
TATSUHITO WORE A GLOVE AND SHOT HIS WIFE FROM THE OTHER SIDE OF THE CURTAIN...
...TO AVOID GETTING GUNPOWDER RESIDUE ON HIMSELF. I KNOW WHERE TO FIND THE GLOVE.
WHERE?
I NOTICED A PIECE OF GREEN ONION STUCK TO THE HAND RIM OF THE WHEELCHAIR.
SAY WHAT?
I'M GUESSING THERE WERE BITS OF GREEN ONION ON THE GLOVE HE USED, AND HE DIDN'T NOTICE WHEN THEY GOT ON HIS FINGERS.
THAT'S RIGHT.

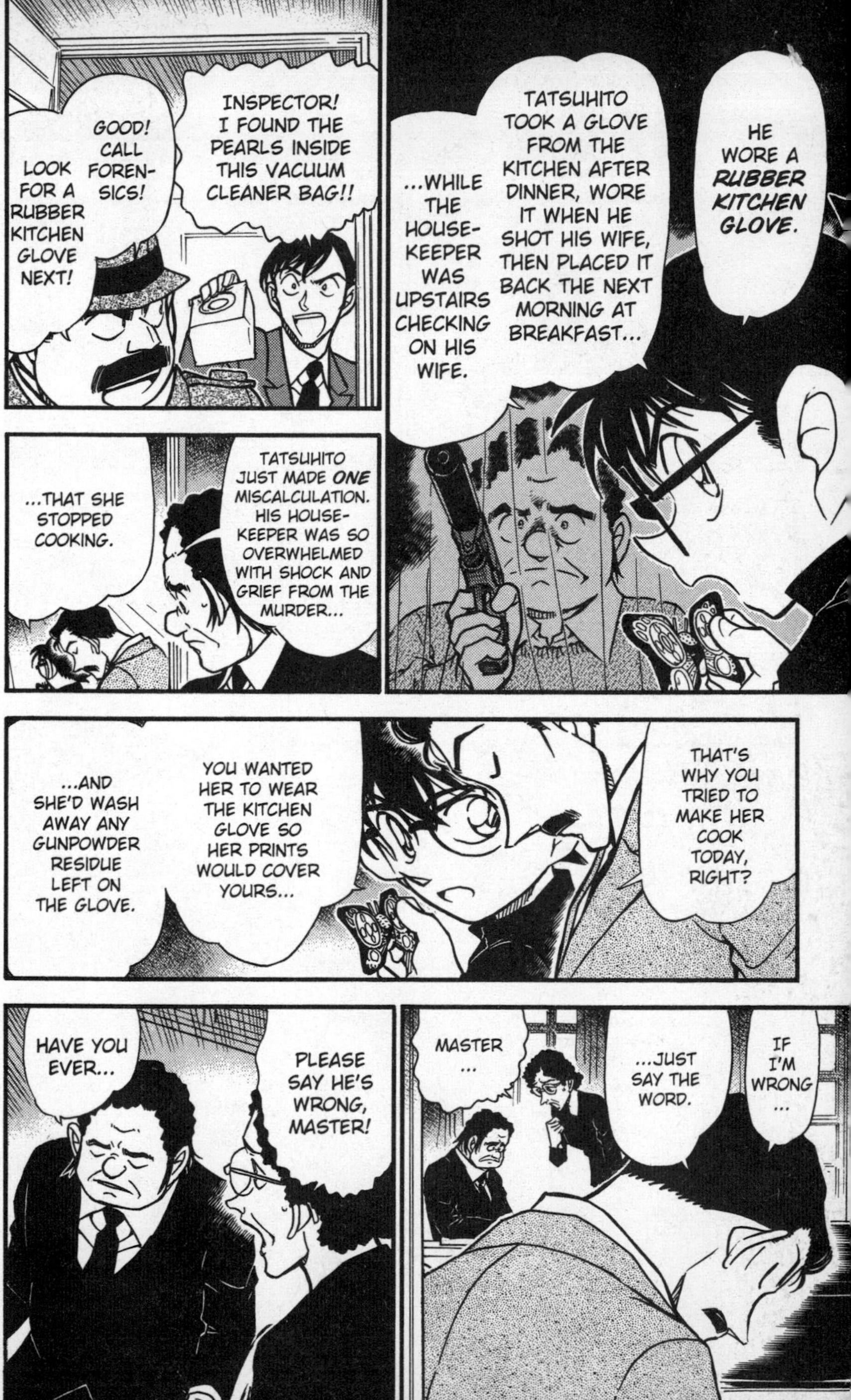
HE WORE A ***RUBBER KITCHEN GLOVE***.
TATSUHITO TOOK A GLOVE FROM THE KITCHEN AFTER DINNER, WORE IT WHEN HE SHOT HIS WIFE, THEN PLACED IT BACK THE NEXT MORNING AT BREAKFAST...
...WHILE THE HOUSEKEEPER WAS UPSTAIRS CHECKING ON HIS WIFE.
INSPECTOR! I FOUND THE PEARLS INSIDE THIS VACUUM CLEANER BAG!!
GOOD! CALL FORENSICS!
LOOK FOR A RUBBER KITCHEN GLOVE NEXT!
TATSUHITO JUST MADE ***ONE*** MISCALCULATION. HIS HOUSEKEEPER WAS SO OVERWHELMED WITH SHOCK AND GRIEF FROM THE MURDER...
...THAT SHE STOPPED COOKING.
THAT'S WHY YOU TRIED TO MAKE HER COOK TODAY, RIGHT?
YOU WANTED HER TO WEAR THE KITCHEN GLOVE SO HER PRINTS WOULD COVER YOURS...
...AND SHE'D WASH AWAY ANY GUNPOWDER RESIDUE LEFT ON THE GLOVE.
IF I'M WRONG...
...JUST SAY THE WORD.
MASTER...
PLEASE SAY HE'S WRONG, MASTER!
HAVE YOU EVER...

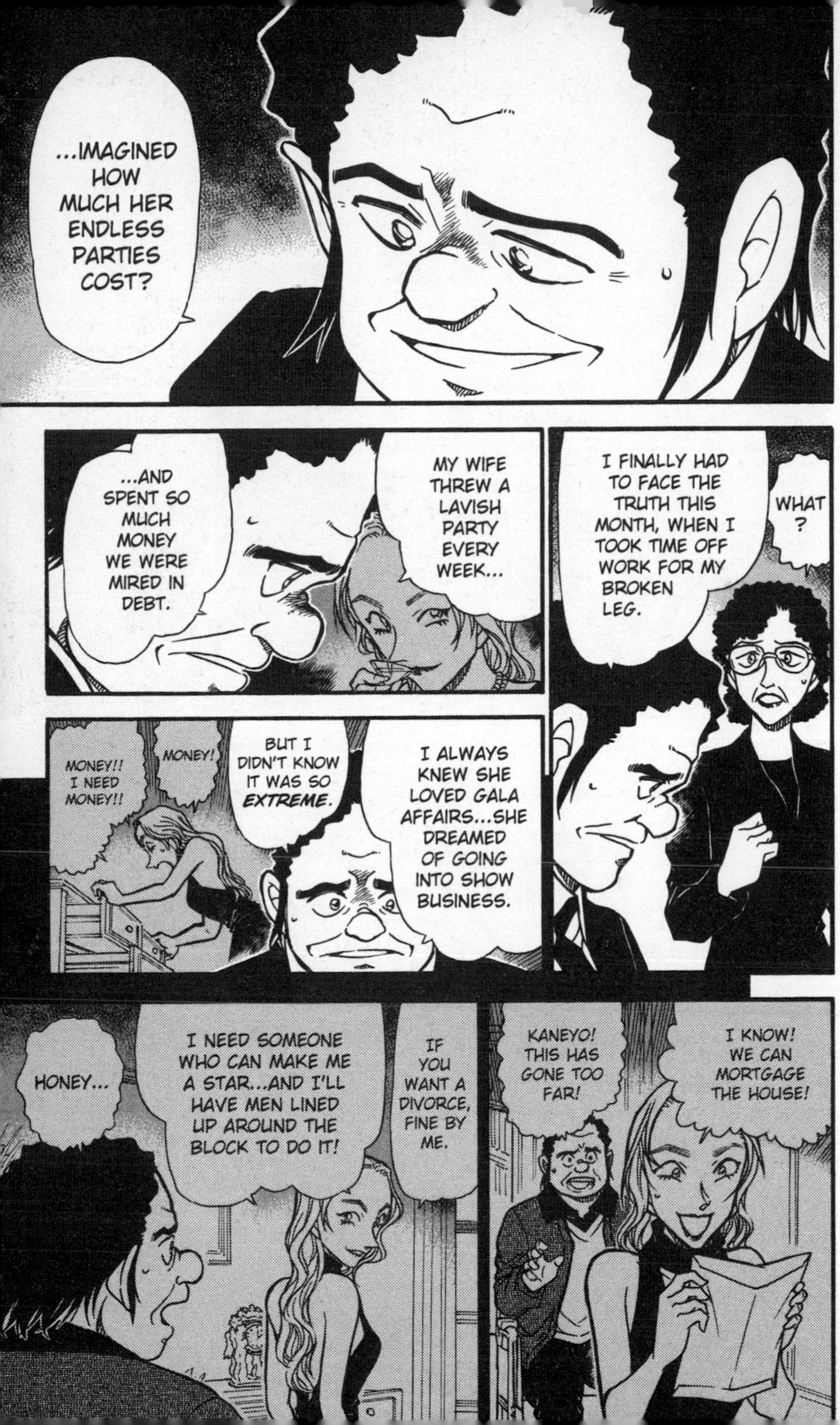
...IMAGINED HOW MUCH HER ENDLESS PARTIES COST?
I FINALLY HAD TO FACE THE TRUTH THIS MONTH, WHEN I TOOK TIME OFF WORK FOR MY BROKEN LEG.
WHAT?
MY WIFE THREW A LAVISH PARTY EVERY WEEK...
...AND SPENT SO MUCH MONEY WE WERE MIRED IN DEBT.
I ALWAYS KNEW SHE LOVED GALA AFFAIRS...SHE DREAMED OF GOING INTO SHOW BUSINESS.
BUT I DIDN'T KNOW IT WAS SO *EXTREME*.
MONEY!
MONEY!! I NEED MONEY!!
I KNOW! WE CAN MORTGAGE THE HOUSE!
KANEYO! THIS HAS GONE TOO FAR!
IF YOU WANT A DIVORCE, FINE BY ME.
I NEED SOMEONE WHO CAN MAKE ME A STAR...AND I'LL HAVE MEN LINED UP AROUND THE BLOCK TO DO IT!
HONEY...

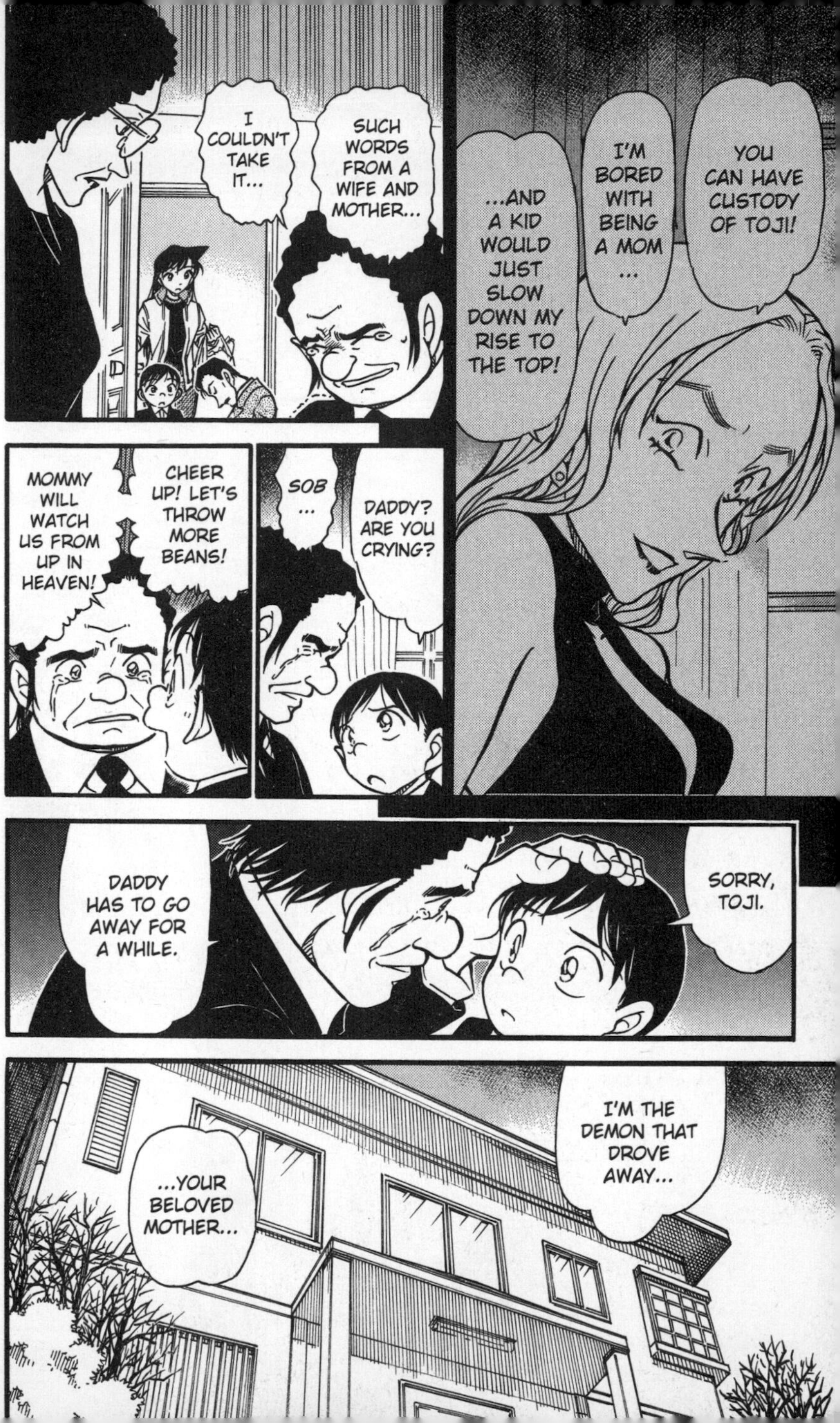
YOU CAN HAVE CUSTODY OF TOJI!
I'M BORED WITH BEING A MOM ...
...AND A KID WOULD JUST SLOW DOWN MY RISE TO THE TOP!
SUCH WORDS FROM A WIFE AND MOTHER...
I COULDN'T TAKE IT...
DADDY? ARE YOU CRYING?
SOB ...
CHEER UP! LET'S THROW MORE BEANS!
MOMMY WILL WATCH US FROM UP IN HEAVEN!
SORRY, TOJI.
DADDY HAS TO GO AWAY FOR A WHILE.
I'M THE DEMON THAT DROVE AWAY...
...YOUR BELOVED MOTHER...

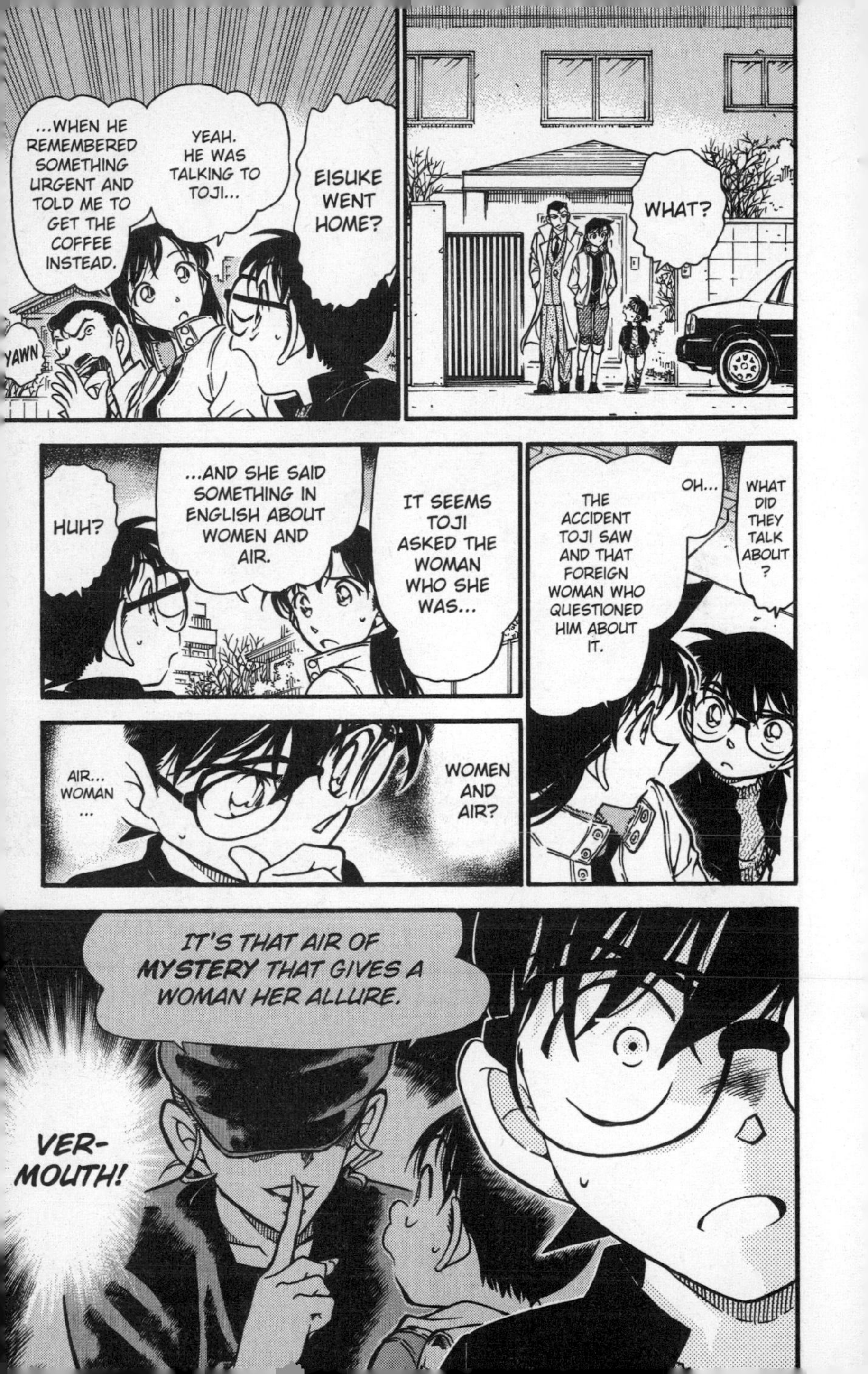
WHAT?
EISUKE WENT HOME?
YEAH. HE WAS TALKING TO TOJI...
...WHEN HE REMEMBERED SOMETHING URGENT AND TOLD ME TO GET THE COFFEE INSTEAD.
YAWN
WHAT DID THEY TALK ABOUT?
OH...
THE ACCIDENT TOJI SAW AND THAT FOREIGN WOMAN WHO QUESTIONED HIM ABOUT IT.
IT SEEMS TOJI ASKED THE WOMAN WHO SHE WAS...
...AND SHE SAID SOMETHING IN ENGLISH ABOUT WOMEN AND AIR.
HUH?
WOMEN AND AIR?
AIR... WOMAN ...
IT'S THAT AIR OF MYSTERY THAT GIVES A WOMAN HER ALLURE.
VER-MOUTH!

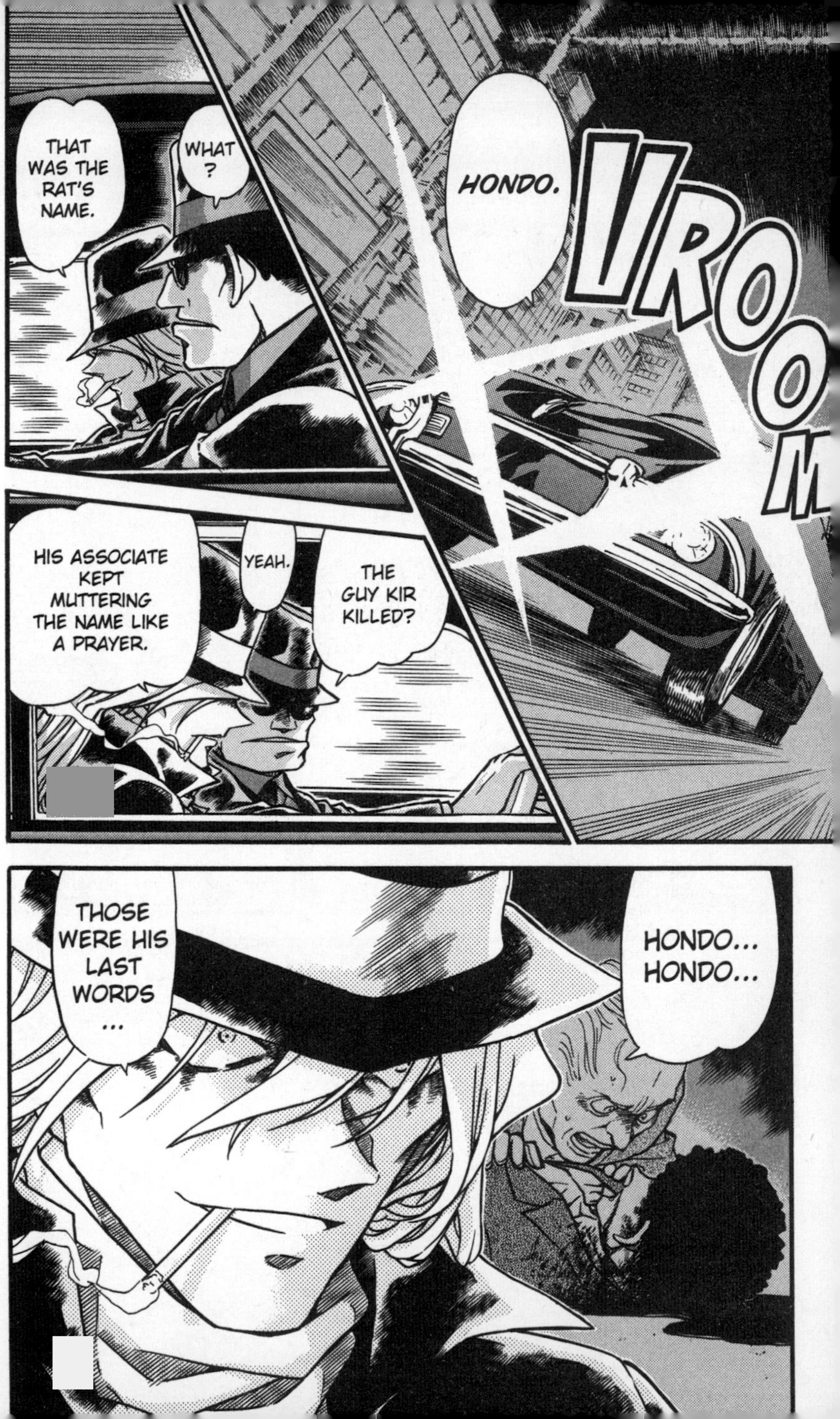
HONDO.
VROOOM
WHAT?
THAT WAS THE RAT'S NAME.
THE GUY KIR KILLED?
YEAH.
HIS ASSOCIATE KEPT MUTTERING THE NAME LIKE A PRAYER.
HONDO... HONDO...
THOSE WERE HIS LAST WORDS...

FILE 3:
THE DETECTIVE LEAGUE'S
SNOWMAN

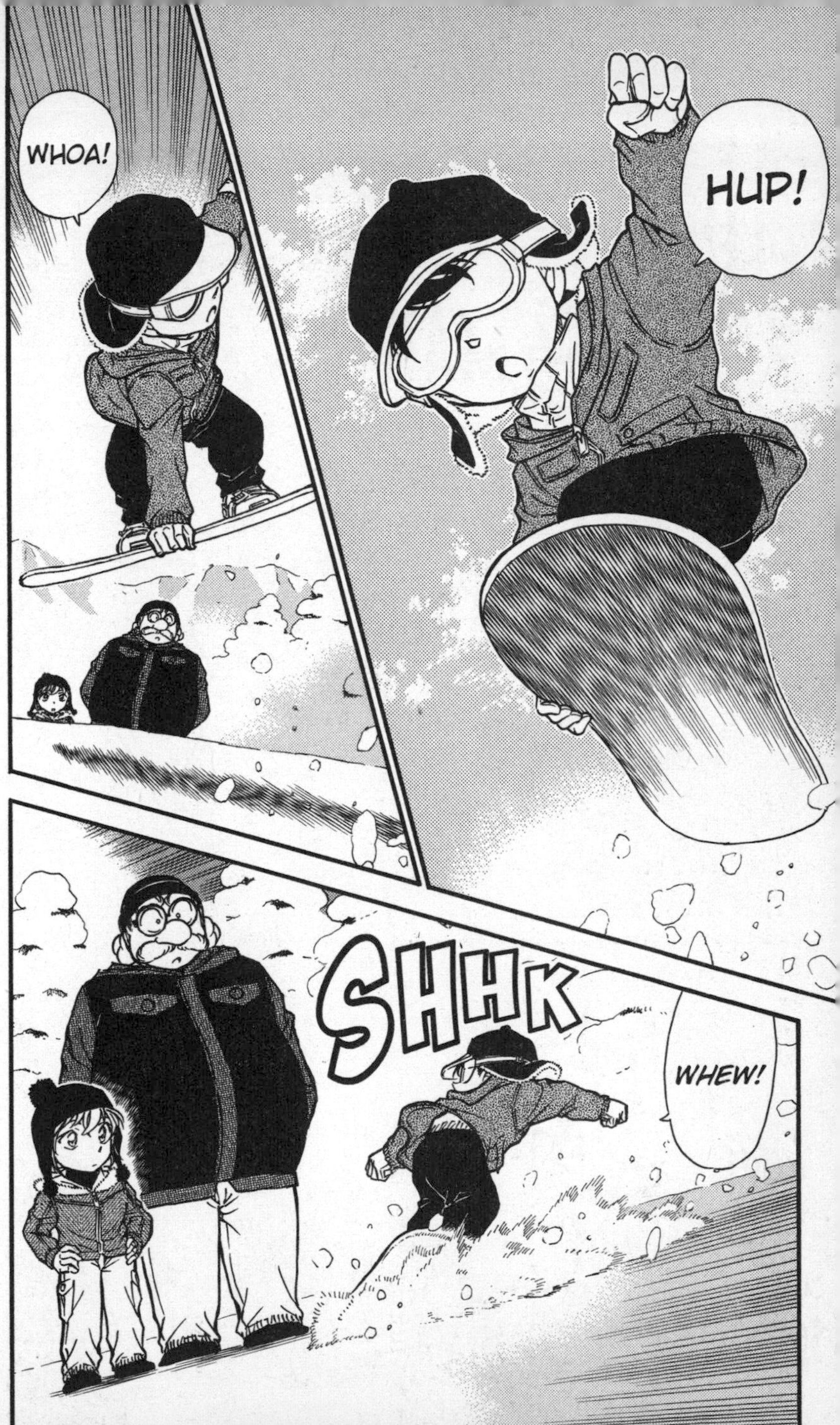
HUP!
WHOA!
SHHK
WHEW!

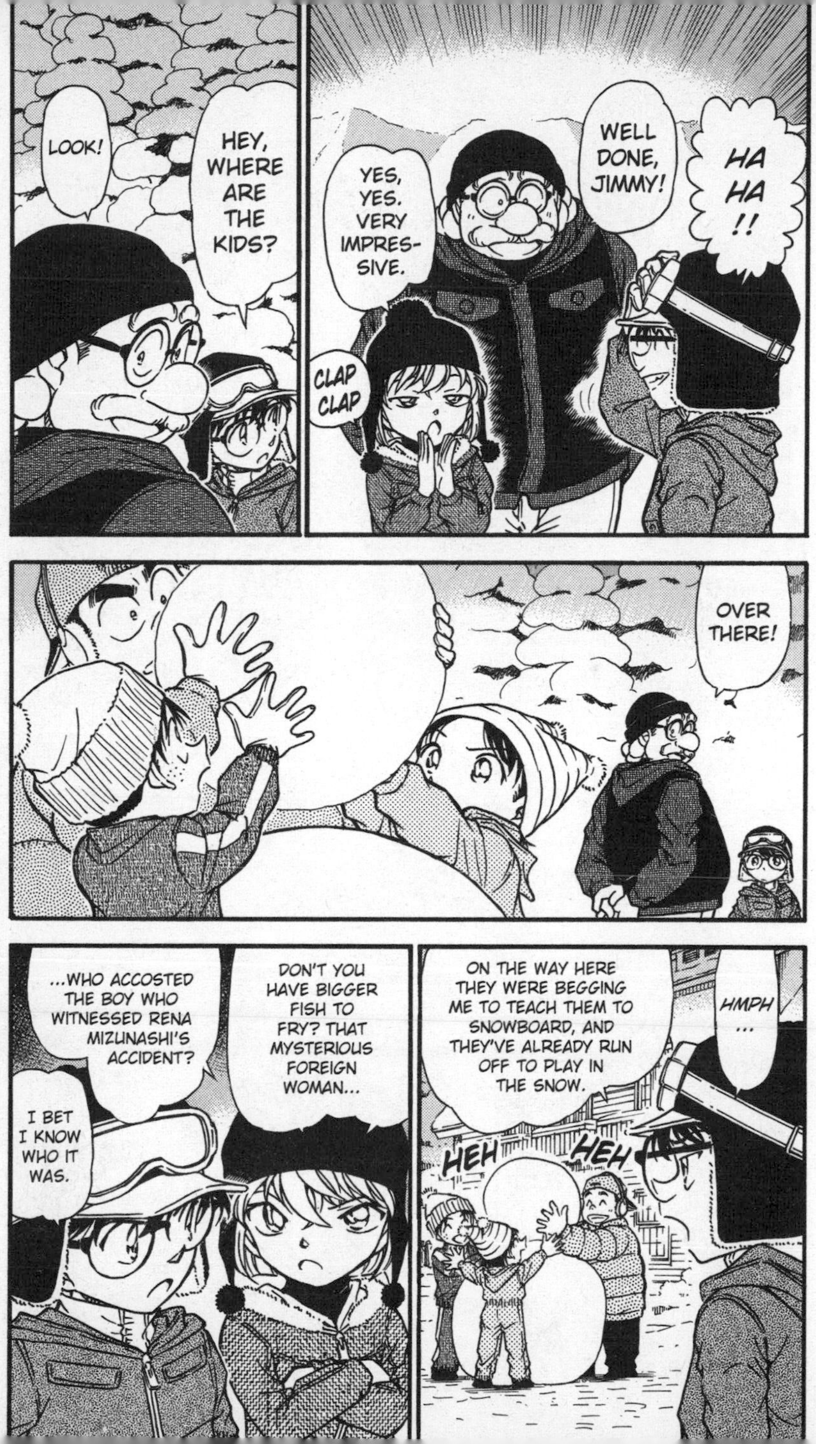
HA HA!!
WELL DONE, JIMMY!
YES, YES. VERY IMPRES-SIVE.
CLAP CLAP
HEY, WHERE ARE THE KIDS?
LOOK!
OVER THERE!
HMPH...
ON THE WAY HERE THEY WERE BEGGING ME TO TEACH THEM TO SNOWBOARD, AND THEY'VE ALREADY RUN OFF TO PLAY IN THE SNOW.
HEH HEH
DON'T YOU HAVE BIGGER FISH TO FRY? THAT MYSTERIOUS FOREIGN WOMAN...
...WHO ACCOSTED THE BOY WHO WITNESSED RENA MIZUNASHI'S ACCIDENT?
I BET I KNOW WHO IT WAS.

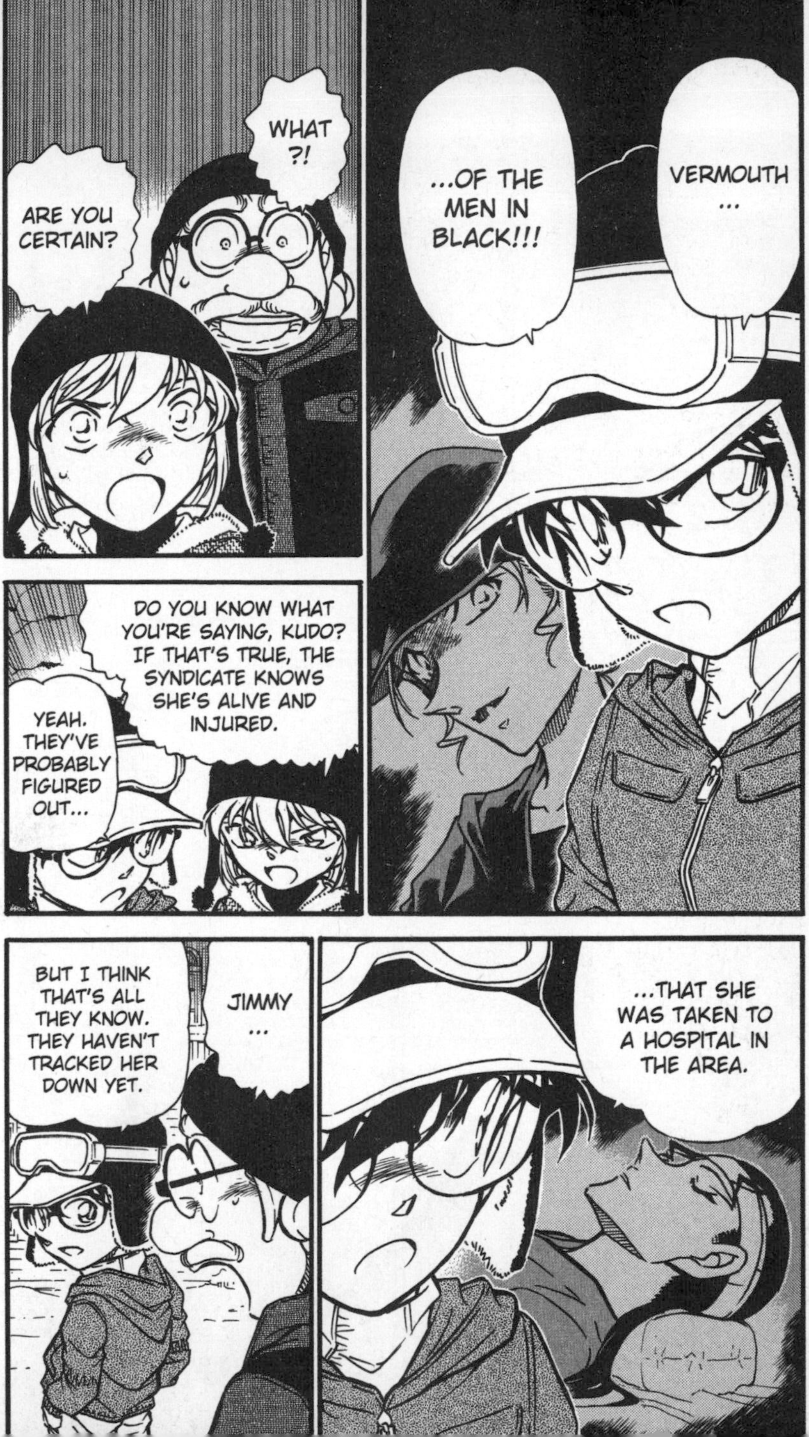
VERMOUTH ...
...OF THE MEN IN BLACK!!!
WHAT ?!
ARE YOU CERTAIN?
DO YOU KNOW WHAT YOU'RE SAYING, KUDO? IF THAT'S TRUE, THE SYNDICATE KNOWS SHE'S ALIVE AND INJURED.
YEAH. THEY'VE PROBABLY FIGURED OUT...
...THAT SHE WAS TAKEN TO A HOSPITAL IN THE AREA.
JIMMY ...
BUT I THINK THAT'S ALL THEY KNOW. THEY HAVEN'T TRACKED HER DOWN YET.

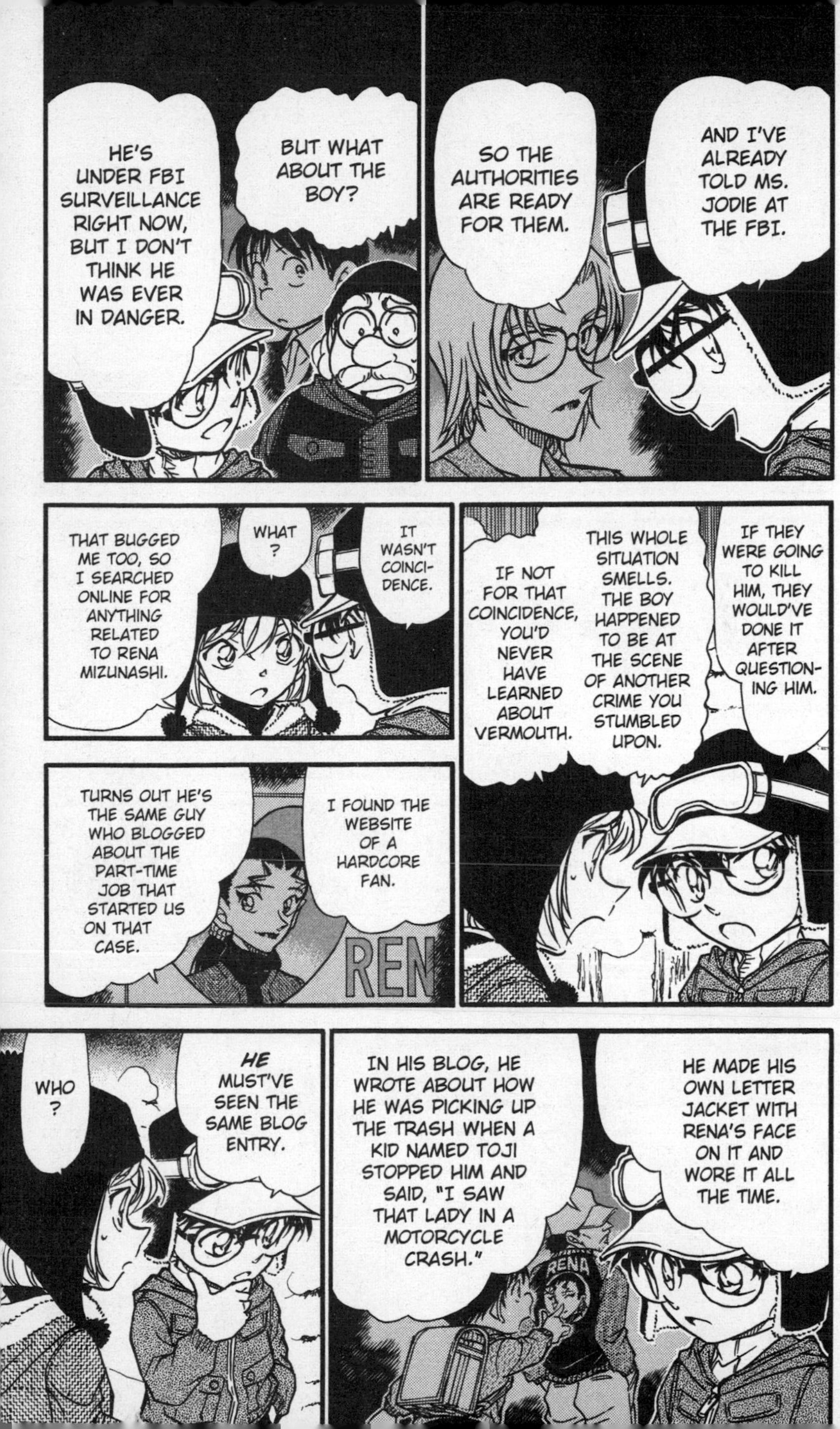
AND I'VE ALREADY TOLD MS. JODIE AT THE FBI.
SO THE AUTHORITIES ARE READY FOR THEM.
BUT WHAT ABOUT THE BOY?
HE'S UNDER FBI SURVEILLANCE RIGHT NOW, BUT I DON'T THINK HE WAS EVER IN DANGER.
IF THEY WERE GOING TO KILL HIM, THEY WOULD'VE DONE IT AFTER QUESTIONING HIM.
THIS WHOLE SITUATION SMELLS. THE BOY HAPPENED TO BE AT THE SCENE OF ANOTHER CRIME YOU STUMBLED UPON.
IF NOT FOR THAT COINCIDENCE, YOU'D NEVER HAVE LEARNED ABOUT VERMOUTH.
IT WASN'T COINCIDENCE.
WHAT?
THAT BUGGED ME TOO, SO I SEARCHED ONLINE FOR ANYTHING RELATED TO RENA MIZUNASHI.
I FOUND THE WEBSITE OF A HARDCORE FAN.
TURNS OUT HE'S THE SAME GUY WHO BLOGGED ABOUT THE PART-TIME JOB THAT STARTED US ON THAT CASE.
REN
HE MADE HIS OWN LETTER JACKET WITH RENA'S FACE ON IT AND WORE IT ALL THE TIME.
IN HIS BLOG, HE WROTE ABOUT HOW HE WAS PICKING UP THE TRASH WHEN A KID NAMED TOJI STOPPED HIM AND SAID, "I SAW THAT LADY IN A MOTORCYCLE CRASH."
RENA
HE MUST'VE SEEN THE SAME BLOG ENTRY.
WHO?

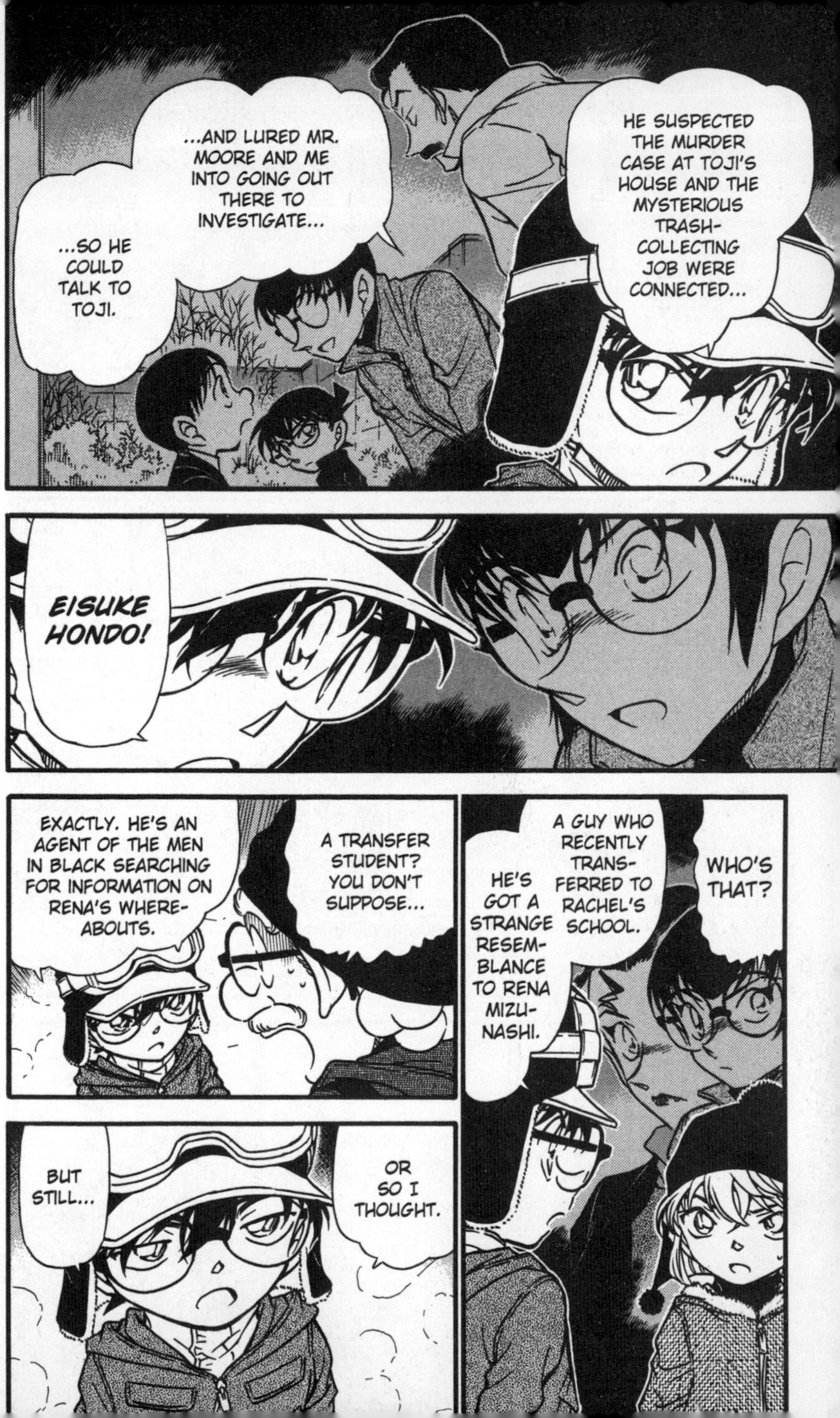
HE SUSPECTED THE MURDER CASE AT TOJI'S HOUSE AND THE MYSTERIOUS TRASH-COLLECTING JOB WERE CONNECTED...
...AND LURED MR. MOORE AND ME INTO GOING OUT THERE TO INVESTIGATE...
...SO HE COULD TALK TO TOJI.
EISUKE HONDO!
WHO'S THAT?
A GUY WHO RECENTLY TRANS-FERRED TO RACHEL'S SCHOOL.
HE'S GOT A STRANGE RESEM-BLANCE TO RENA MIZU-NASHI.
A TRANSFER STUDENT? YOU DON'T SUPPOSE...
EXACTLY. HE'S AN AGENT OF THE MEN IN BLACK SEARCHING FOR INFORMATION ON RENA'S WHERE-ABOUTS.
OR SO I THOUGHT.
BUT STILL...

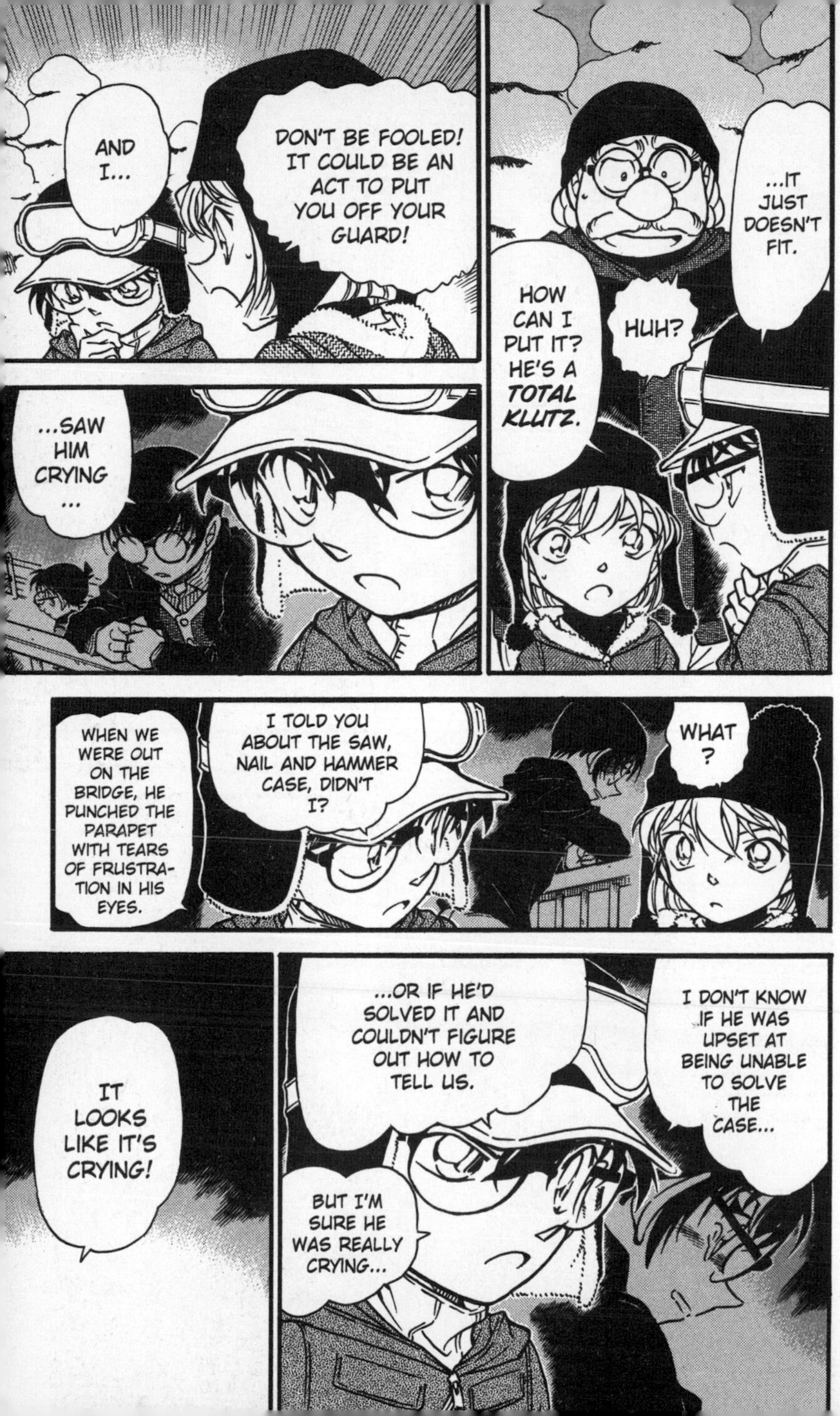
...IT JUST DOESN'T FIT.
HUH?
HOW CAN I PUT IT? HE'S A *TOTAL KLUTZ*.
DON'T BE FOOLED! IT COULD BE AN ACT TO PUT YOU OFF YOUR GUARD!
AND I...
...SAW HIM CRYING...
WHAT?
I TOLD YOU ABOUT THE SAW, NAIL AND HAMMER CASE, DIDN'T I?
WHEN WE WERE OUT ON THE BRIDGE, HE PUNCHED THE PARAPET WITH TEARS OF FRUSTRATION IN HIS EYES.
I DON'T KNOW IF HE WAS UPSET AT BEING UNABLE TO SOLVE THE CASE...
...OR IF HE'D SOLVED IT AND COULDN'T FIGURE OUT HOW TO TELL US.
BUT I'M SURE HE WAS REALLY CRYING...
IT LOOKS LIKE IT'S CRYING!

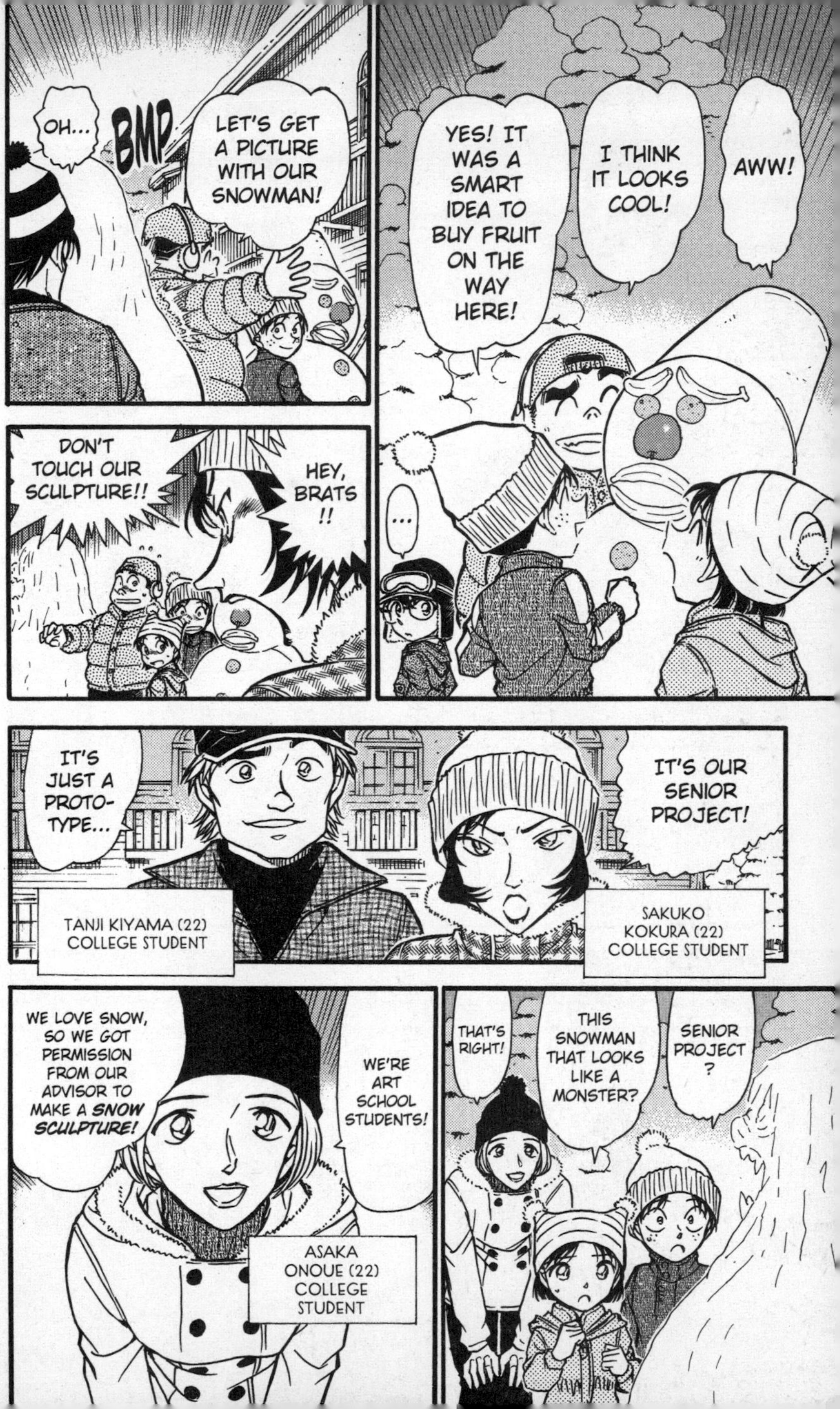
AWW!
I THINK IT LOOKS COOL!
YES! IT WAS A SMART IDEA TO BUY FRUIT ON THE WAY HERE!
...
LET'S GET A PICTURE WITH OUR SNOWMAN!
BMP
OH...
HEY, BRATS!!
DON'T TOUCH OUR SCULPTURE!!
IT'S OUR SENIOR PROJECT!
SAKUKO KOKURA (22) COLLEGE STUDENT
IT'S JUST A PROTOTYPE...
TANJI KIYAMA (22) COLLEGE STUDENT
SENIOR PROJECT?
THIS SNOWMAN THAT LOOKS LIKE A MONSTER?
THAT'S RIGHT!
WE'RE ART SCHOOL STUDENTS!
WE LOVE SNOW, SO WE GOT PERMISSION FROM OUR ADVISOR TO MAKE A *SNOW SCULPTURE!*
ASAKA ONOUE (22) COLLEGE STUDENT

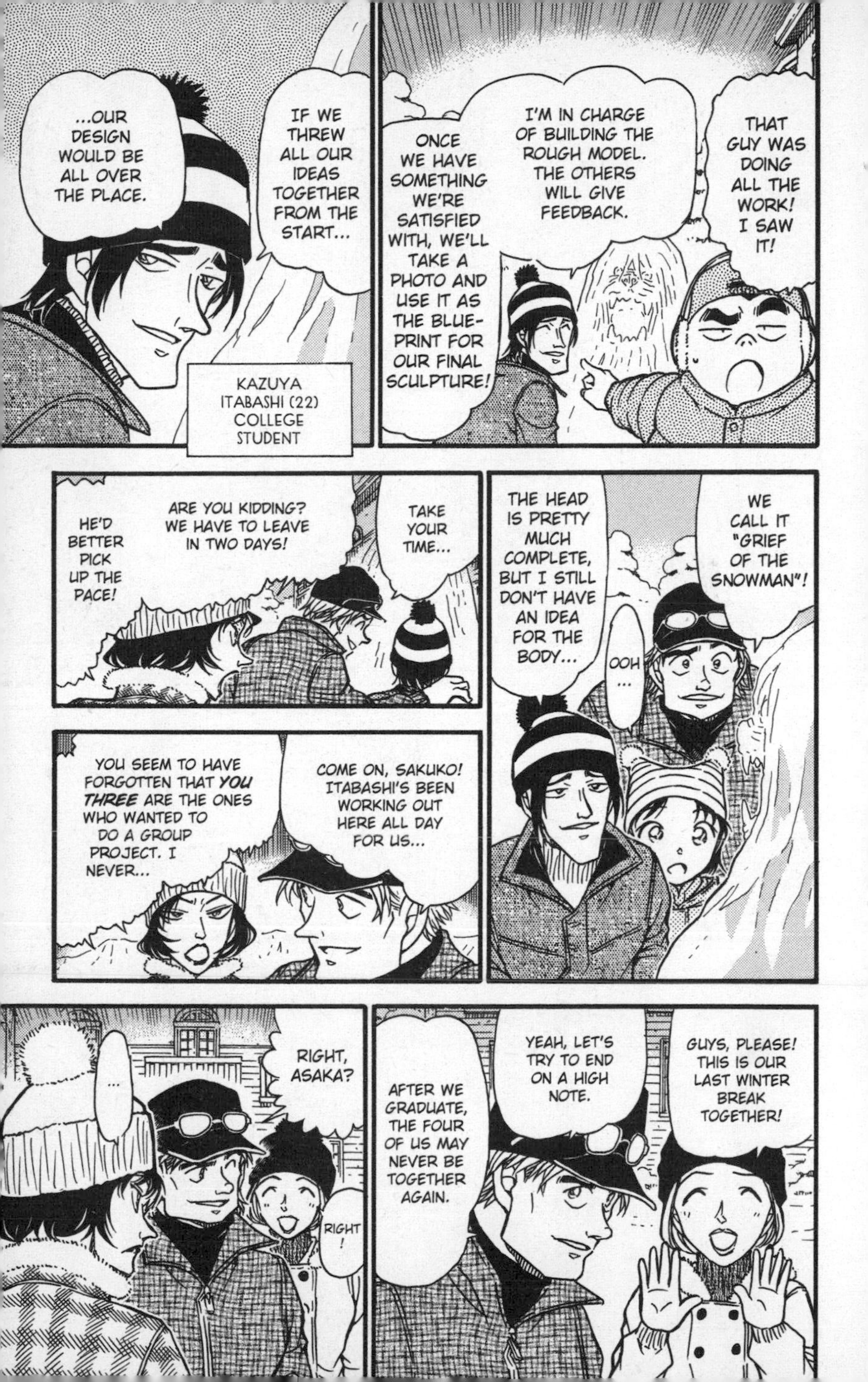
THAT GUY WAS DOING ALL THE WORK! I SAW IT!
I'M IN CHARGE OF BUILDING THE ROUGH MODEL. THE OTHERS WILL GIVE FEEDBACK.
ONCE WE HAVE SOMETHING WE'RE SATISFIED WITH, WE'LL TAKE A PHOTO AND USE IT AS THE BLUE-PRINT FOR OUR FINAL SCULPTURE!
IF WE THREW ALL OUR IDEAS TOGETHER FROM THE START...
...OUR DESIGN WOULD BE ALL OVER THE PLACE.
KAZUYA ITABASHI (22) COLLEGE STUDENT
WE CALL IT "GRIEF OF THE SNOWMAN"!
THE HEAD IS PRETTY MUCH COMPLETE, BUT I STILL DON'T HAVE AN IDEA FOR THE BODY...
OOH ...
TAKE YOUR TIME...
ARE YOU KIDDING? WE HAVE TO LEAVE IN TWO DAYS!
HE'D BETTER PICK UP THE PACE!
COME ON, SAKUKO! ITABASHI'S BEEN WORKING OUT HERE ALL DAY FOR US...
YOU SEEM TO HAVE FORGOTTEN THAT *YOU THREE* ARE THE ONES WHO WANTED TO DO A GROUP PROJECT. I NEVER...
GUYS, PLEASE! THIS IS OUR LAST WINTER BREAK TOGETHER!
YEAH, LET'S TRY TO END ON A HIGH NOTE.
AFTER WE GRADUATE, THE FOUR OF US MAY NEVER BE TOGETHER AGAIN.
RIGHT, ASAKA?
RIGHT!
...

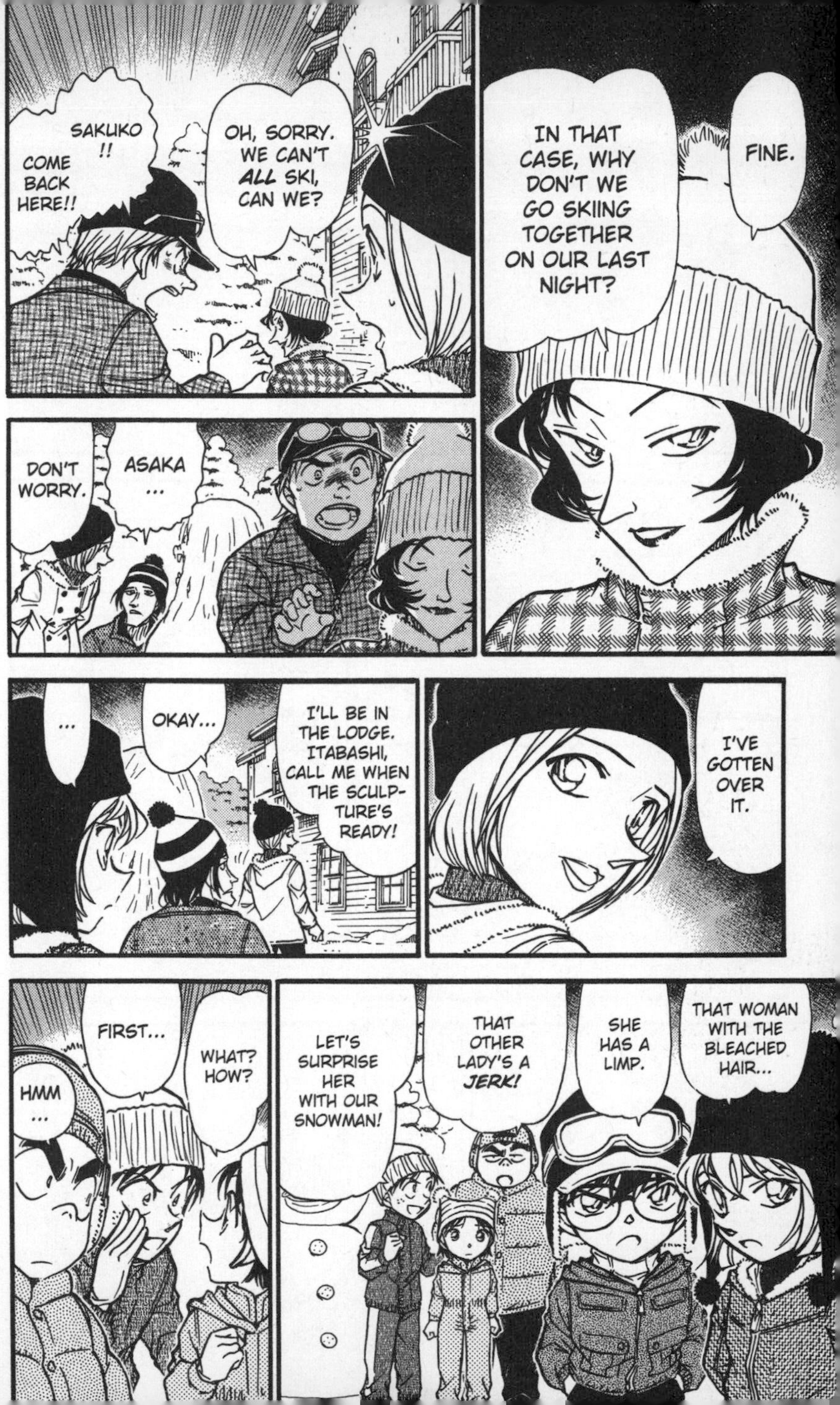
FINE.
IN THAT CASE, WHY DON'T WE GO SKIING TOGETHER ON OUR LAST NIGHT?
OH, SORRY. WE CAN'T ALL SKI, CAN WE?
SAKUKO!!
COME BACK HERE!!
ASAKA...
DON'T WORRY.
I'VE GOTTEN OVER IT.
I'LL BE IN THE LODGE. ITABASHI, CALL ME WHEN THE SCULPTURE'S READY!
OKAY...
...
THAT WOMAN WITH THE BLEACHED HAIR...
SHE HAS A LIMP.
THAT OTHER LADY'S A JERK!
LET'S SURPRISE HER WITH OUR SNOWMAN!
WHAT? HOW?
FIRST...
HMM...

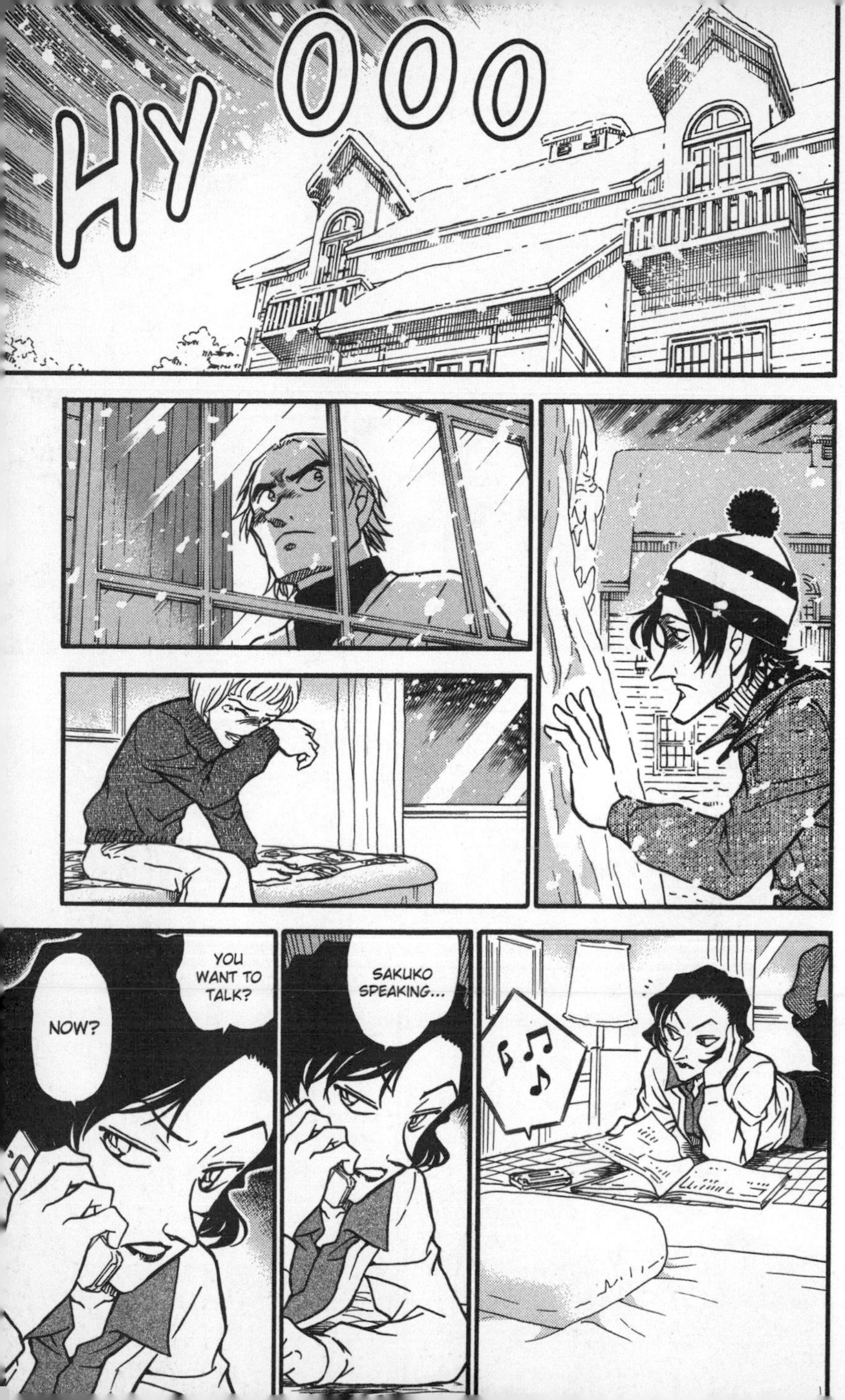
HYOOO
SAKUKO SPEAKING...
YOU WANT TO TALK?
NOW?

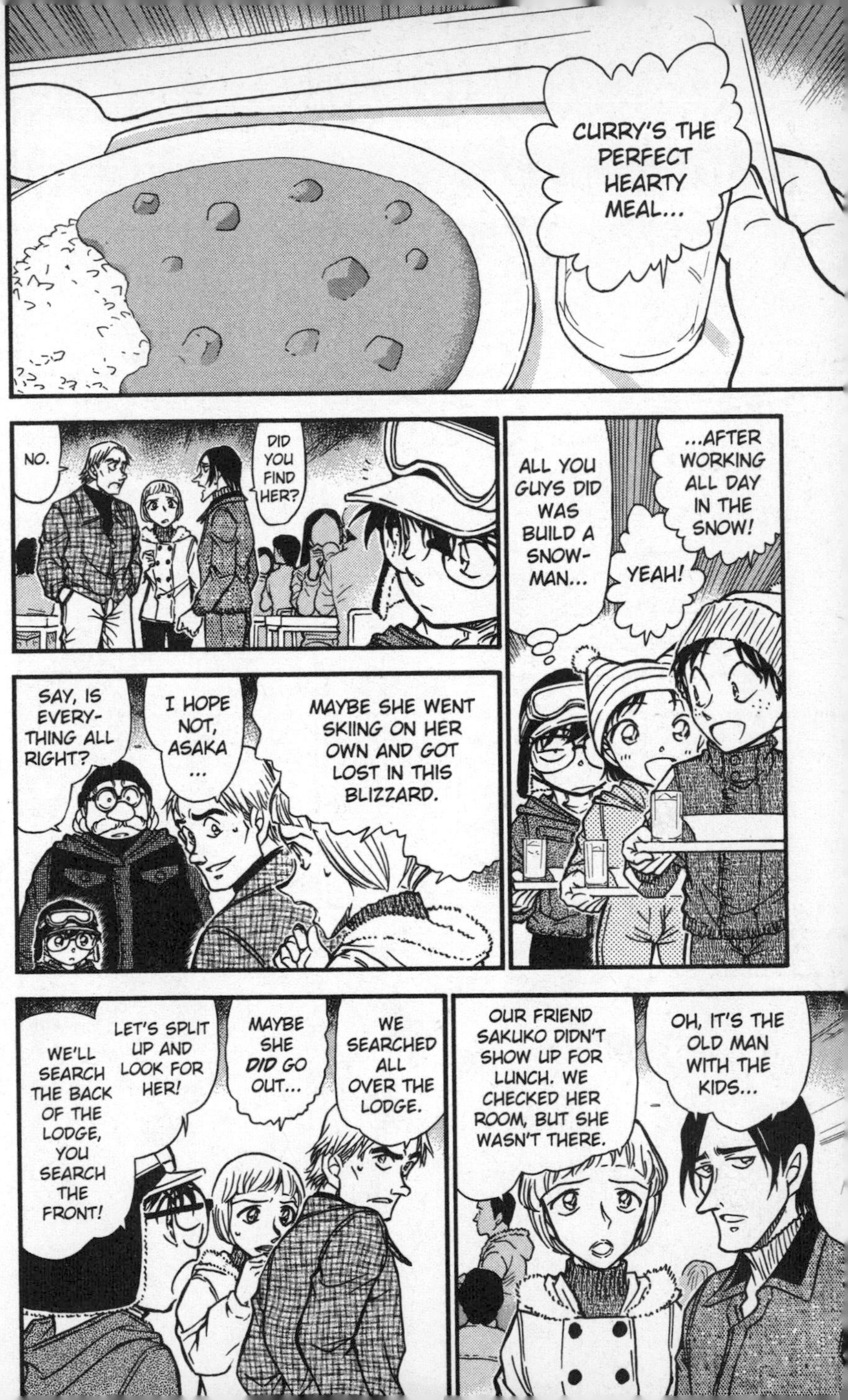
CURRY'S THE PERFECT HEARTY MEAL...
...AFTER WORKING ALL DAY IN THE SNOW!
YEAH!
ALL YOU GUYS DID WAS BUILD A SNOW-MAN...
DID YOU FIND HER?
NO.
MAYBE SHE WENT SKIING ON HER OWN AND GOT LOST IN THIS BLIZZARD.
I HOPE NOT, ASAKA ...
SAY, IS EVERY-THING ALL RIGHT?
OH, IT'S THE OLD MAN WITH THE KIDS...
OUR FRIEND SAKUKO DIDN'T SHOW UP FOR LUNCH. WE CHECKED HER ROOM, BUT SHE WASN'T THERE.
WE SEARCHED ALL OVER THE LODGE.
MAYBE SHE *DID* GO OUT...
LET'S SPLIT UP AND LOOK FOR HER!
WE'LL SEARCH THE BACK OF THE LODGE, YOU SEARCH THE FRONT!

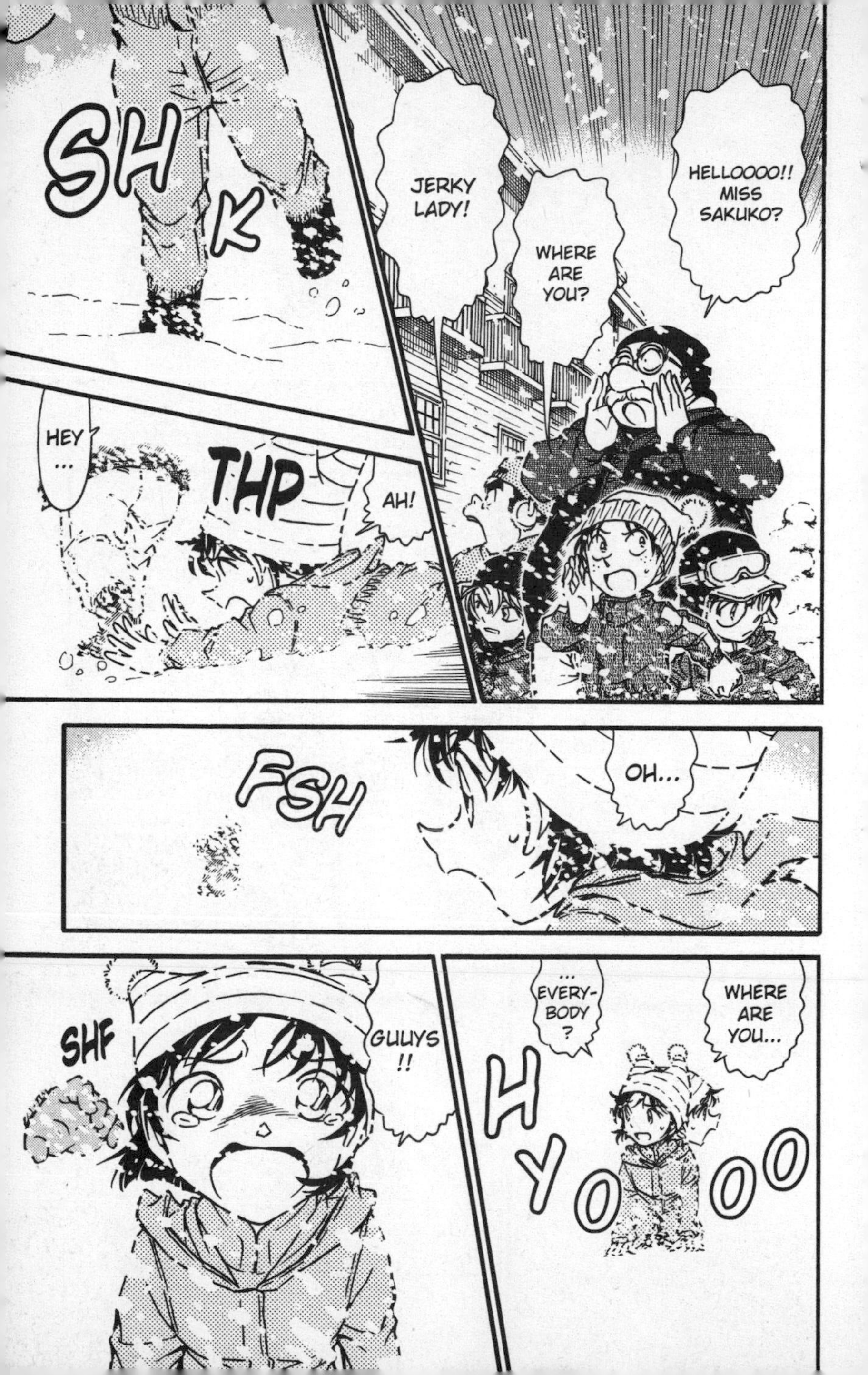
HELLOOOO!! MISS SAKUKO?
WHERE ARE YOU?
JERKY LADY!
SHK
AH!
THP
HEY ...
OH...
FSH
WHERE ARE YOU...
... EVERY-BODY?
HYOOO
GUUYS!!
SHF

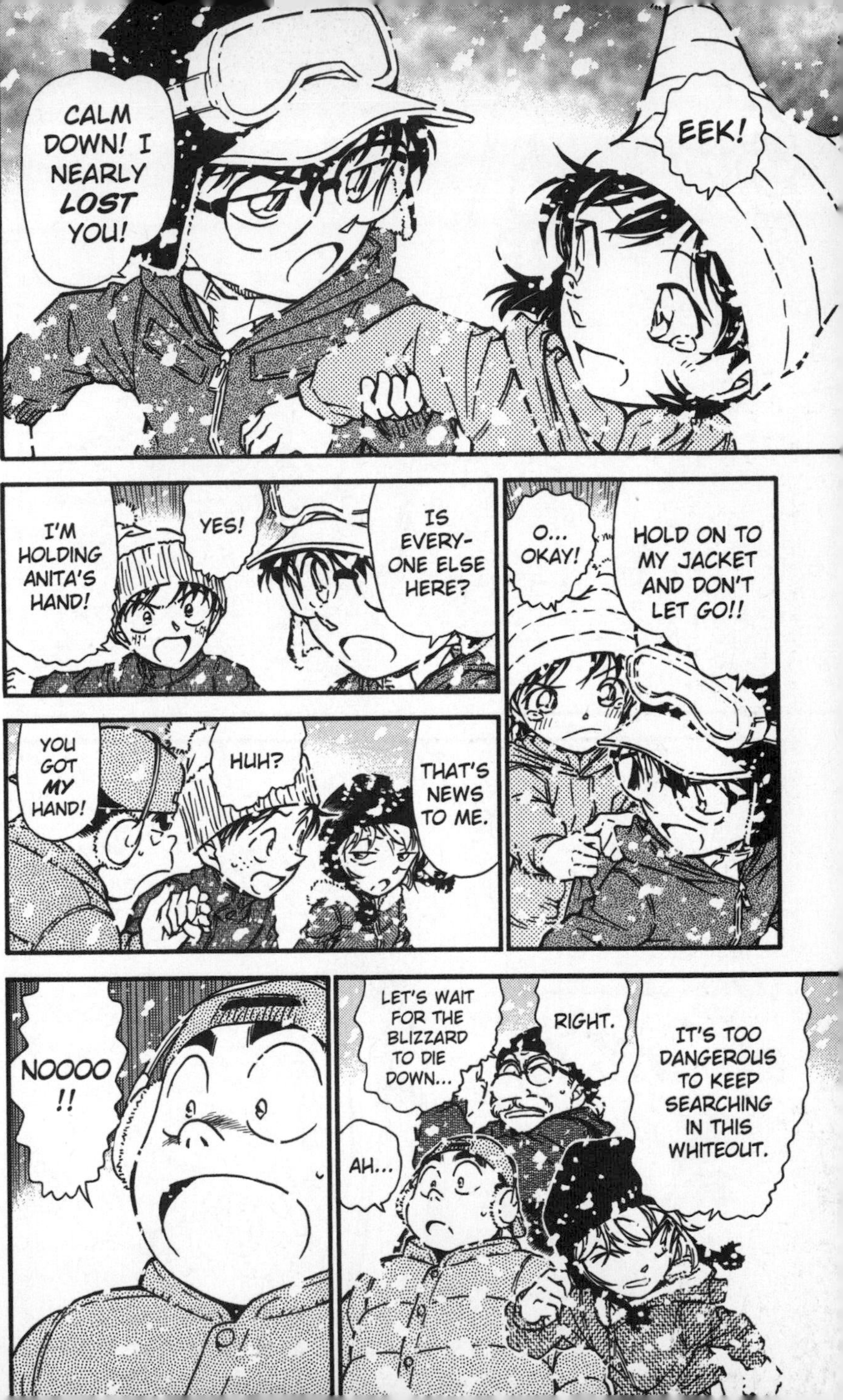
EEK!
CALM DOWN! I NEARLY LOST YOU!
HOLD ON TO MY JACKET AND DON'T LET GO!!
O... OKAY!
IS EVERY-ONE ELSE HERE?
YES!
I'M HOLDING ANITA'S HAND!
THAT'S NEWS TO ME.
HUH?
YOU GOT MY HAND!
IT'S TOO DANGEROUS TO KEEP SEARCHING IN THIS WHITEOUT.
RIGHT.
LET'S WAIT FOR THE BLIZZARD TO DIE DOWN...
AH...
NOOOO!!

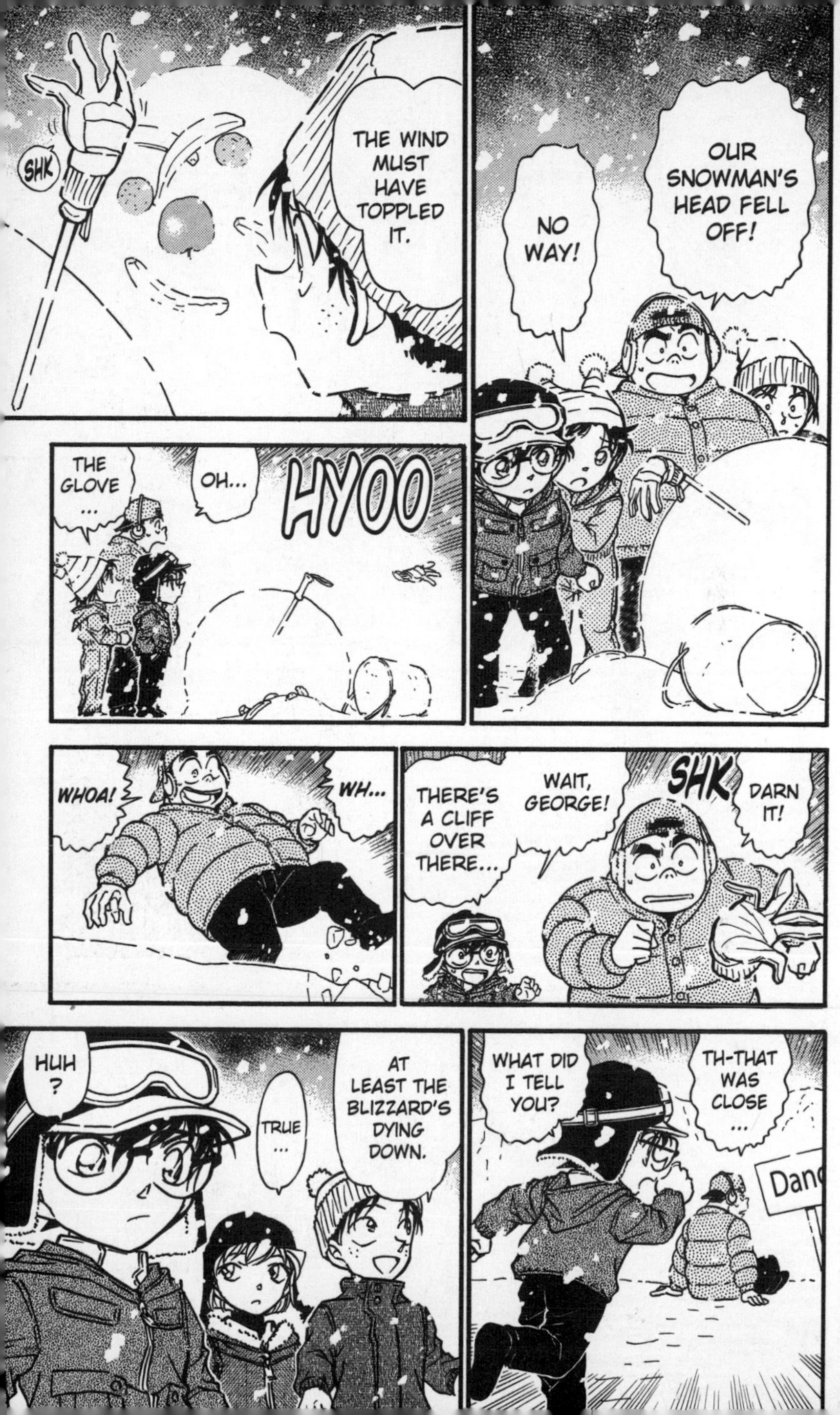
OUR SNOWMAN'S HEAD FELL OFF!
NO WAY!
THE WIND MUST HAVE TOPPLED IT.
SHK
HYOO
OH...
THE GLOVE ...
DARN IT!
SHK
WAIT, GEORGE!
THERE'S A CLIFF OVER THERE...
WH...
WHOA!
TH-THAT WAS CLOSE ...
WHAT DID I TELL YOU?
Dan
AT LEAST THE BLIZZARD'S DYING DOWN.
TRUE ...
HUH ?

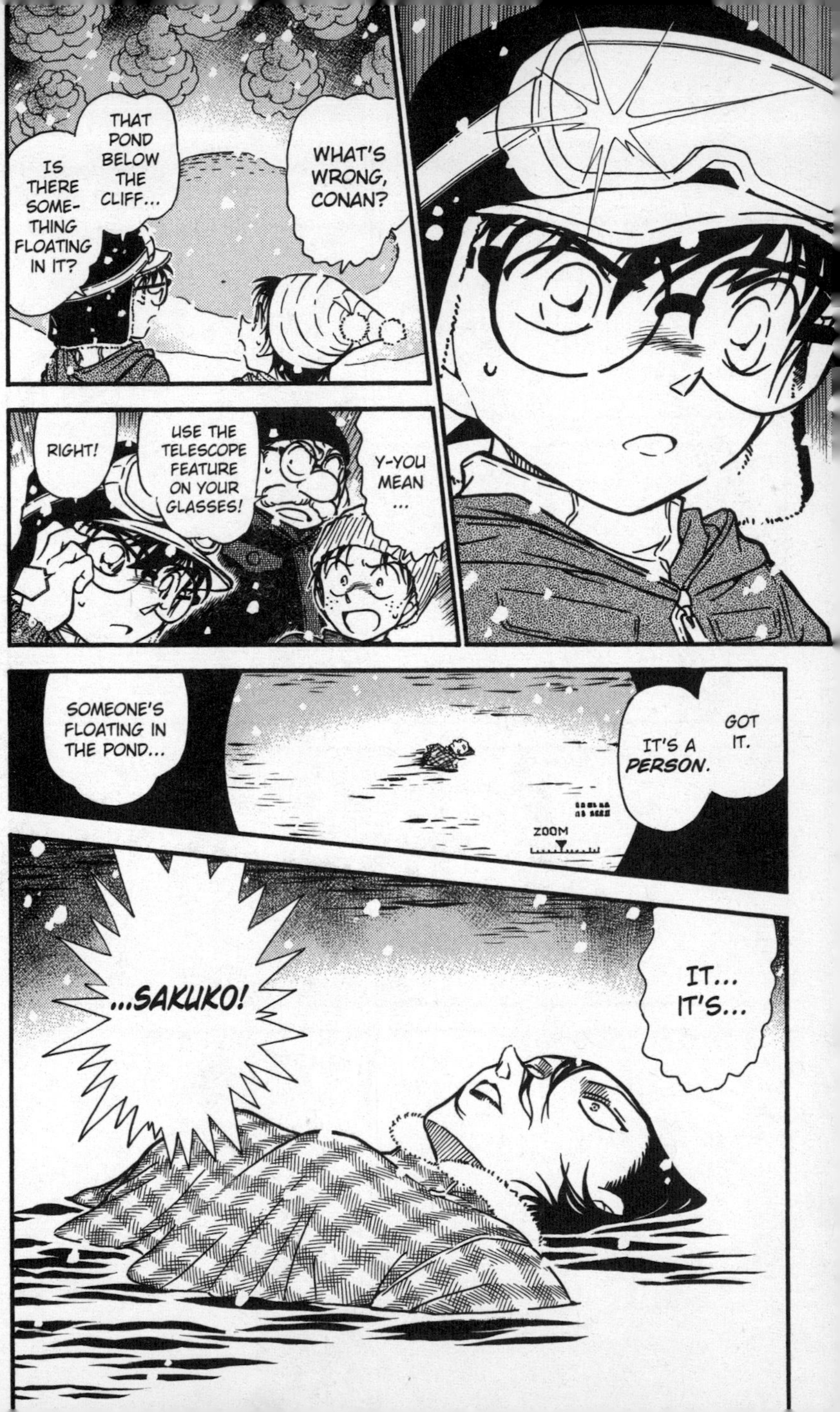
WHAT'S WRONG, CONAN?
THAT POND BELOW THE CLIFF...
IS THERE SOME-THING FLOATING IN IT?
Y-YOU MEAN ...
USE THE TELESCOPE FEATURE ON YOUR GLASSES!
RIGHT!
GOT IT.
IT'S A **PERSON**.
ZOOM
SOMEONE'S FLOATING IN THE POND...
IT... IT'S...
...SAKUKO!

FILE 4:
TRAJECTORY OF THE FALL

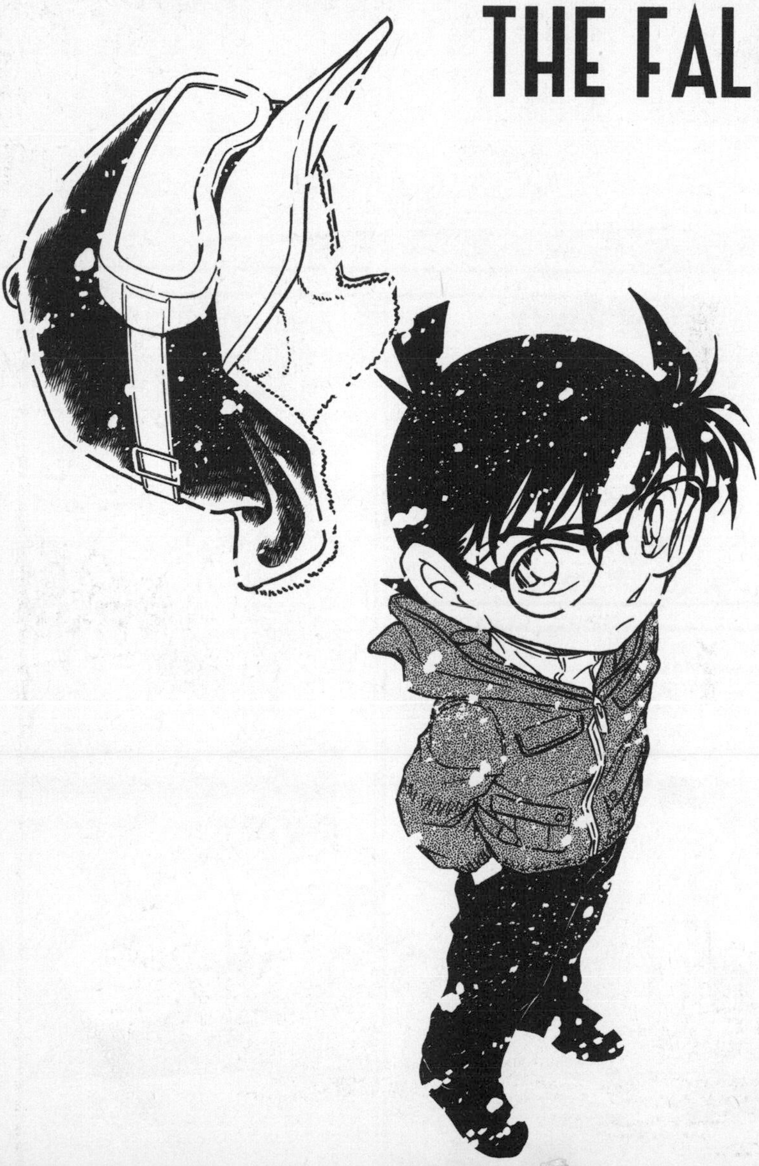

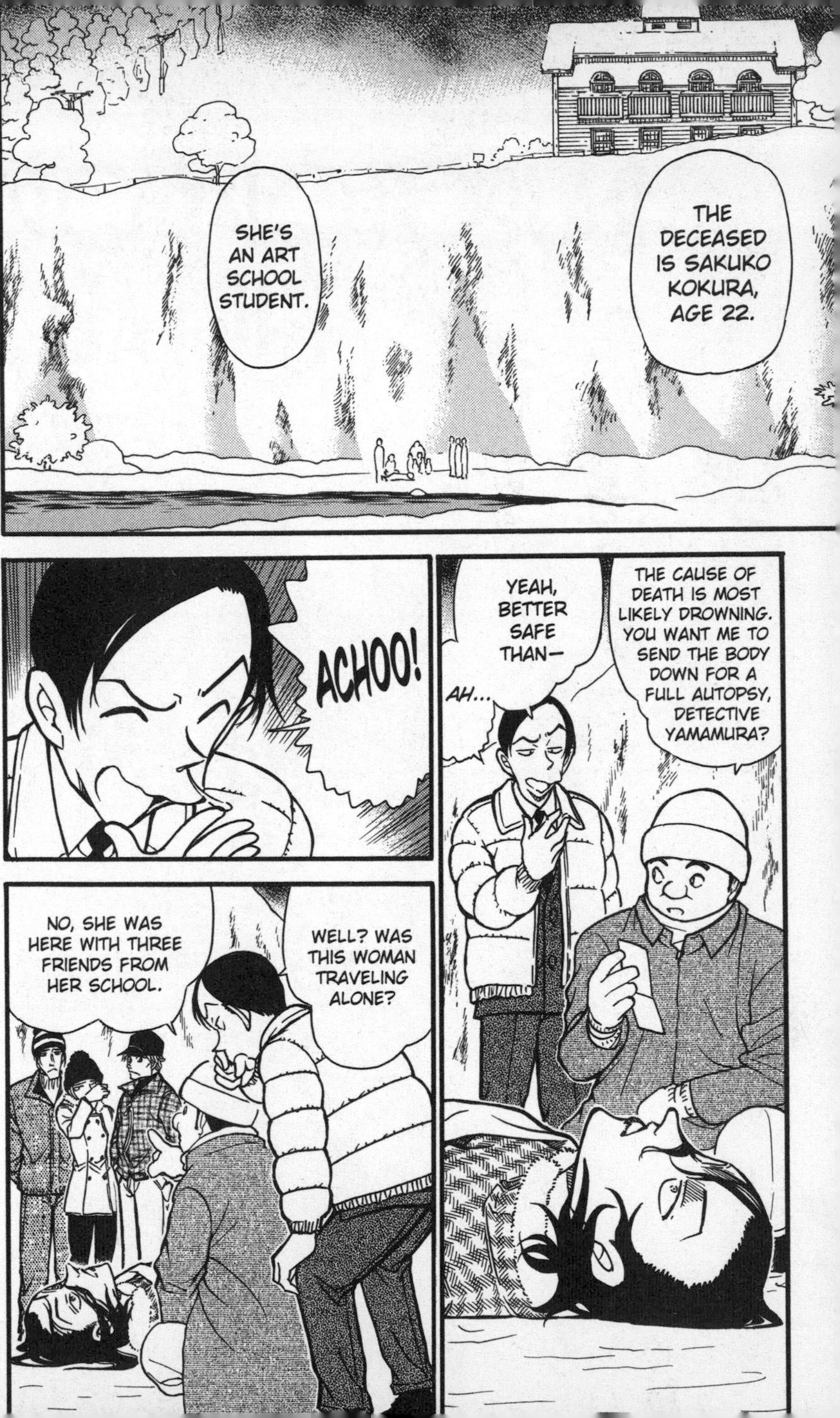
THE DECEASED IS SAKUKO KOKURA, AGE 22.
SHE'S AN ART SCHOOL STUDENT.
THE CAUSE OF DEATH IS MOST LIKELY DROWNING. YOU WANT ME TO SEND THE BODY DOWN FOR A FULL AUTOPSY, DETECTIVE YAMAMURA?
YEAH, BETTER SAFE THAN—
AH...
ACHOO!
WELL? WAS THIS WOMAN TRAVELING ALONE?
NO, SHE WAS HERE WITH THREE FRIENDS FROM HER SCHOOL.

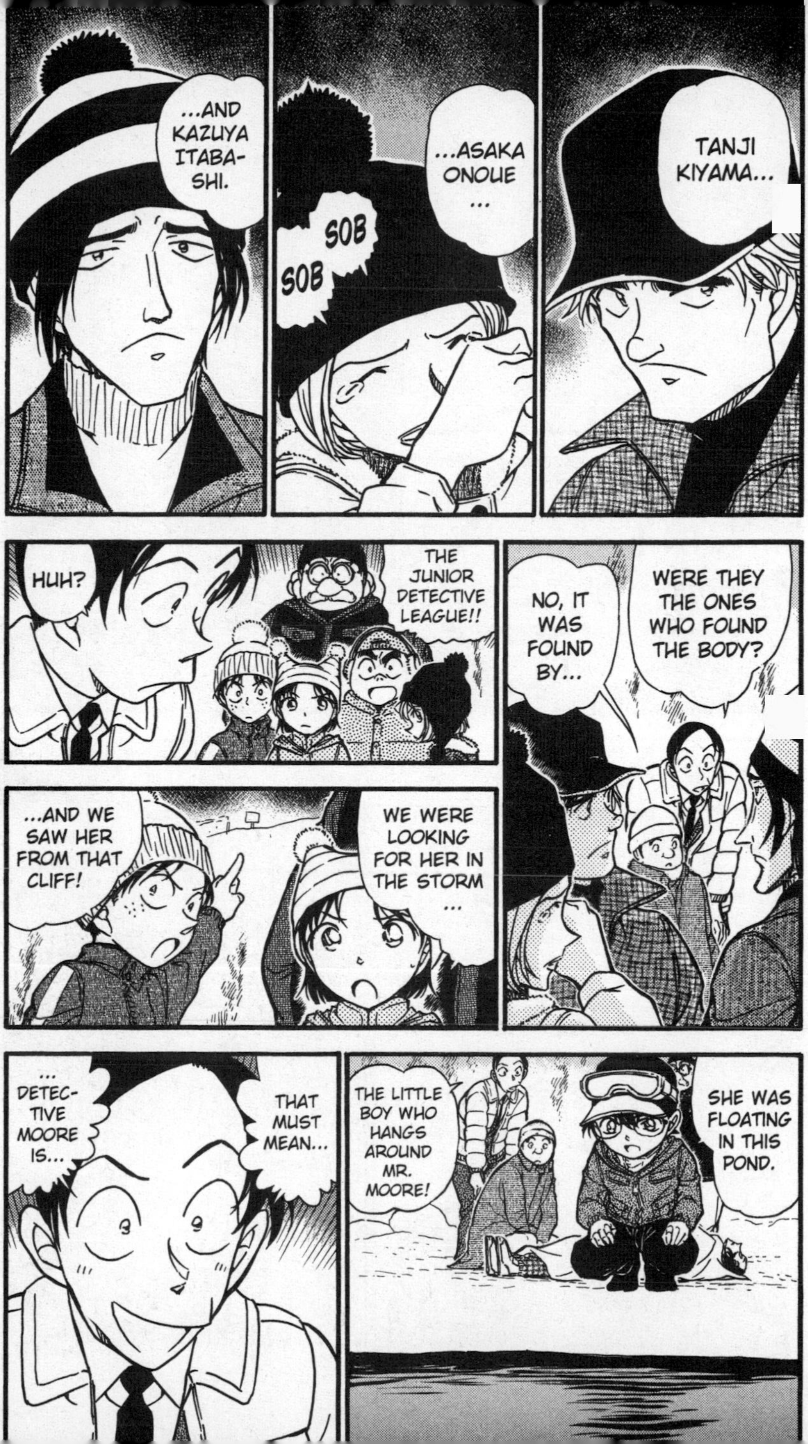
TANJI KIYAMA...
...ASAKA ONOUE ...
SOB SOB
...AND KAZUYA ITABA-SHI.
WERE THEY THE ONES WHO FOUND THE BODY?
NO, IT WAS FOUND BY...
THE JUNIOR DETECTIVE LEAGUE!!
HUH?
WE WERE LOOKING FOR HER IN THE STORM ...
...AND WE SAW HER FROM THAT CLIFF!
SHE WAS FLOATING IN THIS POND.
THE LITTLE BOY WHO HANGS AROUND MR. MOORE!
THAT MUST MEAN...
...DETECTIVE MOORE IS...

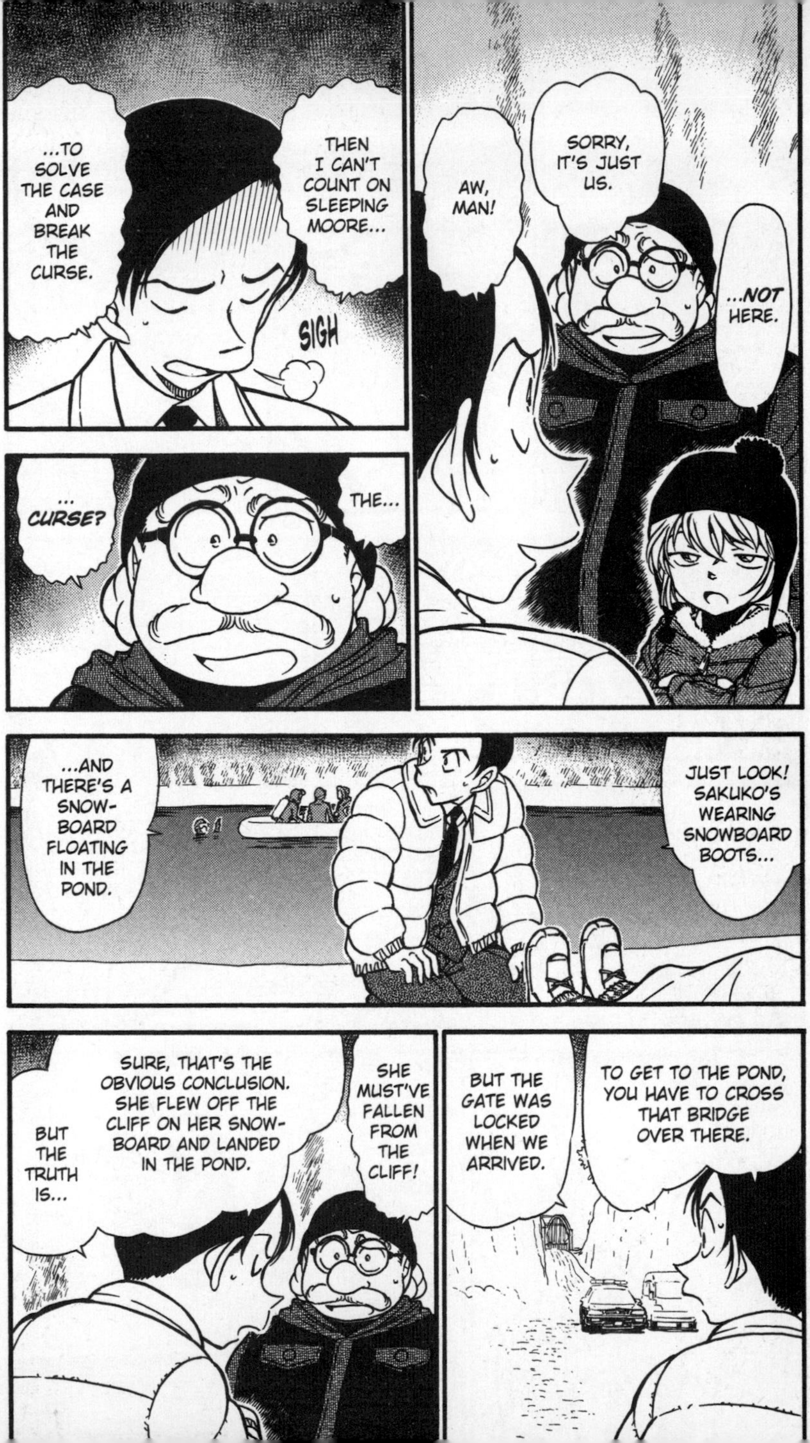
SORRY, IT'S JUST US.
...NOT HERE.
AW, MAN!
THEN I CAN'T COUNT ON SLEEPING MOORE...
...TO SOLVE THE CASE AND BREAK THE CURSE.
SIGH
THE...
...CURSE?
JUST LOOK! SAKUKO'S WEARING SNOWBOARD BOOTS...
...AND THERE'S A SNOW-BOARD FLOATING IN THE POND.
TO GET TO THE POND, YOU HAVE TO CROSS THAT BRIDGE OVER THERE.
BUT THE GATE WAS LOCKED WHEN WE ARRIVED.
SHE MUST'VE FALLEN FROM THE CLIFF!
SURE, THAT'S THE OBVIOUS CONCLUSION. SHE FLEW OFF THE CLIFF ON HER SNOW-BOARD AND LANDED IN THE POND.
BUT THE TRUTH IS...

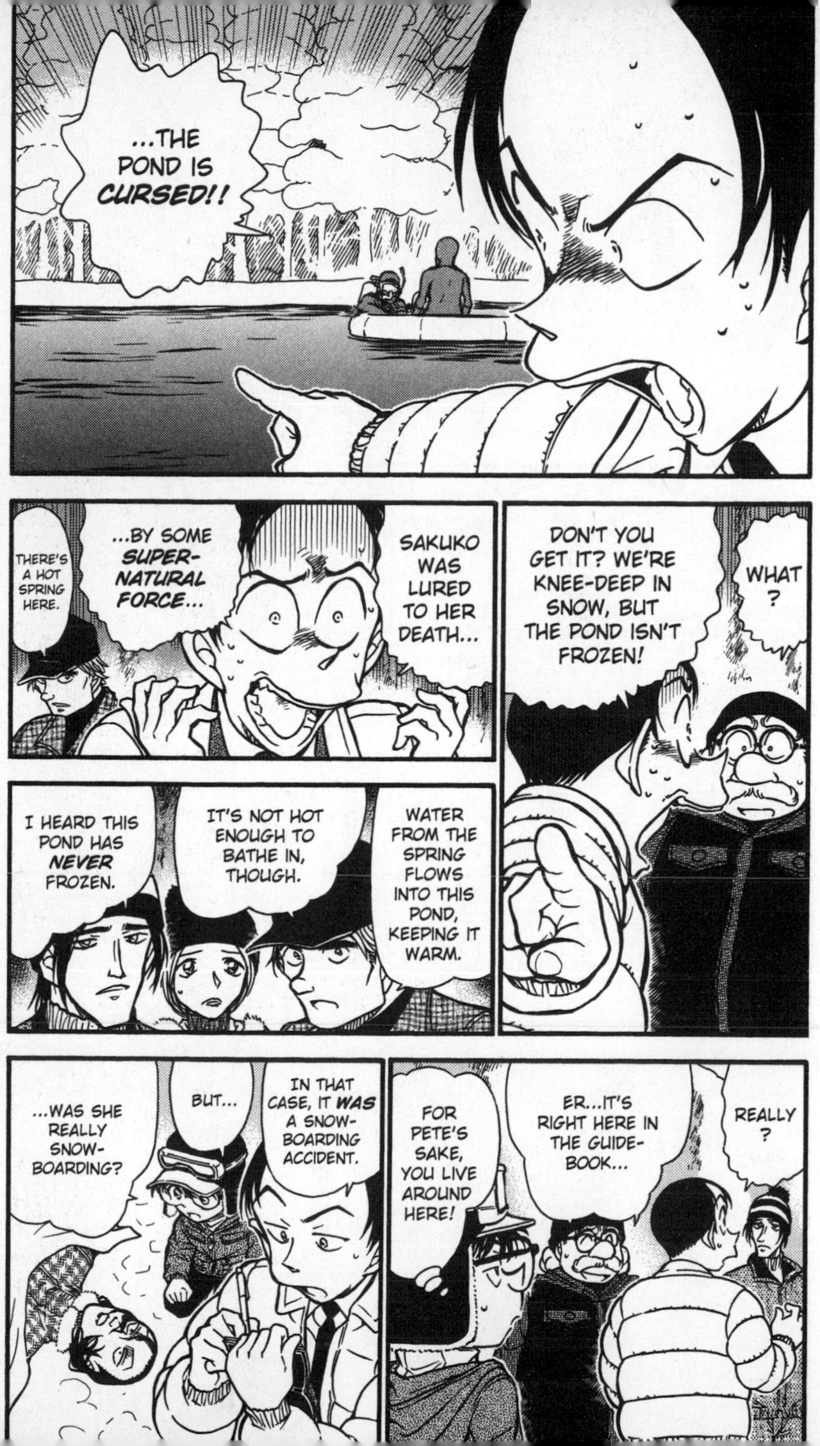
...THE POND IS CURSED!!
WHAT?
DON'T YOU GET IT? WE'RE KNEE-DEEP IN SNOW, BUT THE POND ISN'T FROZEN!
SAKUKO WAS LURED TO HER DEATH...
...BY SOME SUPER-NATURAL FORCE...
THERE'S A HOT SPRING HERE.
WATER FROM THE SPRING FLOWS INTO THIS POND, KEEPING IT WARM.
IT'S NOT HOT ENOUGH TO BATHE IN, THOUGH.
I HEARD THIS POND HAS NEVER FROZEN.
REALLY?
ER...IT'S RIGHT HERE IN THE GUIDE-BOOK...
FOR PETE'S SAKE, YOU LIVE AROUND HERE!
IN THAT CASE, IT WAS A SNOW-BOARDING ACCIDENT.
BUT...
...WAS SHE REALLY SNOW-BOARDING?

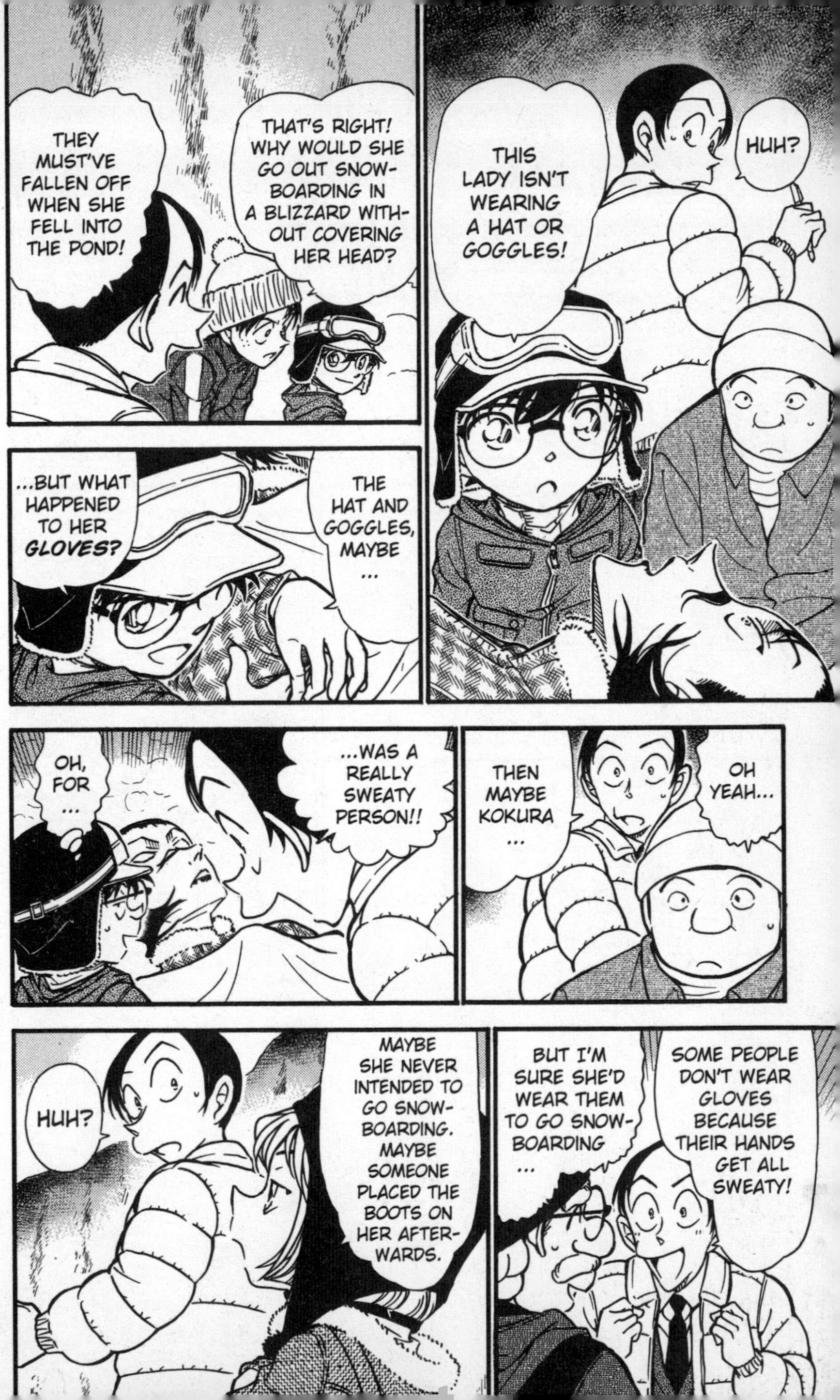
HUH?
THIS LADY ISN'T WEARING A HAT OR GOGGLES!
THAT'S RIGHT! WHY WOULD SHE GO OUT SNOW-BOARDING IN A BLIZZARD WITH-OUT COVERING HER HEAD?
THEY MUST'VE FALLEN OFF WHEN SHE FELL INTO THE POND!
THE HAT AND GOGGLES, MAYBE ...
...BUT WHAT HAPPENED TO HER *GLOVES?*
OH YEAH...
THEN MAYBE KOKURA ...
...WAS A REALLY SWEATY PERSON!!
OH, FOR ...
SOME PEOPLE DON'T WEAR GLOVES BECAUSE THEIR HANDS GET ALL SWEATY!
BUT I'M SURE SHE'D WEAR THEM TO GO SNOW-BOARDING ...
MAYBE SHE NEVER INTENDED TO GO SNOW-BOARDING. MAYBE SOMEONE PLACED THE BOOTS ON HER AFTER-WARDS.
HUH?

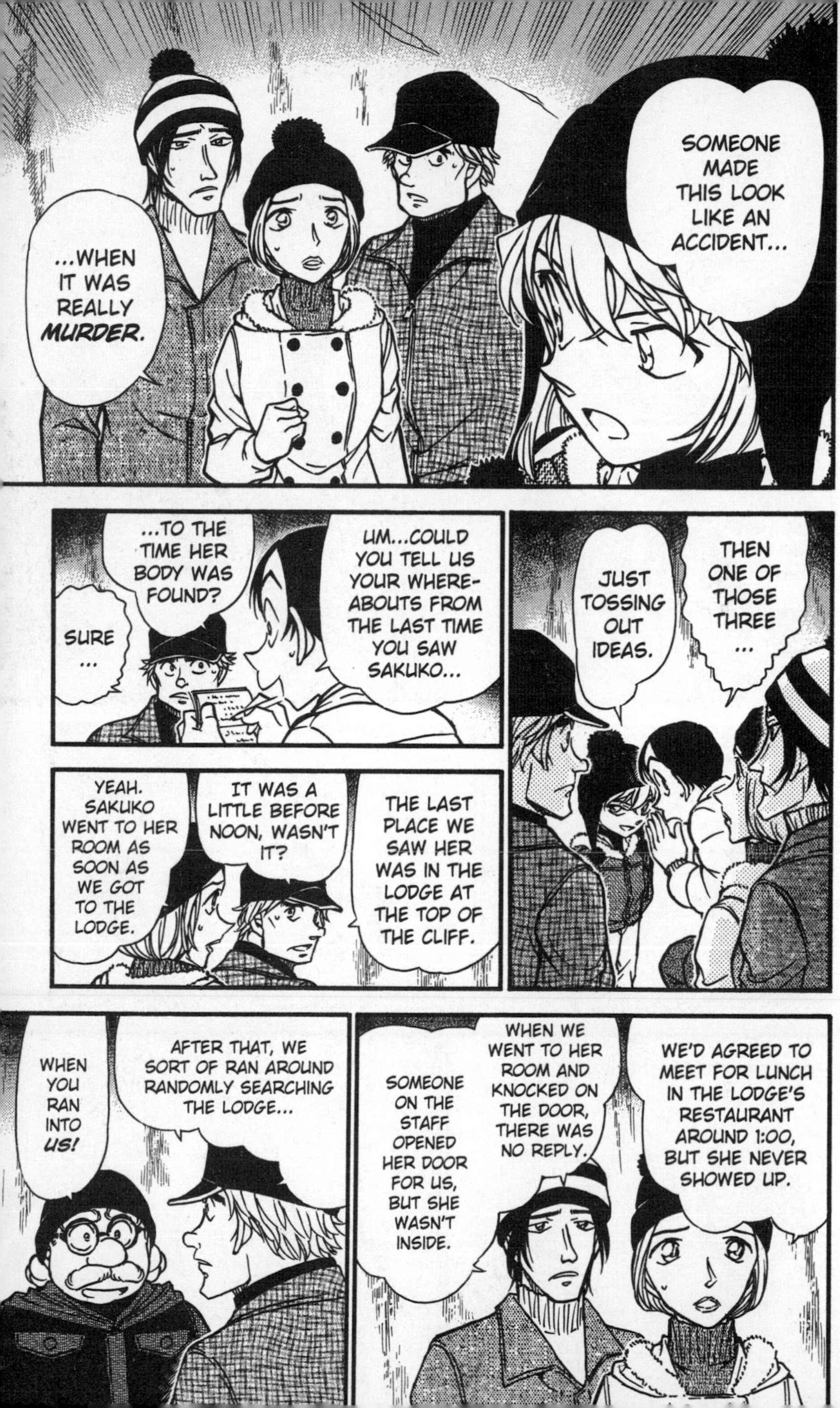
SOMEONE MADE THIS LOOK LIKE AN ACCIDENT...
...WHEN IT WAS REALLY *MURDER*.
THEN ONE OF THOSE THREE ...
JUST TOSSING OUT IDEAS.
UM...COULD YOU TELL US YOUR WHERE-ABOUTS FROM THE LAST TIME YOU SAW SAKUKO...
...TO THE TIME HER BODY WAS FOUND?
SURE ...
THE LAST PLACE WE SAW HER WAS IN THE LODGE AT THE TOP OF THE CLIFF.
IT WAS A LITTLE BEFORE NOON, WASN'T IT?
YEAH. SAKUKO WENT TO HER ROOM AS SOON AS WE GOT TO THE LODGE.
WE'D AGREED TO MEET FOR LUNCH IN THE LODGE'S RESTAURANT AROUND 1:00, BUT SHE NEVER SHOWED UP.
WHEN WE WENT TO HER ROOM AND KNOCKED ON THE DOOR, THERE WAS NO REPLY.
SOMEONE ON THE STAFF OPENED HER DOOR FOR US, BUT SHE WASN'T INSIDE.
AFTER THAT, WE SORT OF RAN AROUND RANDOMLY SEARCHING THE LODGE...
WHEN YOU RAN INTO *US!*

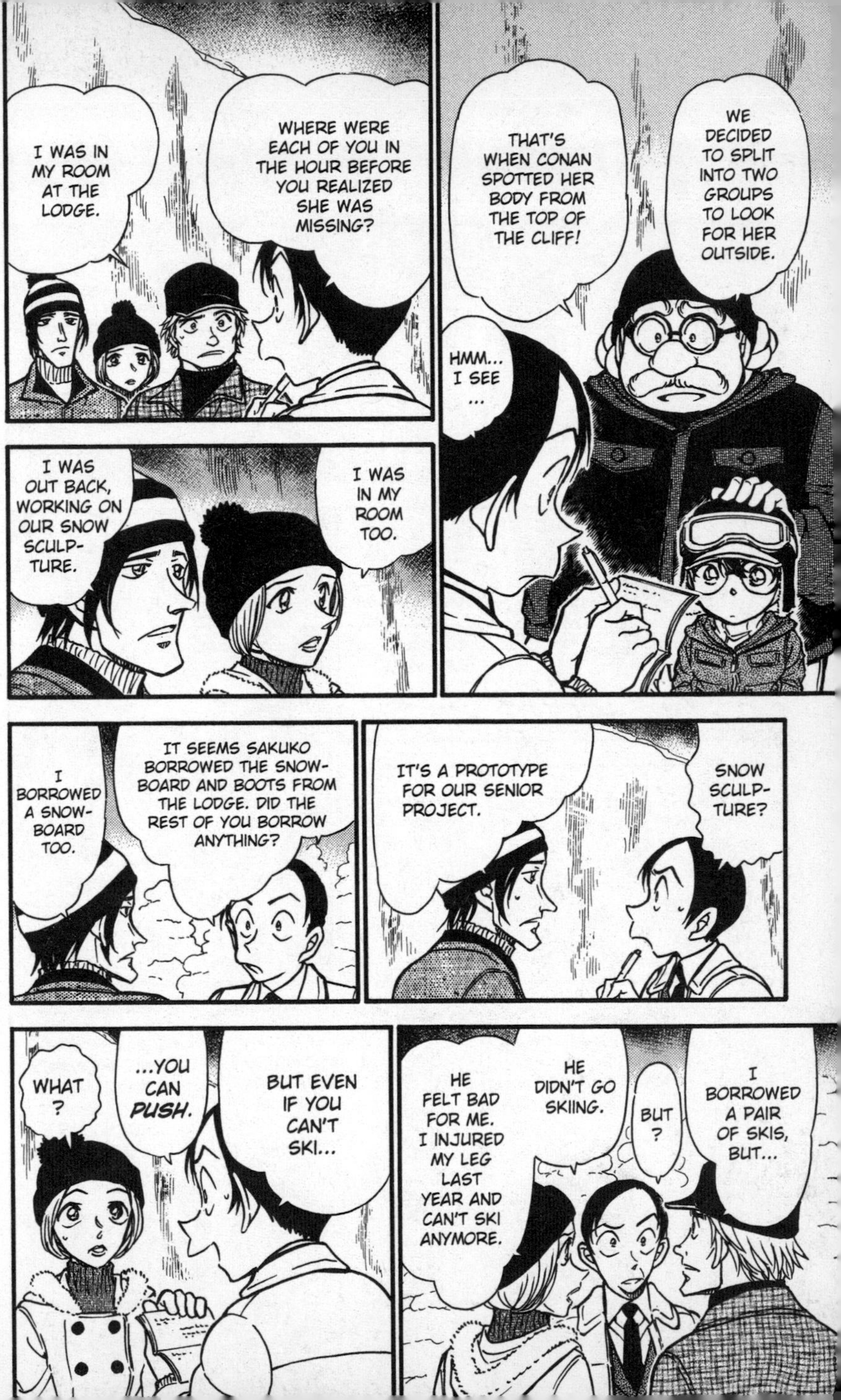
WE DECIDED TO SPLIT INTO TWO GROUPS TO LOOK FOR HER OUTSIDE.
THAT'S WHEN CONAN SPOTTED HER BODY FROM THE TOP OF THE CLIFF!
HMM... I SEE ...
WHERE WERE EACH OF YOU IN THE HOUR BEFORE YOU REALIZED SHE WAS MISSING?
I WAS IN MY ROOM AT THE LODGE.
I WAS IN MY ROOM TOO.
I WAS OUT BACK, WORKING ON OUR SNOW SCULP-TURE.
SNOW SCULP-TURE?
IT'S A PROTOTYPE FOR OUR SENIOR PROJECT.
IT SEEMS SAKUKO BORROWED THE SNOW-BOARD AND BOOTS FROM THE LODGE. DID THE REST OF YOU BORROW ANYTHING?
I BORROWED A SNOW-BOARD TOO.
I BORROWED A PAIR OF SKIS, BUT...
BUT ?
HE DIDN'T GO SKIING.
HE FELT BAD FOR ME. I INJURED MY LEG LAST YEAR AND CAN'T SKI ANYMORE.
BUT EVEN IF YOU CAN'T SKI...
...YOU CAN *PUSH*.
WHAT ?

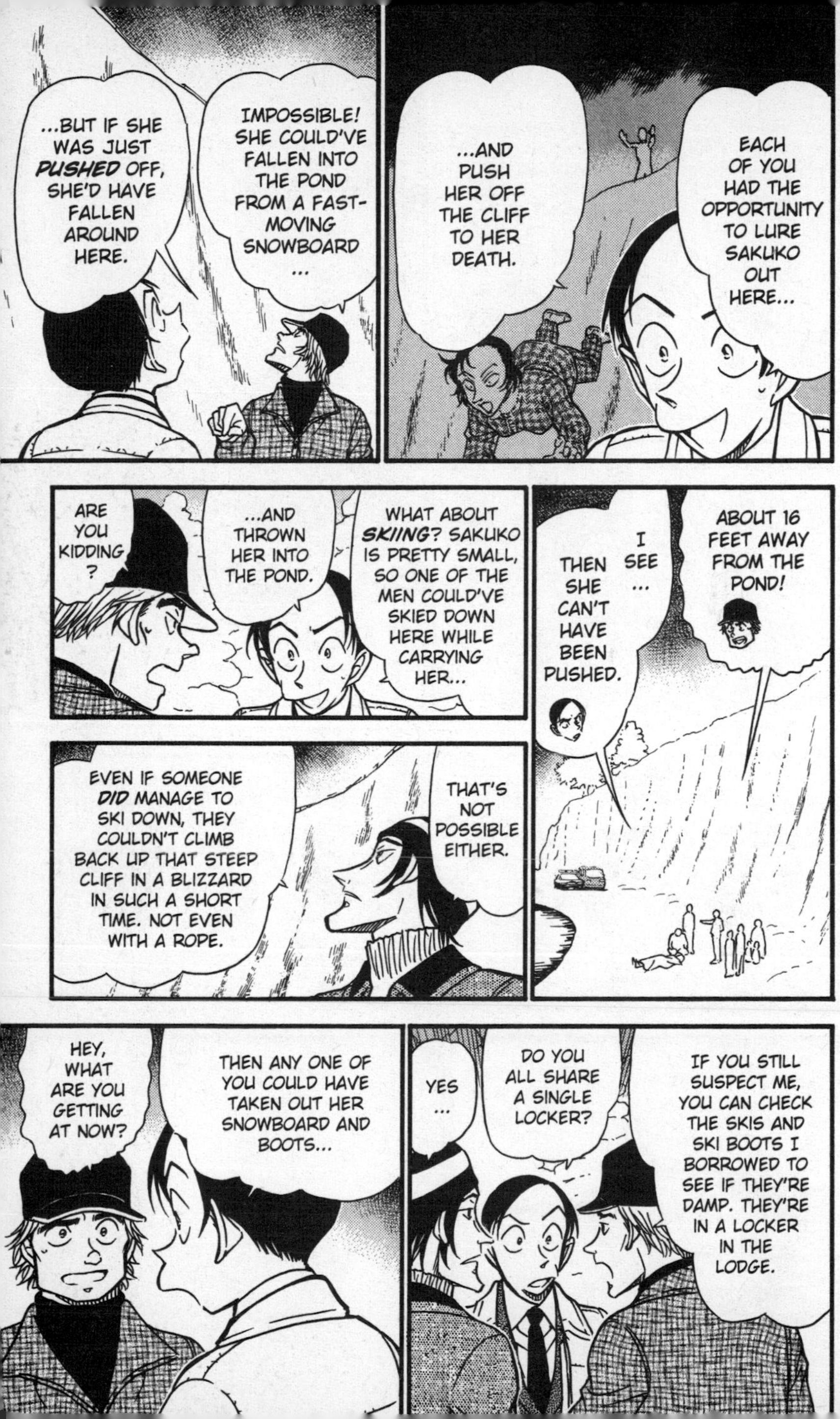
EACH OF YOU HAD THE OPPORTUNITY TO LURE SAKUKO OUT HERE...
...AND PUSH HER OFF THE CLIFF TO HER DEATH.
IMPOSSIBLE! SHE COULD'VE FALLEN INTO THE POND FROM A FAST-MOVING SNOWBOARD...
...BUT IF SHE WAS JUST PUSHED OFF, SHE'D HAVE FALLEN AROUND HERE.
ABOUT 16 FEET AWAY FROM THE POND!
I SEE...
THEN SHE CAN'T HAVE BEEN PUSHED.
WHAT ABOUT SKIING? SAKUKO IS PRETTY SMALL, SO ONE OF THE MEN COULD'VE SKIED DOWN HERE WHILE CARRYING HER...
...AND THROWN HER INTO THE POND.
ARE YOU KIDDING?
THAT'S NOT POSSIBLE EITHER.
EVEN IF SOMEONE DID MANAGE TO SKI DOWN, THEY COULDN'T CLIMB BACK UP THAT STEEP CLIFF IN A BLIZZARD IN SUCH A SHORT TIME. NOT EVEN WITH A ROPE.
IF YOU STILL SUSPECT ME, YOU CAN CHECK THE SKIS AND SKI BOOTS I BORROWED TO SEE IF THEY'RE DAMP. THEY'RE IN A LOCKER IN THE LODGE.
DO YOU ALL SHARE A SINGLE LOCKER?
YES...
THEN ANY ONE OF YOU COULD HAVE TAKEN OUT HER SNOWBOARD AND BOOTS...
HEY, WHAT ARE YOU GETTING AT NOW?

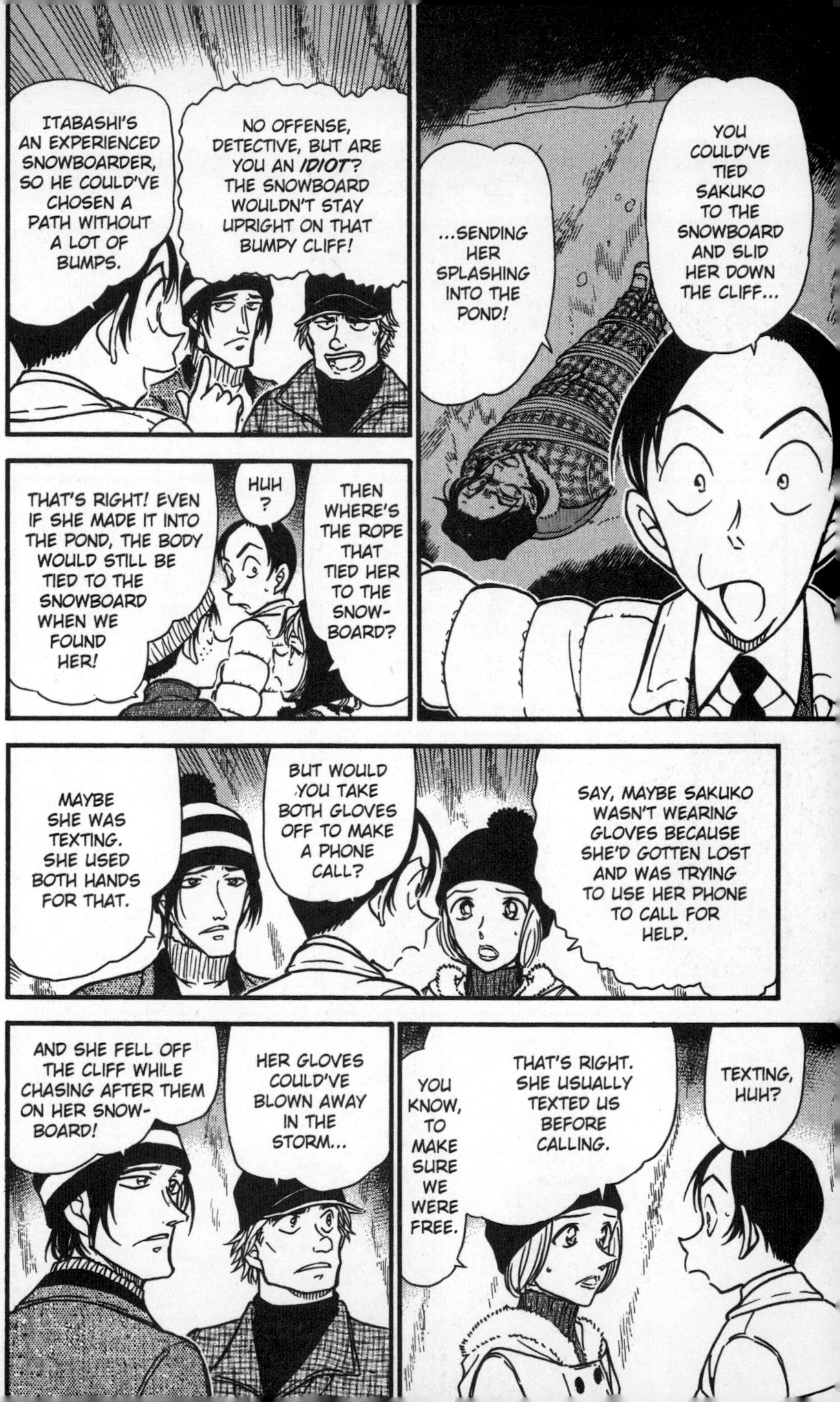
YOU COULD'VE TIED SAKUKO TO THE SNOWBOARD AND SLID HER DOWN THE CLIFF...
...SENDING HER SPLASHING INTO THE POND!
NO OFFENSE, DETECTIVE, BUT ARE YOU AN *IDIOT*? THE SNOWBOARD WOULDN'T STAY UPRIGHT ON THAT BUMPY CLIFF!
ITABASHI'S AN EXPERIENCED SNOWBOARDER, SO HE COULD'VE CHOSEN A PATH WITHOUT A LOT OF BUMPS.
THEN WHERE'S THE ROPE THAT TIED HER TO THE SNOW-BOARD?
HUH?
THAT'S RIGHT! EVEN IF SHE MADE IT INTO THE POND, THE BODY WOULD STILL BE TIED TO THE SNOWBOARD WHEN WE FOUND HER!
SAY, MAYBE SAKUKO WASN'T WEARING GLOVES BECAUSE SHE'D GOTTEN LOST AND WAS TRYING TO USE HER PHONE TO CALL FOR HELP.
BUT WOULD YOU TAKE BOTH GLOVES OFF TO MAKE A PHONE CALL?
MAYBE SHE WAS TEXTING. SHE USED BOTH HANDS FOR THAT.
TEXTING, HUH?
THAT'S RIGHT. SHE USUALLY TEXTED US BEFORE CALLING.
YOU KNOW, TO MAKE SURE WE WERE FREE.
HER GLOVES COULD'VE BLOWN AWAY IN THE STORM...
AND SHE FELL OFF THE CLIFF WHILE CHASING AFTER THEM ON HER SNOW-BOARD!

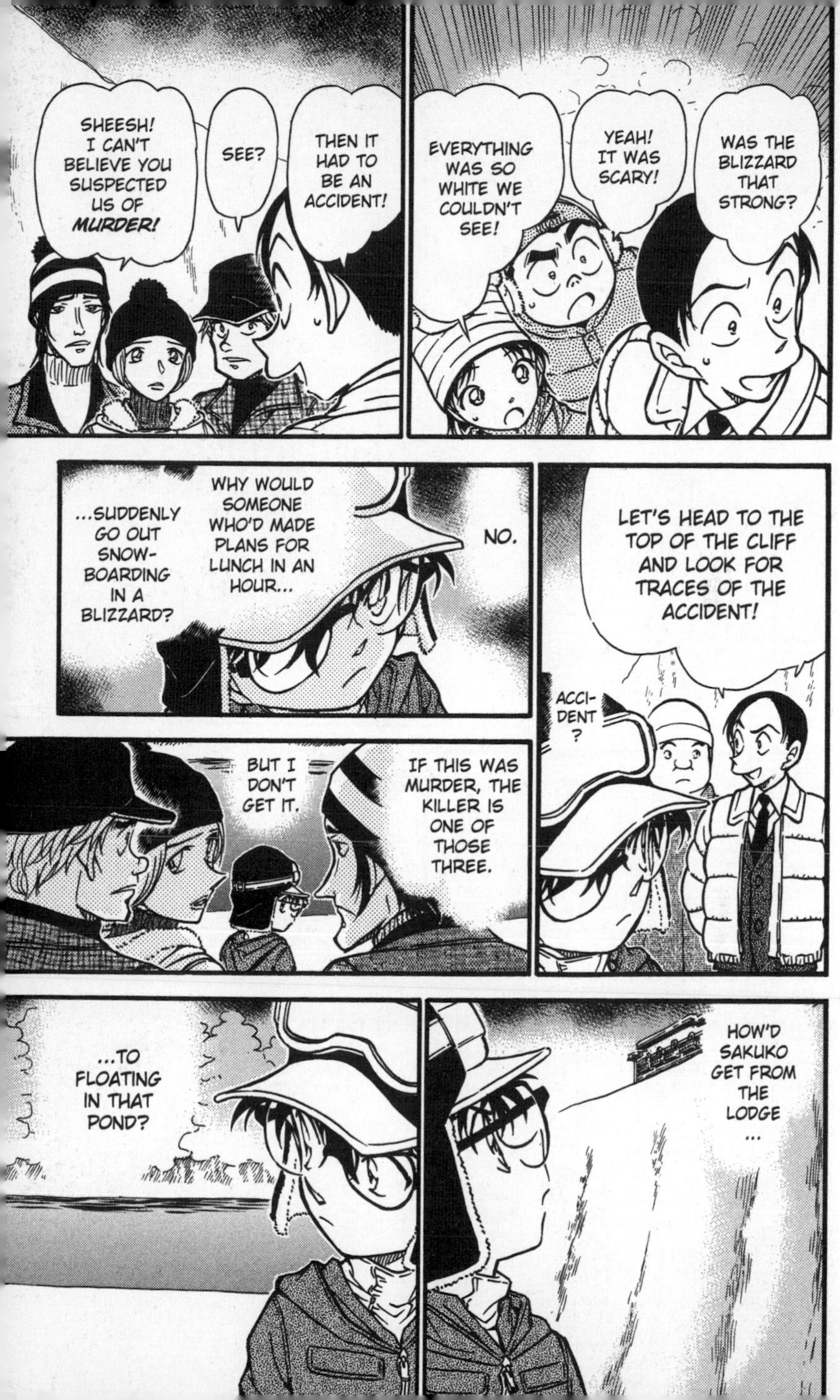
WAS THE BLIZZARD THAT STRONG?
YEAH! IT WAS SCARY!
EVERYTHING WAS SO WHITE WE COULDN'T SEE!
THEN IT HAD TO BE AN ACCIDENT!
SEE?
SHEESH! I CAN'T BELIEVE YOU SUSPECTED US OF ***MURDER!***
LET'S HEAD TO THE TOP OF THE CLIFF AND LOOK FOR TRACES OF THE ACCIDENT!
ACCI-DENT?
NO.
WHY WOULD SOMEONE WHO'D MADE PLANS FOR LUNCH IN AN HOUR...
...SUDDENLY GO OUT SNOW-BOARDING IN A BLIZZARD?
IF THIS WAS MURDER, THE KILLER IS ONE OF THOSE THREE.
BUT I DON'T GET IT.
HOW'D SAKUKO GET FROM THE LODGE ...
...TO FLOATING IN THAT POND?

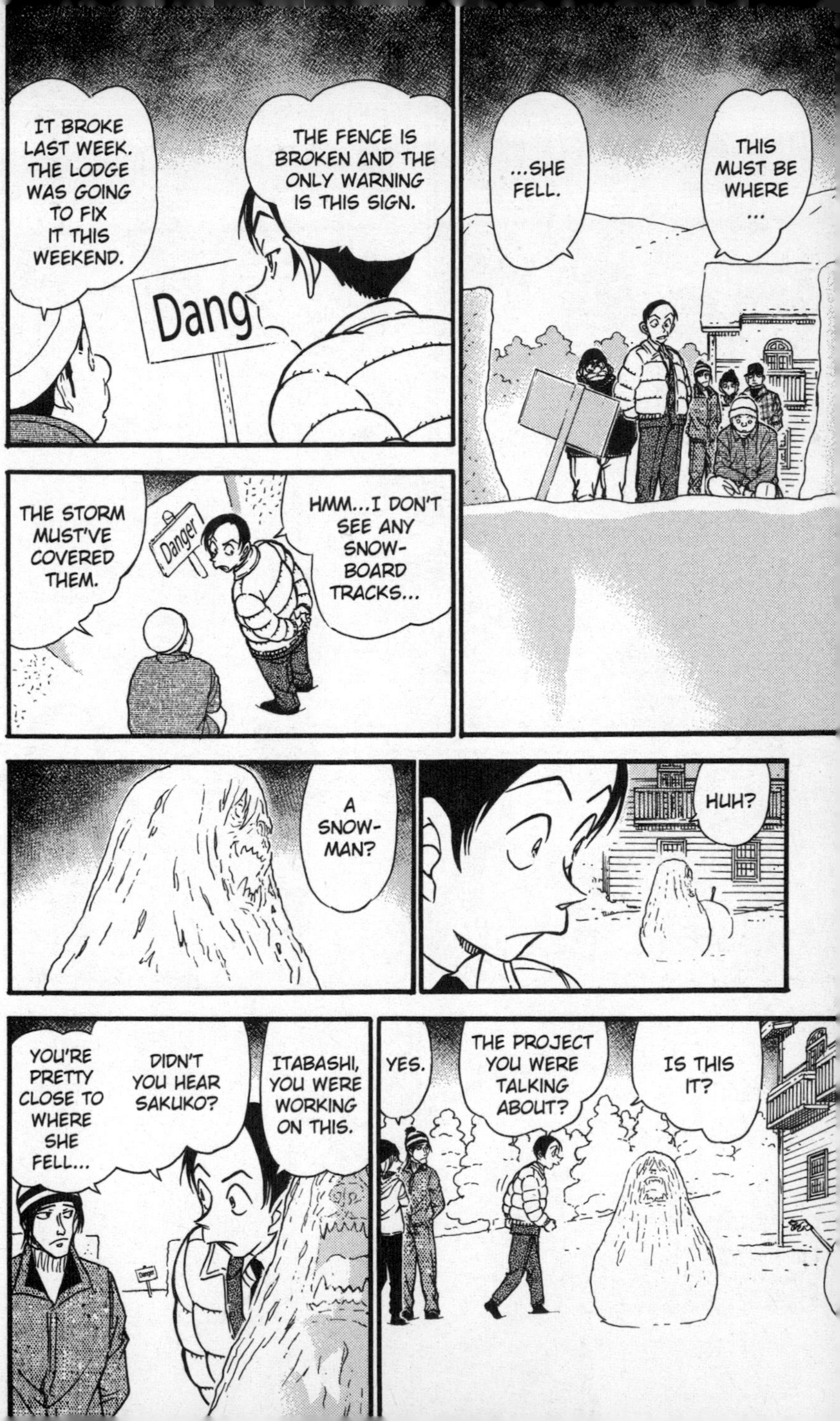
THIS MUST BE WHERE ...
...SHE FELL.
THE FENCE IS BROKEN AND THE ONLY WARNING IS THIS SIGN.
IT BROKE LAST WEEK. THE LODGE WAS GOING TO FIX IT THIS WEEKEND.
Dang
HMM...I DON'T SEE ANY SNOW-BOARD TRACKS...
Danger
THE STORM MUST'VE COVERED THEM.
HUH?
A SNOW-MAN?
IS THIS IT?
THE PROJECT YOU WERE TALKING ABOUT?
YES.
ITABASHI, YOU WERE WORKING ON THIS.
DIDN'T YOU HEAR SAKUKO?
YOU'RE PRETTY CLOSE TO WHERE SHE FELL...
Danger

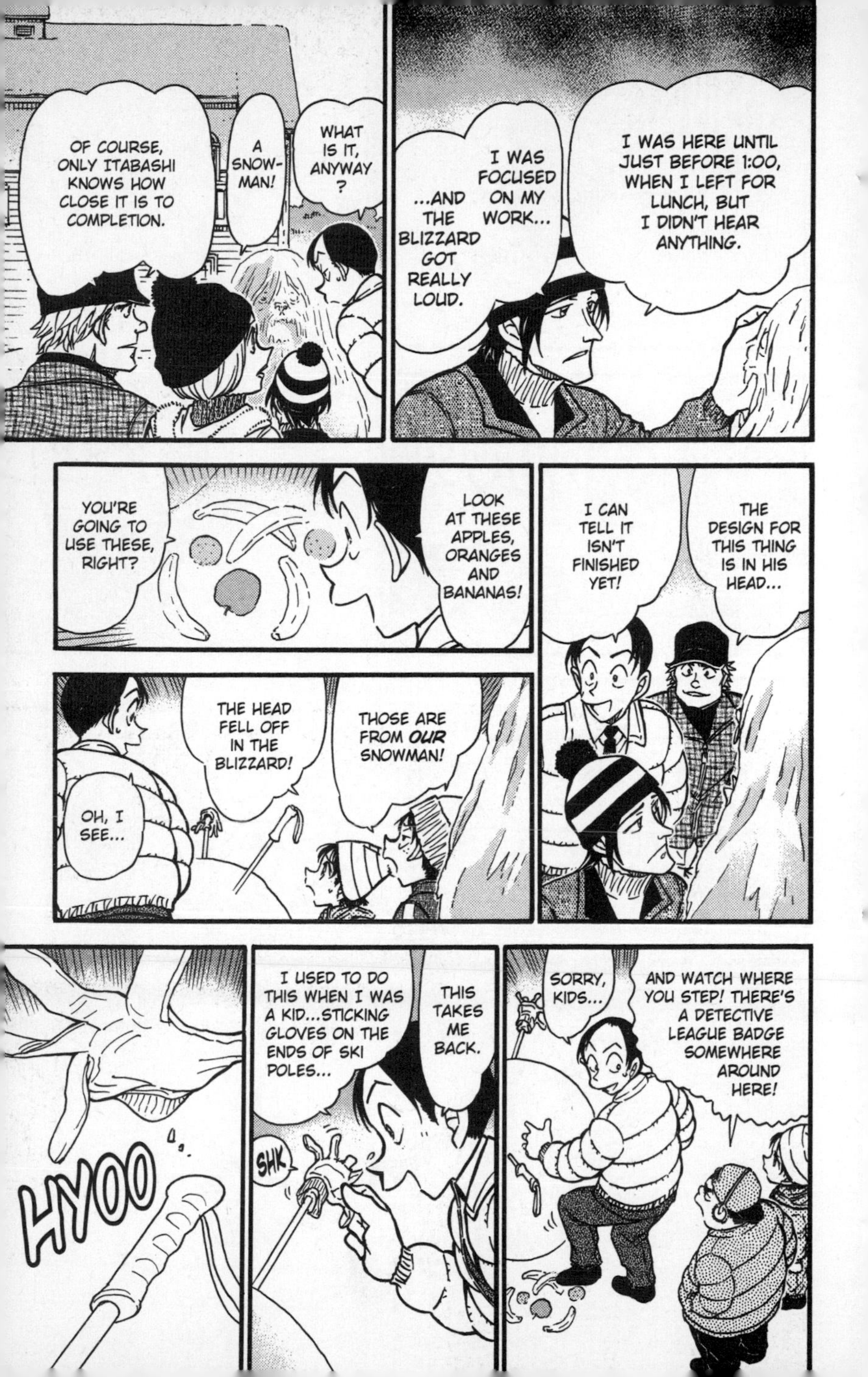
I WAS HERE UNTIL JUST BEFORE 1:00, WHEN I LEFT FOR LUNCH, BUT I DIDN'T HEAR ANYTHING.
I WAS FOCUSED ON MY WORK...
...AND THE BLIZZARD GOT REALLY LOUD.
WHAT IS IT, ANYWAY?
A SNOWMAN!
OF COURSE, ONLY ITABASHI KNOWS HOW CLOSE IT IS TO COMPLETION.
THE DESIGN FOR THIS THING IS IN HIS HEAD...
I CAN TELL IT ISN'T FINISHED YET!
LOOK AT THESE APPLES, ORANGES AND BANANAS!
YOU'RE GOING TO USE THESE, RIGHT?
THOSE ARE FROM *OUR* SNOWMAN!
THE HEAD FELL OFF IN THE BLIZZARD!
OH, I SEE...
SORRY, KIDS...
AND WATCH WHERE YOU STEP! THERE'S A DETECTIVE LEAGUE BADGE SOMEWHERE AROUND HERE!
THIS TAKES ME BACK.
I USED TO DO THIS WHEN I WAS A KID...STICKING GLOVES ON THE ENDS OF SKI POLES...
SHK
HYOO

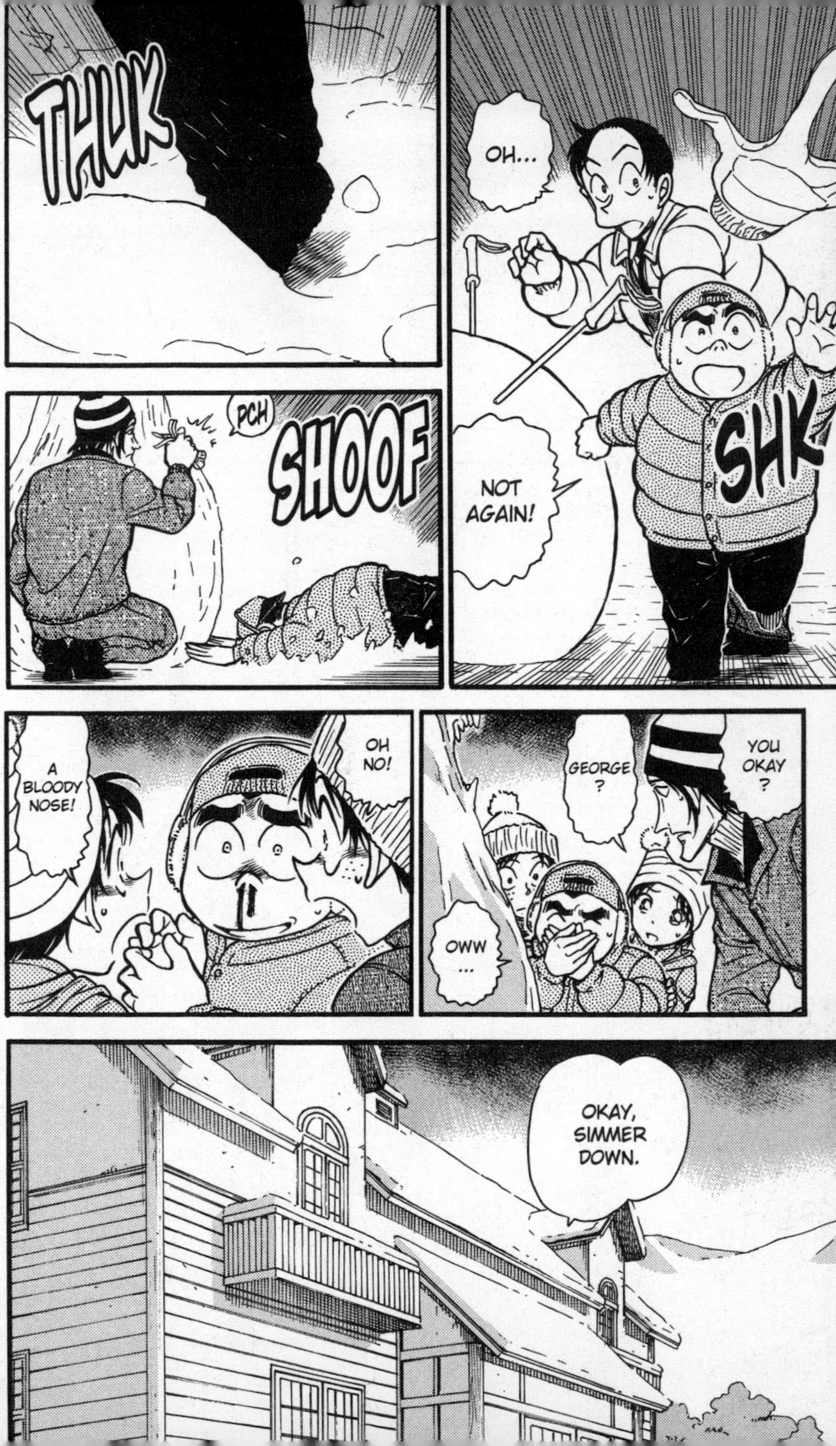
OH...
NOT AGAIN!
SHK
THLK
PCH
SHOOF
YOU OKAY?
GEORGE?
OWW...
OH NO!
A BLOODY NOSE!
OKAY, SIMMER DOWN.

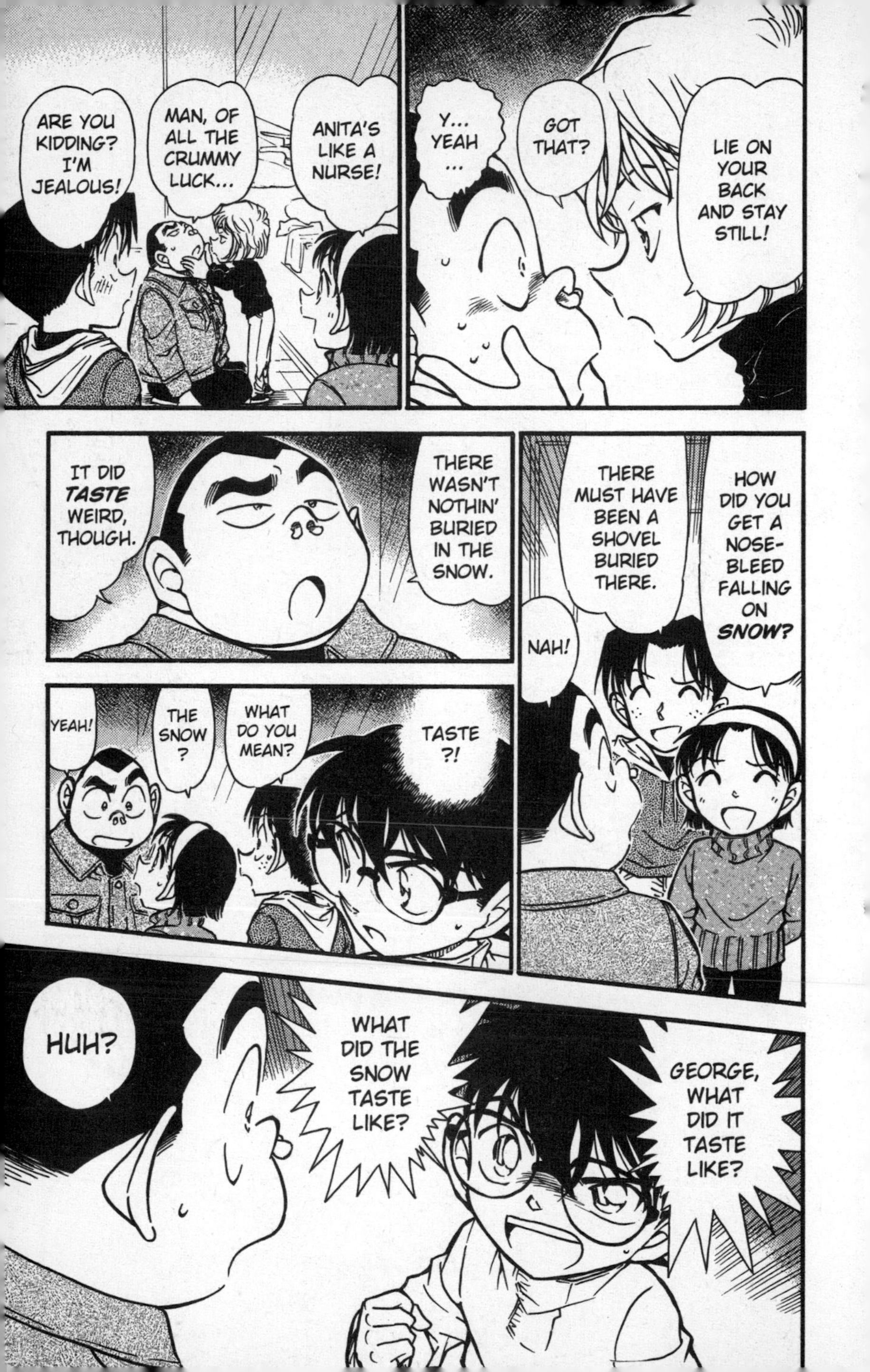
LIE ON YOUR BACK AND STAY STILL!
GOT THAT?
Y... YEAH ...
ANITA'S LIKE A NURSE!
MAN, OF ALL THE CRUMMY LUCK...
ARE YOU KIDDING? I'M JEALOUS!
HOW DID YOU GET A NOSE-BLEED FALLING ON *SNOW?*
THERE MUST HAVE BEEN A SHOVEL BURIED THERE.
NAH!
THERE WASN'T NOTHIN' BURIED IN THE SNOW.
IT DID *TASTE* WEIRD, THOUGH.
TASTE ?!
WHAT DO YOU MEAN?
THE SNOW ?
YEAH!
GEORGE, WHAT DID IT TASTE LIKE?
WHAT DID THE SNOW TASTE LIKE?
HUH?

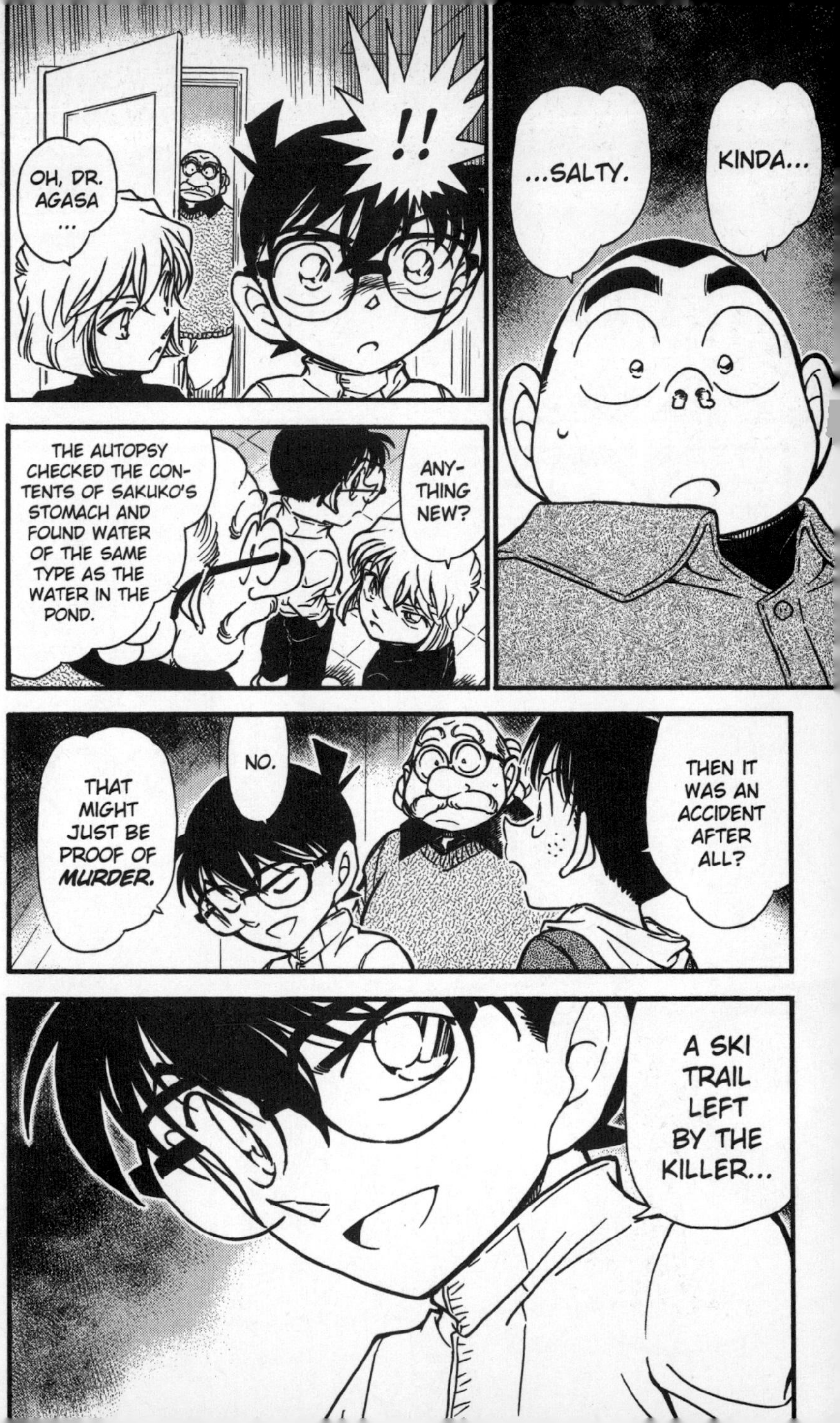
KINDA...
...SALTY.
!!
OH, DR. AGASA ...
ANY-THING NEW?
THE AUTOPSY CHECKED THE CON-TENTS OF SAKUKO'S STOMACH AND FOUND WATER OF THE SAME TYPE AS THE WATER IN THE POND.
THEN IT WAS AN ACCIDENT AFTER ALL?
NO.
THAT MIGHT JUST BE PROOF OF *MURDER.*
A SKI TRAIL LEFT BY THE KILLER...

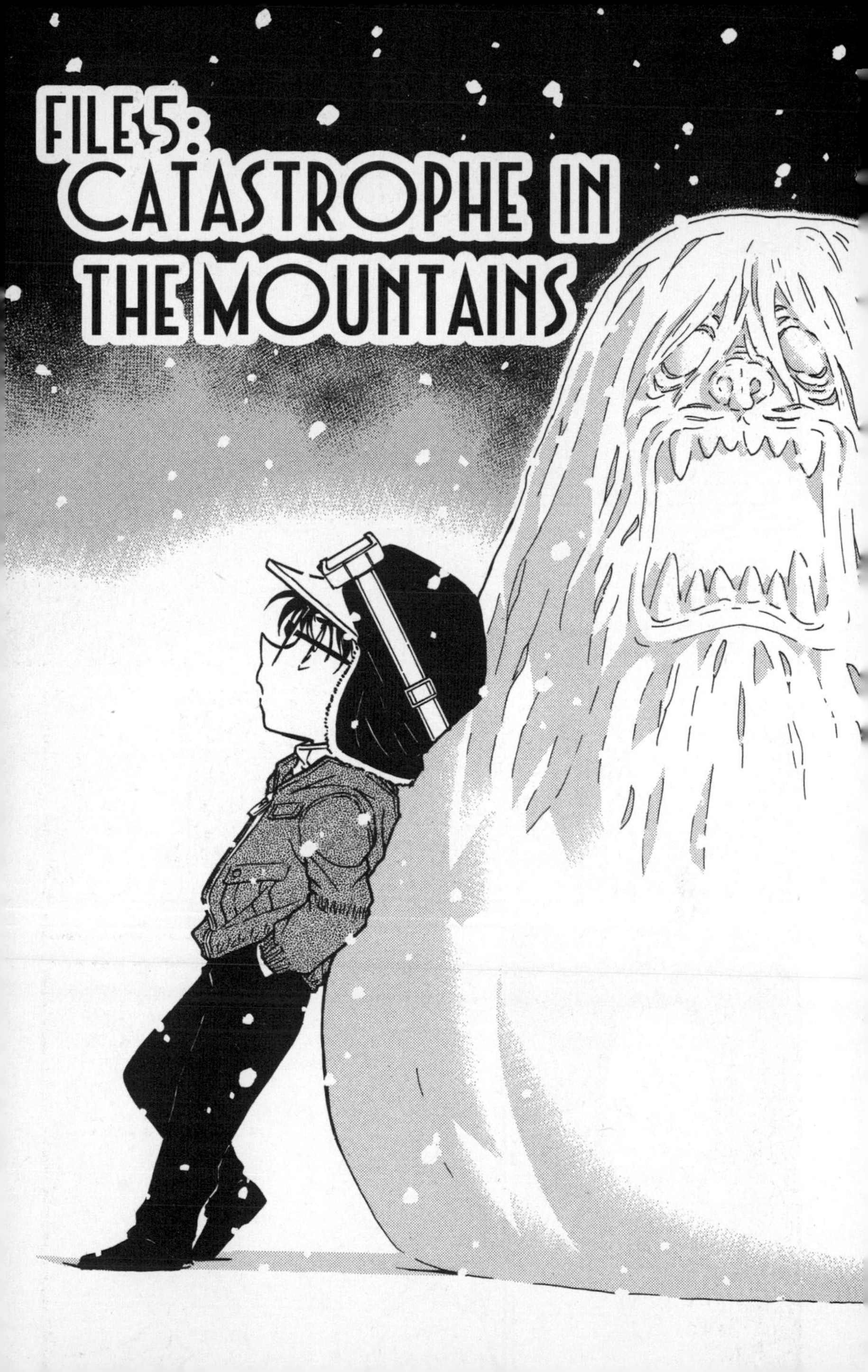
FILE 5:
CATASTROPHE IN THE MOUNTAINS

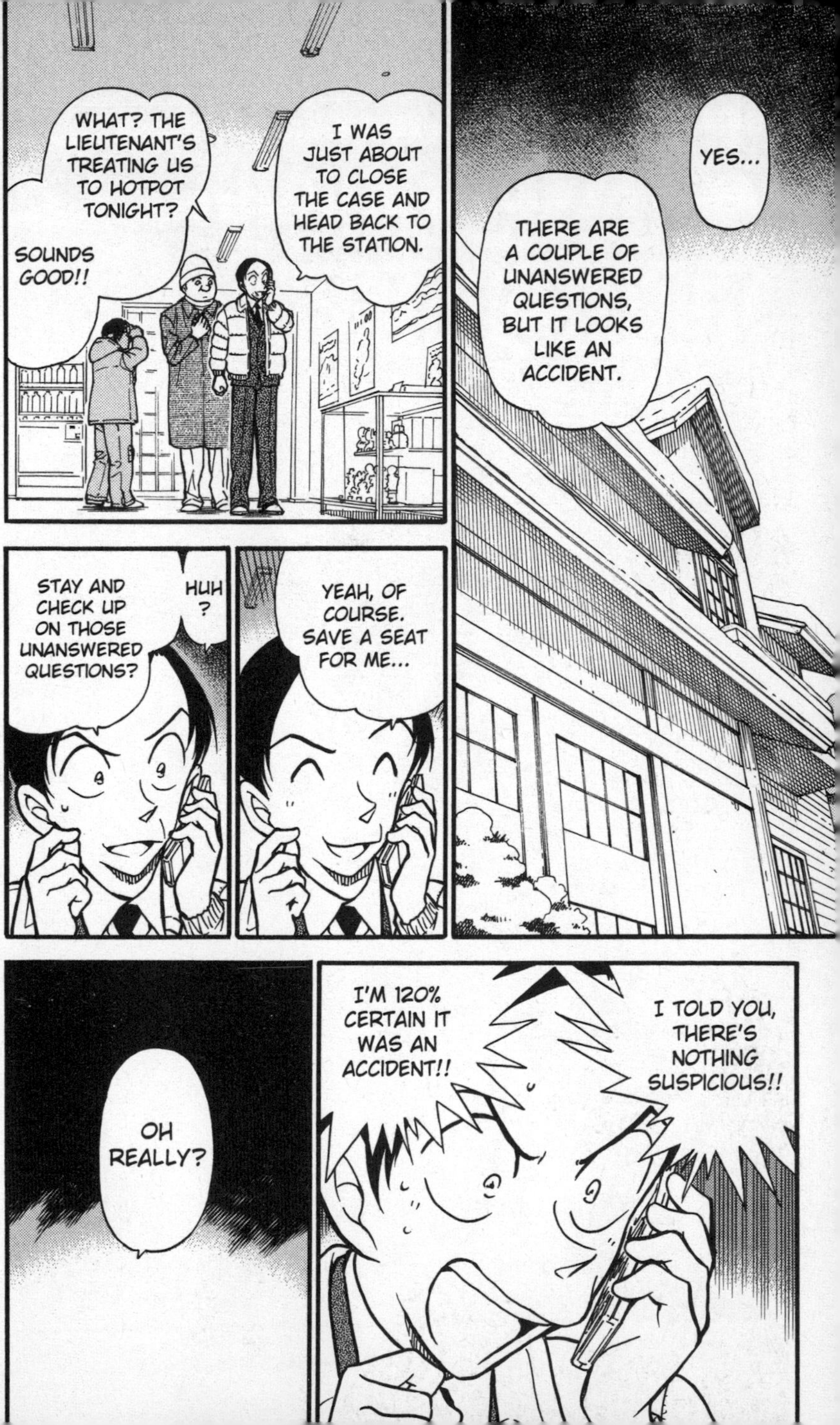
YES...
THERE ARE A COUPLE OF UNANSWERED QUESTIONS, BUT IT LOOKS LIKE AN ACCIDENT.
I WAS JUST ABOUT TO CLOSE THE CASE AND HEAD BACK TO THE STATION.
WHAT? THE LIEUTENANT'S TREATING US TO HOTPOT TONIGHT?
SOUNDS GOOD!!
YEAH, OF COURSE. SAVE A SEAT FOR ME...
HUH?
STAY AND CHECK UP ON THOSE UNANSWERED QUESTIONS?
I TOLD YOU, THERE'S NOTHING SUSPICIOUS!!
I'M 120% CERTAIN IT WAS AN ACCIDENT!!
OH REALLY?

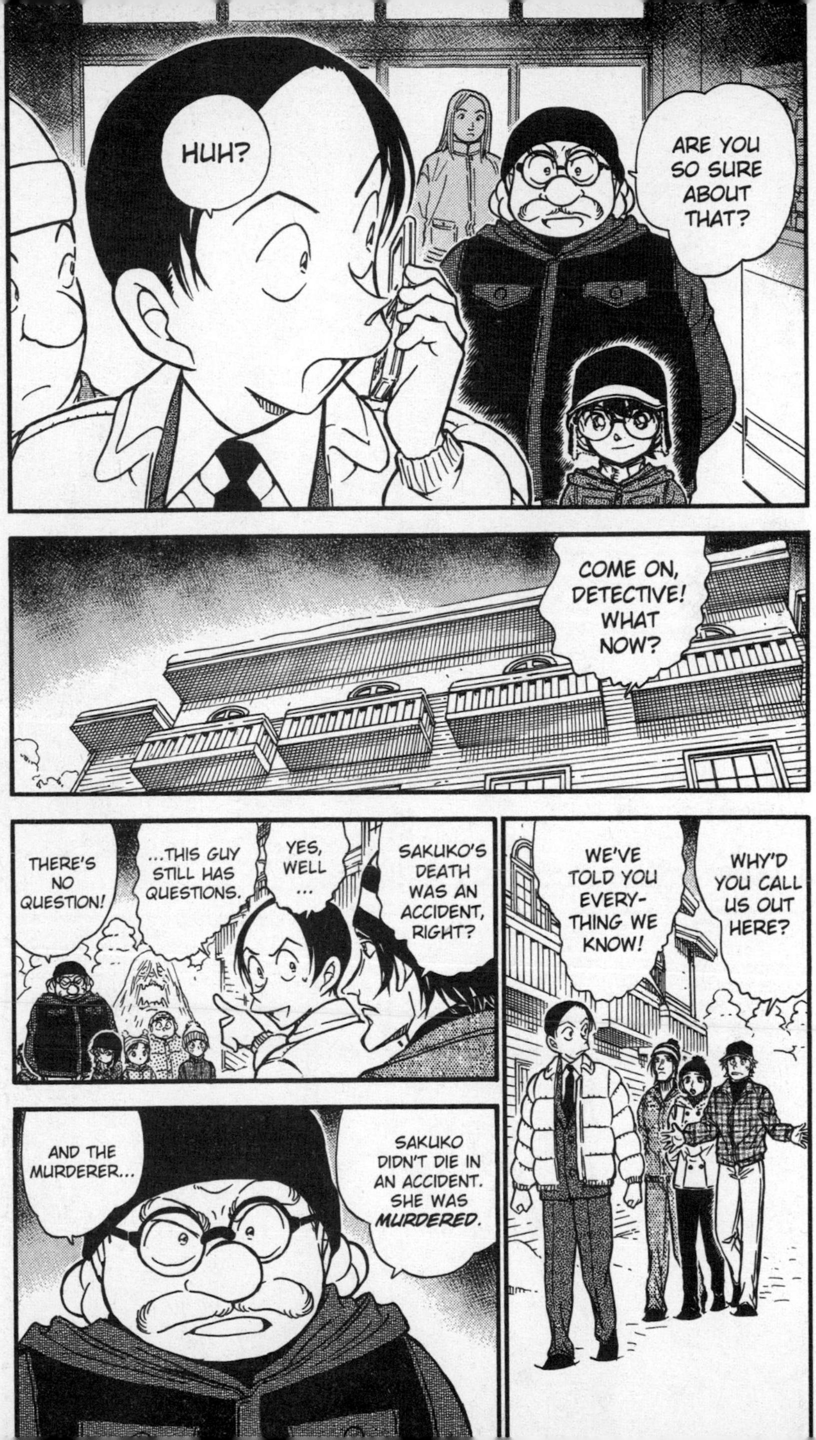
ARE YOU SO SURE ABOUT THAT?
HUH?
COME ON, DETECTIVE! WHAT NOW?
WHY'D YOU CALL US OUT HERE?
WE'VE TOLD YOU EVERY-THING WE KNOW!
SAKUKO'S DEATH WAS AN ACCIDENT, RIGHT?
YES, WELL...
...THIS GUY STILL HAS QUESTIONS.
THERE'S NO QUESTION!
SAKUKO DIDN'T DIE IN AN ACCIDENT. SHE WAS *MURDERED*.
AND THE MURDERER...

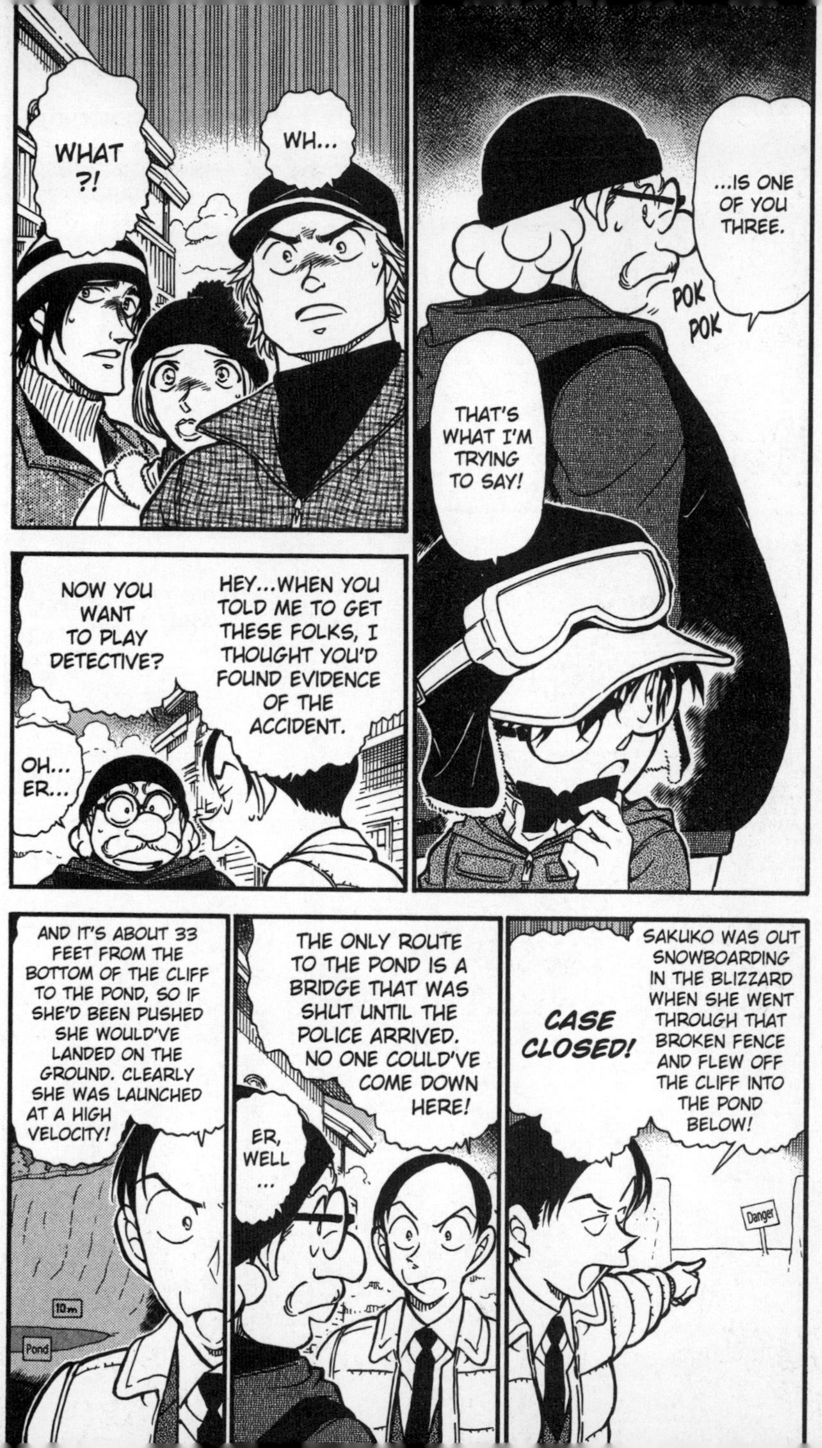
...IS ONE OF YOU THREE.
POK POK
THAT'S WHAT I'M TRYING TO SAY!
WH...
WHAT ?!
HEY...WHEN YOU TOLD ME TO GET THESE FOLKS, I THOUGHT YOU'D FOUND EVIDENCE OF THE ACCIDENT.
NOW YOU WANT TO PLAY DETECTIVE?
OH... ER...
SAKUKO WAS OUT SNOWBOARDING IN THE BLIZZARD WHEN SHE WENT THROUGH THAT BROKEN FENCE AND FLEW OFF THE CLIFF INTO THE POND BELOW!
CASE CLOSED!
Danger
THE ONLY ROUTE TO THE POND IS A BRIDGE THAT WAS SHUT UNTIL THE POLICE ARRIVED. NO ONE COULD'VE COME DOWN HERE!
ER, WELL ...
AND IT'S ABOUT 33 FEET FROM THE BOTTOM OF THE CLIFF TO THE POND, SO IF SHE'D BEEN PUSHED SHE WOULD'VE LANDED ON THE GROUND. CLEARLY SHE WAS LAUNCHED AT A HIGH VELOCITY!
10m
Pond

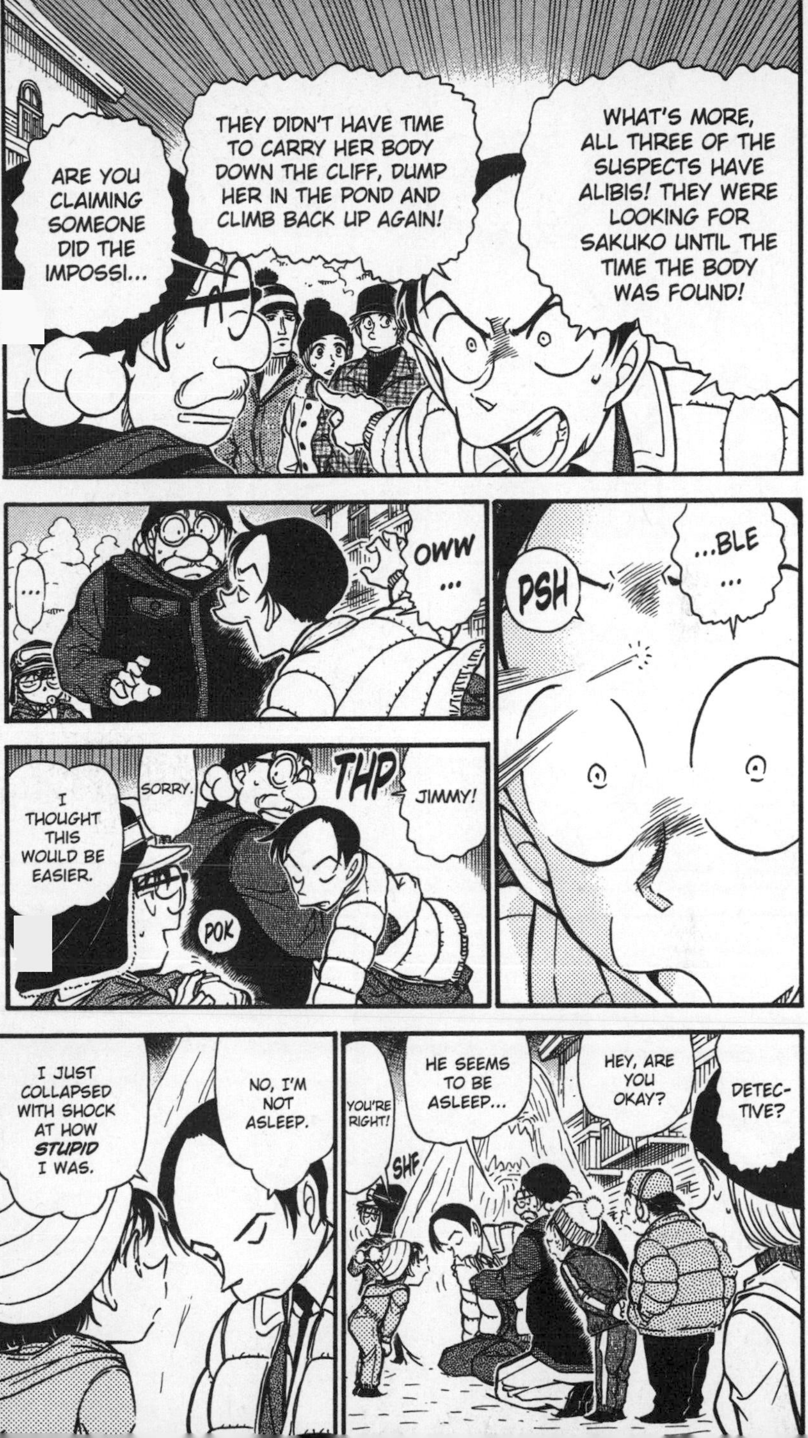
WHAT'S MORE, ALL THREE OF THE SUSPECTS HAVE ALIBIS! THEY WERE LOOKING FOR SAKUKO UNTIL THE TIME THE BODY WAS FOUND!
THEY DIDN'T HAVE TIME TO CARRY HER BODY DOWN THE CLIFF, DUMP HER IN THE POND AND CLIMB BACK UP AGAIN!
ARE YOU CLAIMING SOMEONE DID THE IMPOSSI...
...BLE ...
PSH
OWW ...
...
JIMMY!
THP
SORRY.
I THOUGHT THIS WOULD BE EASIER.
POK
DETEC-TIVE?
HEY, ARE YOU OKAY?
HE SEEMS TO BE ASLEEP...
YOU'RE RIGHT!
SHF
NO, I'M NOT ASLEEP.
I JUST COLLAPSED WITH SHOCK AT HOW STUPID I WAS.

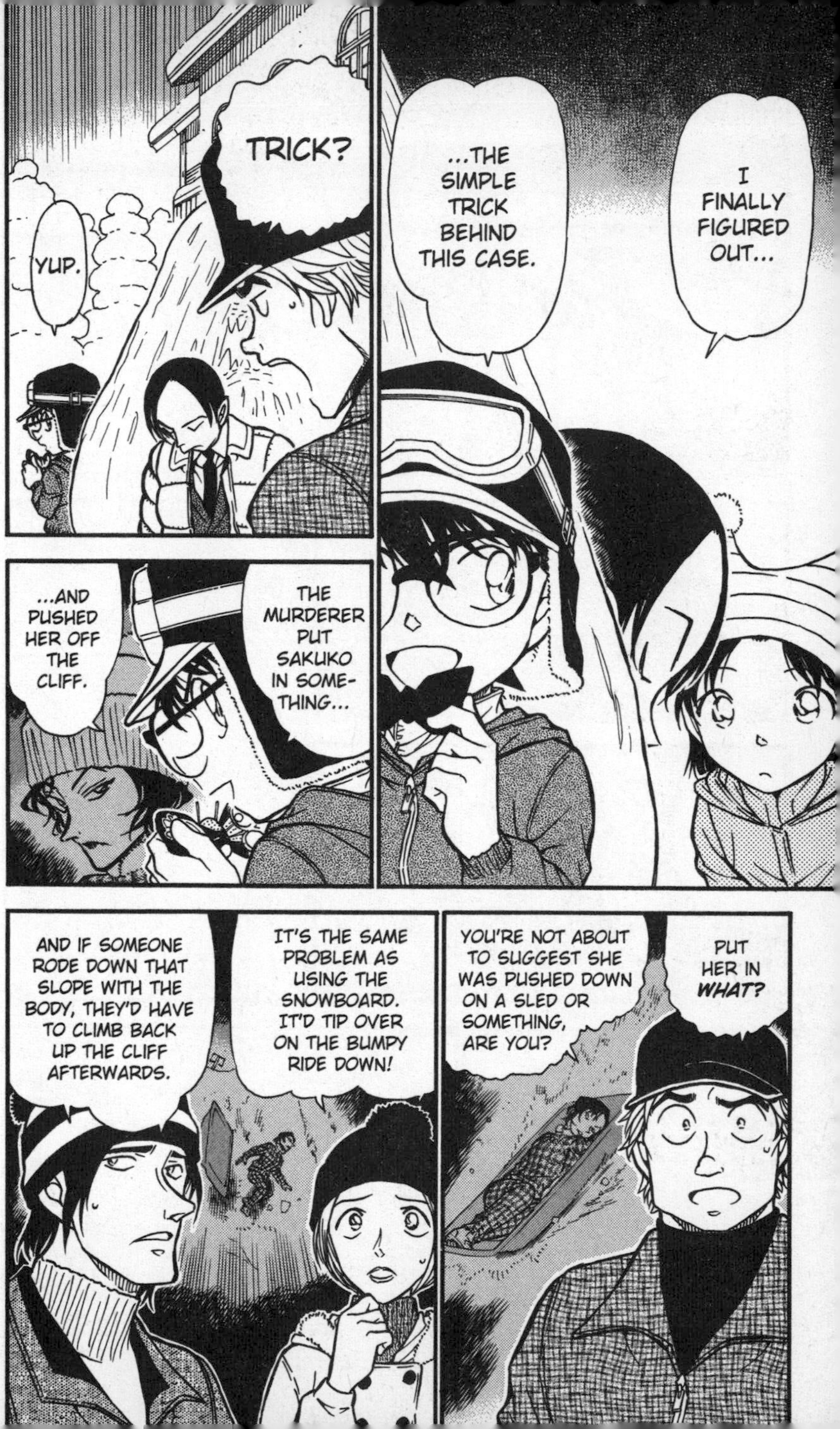
I FINALLY FIGURED OUT...
...THE SIMPLE TRICK BEHIND THIS CASE.
TRICK?
YUP.
THE MURDERER PUT SAKUKO IN SOMETHING...
...AND PUSHED HER OFF THE CLIFF.
PUT HER IN *WHAT?*
YOU'RE NOT ABOUT TO SUGGEST SHE WAS PUSHED DOWN ON A SLED OR SOMETHING, ARE YOU?
IT'S THE SAME PROBLEM AS USING THE SNOWBOARD. IT'D TIP OVER ON THE BUMPY RIDE DOWN!
AND IF SOMEONE RODE DOWN THAT SLOPE WITH THE BODY, THEY'D HAVE TO CLIMB BACK UP THE CLIFF AFTERWARDS.

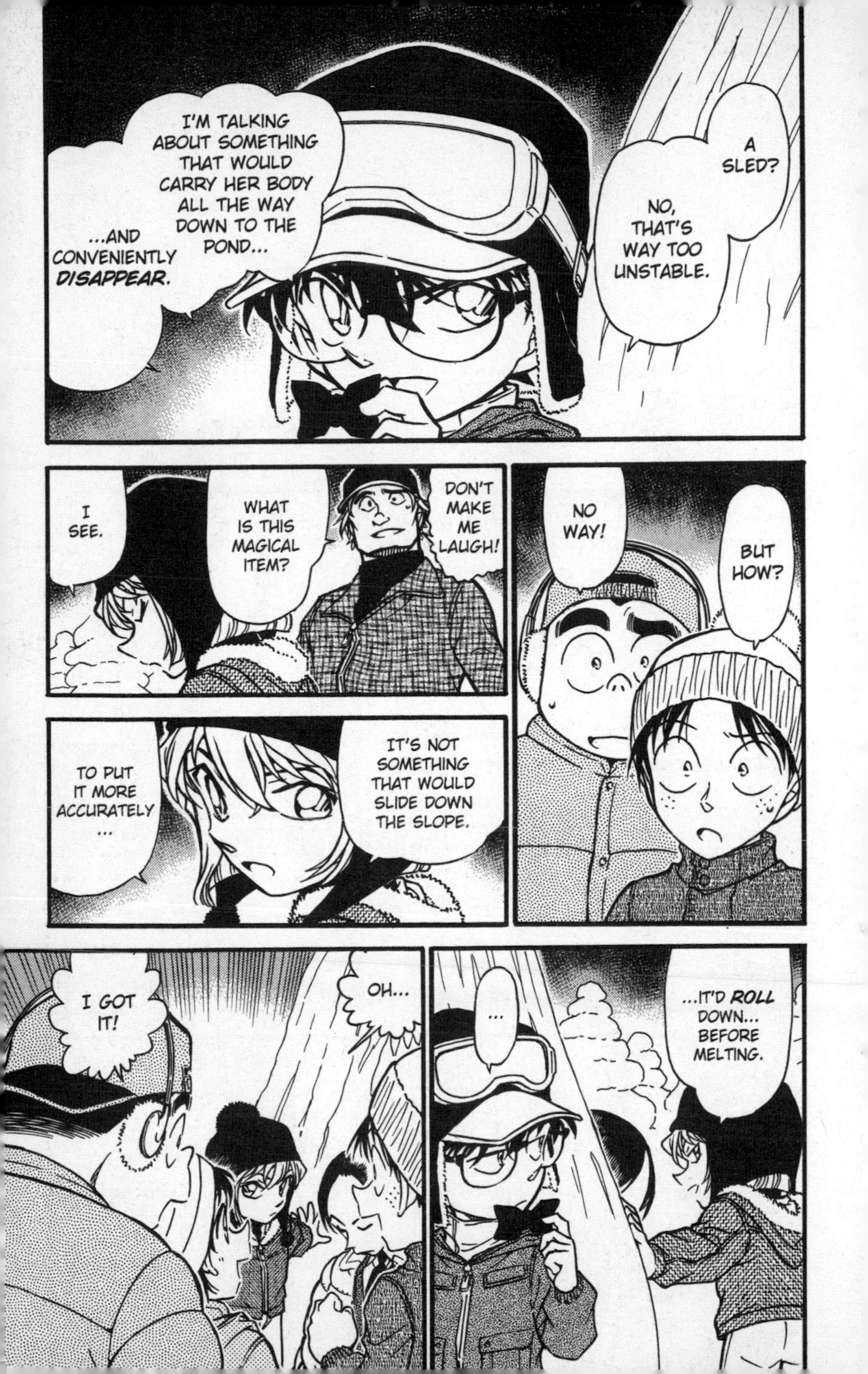
A SLED?
NO, THAT'S WAY TOO UNSTABLE.
I'M TALKING ABOUT SOMETHING THAT WOULD CARRY HER BODY ALL THE WAY DOWN TO THE POND...
...AND CONVENIENTLY *DISAPPEAR*.
BUT HOW?
NO WAY!
DON'T MAKE ME LAUGH!
WHAT IS THIS MAGICAL ITEM?
I SEE.
IT'S NOT SOMETHING THAT WOULD SLIDE DOWN THE SLOPE.
TO PUT IT MORE ACCURATELY...
...IT'D ***ROLL*** DOWN... BEFORE MELTING.
...
OH...
I GOT IT!

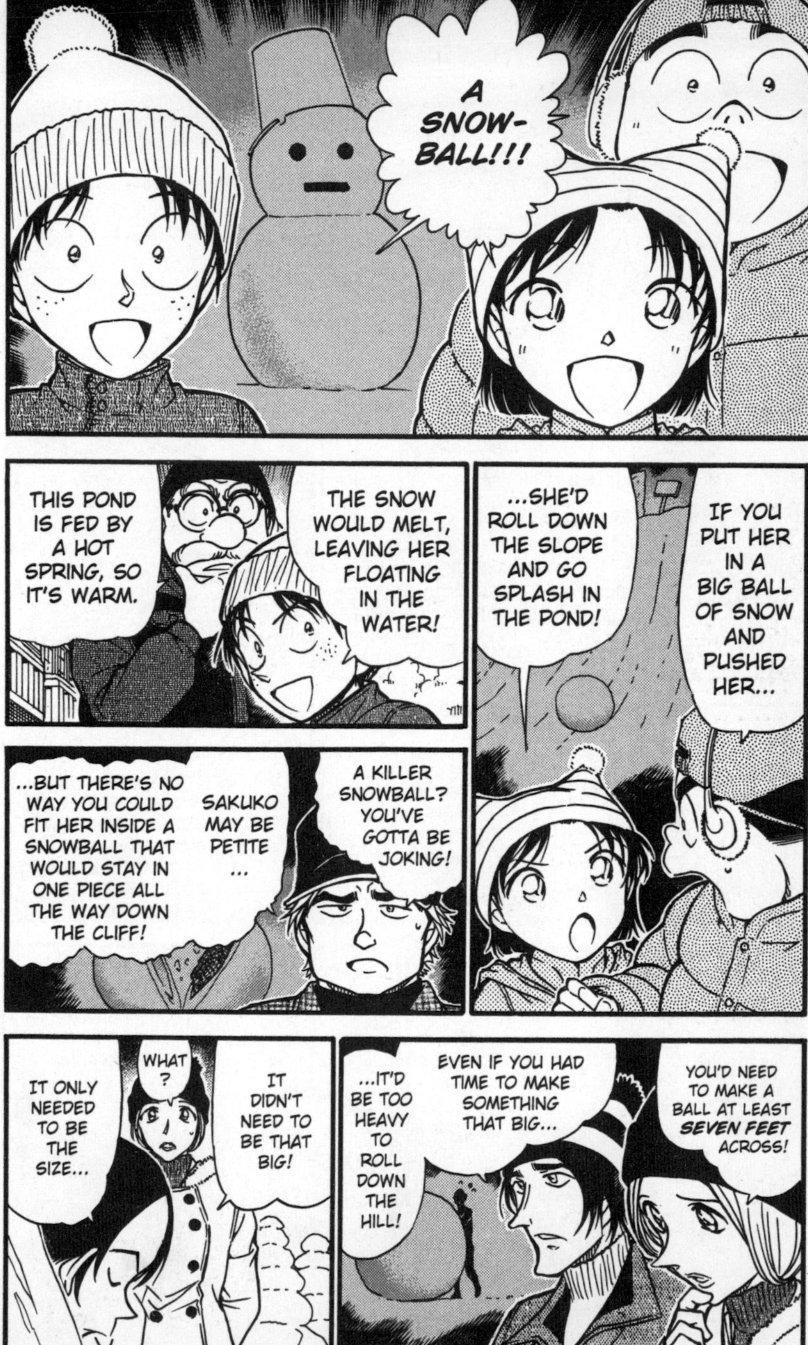
A SNOW-BALL!!!
IF YOU PUT HER IN A BIG BALL OF SNOW AND PUSHED HER...
...SHE'D ROLL DOWN THE SLOPE AND GO SPLASH IN THE POND!
THE SNOW WOULD MELT, LEAVING HER FLOATING IN THE WATER!
THIS POND IS FED BY A HOT SPRING, SO IT'S WARM.
A KILLER SNOWBALL? YOU'VE GOTTA BE JOKING!
SAKUKO MAY BE PETITE ...
...BUT THERE'S NO WAY YOU COULD FIT HER INSIDE A SNOWBALL THAT WOULD STAY IN ONE PIECE ALL THE WAY DOWN THE CLIFF!
YOU'D NEED TO MAKE A BALL AT LEAST *SEVEN FEET* ACROSS!
EVEN IF YOU HAD TIME TO MAKE SOMETHING THAT BIG...
...IT'D BE TOO HEAVY TO ROLL DOWN THE HILL!
IT DIDN'T NEED TO BE THAT BIG!
WHAT?
IT ONLY NEEDED TO BE THE SIZE...

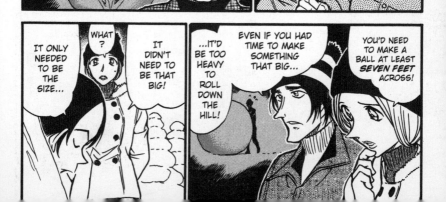

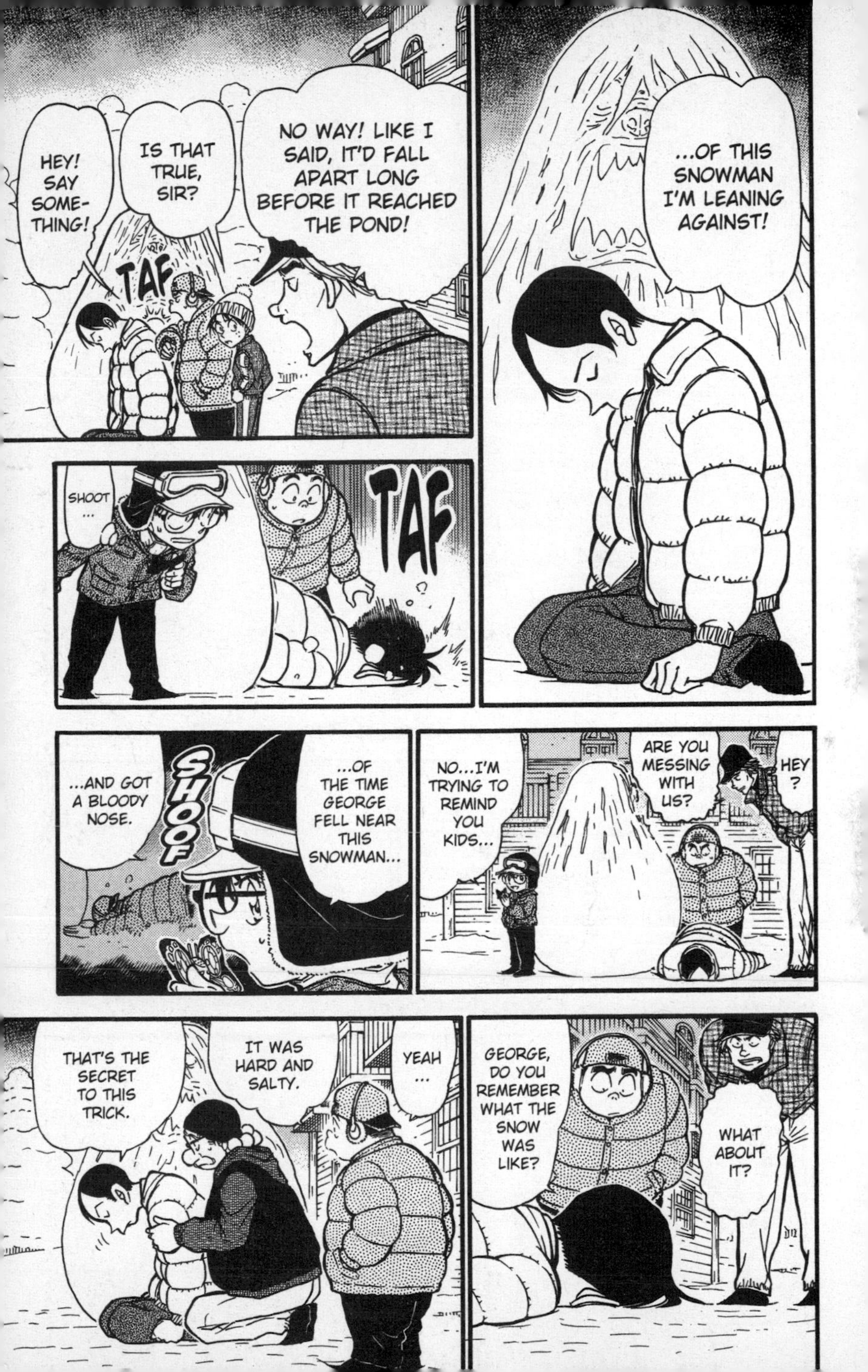
...OF THIS SNOWMAN I'M LEANING AGAINST!
NO WAY! LIKE I SAID, IT'D FALL APART LONG BEFORE IT REACHED THE POND!
IS THAT TRUE, SIR?
HEY! SAY SOME-THING!
TAF
TAF
SHOOT ...
HEY ?
ARE YOU MESSING WITH US?
NO...I'M TRYING TO REMIND YOU KIDS...
...OF THE TIME GEORGE FELL NEAR THIS SNOWMAN...
SHOOF
...AND GOT A BLOODY NOSE.
WHAT ABOUT IT?
GEORGE, DO YOU REMEMBER WHAT THE SNOW WAS LIKE?
YEAH ...
IT WAS HARD AND SALTY.
THAT'S THE SECRET TO THIS TRICK.

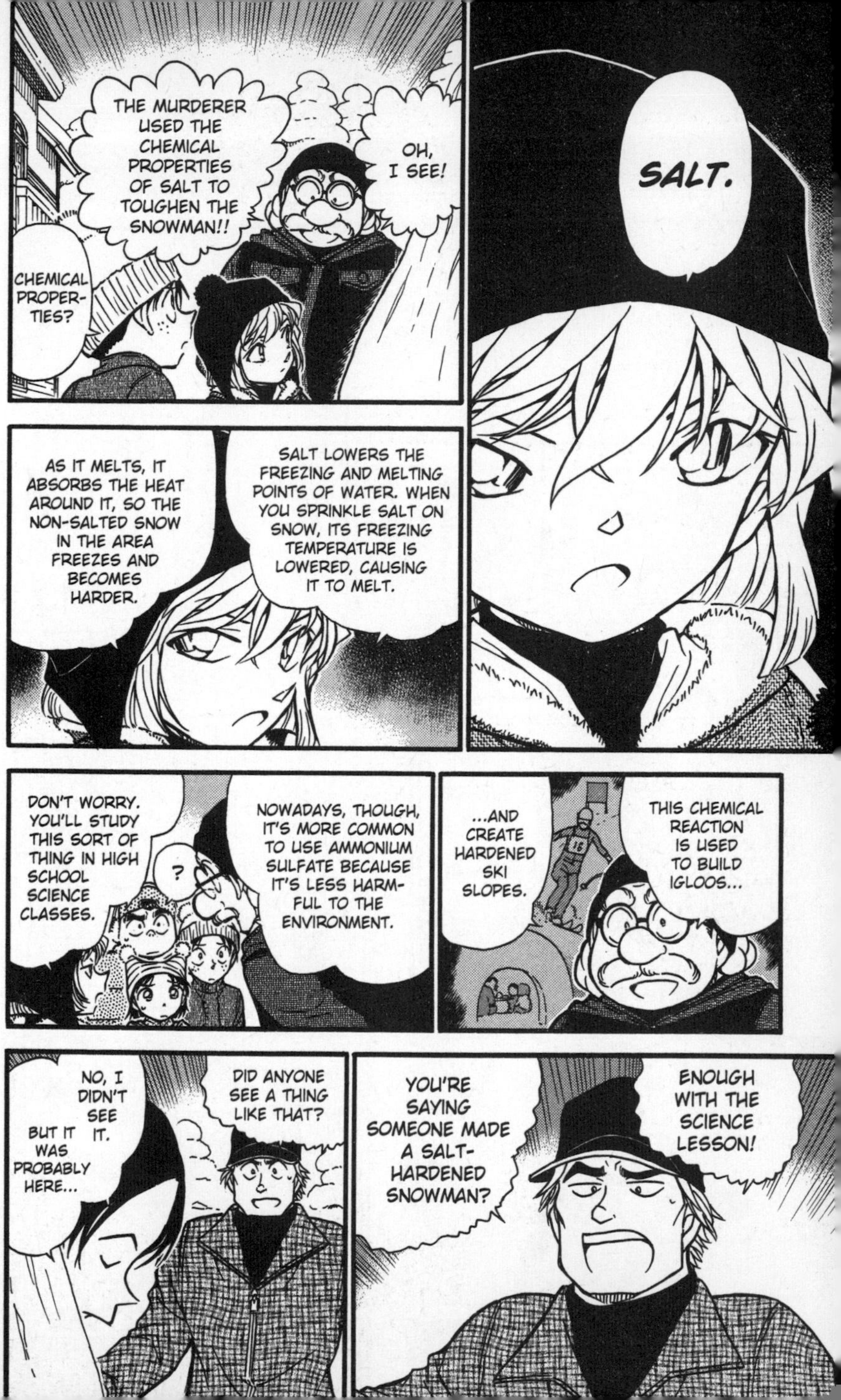
SALT.
OH, I SEE!
THE MURDERER USED THE CHEMICAL PROPERTIES OF SALT TO TOUGHEN THE SNOWMAN!!
CHEMICAL PROPER-TIES?
SALT LOWERS THE FREEZING AND MELTING POINTS OF WATER. WHEN YOU SPRINKLE SALT ON SNOW, ITS FREEZING TEMPERATURE IS LOWERED, CAUSING IT TO MELT.
AS IT MELTS, IT ABSORBS THE HEAT AROUND IT, SO THE NON-SALTED SNOW IN THE AREA FREEZES AND BECOMES HARDER.
THIS CHEMICAL REACTION IS USED TO BUILD IGLOOS...
...AND CREATE HARDENED SKI SLOPES.
NOWADAYS, THOUGH, IT'S MORE COMMON TO USE AMMONIUM SULFATE BECAUSE IT'S LESS HARM-FUL TO THE ENVIRONMENT.
?
DON'T WORRY. YOU'LL STUDY THIS SORT OF THING IN HIGH SCHOOL SCIENCE CLASSES.
ENOUGH WITH THE SCIENCE LESSON!
YOU'RE SAYING SOMEONE MADE A SALT-HARDENED SNOWMAN?
DID ANYONE SEE A THING LIKE THAT?
NO, I DIDN'T SEE IT.
BUT IT WAS PROBABLY HERE...

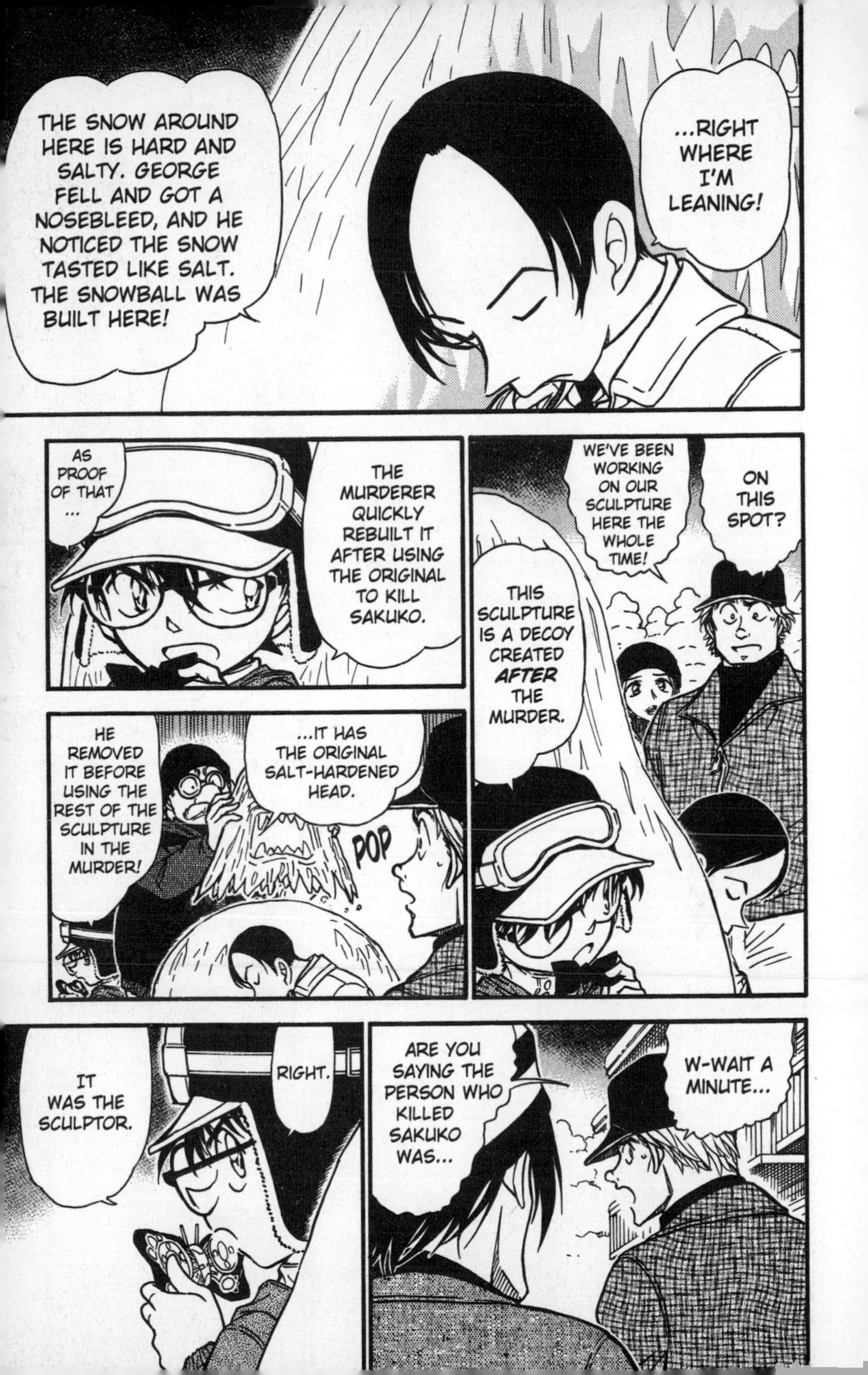
...RIGHT WHERE I'M LEANING!
THE SNOW AROUND HERE IS HARD AND SALTY. GEORGE FELL AND GOT A NOSEBLEED, AND HE NOTICED THE SNOW TASTED LIKE SALT. THE SNOWBALL WAS BUILT HERE!
ON THIS SPOT?
WE'VE BEEN WORKING ON OUR SCULPTURE HERE THE WHOLE TIME!
THIS SCULPTURE IS A DECOY CREATED *AFTER* THE MURDER.
THE MURDERER QUICKLY REBUILT IT AFTER USING THE ORIGINAL TO KILL SAKUKO.
AS PROOF OF THAT...
...IT HAS THE ORIGINAL SALT-HARDENED HEAD.
POP
HE REMOVED IT BEFORE USING THE REST OF THE SCULPTURE IN THE MURDER!
W-WAIT A MINUTE...
ARE YOU SAYING THE PERSON WHO KILLED SAKUKO WAS...
RIGHT.
IT WAS THE SCULPTOR.

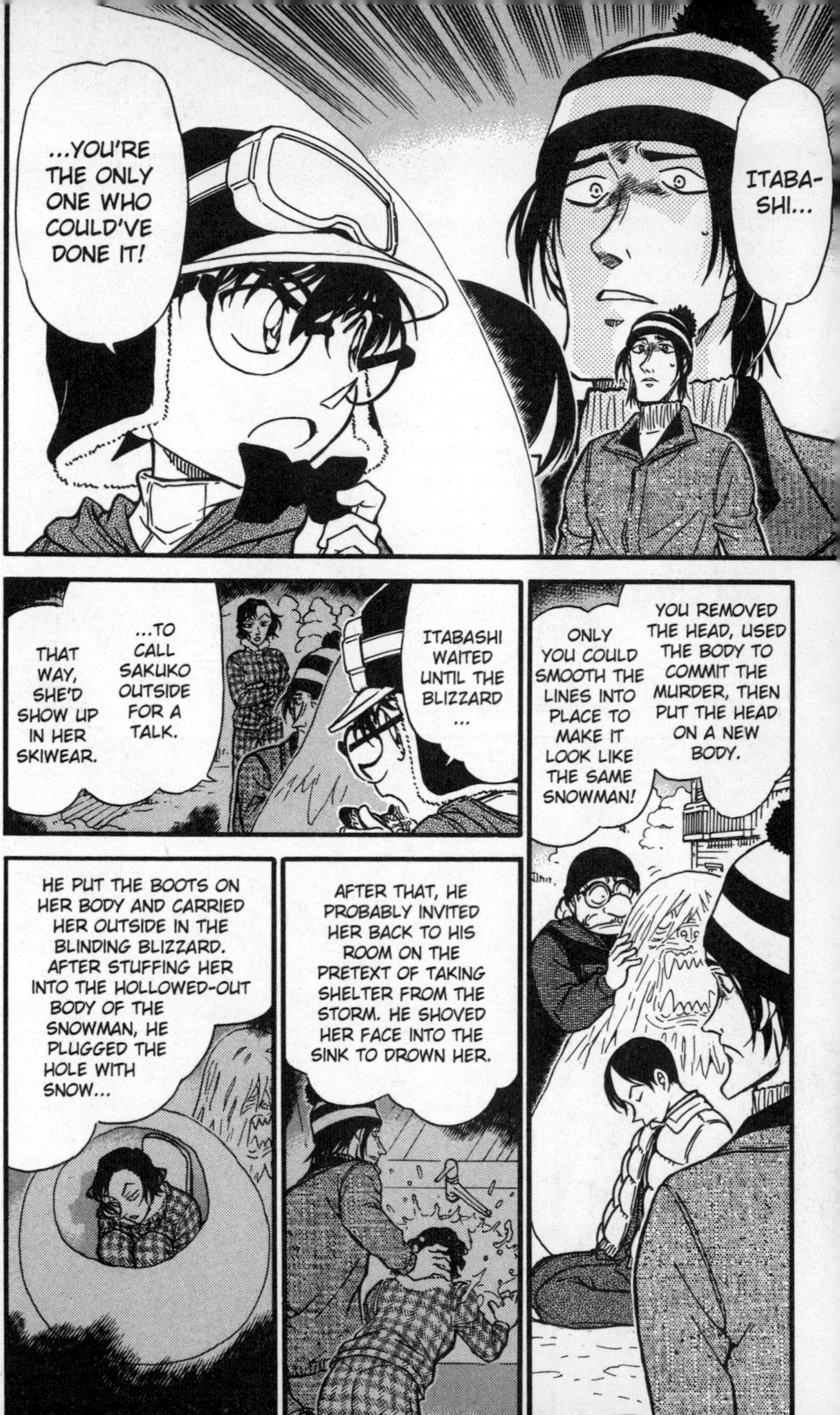
ITABA-SHI...
...YOU'RE THE ONLY ONE WHO COULD'VE DONE IT!
YOU REMOVED THE HEAD, USED THE BODY TO COMMIT THE MURDER, THEN PUT THE HEAD ON A NEW BODY.
ONLY YOU COULD SMOOTH THE LINES INTO PLACE TO MAKE IT LOOK LIKE THE SAME SNOWMAN!
ITABASHI WAITED UNTIL THE BLIZZARD...
...TO CALL SAKUKO OUTSIDE FOR A TALK.
THAT WAY, SHE'D SHOW UP IN HER SKIWEAR.
AFTER THAT, HE PROBABLY INVITED HER BACK TO HIS ROOM ON THE PRETEXT OF TAKING SHELTER FROM THE STORM. HE SHOVED HER FACE INTO THE SINK TO DROWN HER.
HE PUT THE BOOTS ON HER BODY AND CARRIED HER OUTSIDE IN THE BLINDING BLIZZARD. AFTER STUFFING HER INTO THE HOLLOWED-OUT BODY OF THE SNOWMAN, HE PLUGGED THE HOLE WITH SNOW...

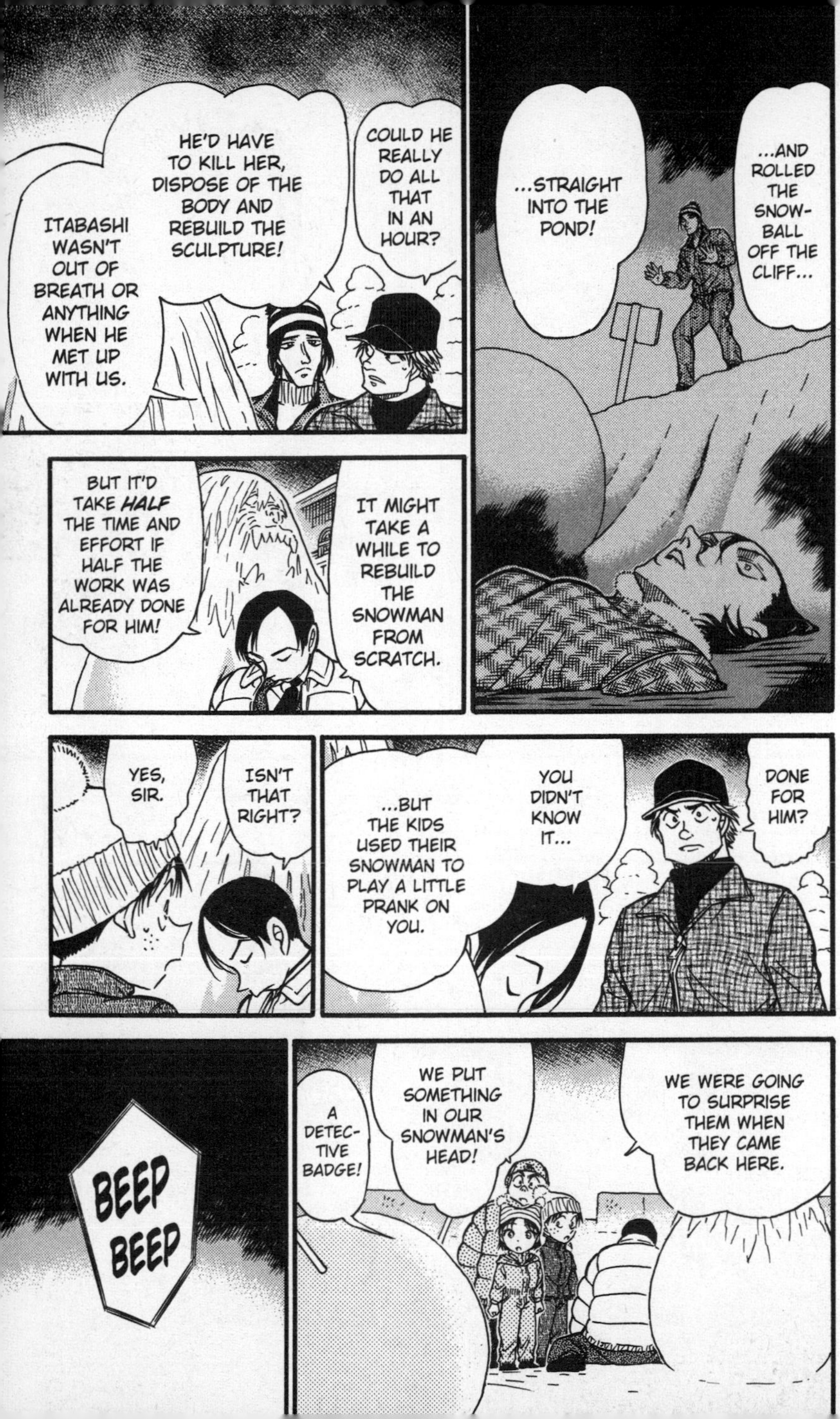
...AND ROLLED THE SNOW-BALL OFF THE CLIFF...
...STRAIGHT INTO THE POND!
COULD HE REALLY DO ALL THAT IN AN HOUR?
HE'D HAVE TO KILL HER, DISPOSE OF THE BODY AND REBUILD THE SCULPTURE!
ITABASHI WASN'T OUT OF BREATH OR ANYTHING WHEN HE MET UP WITH US.
IT MIGHT TAKE A WHILE TO REBUILD THE SNOWMAN FROM SCRATCH.
BUT IT'D TAKE HALF THE TIME AND EFFORT IF HALF THE WORK WAS ALREADY DONE FOR HIM!
DONE FOR HIM?
YOU DIDN'T KNOW IT...
...BUT THE KIDS USED THEIR SNOWMAN TO PLAY A LITTLE PRANK ON YOU.
ISN'T THAT RIGHT?
YES, SIR.
WE WERE GOING TO SURPRISE THEM WHEN THEY CAME BACK HERE.
WE PUT SOMETHING IN OUR SNOWMAN'S HEAD!
A DETECTIVE BADGE!
BEEP BEEP

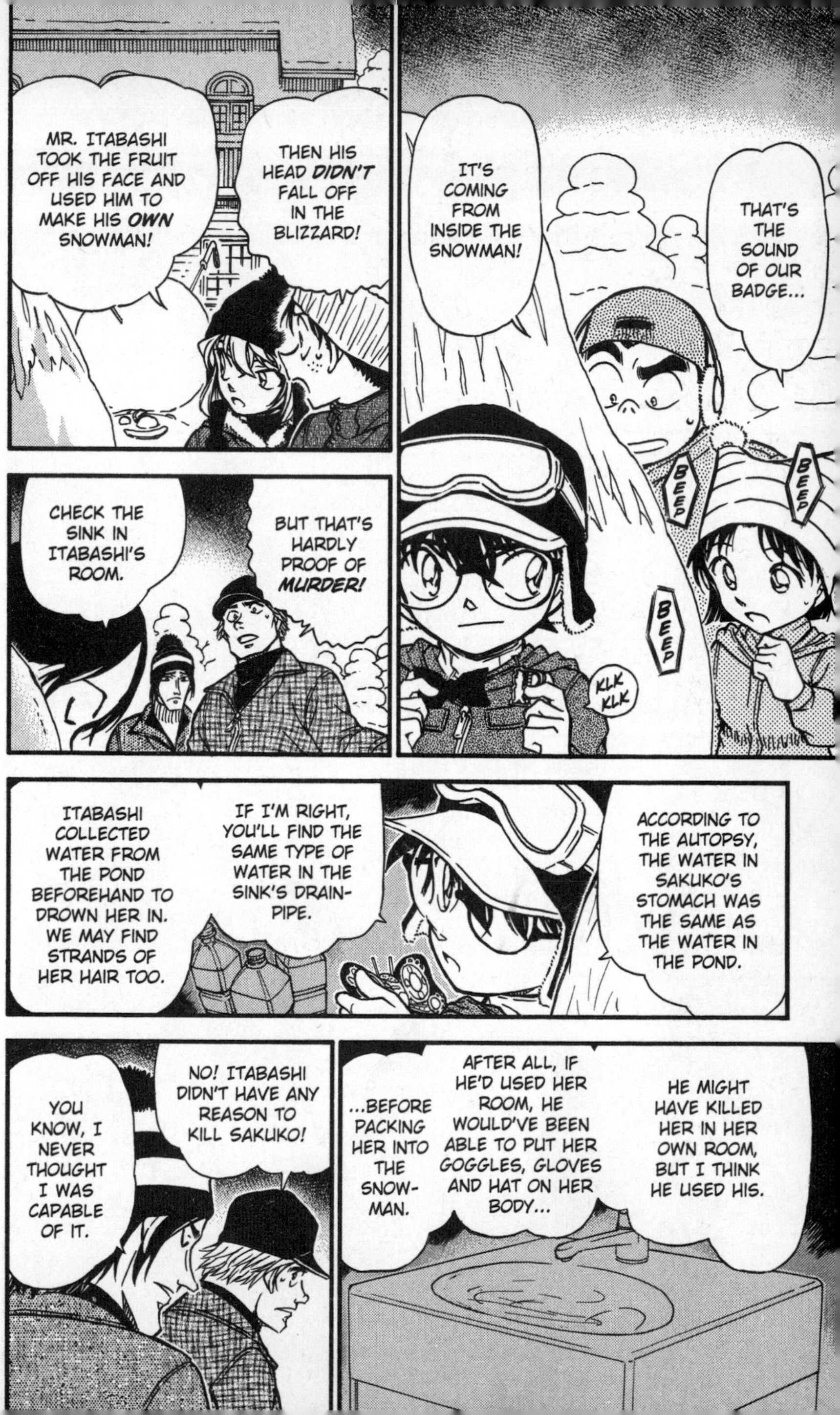
THAT'S THE SOUND OF OUR BADGE...
IT'S COMING FROM INSIDE THE SNOWMAN!
BEEP
BEEP
BEEP
KLK KLK
THEN HIS HEAD *DIDN'T* FALL OFF IN THE BLIZZARD!
MR. ITABASHI TOOK THE FRUIT OFF HIS FACE AND USED HIM TO MAKE HIS *OWN* SNOWMAN!
BUT THAT'S HARDLY PROOF OF *MURDER!*
CHECK THE SINK IN ITABASHI'S ROOM.
ACCORDING TO THE AUTOPSY, THE WATER IN SAKUKO'S STOMACH WAS THE SAME AS THE WATER IN THE POND.
IF I'M RIGHT, YOU'LL FIND THE SAME TYPE OF WATER IN THE SINK'S DRAIN-PIPE.
ITABASHI COLLECTED WATER FROM THE POND BEFOREHAND TO DROWN HER IN. WE MAY FIND STRANDS OF HER HAIR TOO.
HE MIGHT HAVE KILLED HER IN HER OWN ROOM, BUT I THINK HE USED HIS.
AFTER ALL, IF HE'D USED HER ROOM, HE WOULD'VE BEEN ABLE TO PUT HER GOGGLES, GLOVES AND HAT ON HER BODY...
...BEFORE PACKING HER INTO THE SNOW-MAN.
NO! ITABASHI DIDN'T HAVE ANY REASON TO KILL SAKUKO!
YOU KNOW, I NEVER THOUGHT I WAS CAPABLE OF IT.

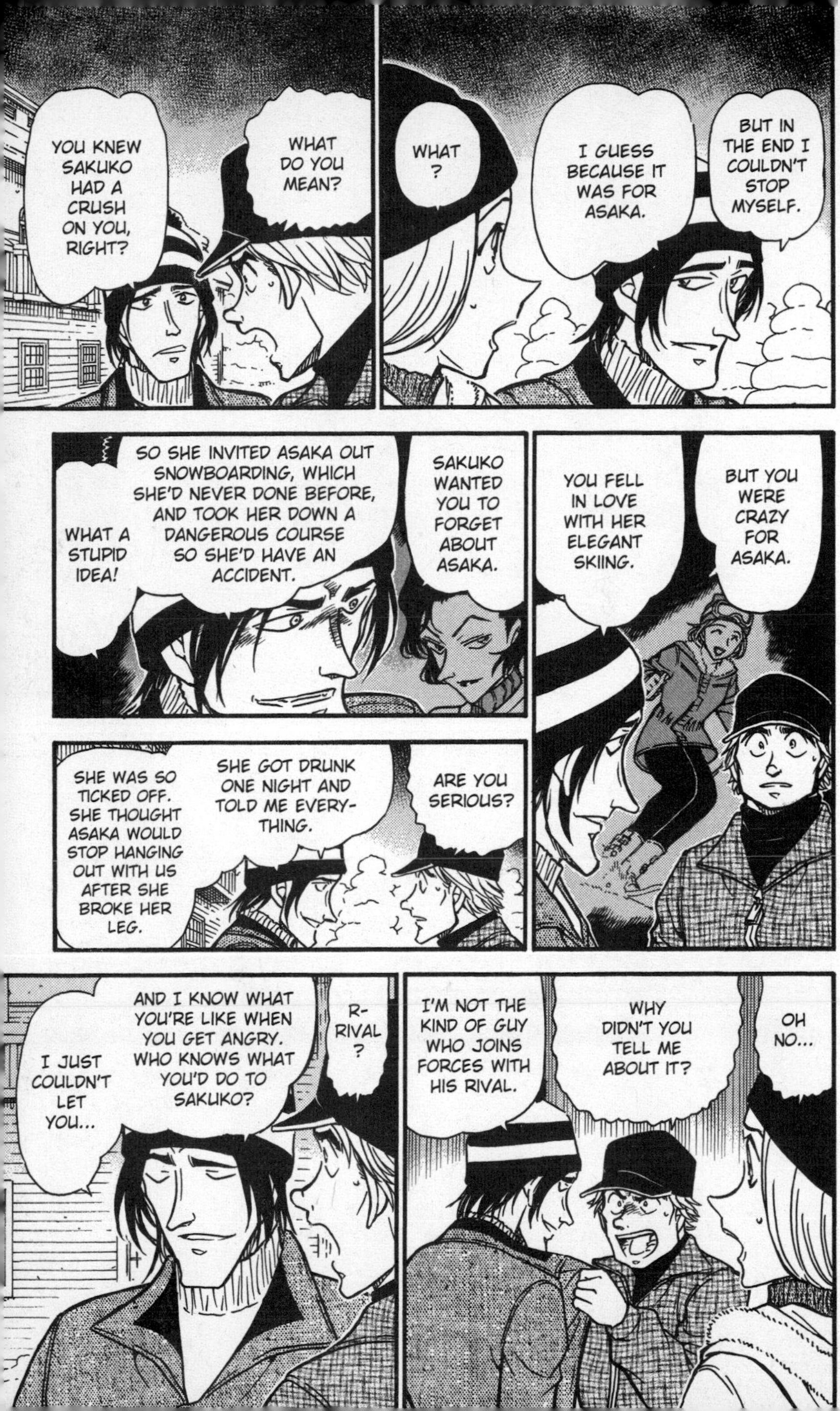
BUT IN THE END I COULDN'T STOP MYSELF.
I GUESS BECAUSE IT WAS FOR ASAKA.
WHAT?
WHAT DO YOU MEAN?
YOU KNEW SAKUKO HAD A CRUSH ON YOU, RIGHT?
BUT YOU WERE CRAZY FOR ASAKA.
YOU FELL IN LOVE WITH HER ELEGANT SKIING.
SAKUKO WANTED YOU TO FORGET ABOUT ASAKA.
SO SHE INVITED ASAKA OUT SNOWBOARDING, WHICH SHE'D NEVER DONE BEFORE, AND TOOK HER DOWN A DANGEROUS COURSE SO SHE'D HAVE AN ACCIDENT.
WHAT A STUPID IDEA!
ARE YOU SERIOUS?
SHE GOT DRUNK ONE NIGHT AND TOLD ME EVERY-THING.
SHE WAS SO TICKED OFF. SHE THOUGHT ASAKA WOULD STOP HANGING OUT WITH US AFTER SHE BROKE HER LEG.
OH NO...
WHY DIDN'T YOU TELL ME ABOUT IT?
I'M NOT THE KIND OF GUY WHO JOINS FORCES WITH HIS RIVAL.
R-RIVAL?
AND I KNOW WHAT YOU'RE LIKE WHEN YOU GET ANGRY. WHO KNOWS WHAT YOU'D DO TO SAKUKO?
I JUST COULDN'T LET YOU...

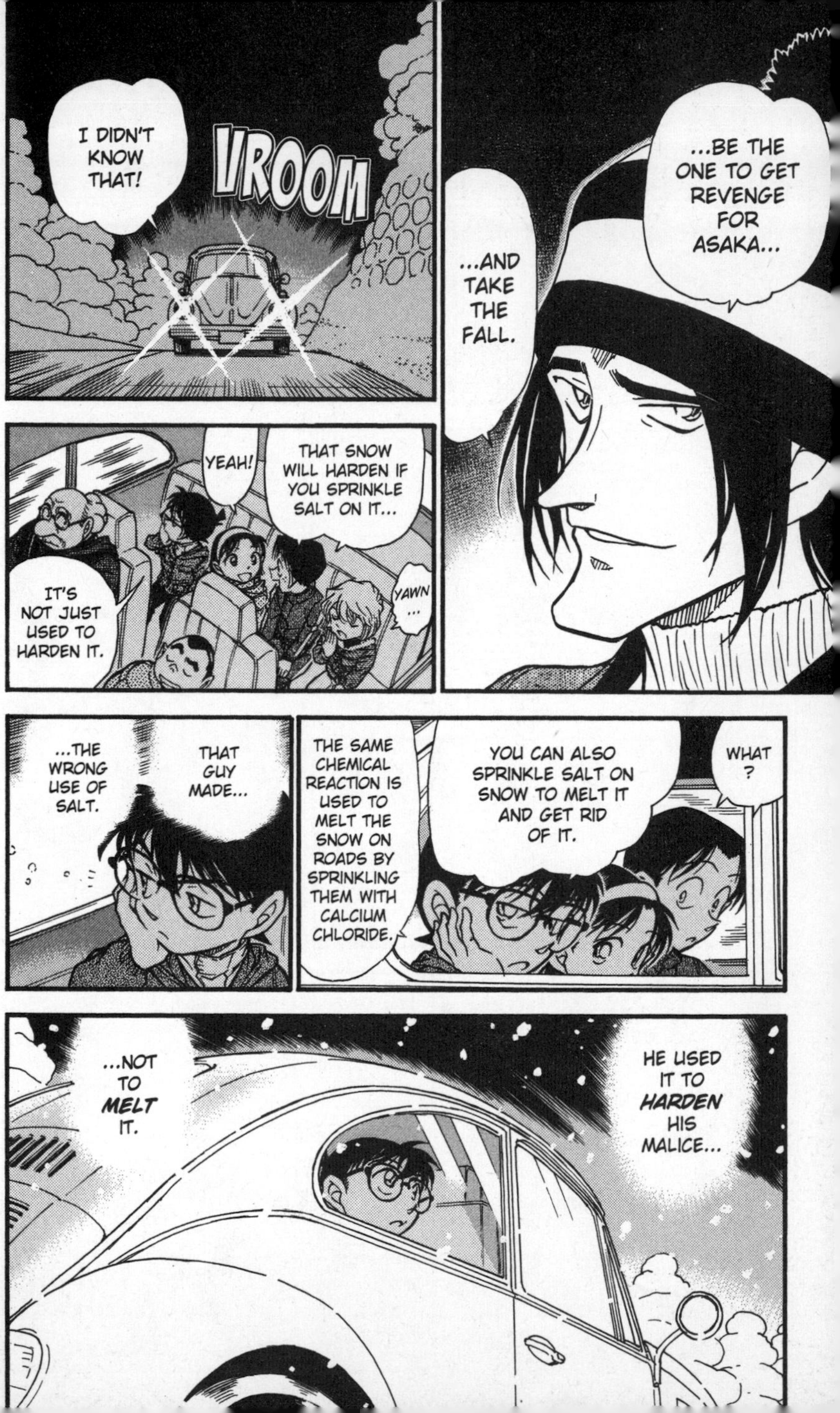
...BE THE ONE TO GET REVENGE FOR ASAKA...
...AND TAKE THE FALL.
I DIDN'T KNOW THAT!
VROOM
THAT SNOW WILL HARDEN IF YOU SPRINKLE SALT ON IT...
YEAH!
YAWN...
IT'S NOT JUST USED TO HARDEN IT.
WHAT?
YOU CAN ALSO SPRINKLE SALT ON SNOW TO MELT IT AND GET RID OF IT.
THE SAME CHEMICAL REACTION IS USED TO MELT THE SNOW ON ROADS BY SPRINKLING THEM WITH CALCIUM CHLORIDE.
THAT GUY MADE...
...THE WRONG USE OF SALT.
HE USED IT TO HARDEN HIS MALICE...
...NOT TO MELT IT.

FILE 6: THE DEVOURING ROOM

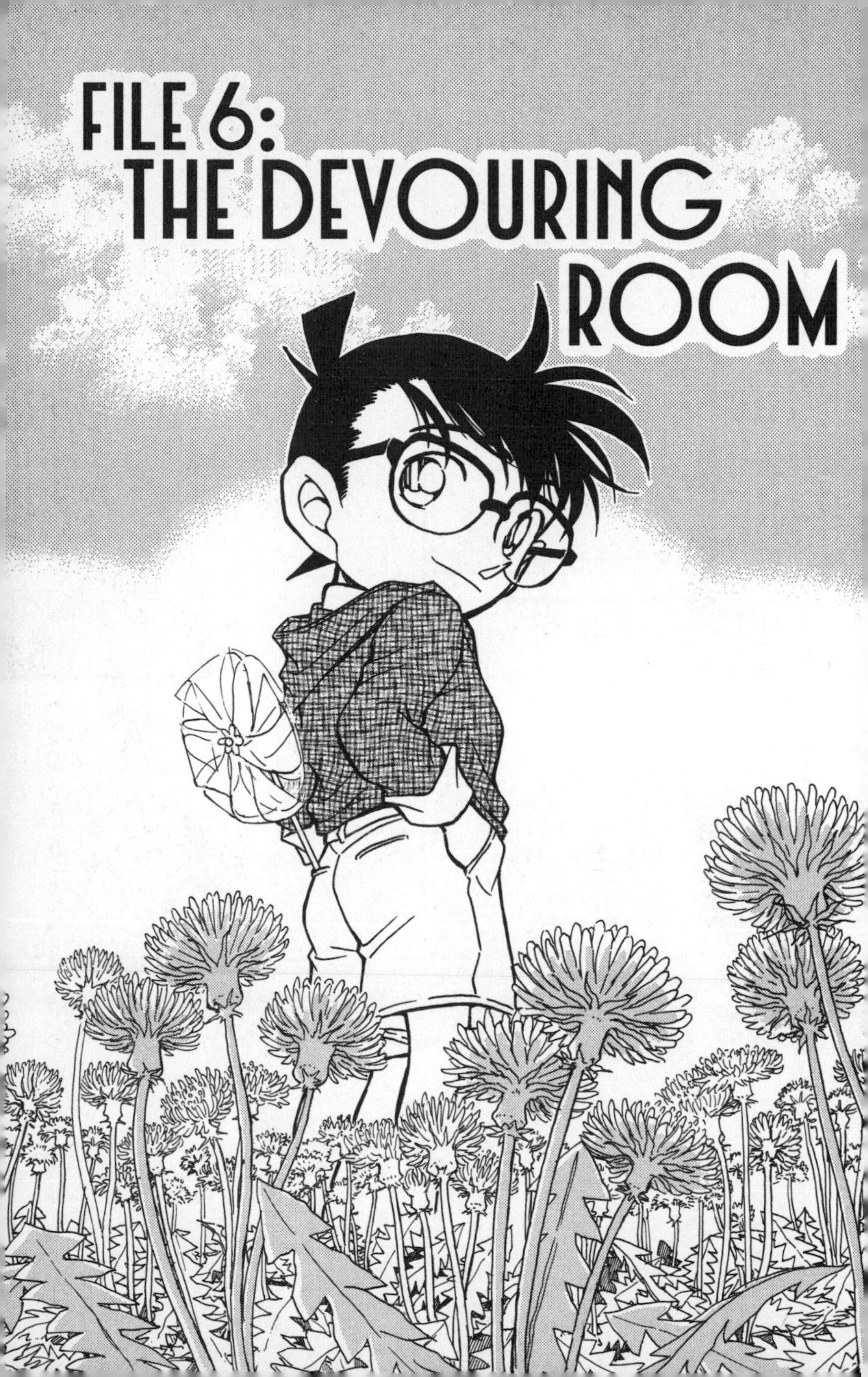

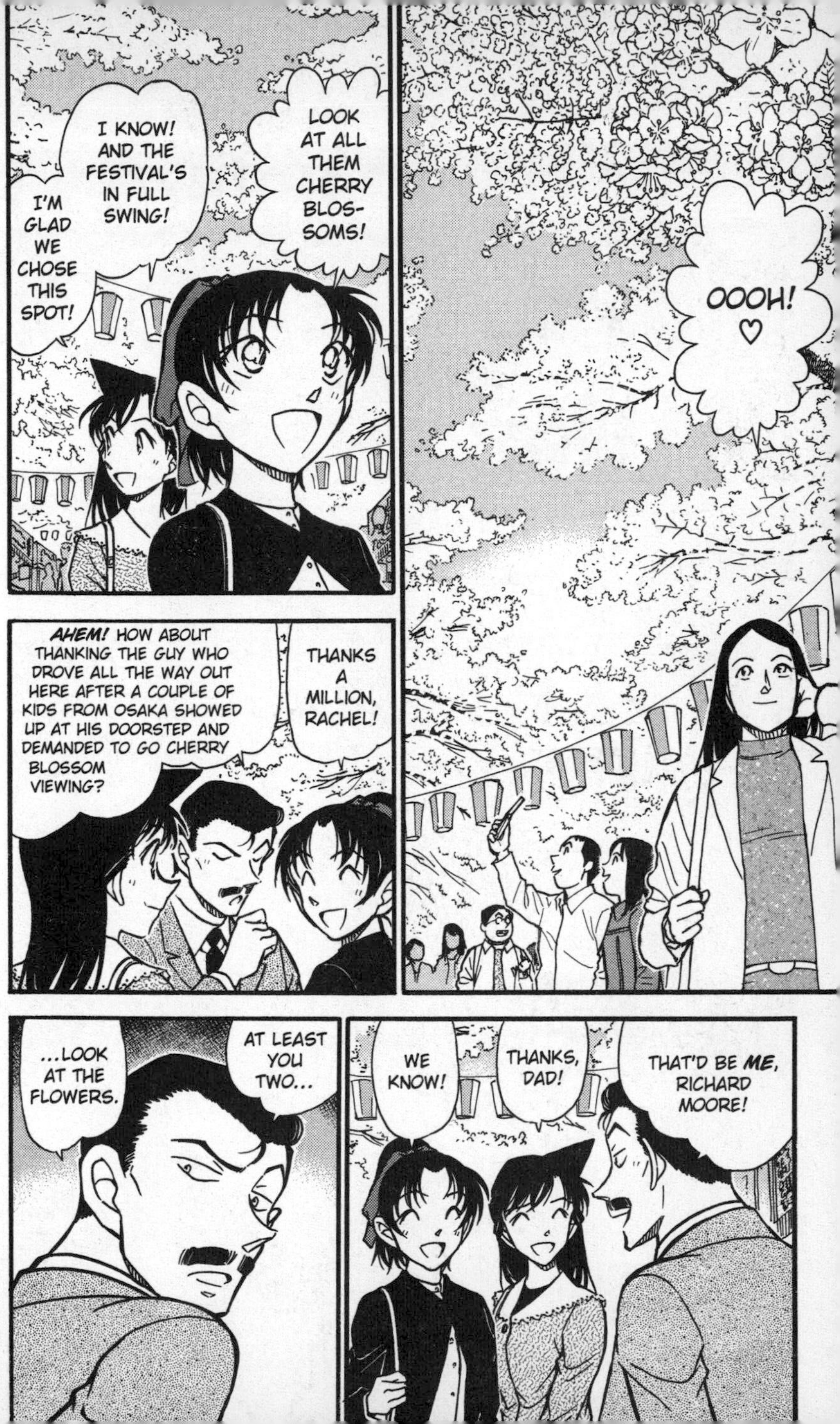
OOOH! ♥
LOOK AT ALL THEM CHERRY BLOSSOMS!
I KNOW! AND THE FESTIVAL'S IN FULL SWING!
I'M GLAD WE CHOSE THIS SPOT!
THANKS A MILLION, RACHEL!
AHEM! HOW ABOUT THANKING THE GUY WHO DROVE ALL THE WAY OUT HERE AFTER A COUPLE OF KIDS FROM OSAKA SHOWED UP AT HIS DOORSTEP AND DEMANDED TO GO CHERRY BLOSSOM VIEWING?
THAT'D BE *ME*, RICHARD MOORE!
THANKS, DAD!
WE KNOW!
AT LEAST YOU TWO...
...LOOK AT THE FLOWERS.

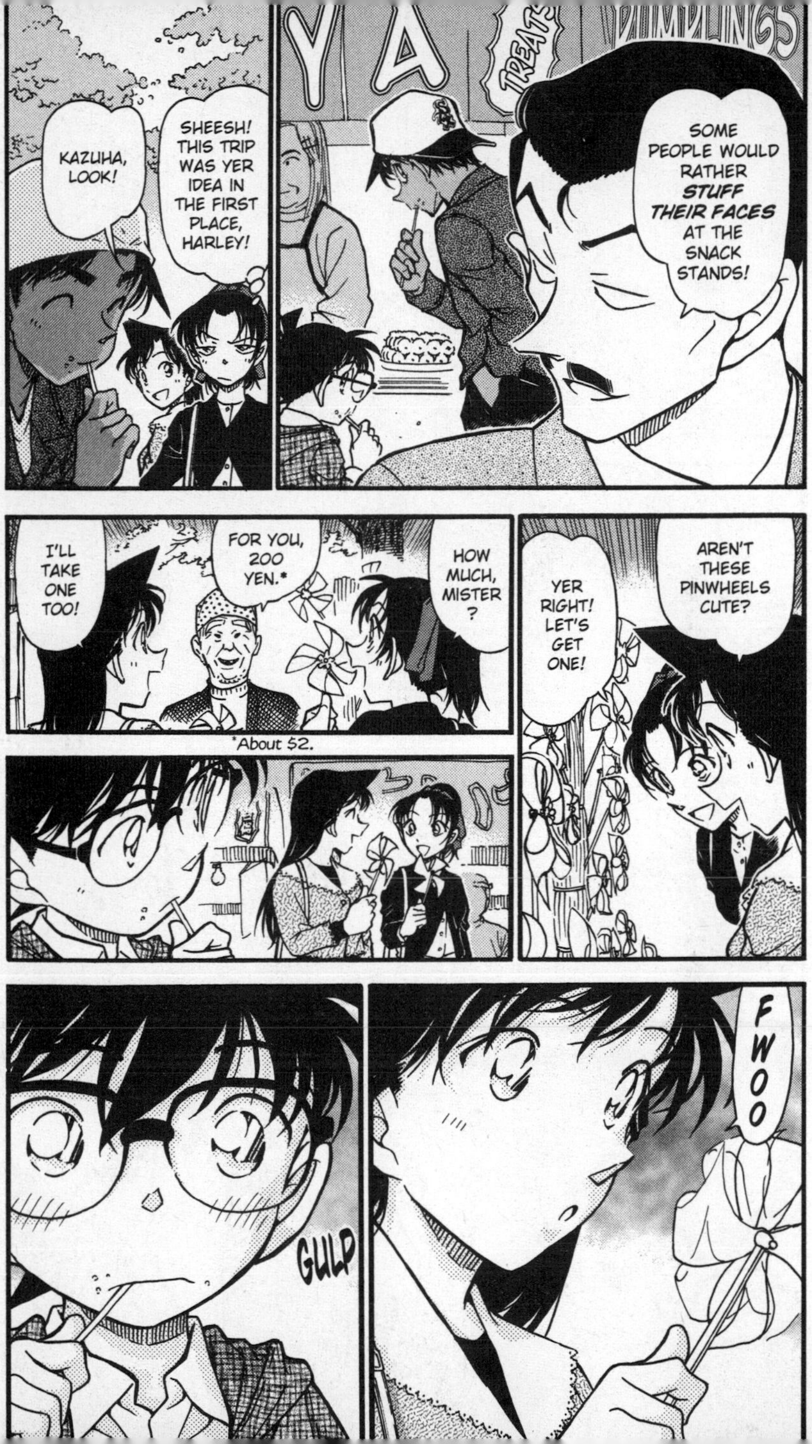
TREATS
SOME PEOPLE WOULD RATHER **STUFF THEIR FACES** AT THE SNACK STANDS!
SHEESH! THIS TRIP WAS YER IDEA IN THE FIRST PLACE, HARLEY!
KAZUHA, LOOK!
AREN'T THESE PINWHEELS CUTE?
YER RIGHT! LET'S GET ONE!
HOW MUCH, MISTER?
FOR YOU, 200 YEN.*
I'LL TAKE ONE TOO!
*About $2.
FWOO
GULP

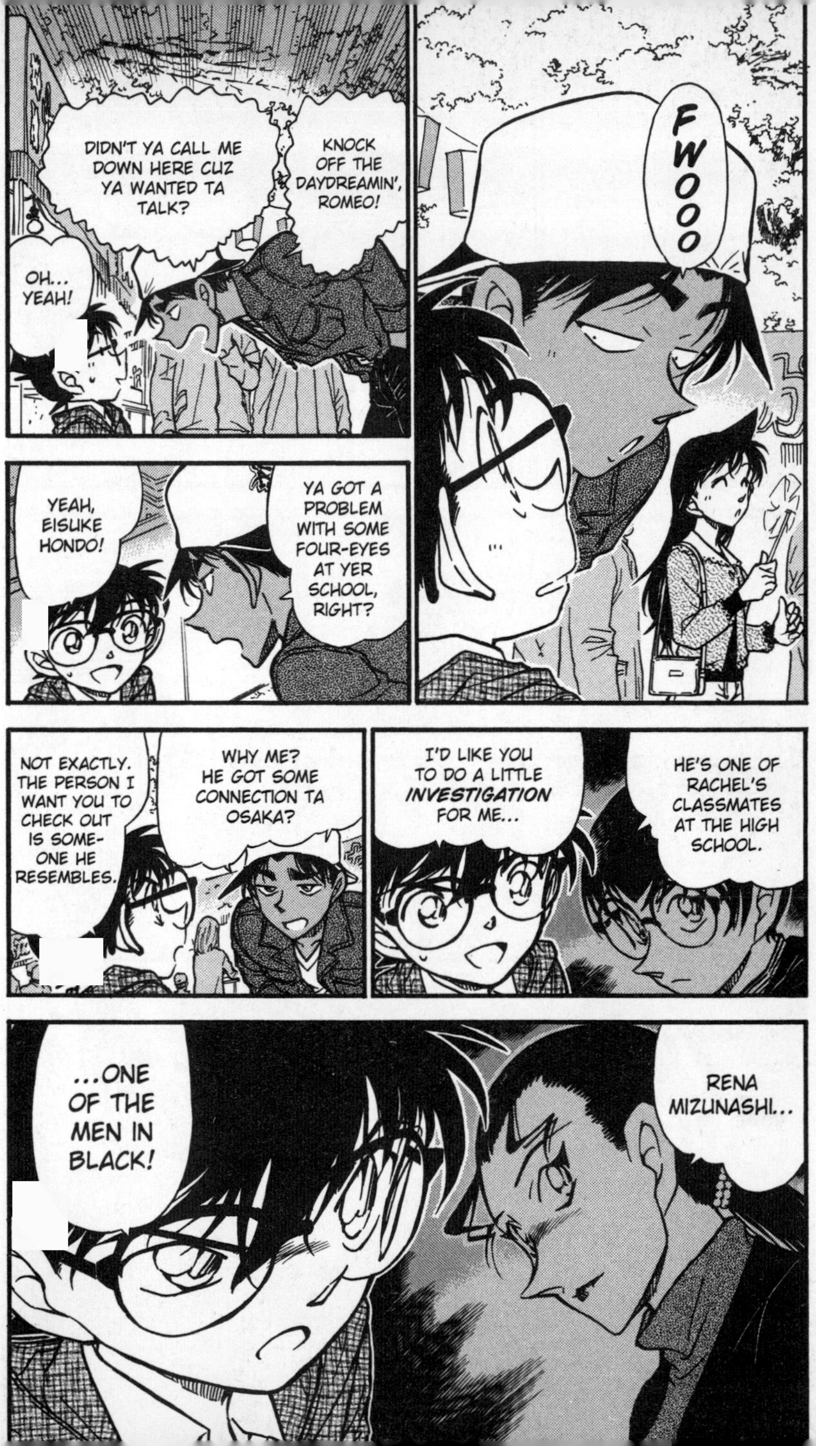
FWOOO
KNOCK OFF THE DAYDREAMIN', ROMEO!
DIDN'T YA CALL ME DOWN HERE CUZ YA WANTED TA TALK?
OH... YEAH!
YA GOT A PROBLEM WITH SOME FOUR-EYES AT YER SCHOOL, RIGHT?
YEAH, EISUKE HONDO!
HE'S ONE OF RACHEL'S CLASSMATES AT THE HIGH SCHOOL.
I'D LIKE YOU TO DO A LITTLE *INVESTIGATION* FOR ME...
WHY ME? HE GOT SOME CONNECTION TA OSAKA?
NOT EXACTLY. THE PERSON I WANT YOU TO CHECK OUT IS SOME-ONE HE RESEMBLES.
RENA MIZUNASHI...
...ONE OF THE MEN IN BLACK!

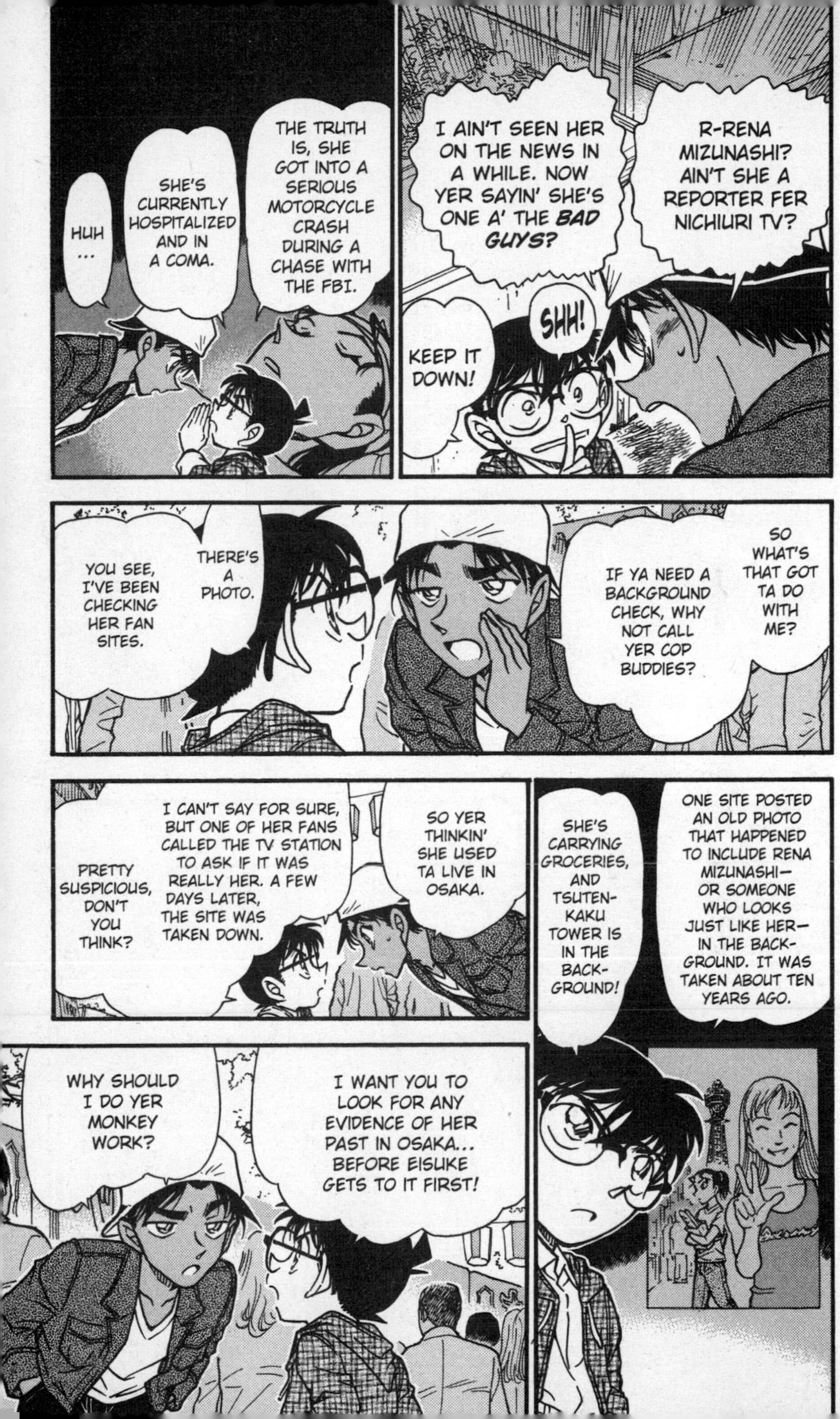
R-RENA MIZUNASHI? AIN'T SHE A REPORTER FER NICHIURI TV?
I AIN'T SEEN HER ON THE NEWS IN A WHILE. NOW YER SAYIN' SHE'S ONE A' THE *BAD GUYS?*
SHH!
KEEP IT DOWN!
THE TRUTH IS, SHE GOT INTO A SERIOUS MOTORCYCLE CRASH DURING A CHASE WITH THE FBI.
SHE'S CURRENTLY HOSPITALIZED AND IN A COMA.
HUH ...
SO WHAT'S THAT GOT TA DO WITH ME?
IF YA NEED A BACKGROUND CHECK, WHY NOT CALL YER COP BUDDIES?
THERE'S A PHOTO.
YOU SEE, I'VE BEEN CHECKING HER FAN SITES.
ONE SITE POSTED AN OLD PHOTO THAT HAPPENED TO INCLUDE RENA MIZUNASHI—OR SOMEONE WHO LOOKS JUST LIKE HER—IN THE BACKGROUND. IT WAS TAKEN ABOUT TEN YEARS AGO.
SHE'S CARRYING GROCERIES, AND TSUTENKAKU TOWER IS IN THE BACKGROUND!
SO YER THINKIN' SHE USED TA LIVE IN OSAKA.
I CAN'T SAY FOR SURE, BUT ONE OF HER FANS CALLED THE TV STATION TO ASK IF IT WAS REALLY HER. A FEW DAYS LATER, THE SITE WAS TAKEN DOWN.
PRETTY SUSPICIOUS, DON'T YOU THINK?
I WANT YOU TO LOOK FOR ANY EVIDENCE OF HER PAST IN OSAKA... BEFORE EISUKE GETS TO IT FIRST!
WHY SHOULD I DO YER MONKEY WORK?

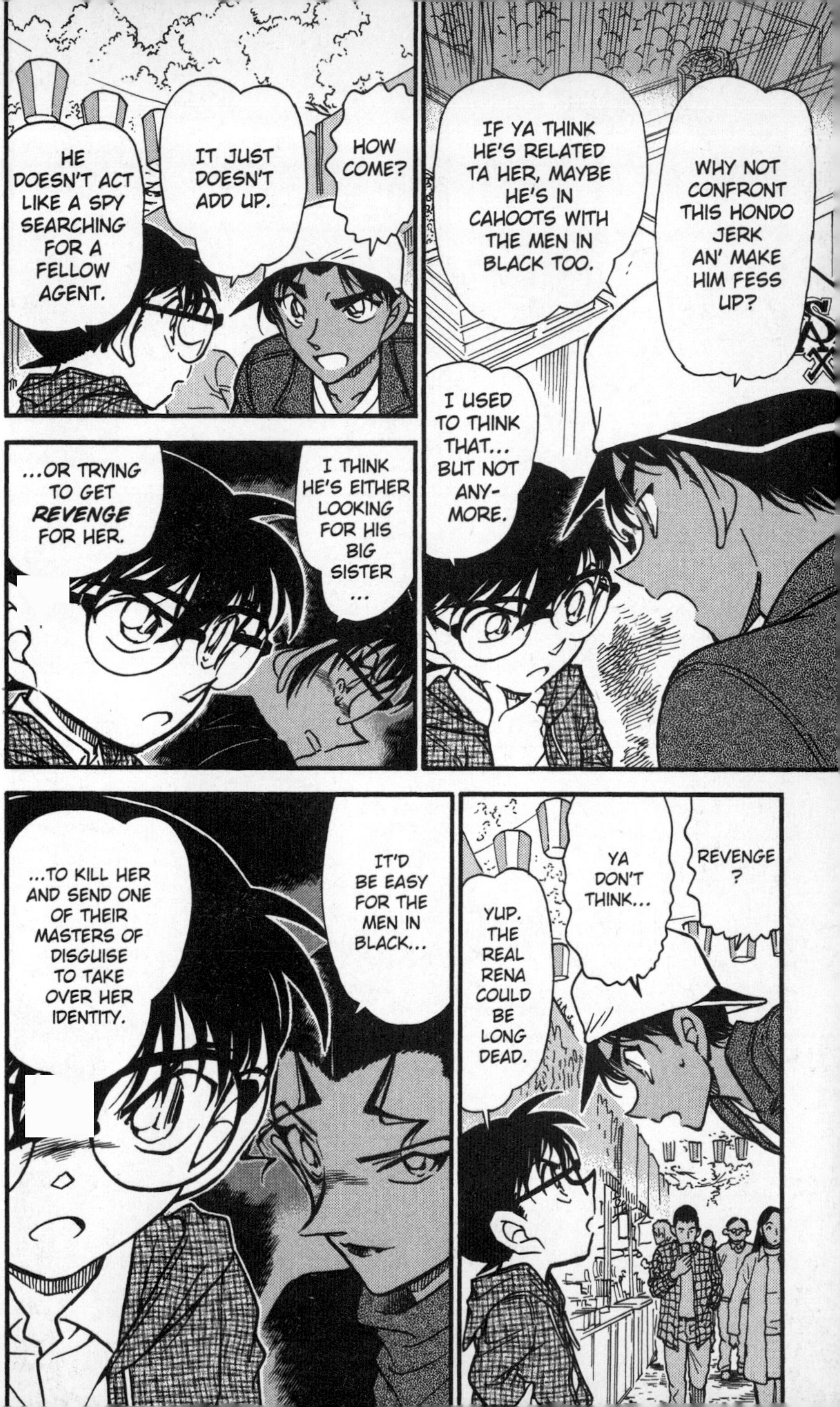
WHY NOT CONFRONT THIS HONDO JERK AN' MAKE HIM FESS UP?
IF YA THINK HE'S RELATED TA HER, MAYBE HE'S IN CAHOOTS WITH THE MEN IN BLACK TOO.
I USED TO THINK THAT... BUT NOT ANY-MORE.
HOW COME?
IT JUST DOESN'T ADD UP.
HE DOESN'T ACT LIKE A SPY SEARCHING FOR A FELLOW AGENT.
I THINK HE'S EITHER LOOKING FOR HIS BIG SISTER...
...OR TRYING TO GET *REVENGE* FOR HER.
REVENGE?
YA DON'T THINK...
YUP. THE REAL RENA COULD BE LONG DEAD.
IT'D BE EASY FOR THE MEN IN BLACK...
...TO KILL HER AND SEND ONE OF THEIR MASTERS OF DISGUISE TO TAKE OVER HER IDENTITY.

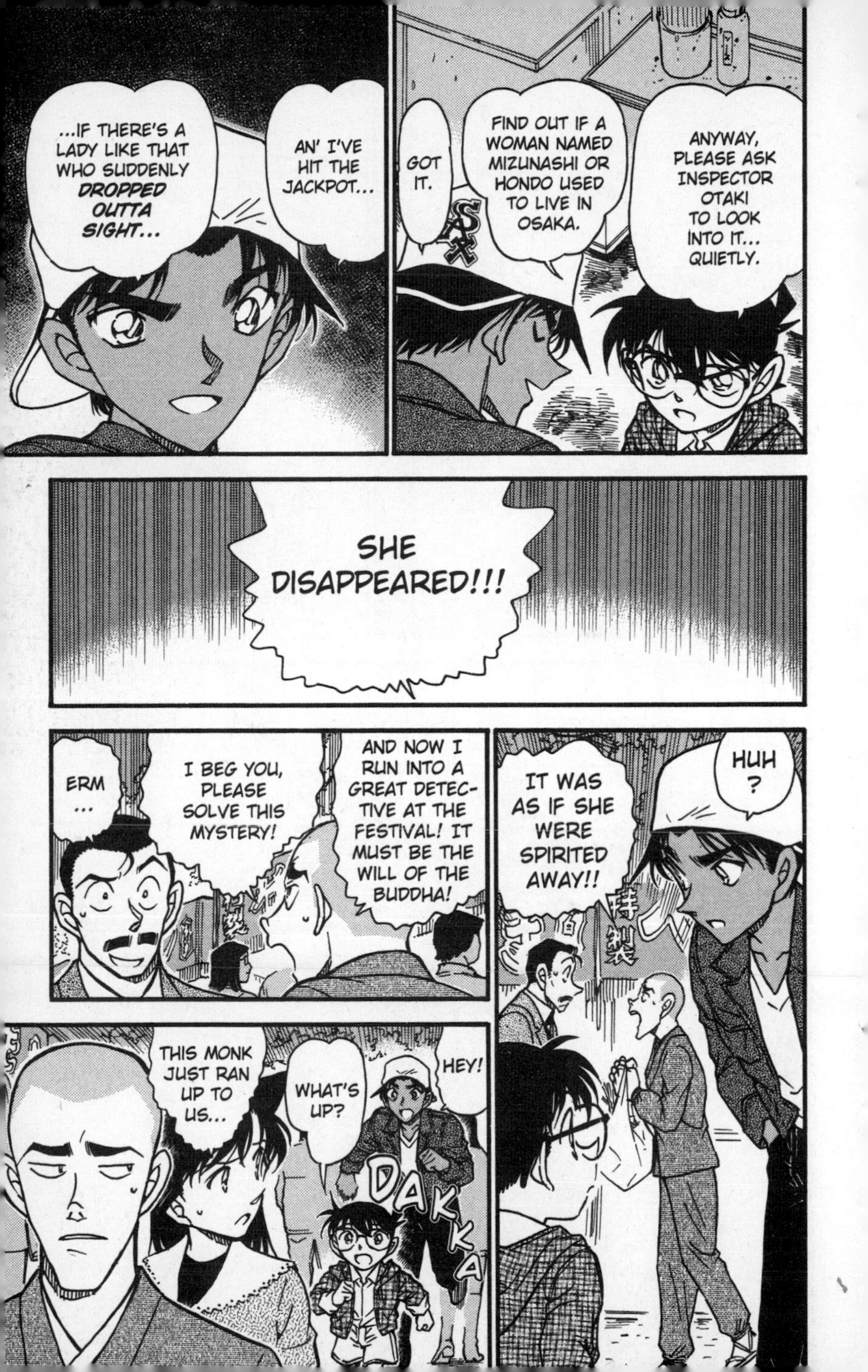
ANYWAY, PLEASE ASK INSPECTOR OTAKI TO LOOK INTO IT... QUIETLY.
FIND OUT IF A WOMAN NAMED MIZUNASHI OR HONDO USED TO LIVE IN OSAKA.
GOT IT.
AN' I'VE HIT THE JACKPOT...
...IF THERE'S A LADY LIKE THAT WHO SUDDENLY DROPPED OUTTA SIGHT...
SHE DISAPPEARED!!!
HUH?
IT WAS AS IF SHE WERE SPIRITED AWAY!!
AND NOW I RUN INTO A GREAT DETECTIVE AT THE FESTIVAL! IT MUST BE THE WILL OF THE BUDDHA!
I BEG YOU, PLEASE SOLVE THIS MYSTERY!
ERM ...
HEY!
WHAT'S UP?
THIS MONK JUST RAN UP TO US...
DAKKA

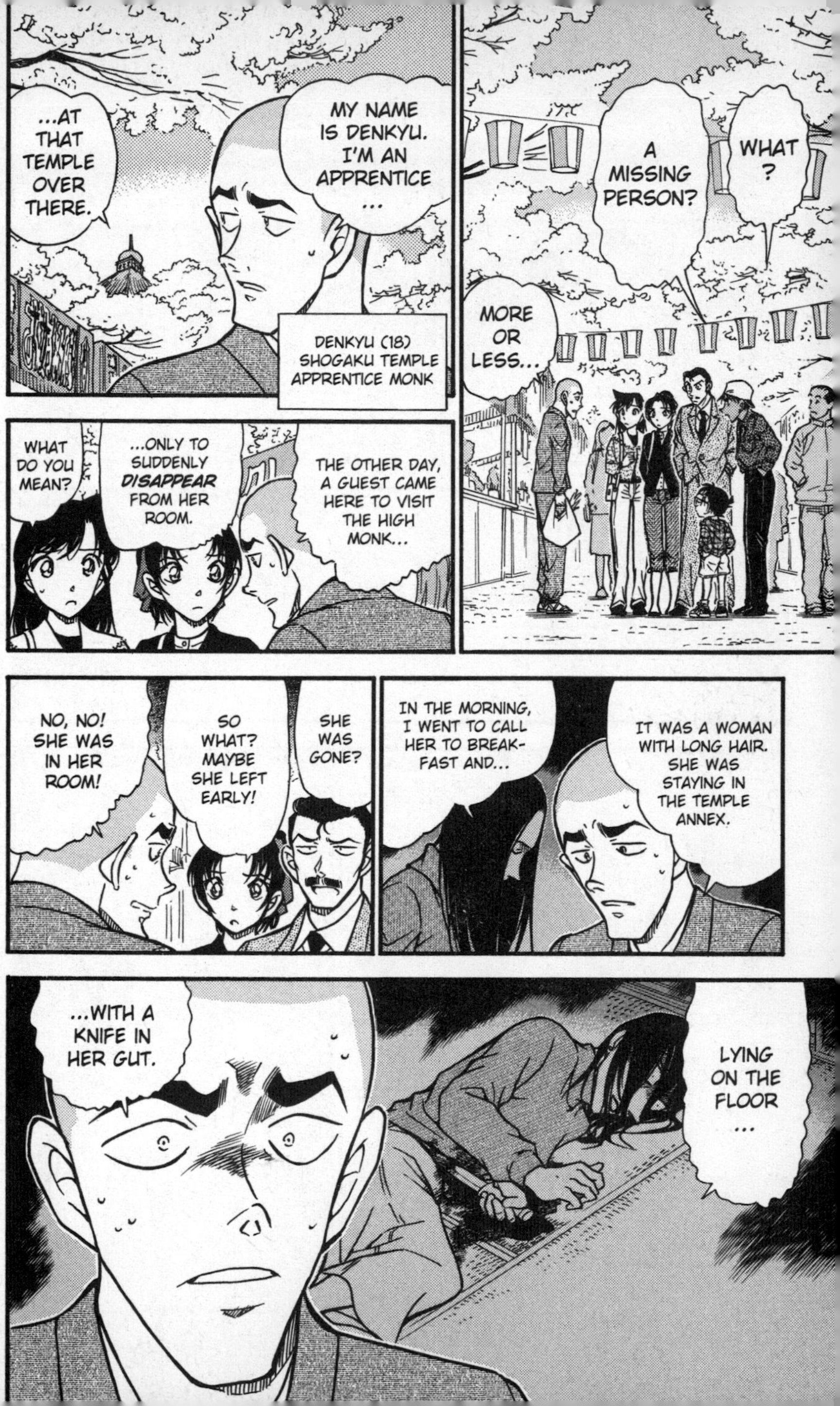
WHAT ?
A MISSING PERSON?
MORE OR LESS...
MY NAME IS DENKYU. I'M AN APPRENTICE ...
...AT THAT TEMPLE OVER THERE.
DENKYU (18) SHOGAKU TEMPLE APPRENTICE MONK
THE OTHER DAY, A GUEST CAME HERE TO VISIT THE HIGH MONK...
...ONLY TO SUDDENLY *DISAPPEAR* FROM HER ROOM.
WHAT DO YOU MEAN?
IT WAS A WOMAN WITH LONG HAIR. SHE WAS STAYING IN THE TEMPLE ANNEX.
IN THE MORNING, I WENT TO CALL HER TO BREAK-FAST AND...
SHE WAS GONE?
SO WHAT? MAYBE SHE LEFT EARLY!
NO, NO! SHE WAS IN HER ROOM!
LYING ON THE FLOOR ...
...WITH A KNIFE IN HER GUT.

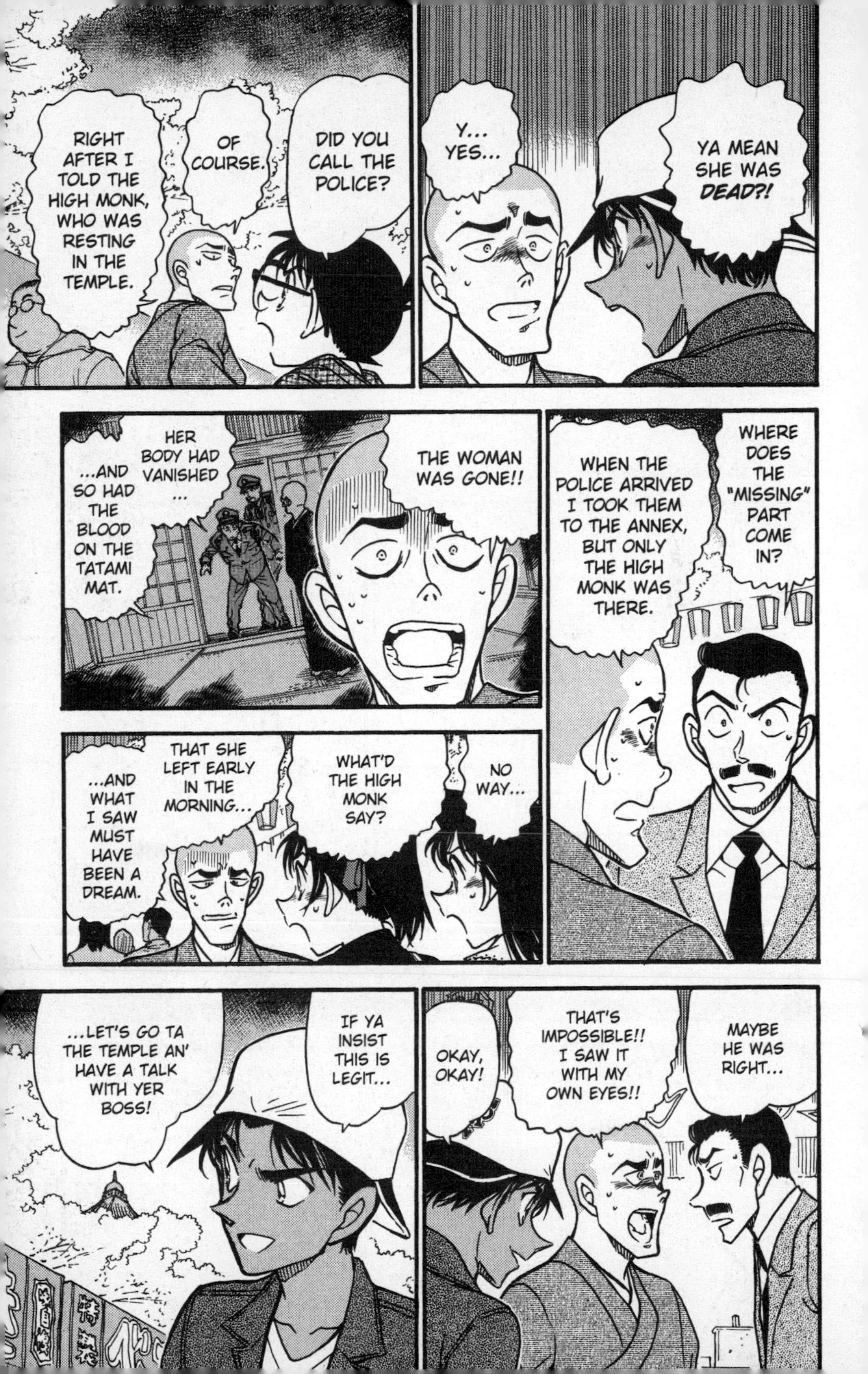
YA MEAN SHE WAS *DEAD?!*
Y... YES...
DID YOU CALL THE POLICE?
OF COURSE.
RIGHT AFTER I TOLD THE HIGH MONK, WHO WAS RESTING IN THE TEMPLE.
WHERE DOES THE "MISSING" PART COME IN?
WHEN THE POLICE ARRIVED I TOOK THEM TO THE ANNEX, BUT ONLY THE HIGH MONK WAS THERE.
THE WOMAN WAS GONE!!
HER BODY HAD VANISHED...
...AND SO HAD THE BLOOD ON THE TATAMI MAT.
NO WAY...
WHAT'D THE HIGH MONK SAY?
THAT SHE LEFT EARLY IN THE MORNING...
...AND WHAT I SAW MUST HAVE BEEN A DREAM.
MAYBE HE WAS RIGHT...
THAT'S IMPOSSIBLE!! I SAW IT WITH MY OWN EYES!!
OKAY, OKAY!
IF YA INSIST THIS IS LEGIT...
...LET'S GO TA THE TEMPLE AN' HAVE A TALK WITH YER BOSS!

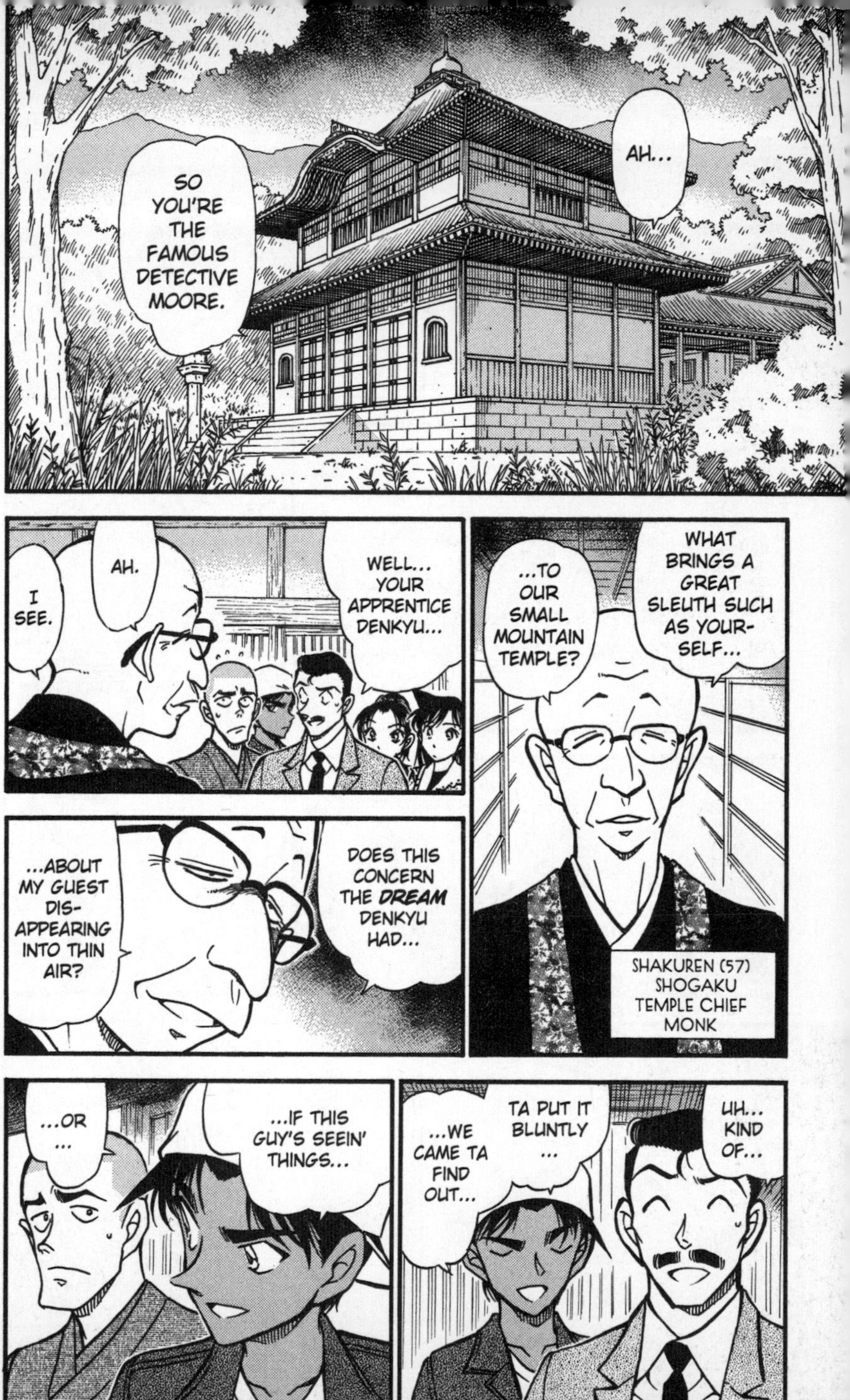
AH...
SO YOU'RE THE FAMOUS DETECTIVE MOORE.
WHAT BRINGS A GREAT SLEUTH SUCH AS YOUR-SELF...
...TO OUR SMALL MOUNTAIN TEMPLE?
SHAKUREN (57) SHOGAKU TEMPLE CHIEF MONK
WELL... YOUR APPRENTICE DENKYU...
AH.
I SEE.
DOES THIS CONCERN THE *DREAM* DENKYU HAD...
...ABOUT MY GUEST DIS-APPEARING INTO THIN AIR?
UH... KIND OF...
TA PUT IT BLUNTLY ...
...WE CAME TA FIND OUT...
...IF THIS GUY'S SEEIN' THINGS...
...OR ...

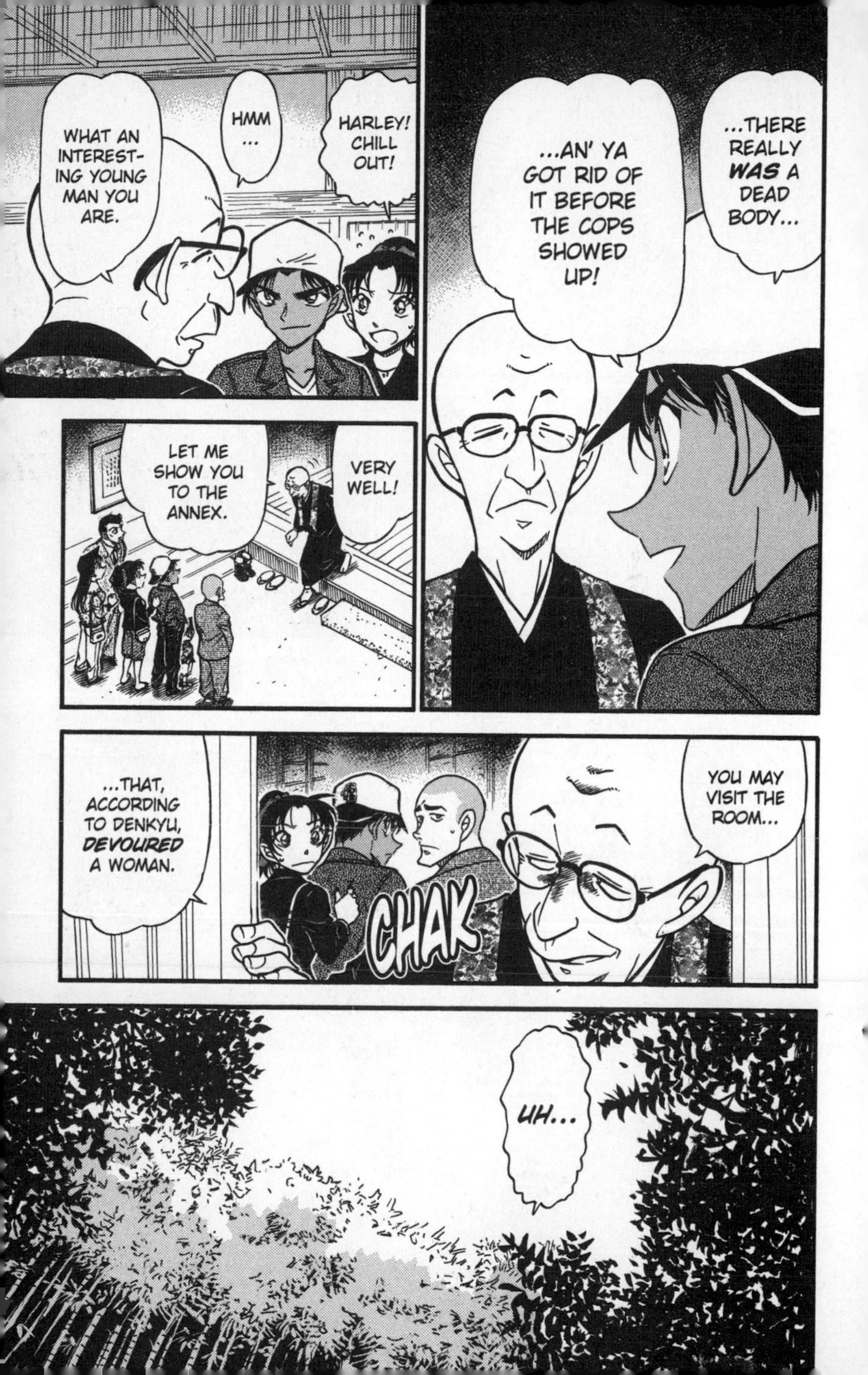
...THERE REALLY WAS A DEAD BODY...
...AN' YA GOT RID OF IT BEFORE THE COPS SHOWED UP!
HARLEY! CHILL OUT!
HMM ...
WHAT AN INTERESTING YOUNG MAN YOU ARE.
VERY WELL!
LET ME SHOW YOU TO THE ANNEX.
YOU MAY VISIT THE ROOM...
CHAK
...THAT, ACCORDING TO DENKYU, DEVOURED A WOMAN.
UH...

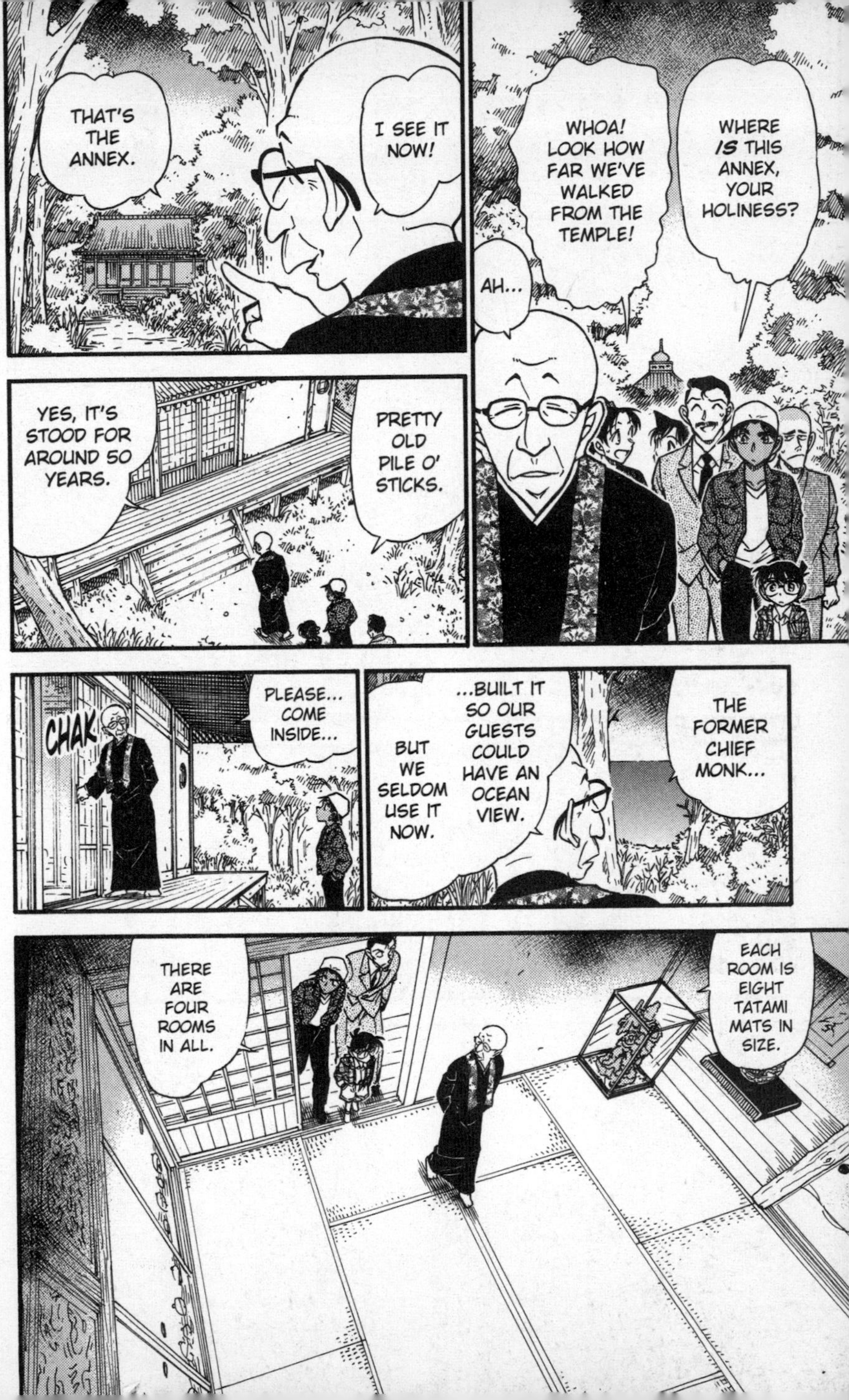
WHERE IS THIS ANNEX, YOUR HOLINESS?
WHOA! LOOK HOW FAR WE'VE WALKED FROM THE TEMPLE!
AH...
I SEE IT NOW!
THAT'S THE ANNEX.
PRETTY OLD PILE O' STICKS.
YES, IT'S STOOD FOR AROUND 50 YEARS.
THE FORMER CHIEF MONK...
...BUILT IT SO OUR GUESTS COULD HAVE AN OCEAN VIEW.
BUT WE SELDOM USE IT NOW.
PLEASE... COME INSIDE...
CHAK
EACH ROOM IS EIGHT TATAMI MATS IN SIZE.
THERE ARE FOUR ROOMS IN ALL.

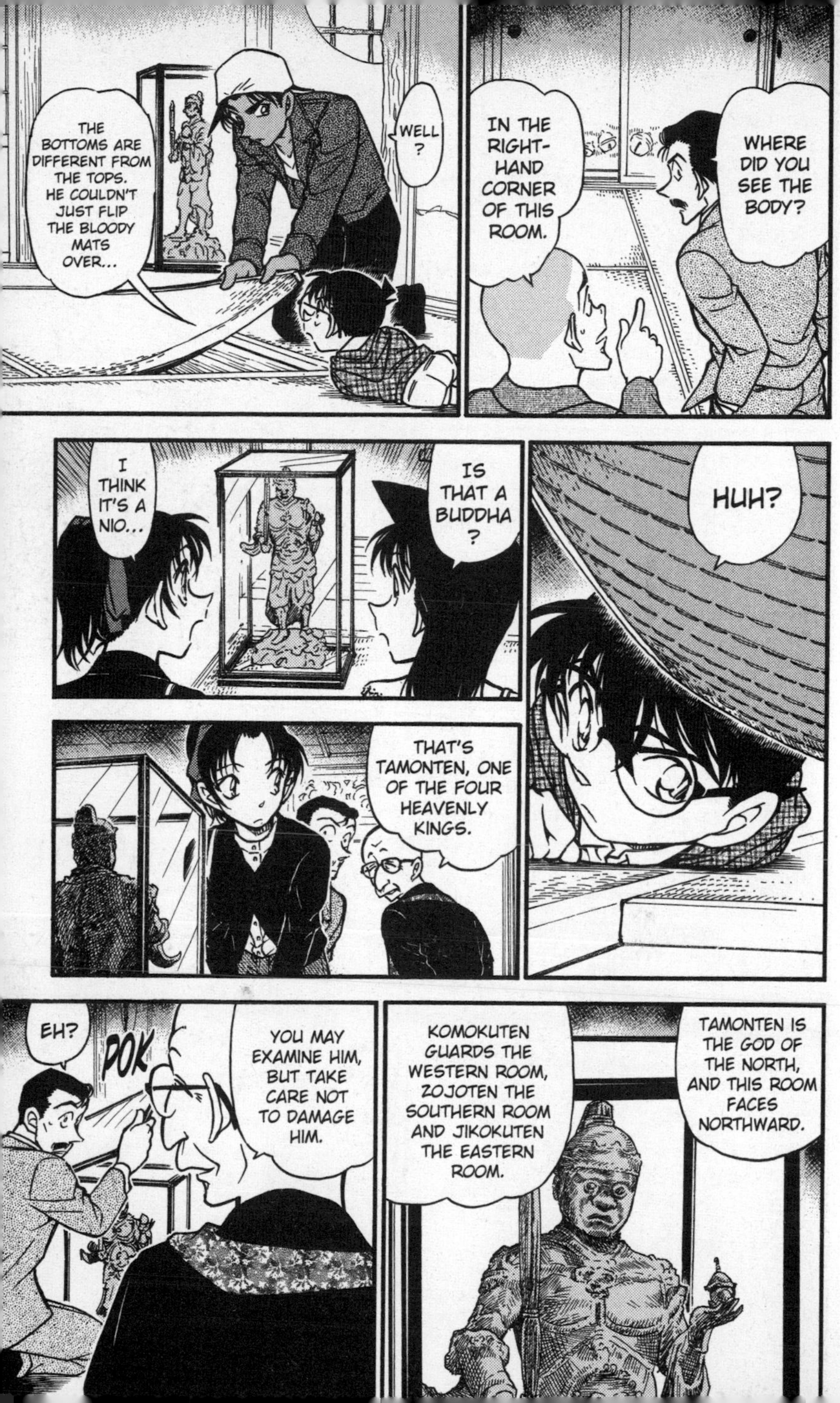
WHERE DID YOU SEE THE BODY?
IN THE RIGHT-HAND CORNER OF THIS ROOM.
WELL?
THE BOTTOMS ARE DIFFERENT FROM THE TOPS. HE COULDN'T JUST FLIP THE BLOODY MATS OVER...
HUH?
IS THAT A BUDDHA?
I THINK IT'S A NIO...
THAT'S TAMONTEN, ONE OF THE FOUR HEAVENLY KINGS.
TAMONTEN IS THE GOD OF THE NORTH, AND THIS ROOM FACES NORTHWARD.
KOMOKUTEN GUARDS THE WESTERN ROOM, ZOJOTEN THE SOUTHERN ROOM AND JIKOKUTEN THE EASTERN ROOM.
YOU MAY EXAMINE HIM, BUT TAKE CARE NOT TO DAMAGE HIM.
POK
EH?

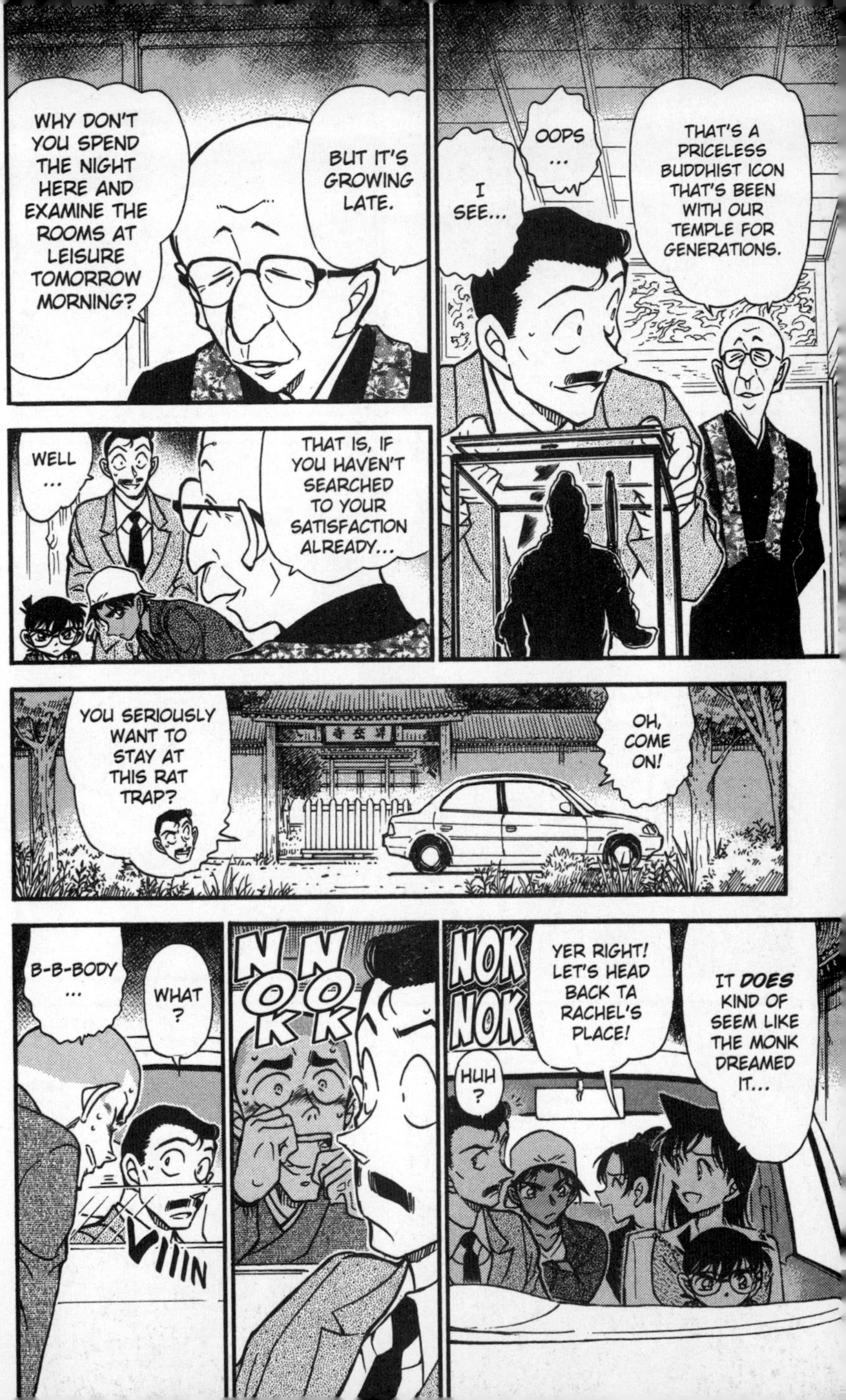
THAT'S A PRICELESS BUDDHIST ICON THAT'S BEEN WITH OUR TEMPLE FOR GENERATIONS.
OOPS ...
I SEE...
BUT IT'S GROWING LATE.
WHY DON'T YOU SPEND THE NIGHT HERE AND EXAMINE THE ROOMS AT LEISURE TOMORROW MORNING?
THAT IS, IF YOU HAVEN'T SEARCHED TO YOUR SATISFACTION ALREADY...
WELL ...
OH, COME ON!
YOU SERIOUSLY WANT TO STAY AT THIS RAT TRAP?
IT DOES KIND OF SEEM LIKE THE MONK DREAMED IT...
YER RIGHT! LET'S HEAD BACK TA RACHEL'S PLACE!
NOK NOK
HUH ?
NOK NOK
WHAT ?
B-B-BODY ...
VIIIN

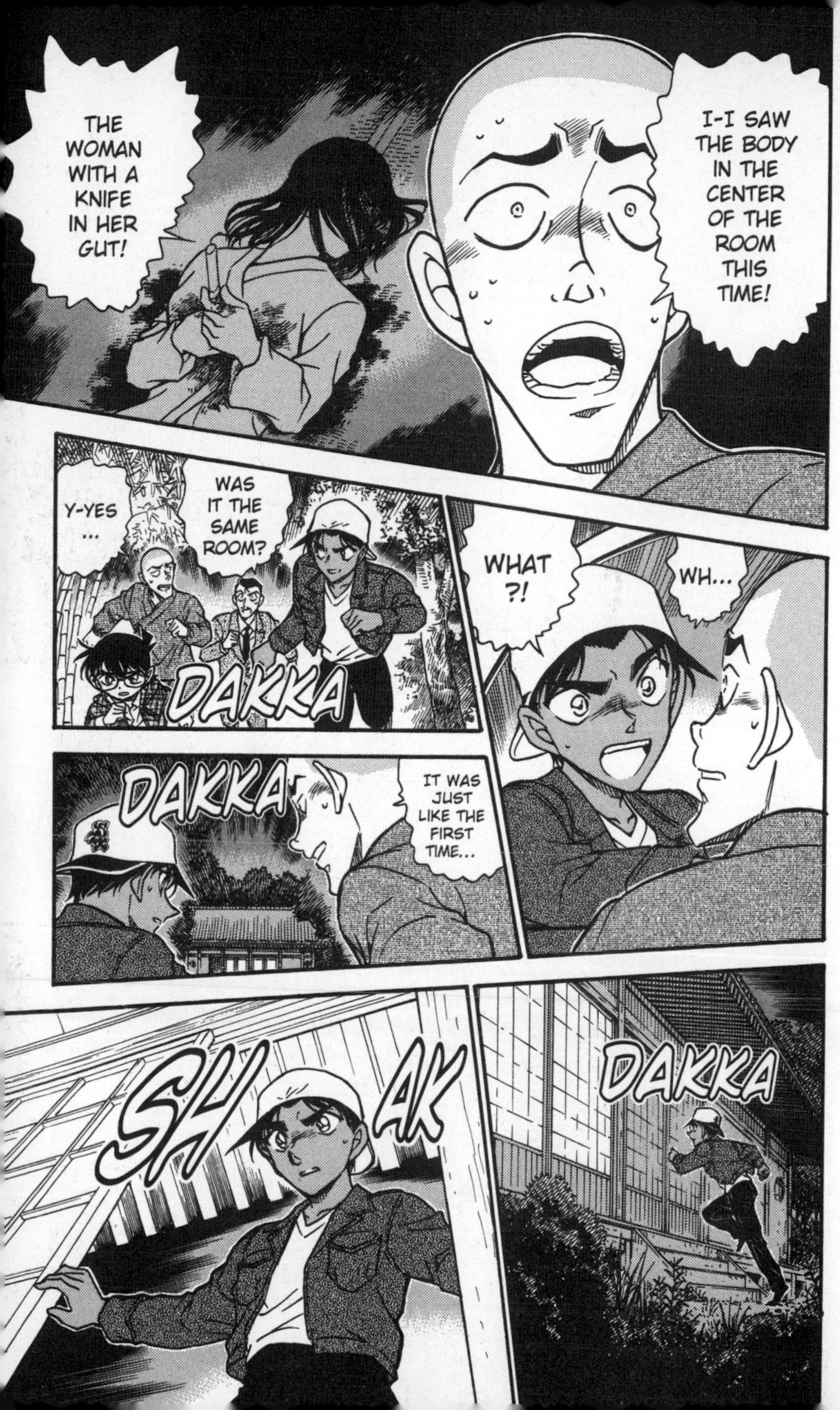
I-I SAW THE BODY IN THE CENTER OF THE ROOM THIS TIME!
THE WOMAN WITH A KNIFE IN HER GUT!
WH...
WHAT ?!
WAS IT THE SAME ROOM?
Y-YES ...
DAKKA
DAKKA
IT WAS JUST LIKE THE FIRST TIME...
DAKKA
SHAK

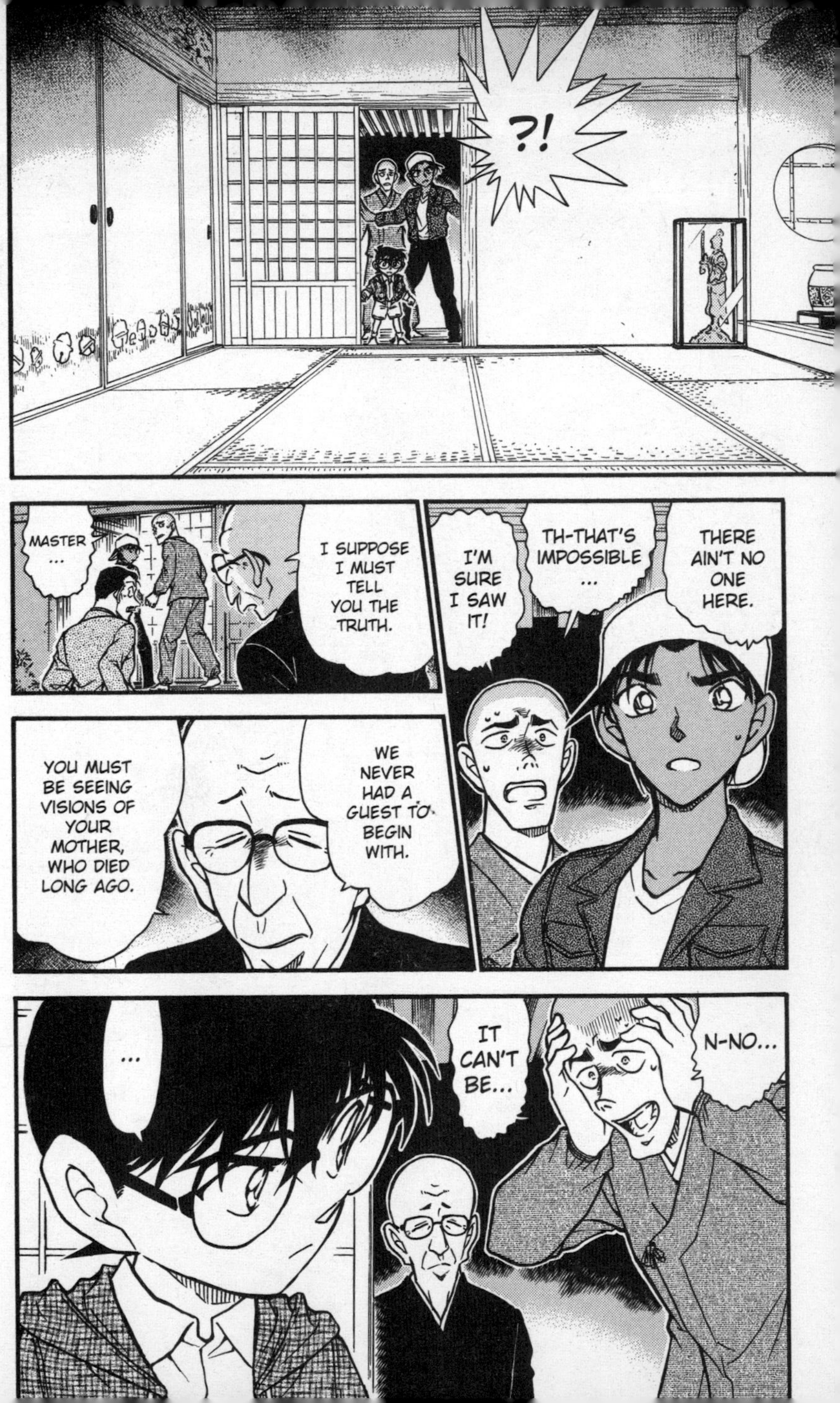
?!
THERE AIN'T NO ONE HERE.
TH-THAT'S IMPOSSIBLE...
I'M SURE I SAW IT!
I SUPPOSE I MUST TELL YOU THE TRUTH.
MASTER...
WE NEVER HAD A GUEST TO BEGIN WITH.
YOU MUST BE SEEING VISIONS OF YOUR MOTHER, WHO DIED LONG AGO.
N-NO...
IT CAN'T BE...
...

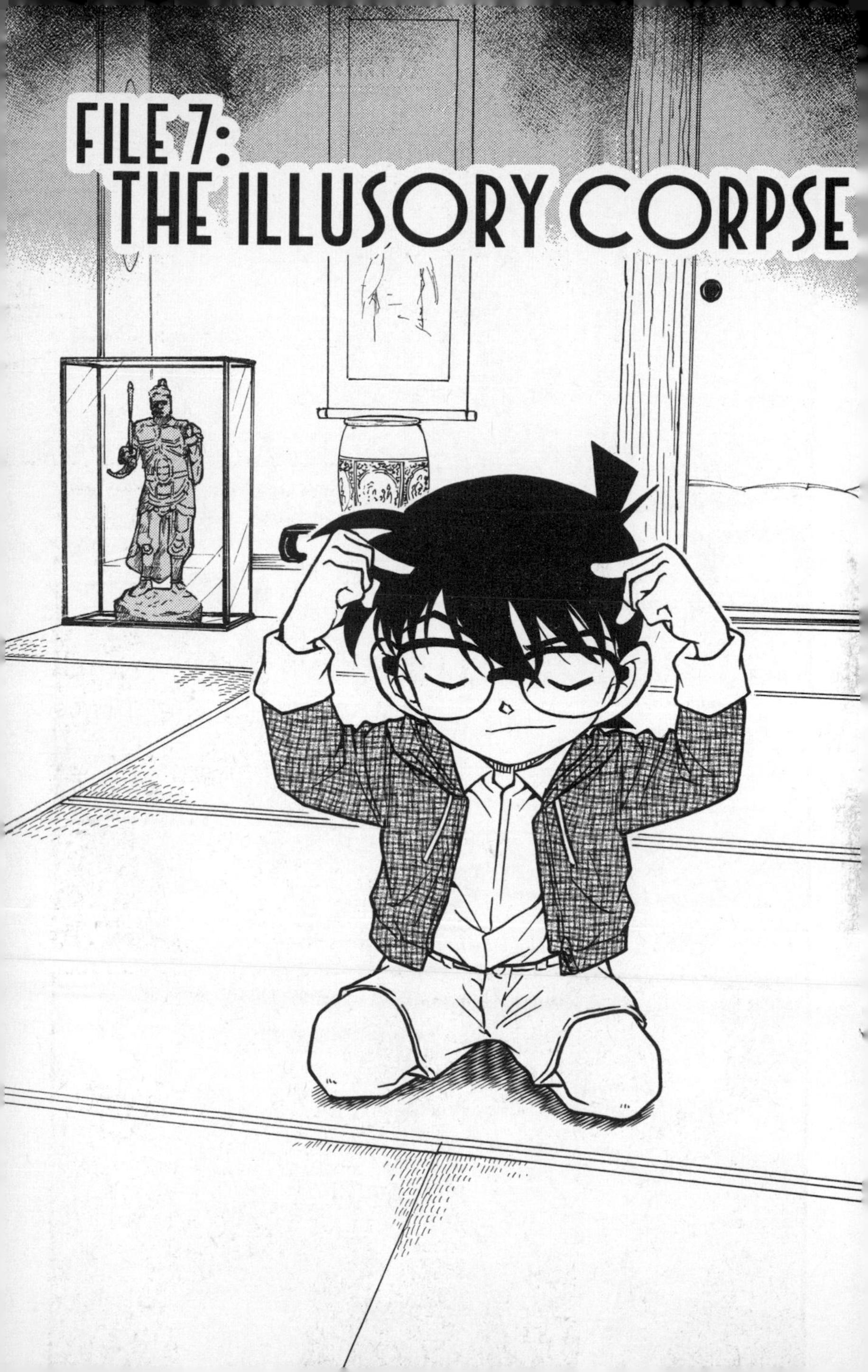
FILE 7:
THE ILLUSORY CORPSE

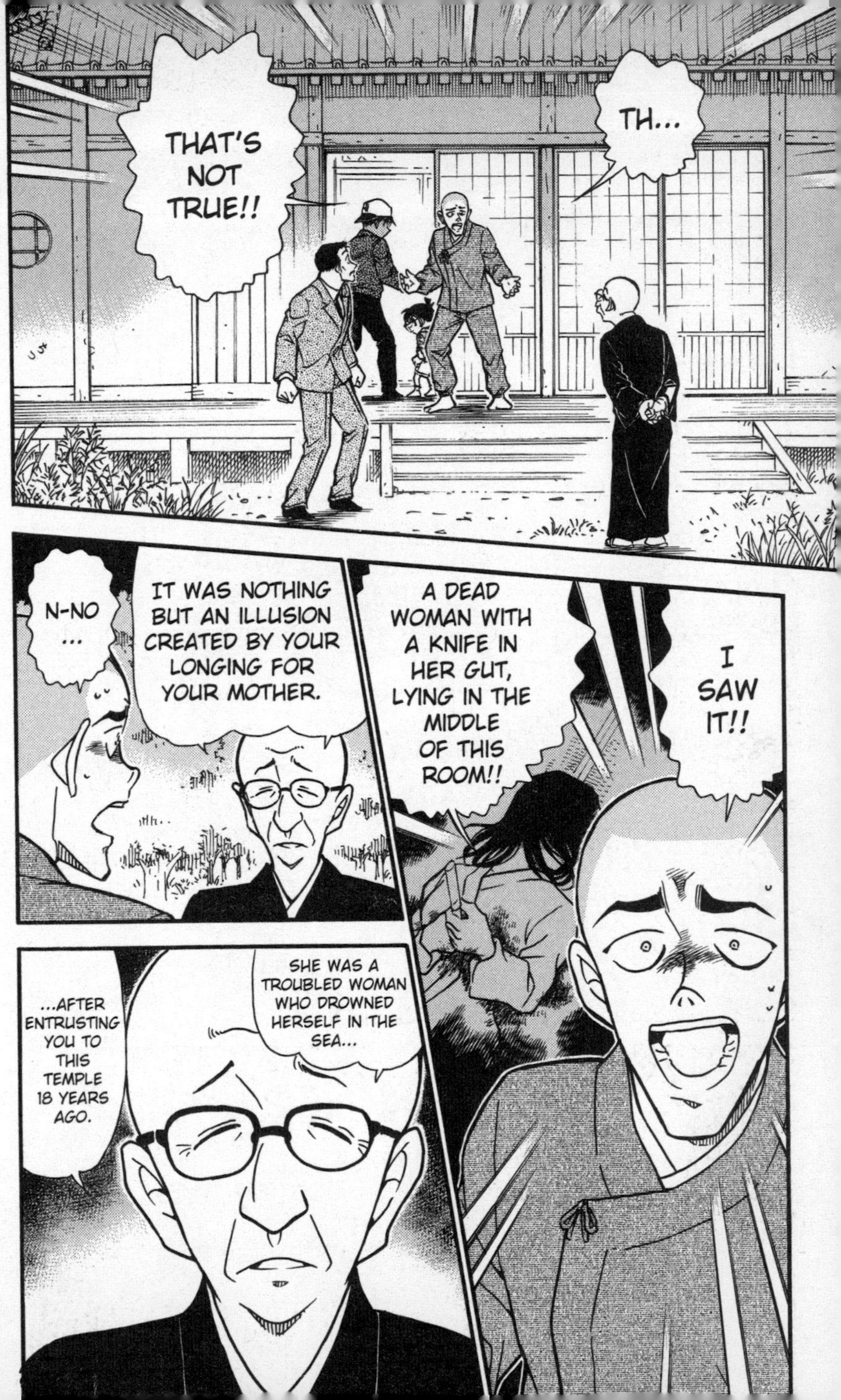
TH...
THAT'S NOT TRUE!!
I SAW IT!!
A DEAD WOMAN WITH A KNIFE IN HER GUT, LYING IN THE MIDDLE OF THIS ROOM!!
IT WAS NOTHING BUT AN ILLUSION CREATED BY YOUR LONGING FOR YOUR MOTHER.
N-NO ...
SHE WAS A TROUBLED WOMAN WHO DROWNED HERSELF IN THE SEA...
...AFTER ENTRUSTING YOU TO THIS TEMPLE 18 YEARS AGO.

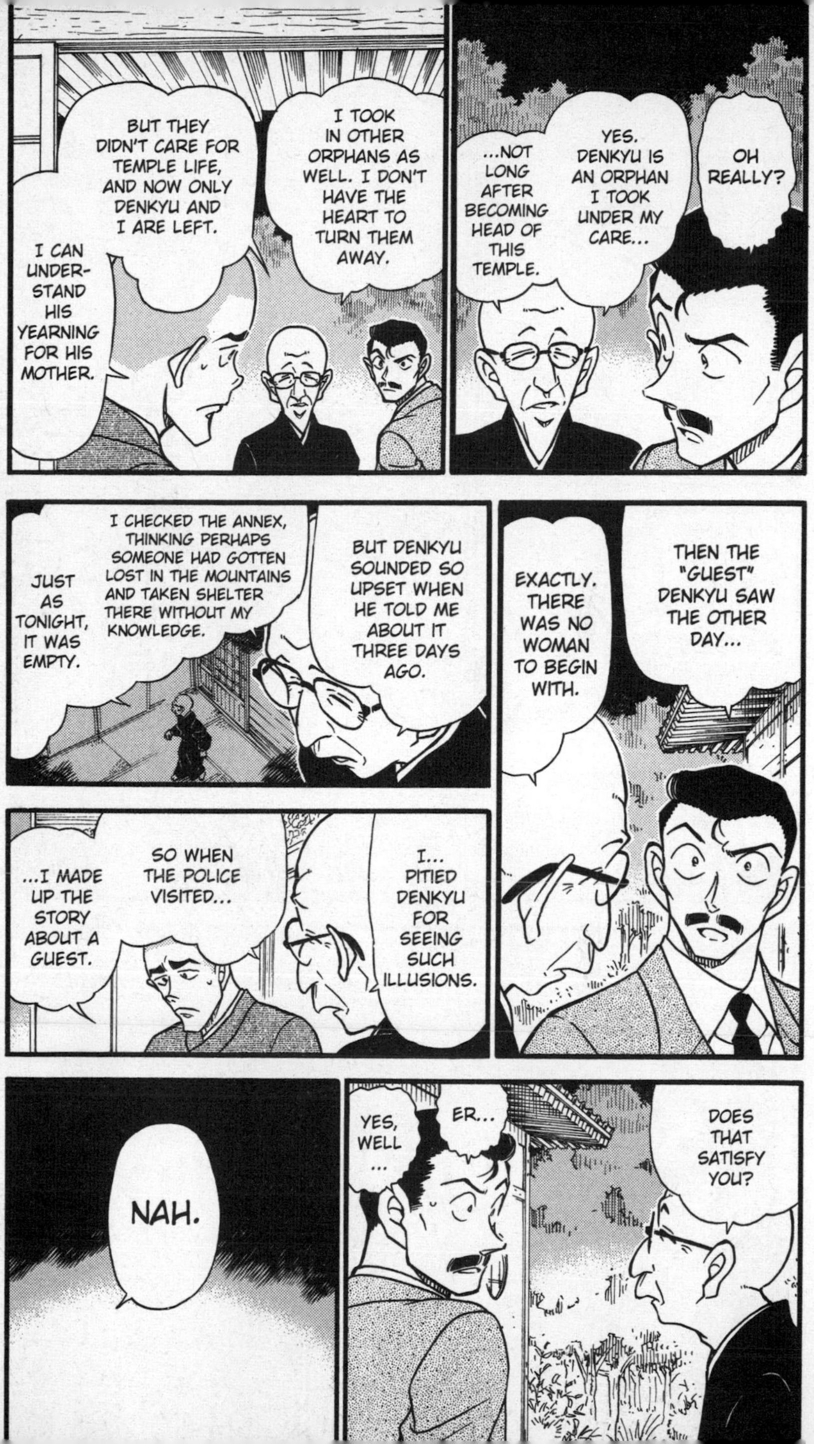
OH REALLY?
YES. DENKYU IS AN ORPHAN I TOOK UNDER MY CARE...
...NOT LONG AFTER BECOMING HEAD OF THIS TEMPLE.
I TOOK IN OTHER ORPHANS AS WELL. I DON'T HAVE THE HEART TO TURN THEM AWAY.
BUT THEY DIDN'T CARE FOR TEMPLE LIFE, AND NOW ONLY DENKYU AND I ARE LEFT.
I CAN UNDERSTAND HIS YEARNING FOR HIS MOTHER.
THEN THE "GUEST" DENKYU SAW THE OTHER DAY...
EXACTLY. THERE WAS NO WOMAN TO BEGIN WITH.
BUT DENKYU SOUNDED SO UPSET WHEN HE TOLD ME ABOUT IT THREE DAYS AGO.
I CHECKED THE ANNEX, THINKING PERHAPS SOMEONE HAD GOTTEN LOST IN THE MOUNTAINS AND TAKEN SHELTER THERE WITHOUT MY KNOWLEDGE.
JUST AS TONIGHT, IT WAS EMPTY.
I... PITIED DENKYU FOR SEEING SUCH ILLUSIONS.
SO WHEN THE POLICE VISITED...
...I MADE UP THE STORY ABOUT A GUEST.
DOES THAT SATISFY YOU?
ER...
YES, WELL ...
NAH.

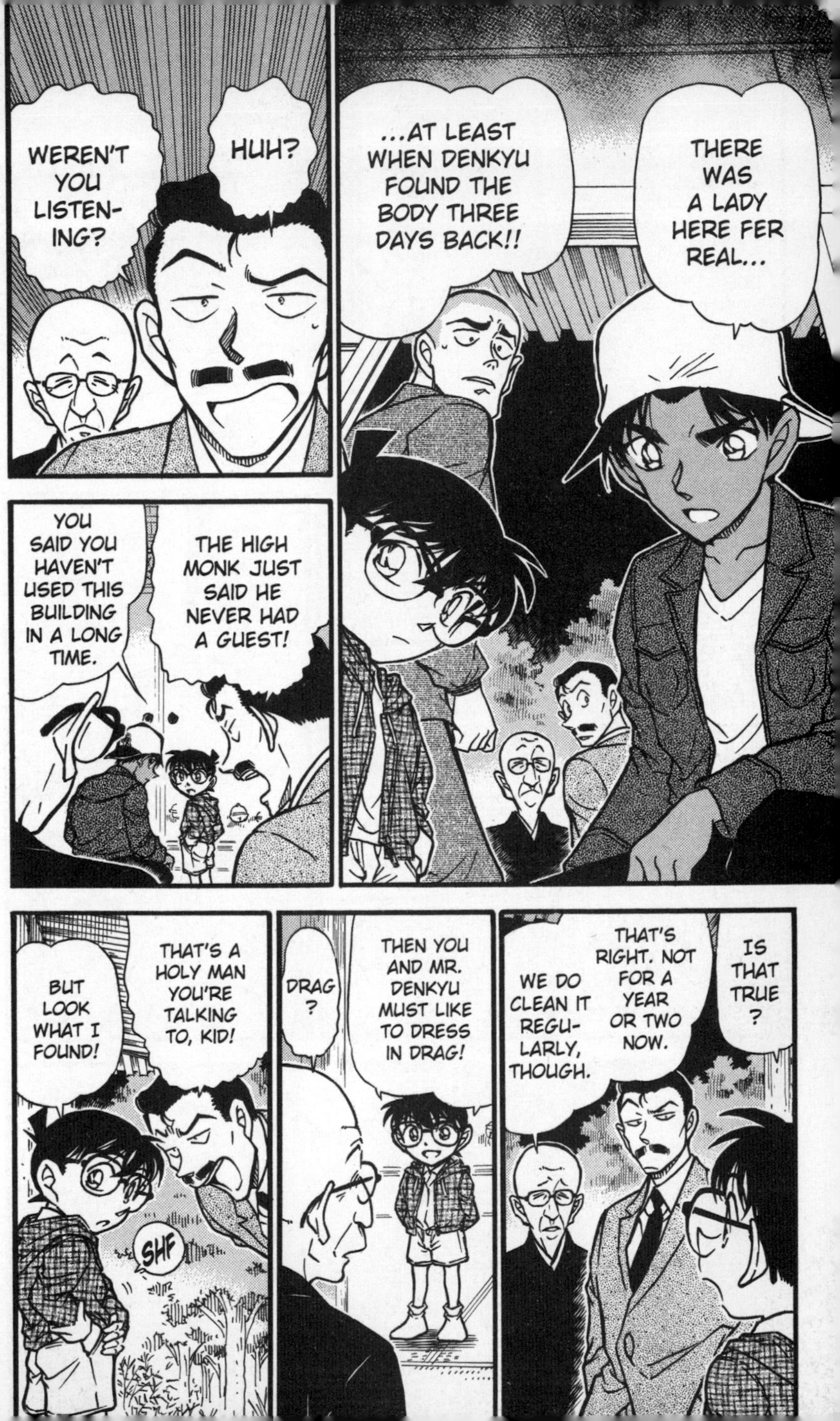
THERE WAS A LADY HERE FER REAL...
...AT LEAST WHEN DENKYU FOUND THE BODY THREE DAYS BACK!!
HUH?
WEREN'T YOU LISTENING?
THE HIGH MONK JUST SAID HE NEVER HAD A GUEST!
YOU SAID YOU HAVEN'T USED THIS BUILDING IN A LONG TIME.
IS THAT TRUE?
THAT'S RIGHT. NOT FOR A YEAR OR TWO NOW.
WE DO CLEAN IT REGULARLY, THOUGH.
THEN YOU AND MR. DENKYU MUST LIKE TO DRESS IN DRAG!
DRAG?
THAT'S A HOLY MAN YOU'RE TALKING TO, KID!
BUT LOOK WHAT I FOUND!
SHF

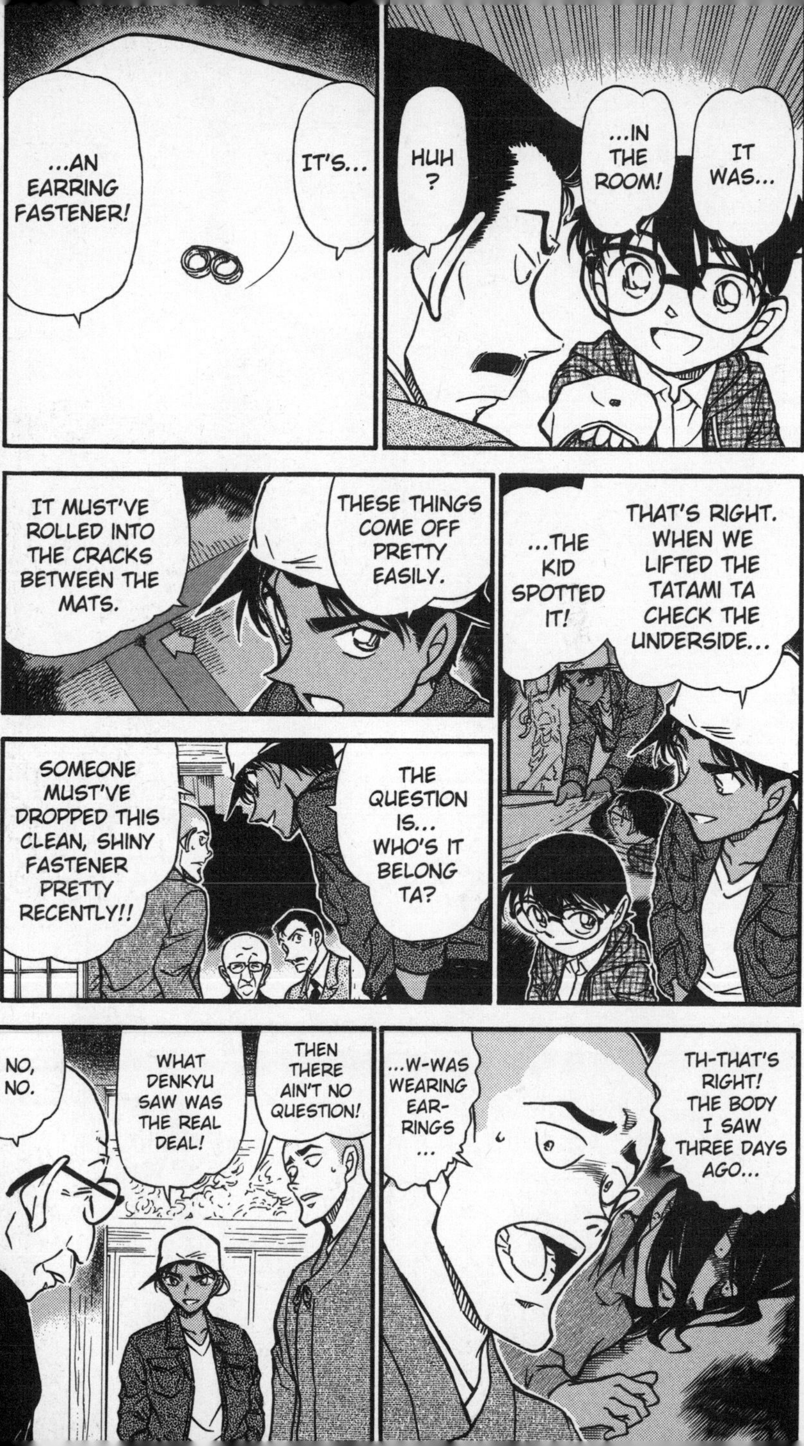
IT WAS...
...IN THE ROOM!
HUH?
IT'S...
...AN EARRING FASTENER!
THAT'S RIGHT. WHEN WE LIFTED THE TATAMI TA CHECK THE UNDERSIDE...
...THE KID SPOTTED IT!
THESE THINGS COME OFF PRETTY EASILY.
IT MUST'VE ROLLED INTO THE CRACKS BETWEEN THE MATS.
THE QUESTION IS... WHO'S IT BELONG TA?
SOMEONE MUST'VE DROPPED THIS CLEAN, SHINY FASTENER PRETTY RECENTLY!!
TH-THAT'S RIGHT! THE BODY I SAW THREE DAYS AGO...
...W-WAS WEARING EAR-RINGS...
THEN THERE AIN'T NO QUESTION!
WHAT DENKYU SAW WAS THE REAL DEAL!
NO, NO.

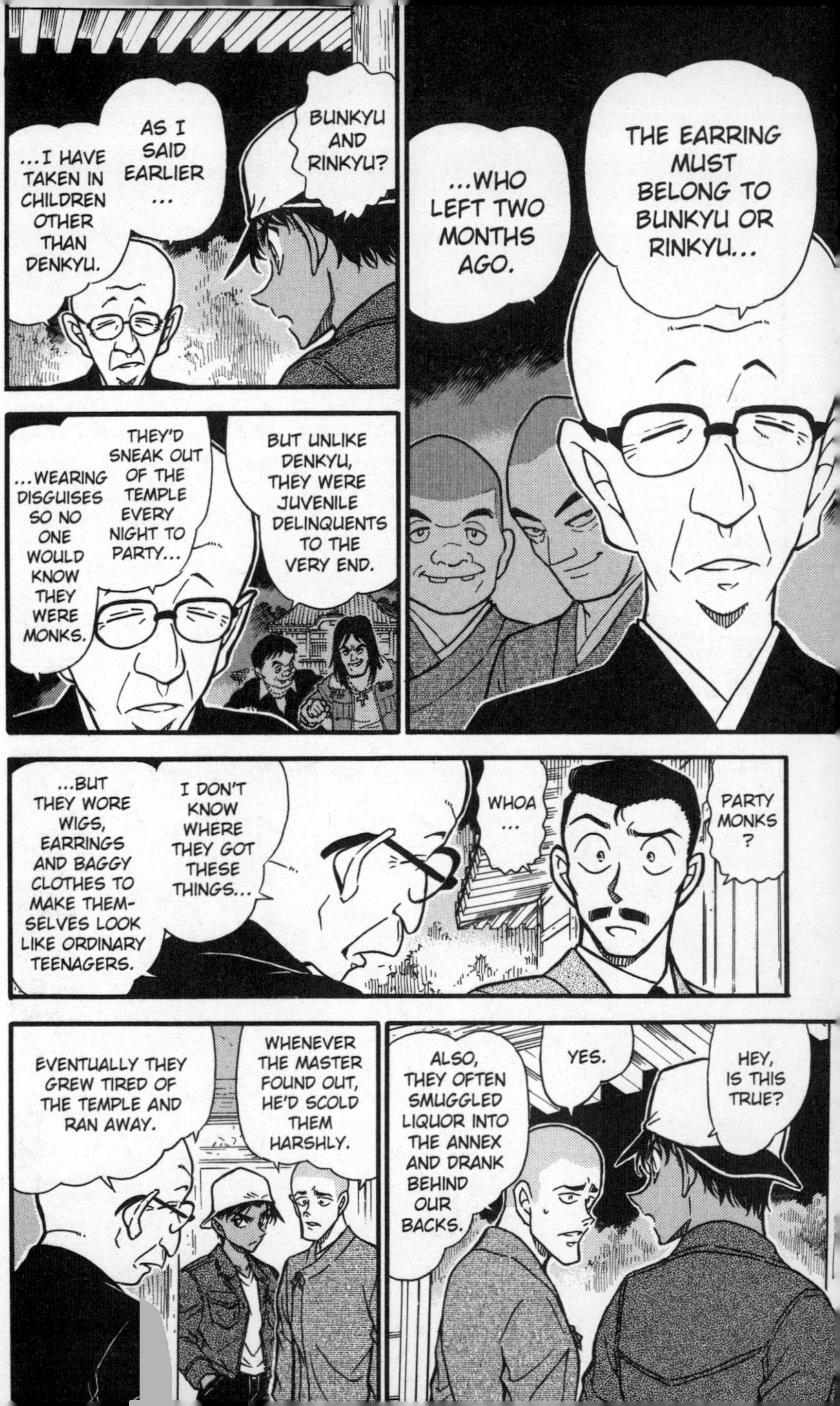
THE EARRING MUST BELONG TO BUNKYU OR RINKYU...
...WHO LEFT TWO MONTHS AGO.
BUNKYU AND RINKYU?
AS I SAID EARLIER...
...I HAVE TAKEN IN CHILDREN OTHER THAN DENKYU.
BUT UNLIKE DENKYU, THEY WERE JUVENILE DELINQUENTS TO THE VERY END.
THEY'D SNEAK OUT OF THE TEMPLE EVERY NIGHT TO PARTY...
...WEARING DISGUISES SO NO ONE WOULD KNOW THEY WERE MONKS.
PARTY MONKS?
WHOA...
I DON'T KNOW WHERE THEY GOT THESE THINGS...
...BUT THEY WORE WIGS, EARRINGS AND BAGGY CLOTHES TO MAKE THEM-SELVES LOOK LIKE ORDINARY TEENAGERS.
HEY, IS THIS TRUE?
YES.
ALSO, THEY OFTEN SMUGGLED LIQUOR INTO THE ANNEX AND DRANK BEHIND OUR BACKS.
WHENEVER THE MASTER FOUND OUT, HE'D SCOLD THEM HARSHLY.
EVENTUALLY THEY GREW TIRED OF THE TEMPLE AND RAN AWAY.

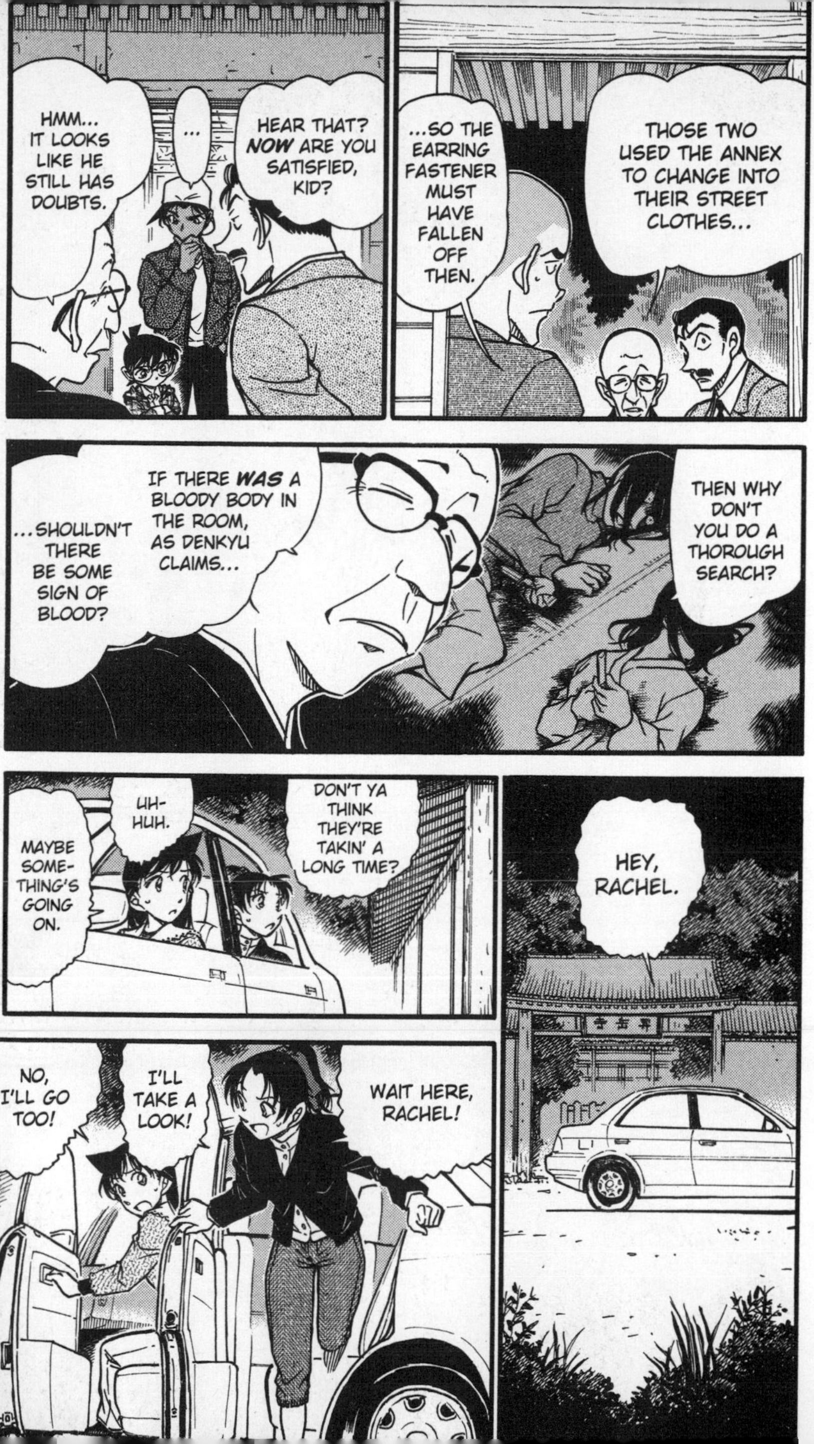
THOSE TWO USED THE ANNEX TO CHANGE INTO THEIR STREET CLOTHES...
...SO THE EARRING FASTENER MUST HAVE FALLEN OFF THEN.
HEAR THAT? NOW ARE YOU SATISFIED, KID?
...
HMM... IT LOOKS LIKE HE STILL HAS DOUBTS.
THEN WHY DON'T YOU DO A THOROUGH SEARCH?
IF THERE WAS A BLOODY BODY IN THE ROOM, AS DENKYU CLAIMS...
...SHOULDN'T THERE BE SOME SIGN OF BLOOD?
HEY, RACHEL.
DON'T YA THINK THEY'RE TAKIN' A LONG TIME?
UH-HUH.
MAYBE SOME-THING'S GOING ON.
WAIT HERE, RACHEL!
I'LL TAKE A LOOK!
NO, I'LL GO TOO!

R-RIGHT...

M-MAYBE WE SHOULD JUST WAIT INSIDE THE CAR...

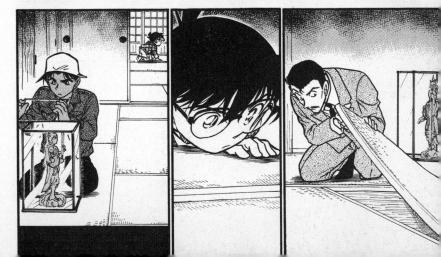

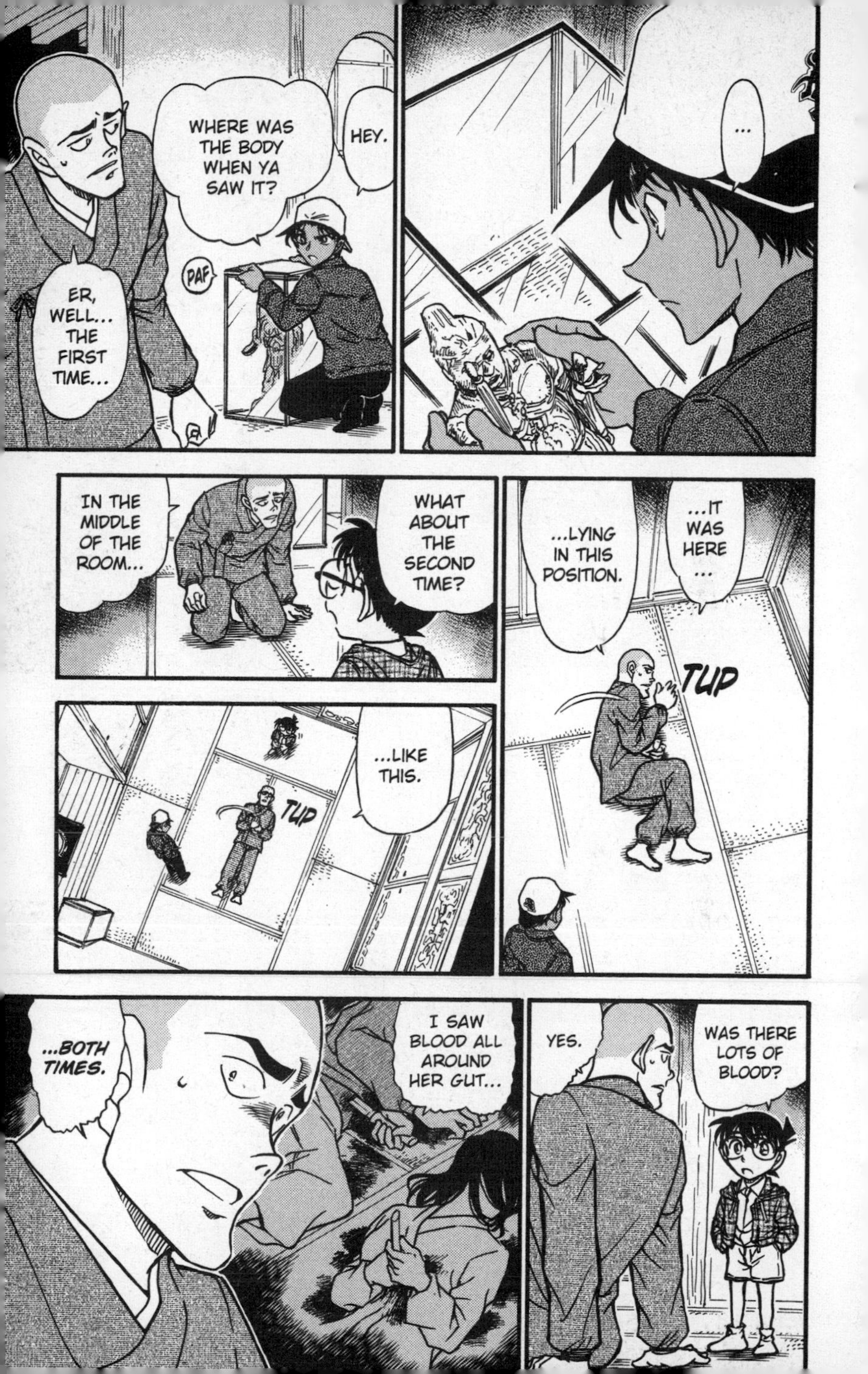
...
HEY.
WHERE WAS THE BODY WHEN YA SAW IT?
PAF
ER, WELL... THE FIRST TIME...
...IT WAS HERE...
...LYING IN THIS POSITION.
TUP
WHAT ABOUT THE SECOND TIME?
IN THE MIDDLE OF THE ROOM...
...LIKE THIS.
TUP
WAS THERE LOTS OF BLOOD?
YES.
I SAW BLOOD ALL AROUND HER GUT...
...BOTH TIMES.

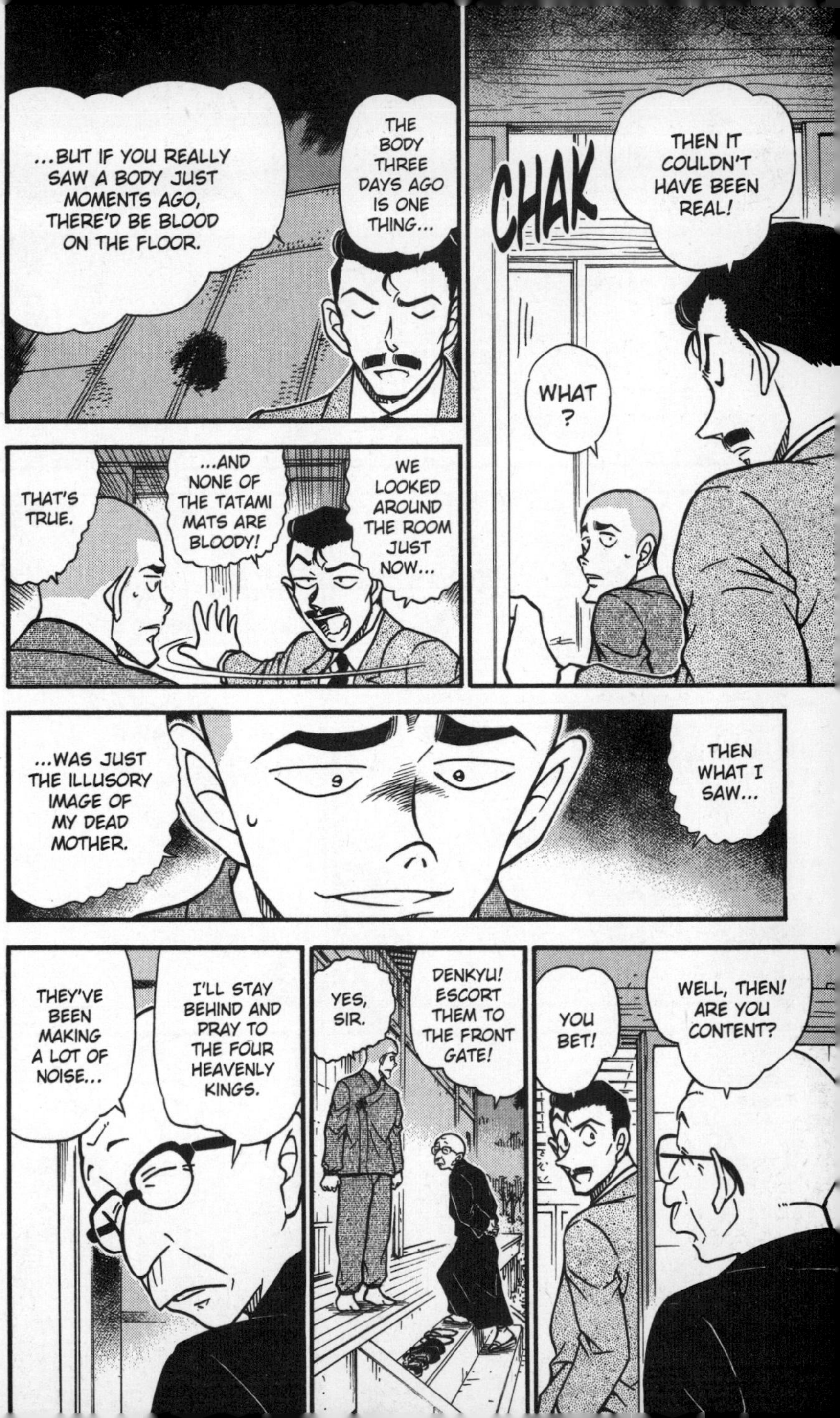
THEN IT COULDN'T HAVE BEEN REAL!
CHAK
WHAT ?
THE BODY THREE DAYS AGO IS ONE THING...
...BUT IF YOU REALLY SAW A BODY JUST MOMENTS AGO, THERE'D BE BLOOD ON THE FLOOR.
WE LOOKED AROUND THE ROOM JUST NOW...
...AND NONE OF THE TATAMI MATS ARE BLOODY!
THAT'S TRUE.
THEN WHAT I SAW...
...WAS JUST THE ILLUSORY IMAGE OF MY DEAD MOTHER.
WELL, THEN! ARE YOU CONTENT?
YOU BET!
DENKYU! ESCORT THEM TO THE FRONT GATE!
YES, SIR.
I'LL STAY BEHIND AND PRAY TO THE FOUR HEAVENLY KINGS.
THEY'VE BEEN MAKING A LOT OF NOISE...

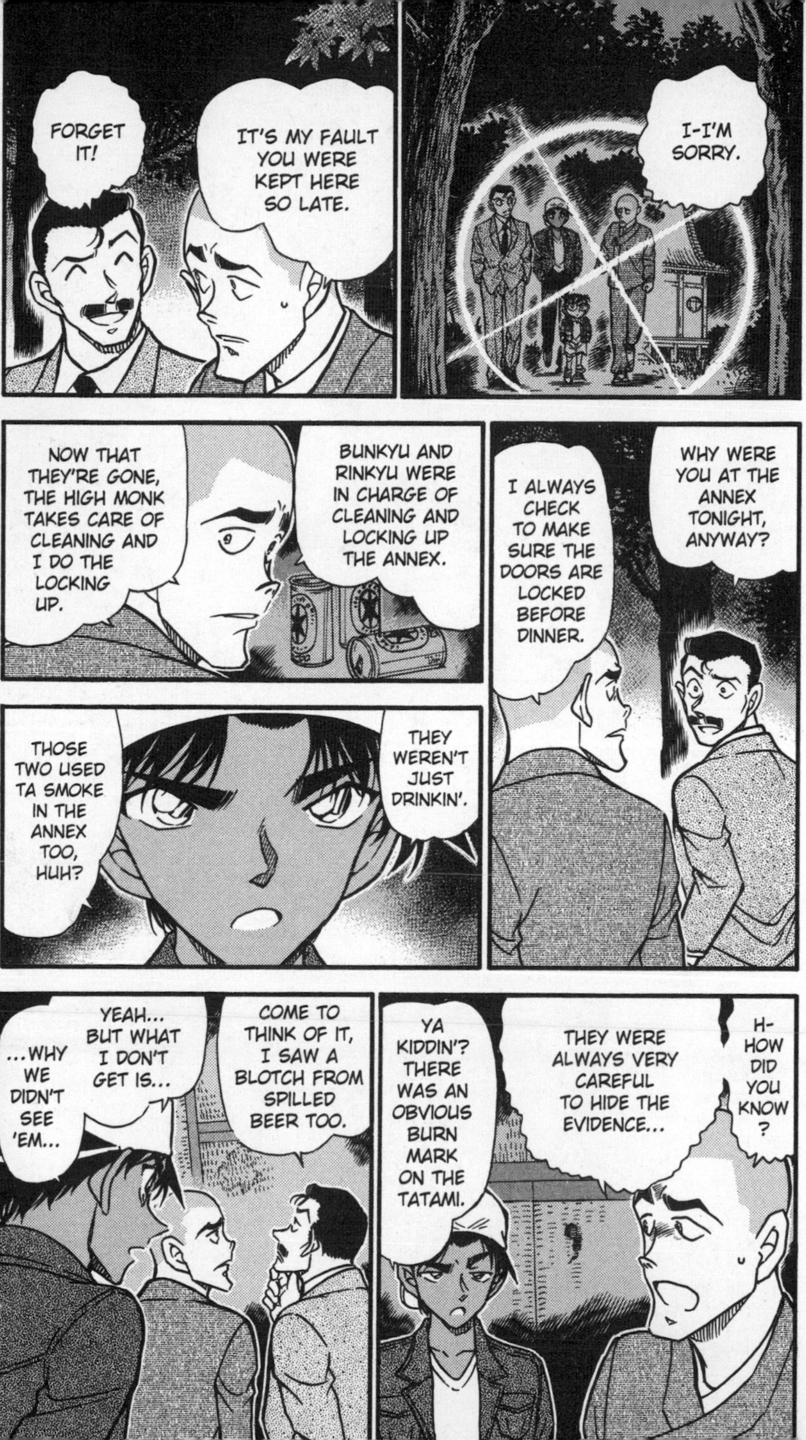
I-I'M SORRY.
IT'S MY FAULT YOU WERE KEPT HERE SO LATE.
FORGET IT!
WHY WERE YOU AT THE ANNEX TONIGHT, ANYWAY?
I ALWAYS CHECK TO MAKE SURE THE DOORS ARE LOCKED BEFORE DINNER.
BUNKYU AND RINKYU WERE IN CHARGE OF CLEANING AND LOCKING UP THE ANNEX.
NOW THAT THEY'RE GONE, THE HIGH MONK TAKES CARE OF CLEANING AND I DO THE LOCKING UP.
THEY WEREN'T JUST DRINKIN'.
THOSE TWO USED TA SMOKE IN THE ANNEX TOO, HUH?
H-HOW DID YOU KNOW?
THEY WERE ALWAYS VERY CAREFUL TO HIDE THE EVIDENCE...
YA KIDDIN'? THERE WAS AN OBVIOUS BURN MARK ON THE TATAMI.
COME TO THINK OF IT, I SAW A BLOTCH FROM SPILLED BEER TOO.
YEAH... BUT WHAT I DON'T GET IS...
...WHY WE DIDN'T SEE 'EM...

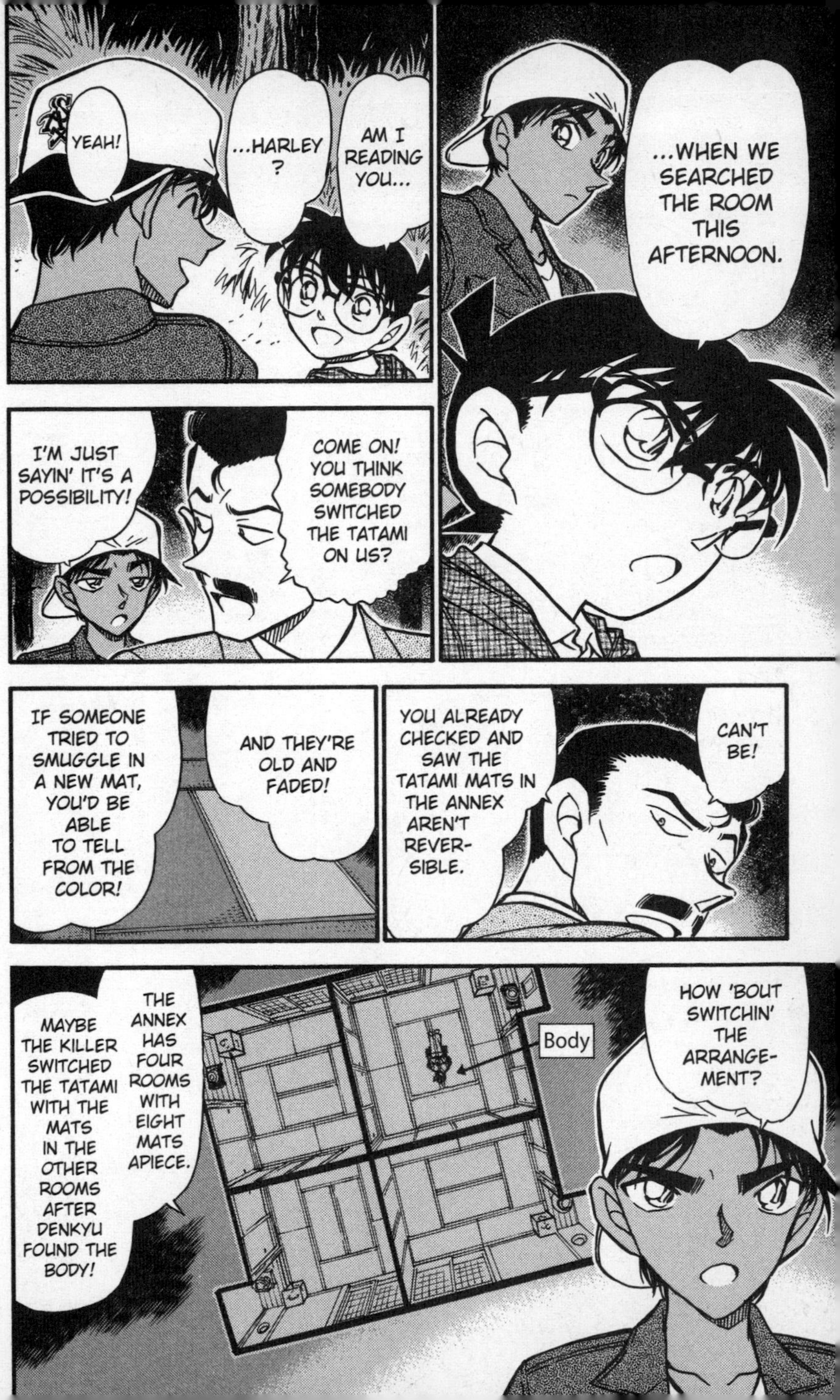
...WHEN WE SEARCHED THE ROOM THIS AFTERNOON.
AM I READING YOU...
...HARLEY?
YEAH!
COME ON! YOU THINK SOMEBODY SWITCHED THE TATAMI ON US?
I'M JUST SAYIN' IT'S A POSSIBILITY!
CAN'T BE!
YOU ALREADY CHECKED AND SAW THE TATAMI MATS IN THE ANNEX AREN'T REVER-SIBLE.
AND THEY'RE OLD AND FADED!
IF SOMEONE TRIED TO SMUGGLE IN A NEW MAT, YOU'D BE ABLE TO TELL FROM THE COLOR!
HOW 'BOUT SWITCHIN' THE ARRANGE-MENT?
Body
THE ANNEX HAS FOUR ROOMS WITH EIGHT MATS APIECE.
MAYBE THE KILLER SWITCHED THE TATAMI WITH THE MATS IN THE OTHER ROOMS AFTER DENKYU FOUND THE BODY!

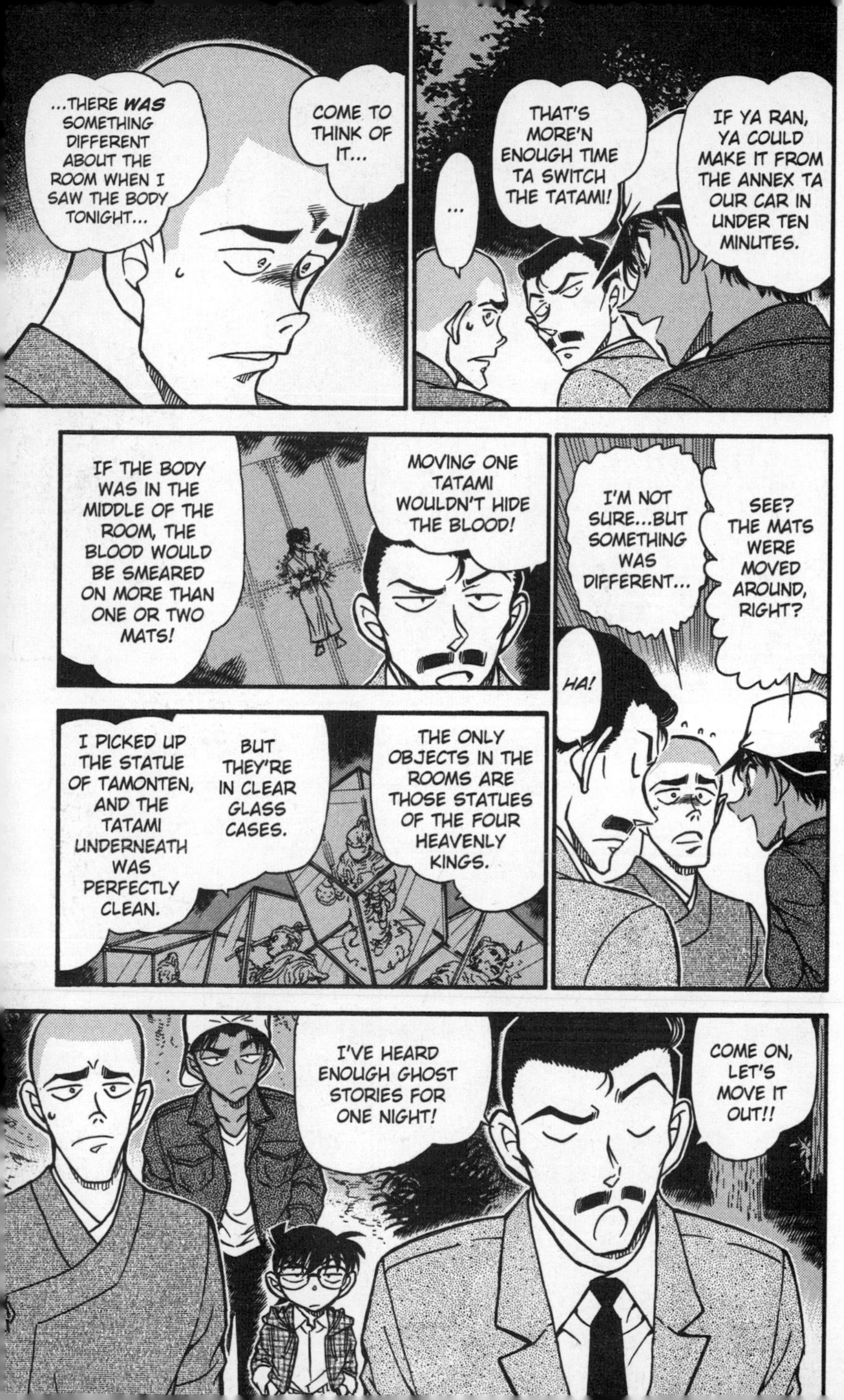
IF YA RAN, YA COULD MAKE IT FROM THE ANNEX TA OUR CAR IN UNDER TEN MINUTES.
THAT'S MORE'N ENOUGH TIME TA SWITCH THE TATAMI!
...
COME TO THINK OF IT...
...THERE ***WAS*** SOMETHING DIFFERENT ABOUT THE ROOM WHEN I SAW THE BODY TONIGHT...
SEE? THE MATS WERE MOVED AROUND, RIGHT?
I'M NOT SURE...BUT SOMETHING WAS DIFFERENT...
HA!
MOVING ONE TATAMI WOULDN'T HIDE THE BLOOD!
IF THE BODY WAS IN THE MIDDLE OF THE ROOM, THE BLOOD WOULD BE SMEARED ON MORE THAN ONE OR TWO MATS!
THE ONLY OBJECTS IN THE ROOMS ARE THOSE STATUES OF THE FOUR HEAVENLY KINGS.
BUT THEY'RE IN CLEAR GLASS CASES.
I PICKED UP THE STATUE OF TAMONTEN, AND THE TATAMI UNDERNEATH WAS PERFECTLY CLEAN.
COME ON, LET'S MOVE IT OUT!!
I'VE HEARD ENOUGH GHOST STORIES FOR ONE NIGHT!

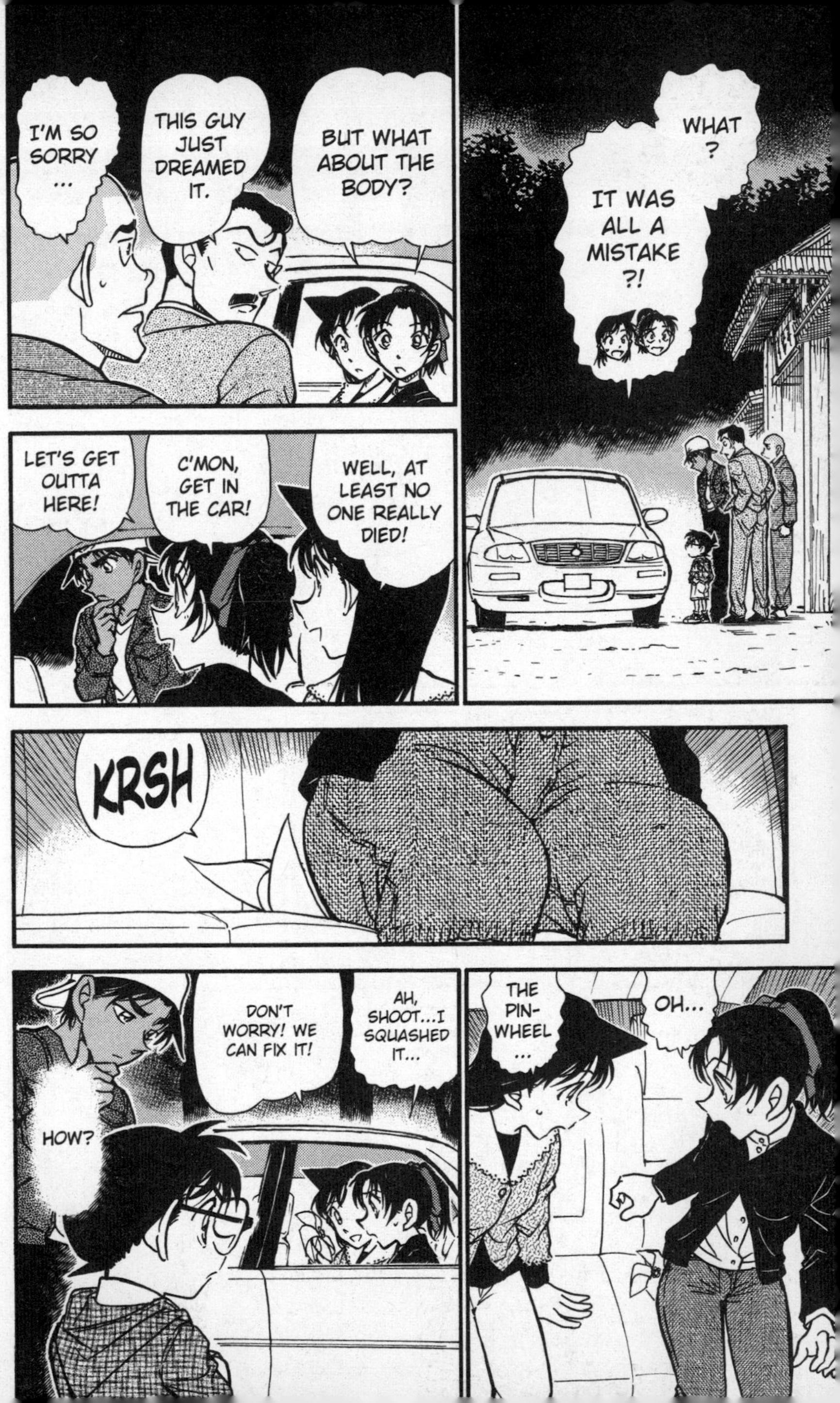
WHAT?
IT WAS ALL A MISTAKE?!
BUT WHAT ABOUT THE BODY?
THIS GUY JUST DREAMED IT.
I'M SO SORRY...
WELL, AT LEAST NO ONE REALLY DIED!
C'MON, GET IN THE CAR!
LET'S GET OUTTA HERE!
KRSH
OH...
THE PIN-WHEEL...
AH, SHOOT...I SQUASHED IT...
DON'T WORRY! WE CAN FIX IT!
HOW?

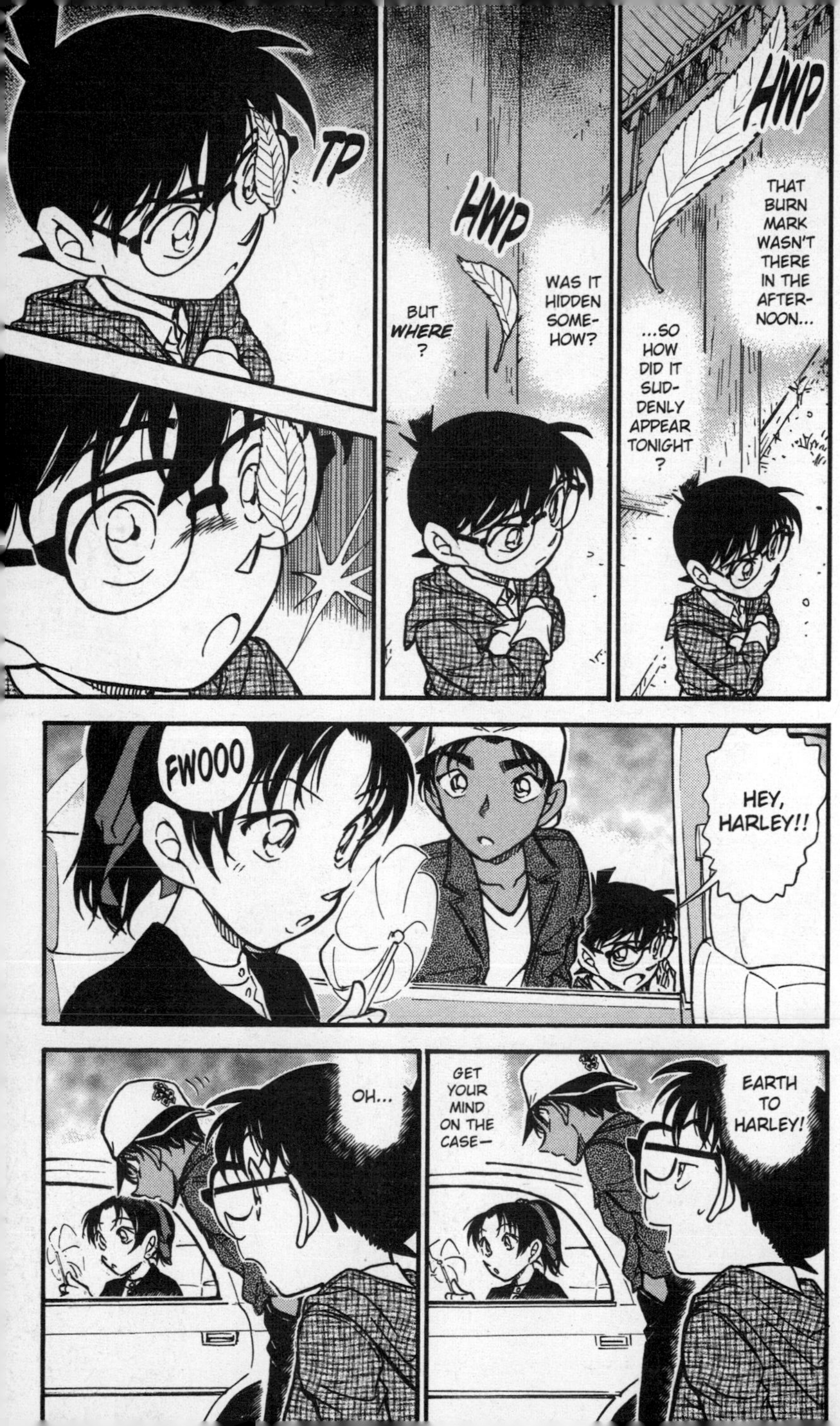
HWP
THAT BURN MARK WASN'T THERE IN THE AFTER-NOON...
...SO HOW DID IT SUD-DENLY APPEAR TONIGHT?
HWP
WAS IT HIDDEN SOME-HOW?
BUT WHERE?
TP
HEY, HARLEY!!
FWOOO
EARTH TO HARLEY!
GET YOUR MIND ON THE CASE—
OH...

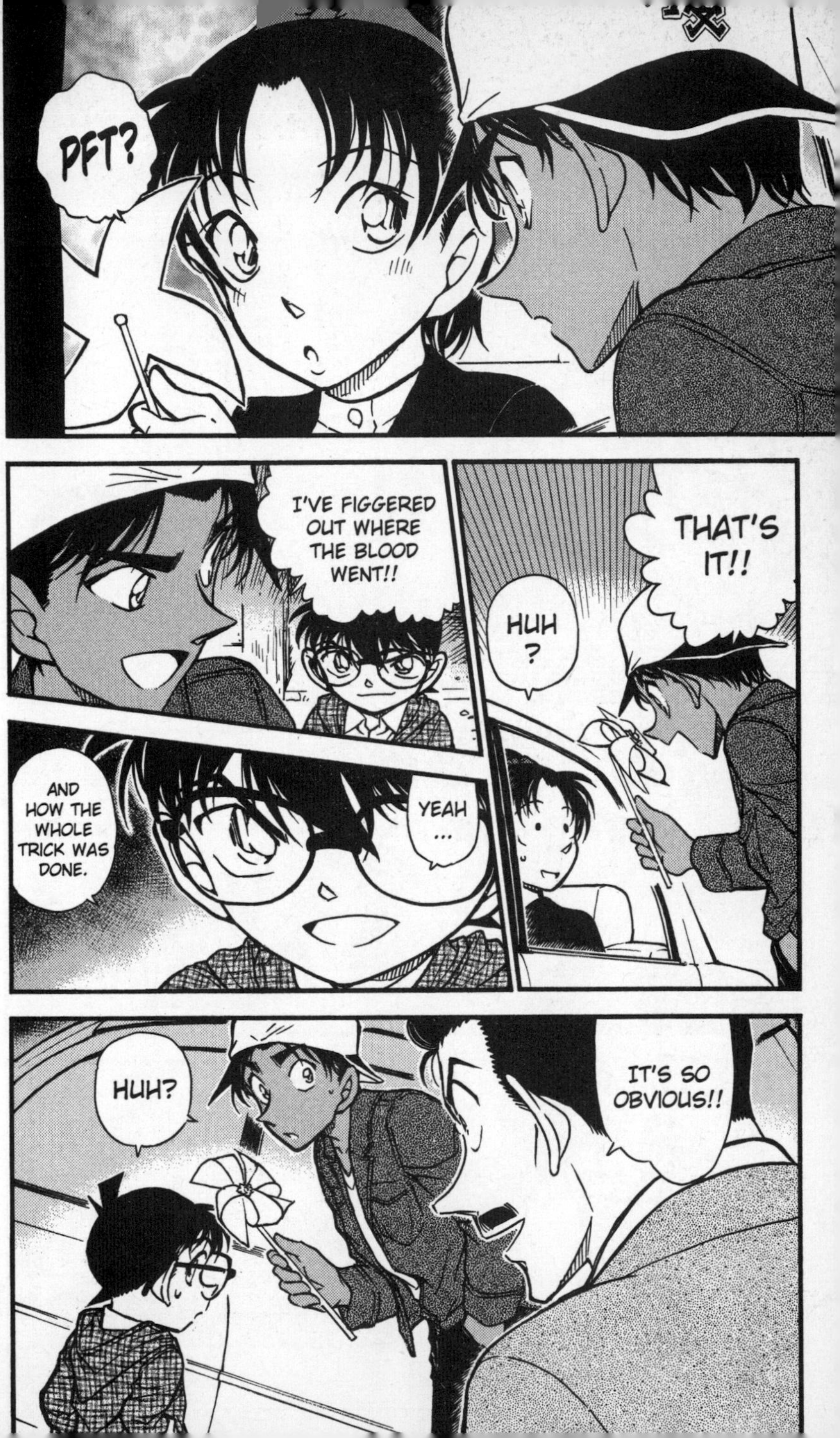
PFT?
THAT'S IT!!
HUH?
I'VE FIGGERED OUT WHERE THE BLOOD WENT!!
YEAH ...
AND HOW THE WHOLE TRICK WAS DONE.
IT'S SO OBVIOUS!!
HUH?

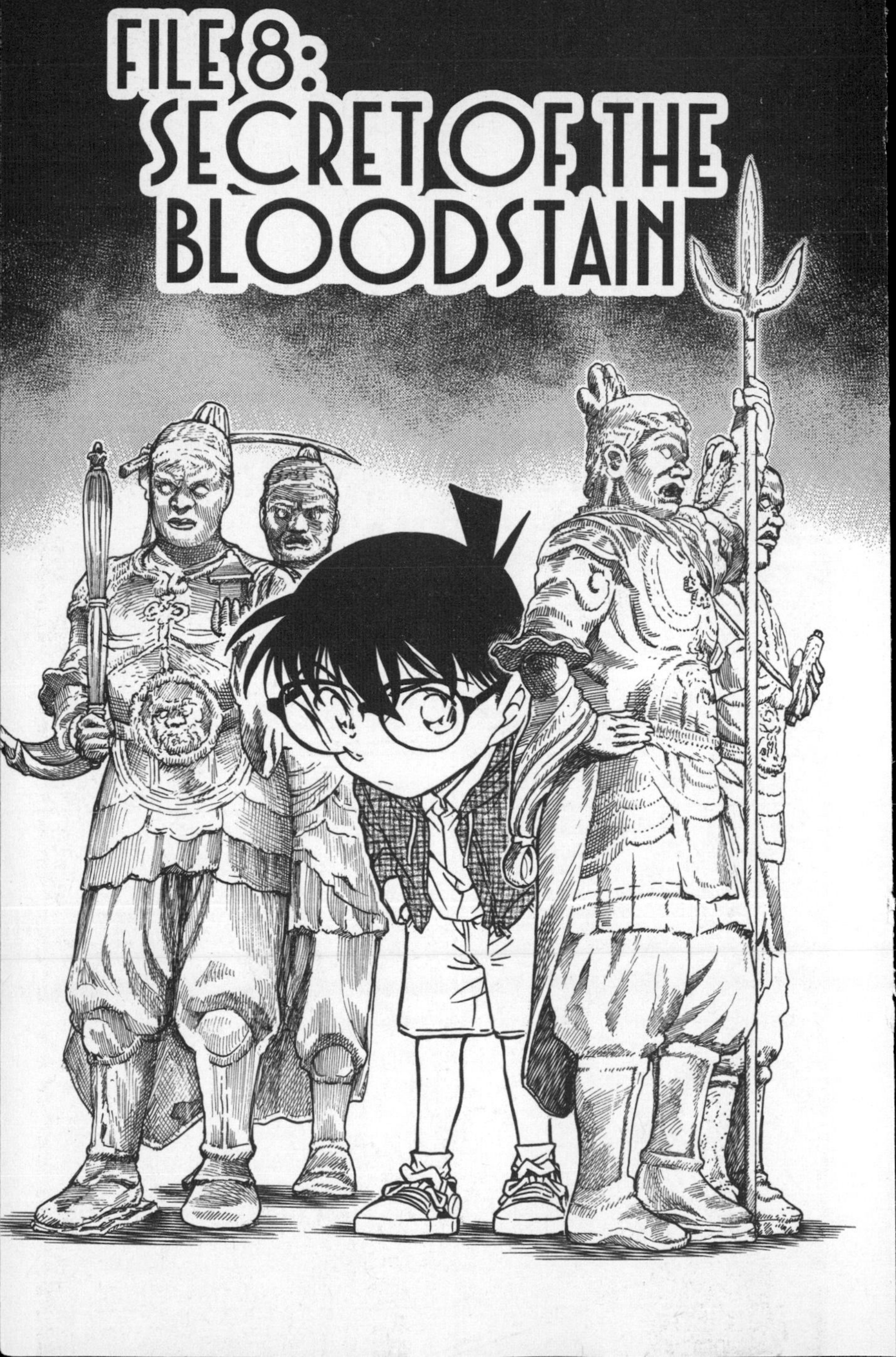
FILE 8:
SECRET OF THE BLOODSTAIN

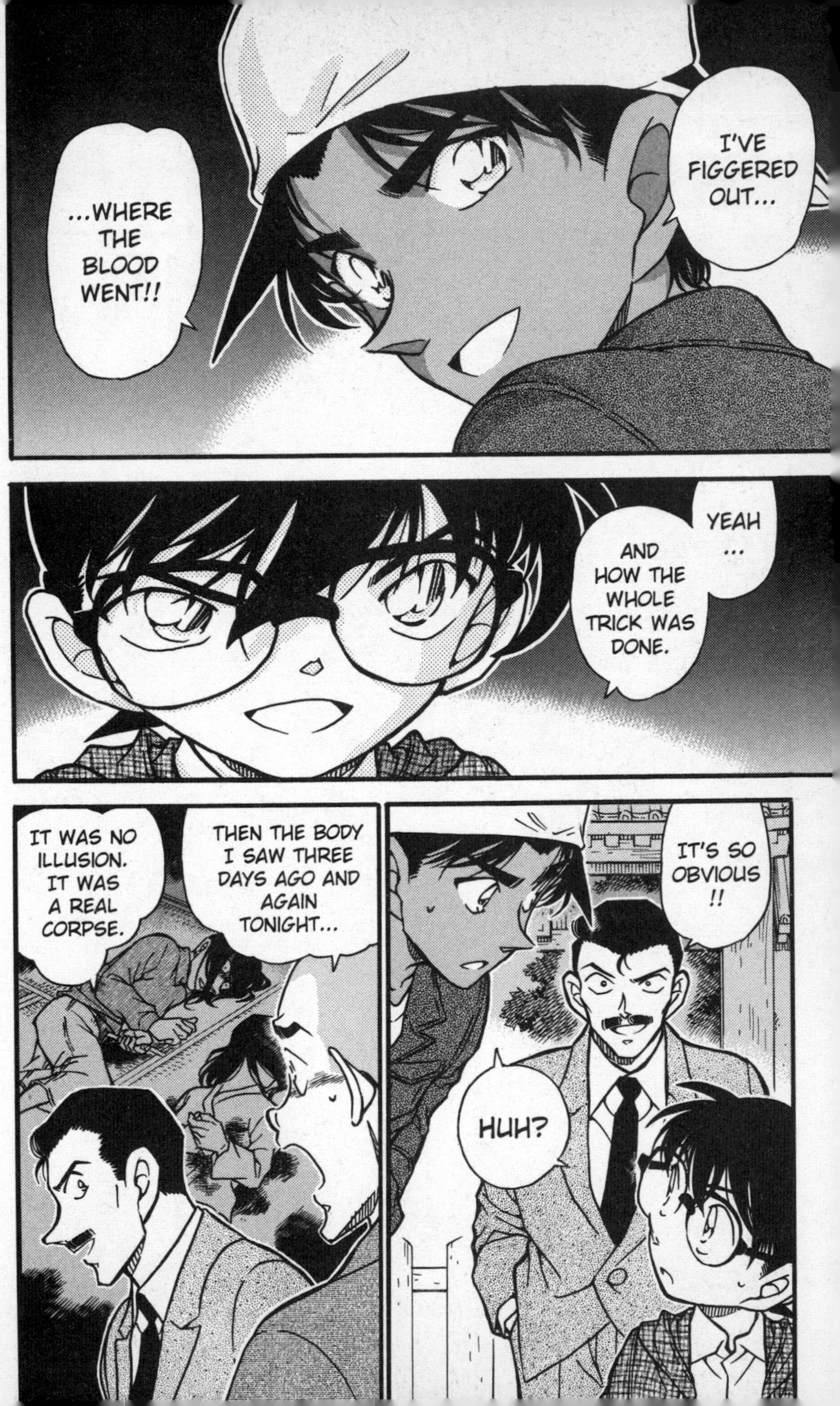
I'VE FIGGERED OUT...
...WHERE THE BLOOD WENT!!
YEAH ...
AND HOW THE WHOLE TRICK WAS DONE.
IT'S SO OBVIOUS !!
HUH?
THEN THE BODY I SAW THREE DAYS AGO AND AGAIN TONIGHT...
IT WAS NO ILLUSION. IT WAS A REAL CORPSE.

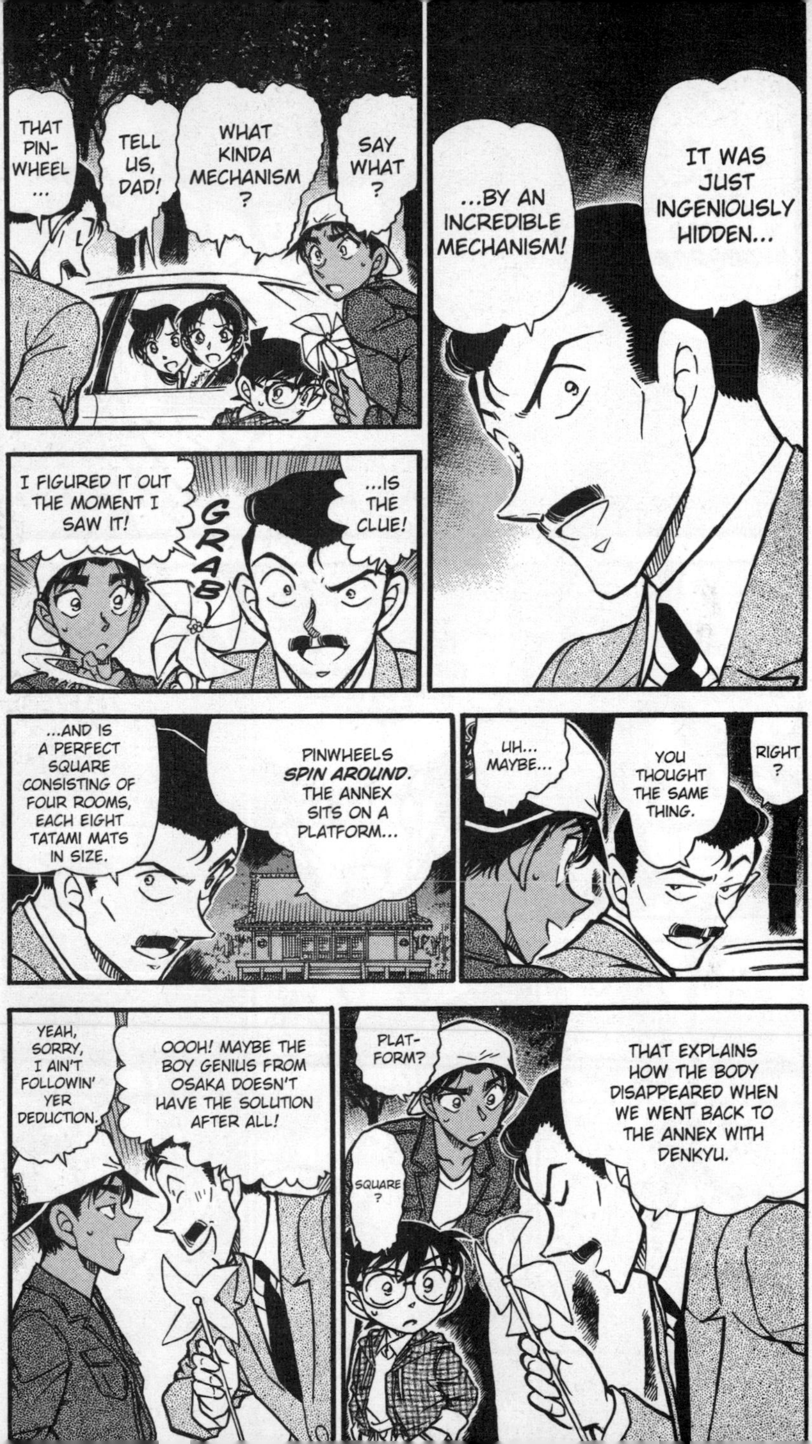
IT WAS JUST INGENIOUSLY HIDDEN...
...BY AN INCREDIBLE MECHANISM!
SAY WHAT?
WHAT KINDA MECHANISM?
TELL US, DAD!
THAT PIN-WHEEL...
...IS THE CLUE!
GRAB
I FIGURED IT OUT THE MOMENT I SAW IT!
RIGHT?
YOU THOUGHT THE SAME THING.
UH... MAYBE...
PINWHEELS *SPIN AROUND*. THE ANNEX SITS ON A PLATFORM...
...AND IS A PERFECT SQUARE CONSISTING OF FOUR ROOMS, EACH EIGHT TATAMI MATS IN SIZE.
THAT EXPLAINS HOW THE BODY DISAPPEARED WHEN WE WENT BACK TO THE ANNEX WITH DENKYU.
PLAT-FORM?
SQUARE?
OOOH! MAYBE THE BOY GENIUS FROM OSAKA DOESN'T HAVE THE SOLUTION AFTER ALL!
YEAH, SORRY, I AIN'T FOLLOWIN' YER DEDUCTION.

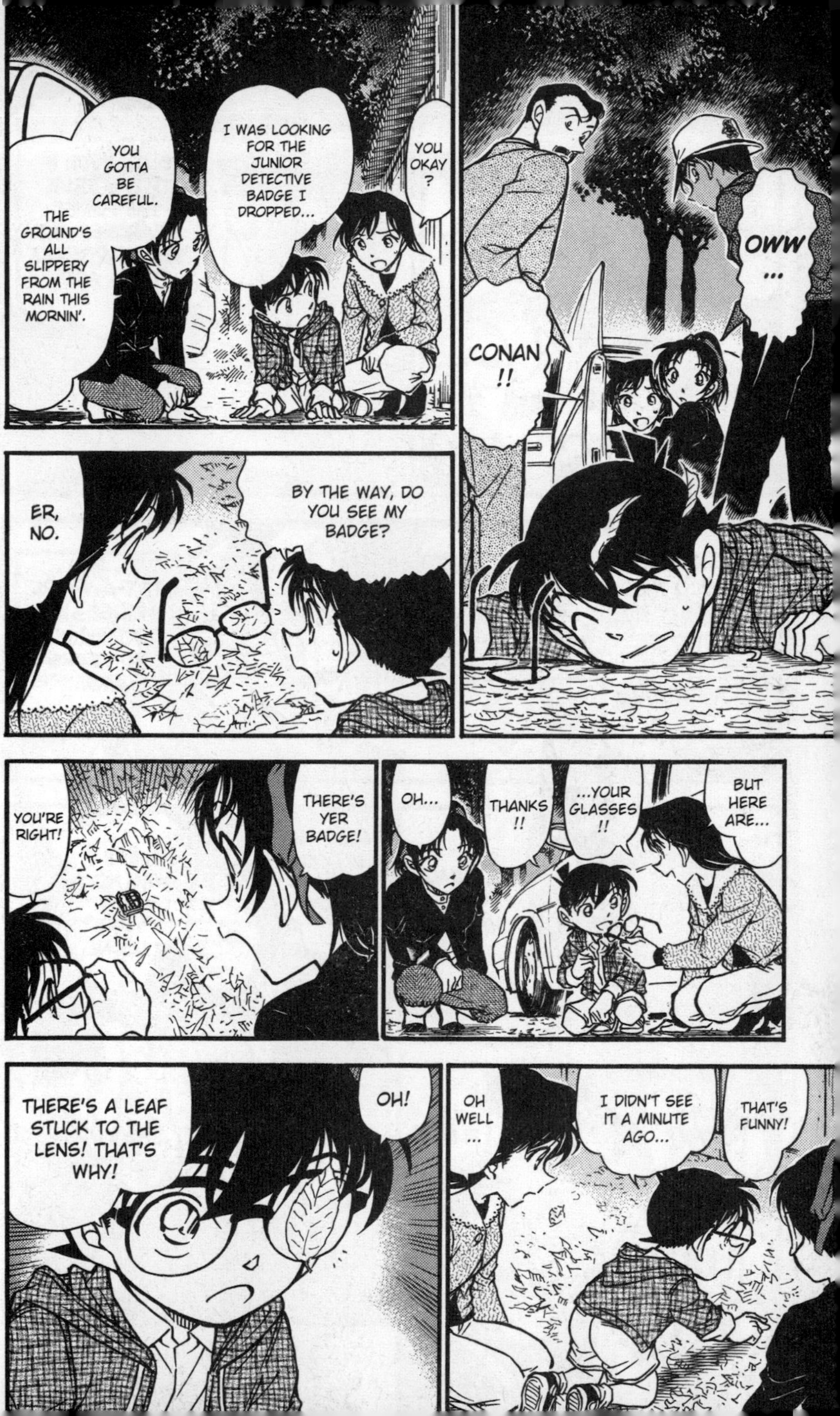
OWW ...
CONAN !!
YOU OKAY ?
I WAS LOOKING FOR THE JUNIOR DETECTIVE BADGE I DROPPED...
YOU GOTTA BE CAREFUL.
THE GROUND'S ALL SLIPPERY FROM THE RAIN THIS MORNIN'.
BY THE WAY, DO YOU SEE MY BADGE?
ER, NO.
BUT HERE ARE...
...YOUR GLASSES !!
THANKS !!
OH...
THERE'S YER BADGE!
YOU'RE RIGHT!
THAT'S FUNNY!
I DIDN'T SEE IT A MINUTE AGO...
OH WELL ...
OH!
THERE'S A LEAF STUCK TO THE LENS! THAT'S WHY!

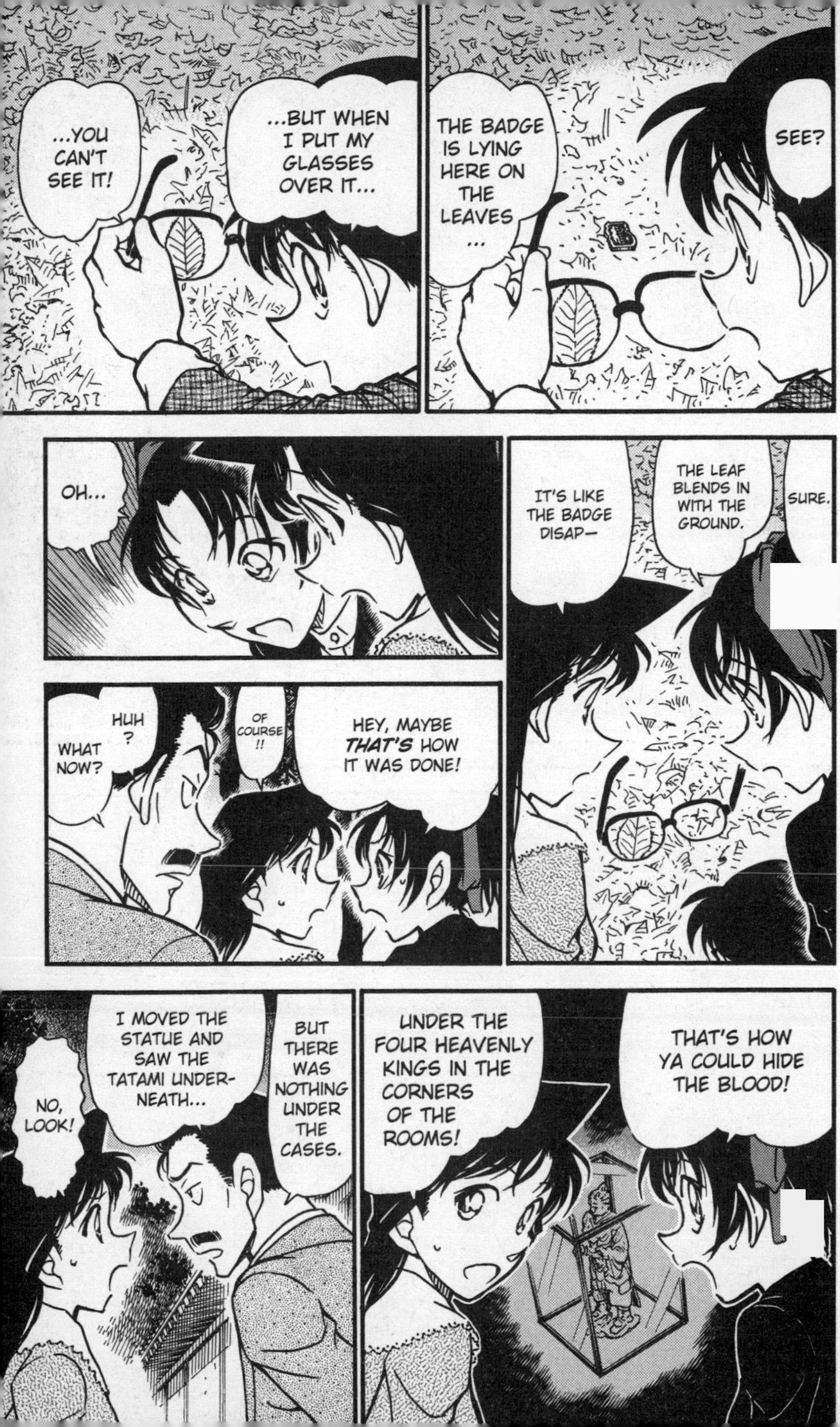
SEE?
THE BADGE IS LYING HERE ON THE LEAVES ...
...BUT WHEN I PUT MY GLASSES OVER IT...
...YOU CAN'T SEE IT!
SURE.
THE LEAF BLENDS IN WITH THE GROUND.
IT'S LIKE THE BADGE DISAP—
OH...
HEY, MAYBE *THAT'S* HOW IT WAS DONE!
OF COURSE!!
HUH?
WHAT NOW?
THAT'S HOW YA COULD HIDE THE BLOOD!
UNDER THE FOUR HEAVENLY KINGS IN THE CORNERS OF THE ROOMS!
BUT THERE WAS NOTHING UNDER THE CASES.
I MOVED THE STATUE AND SAW THE TATAMI UNDERNEATH...
NO, LOOK!

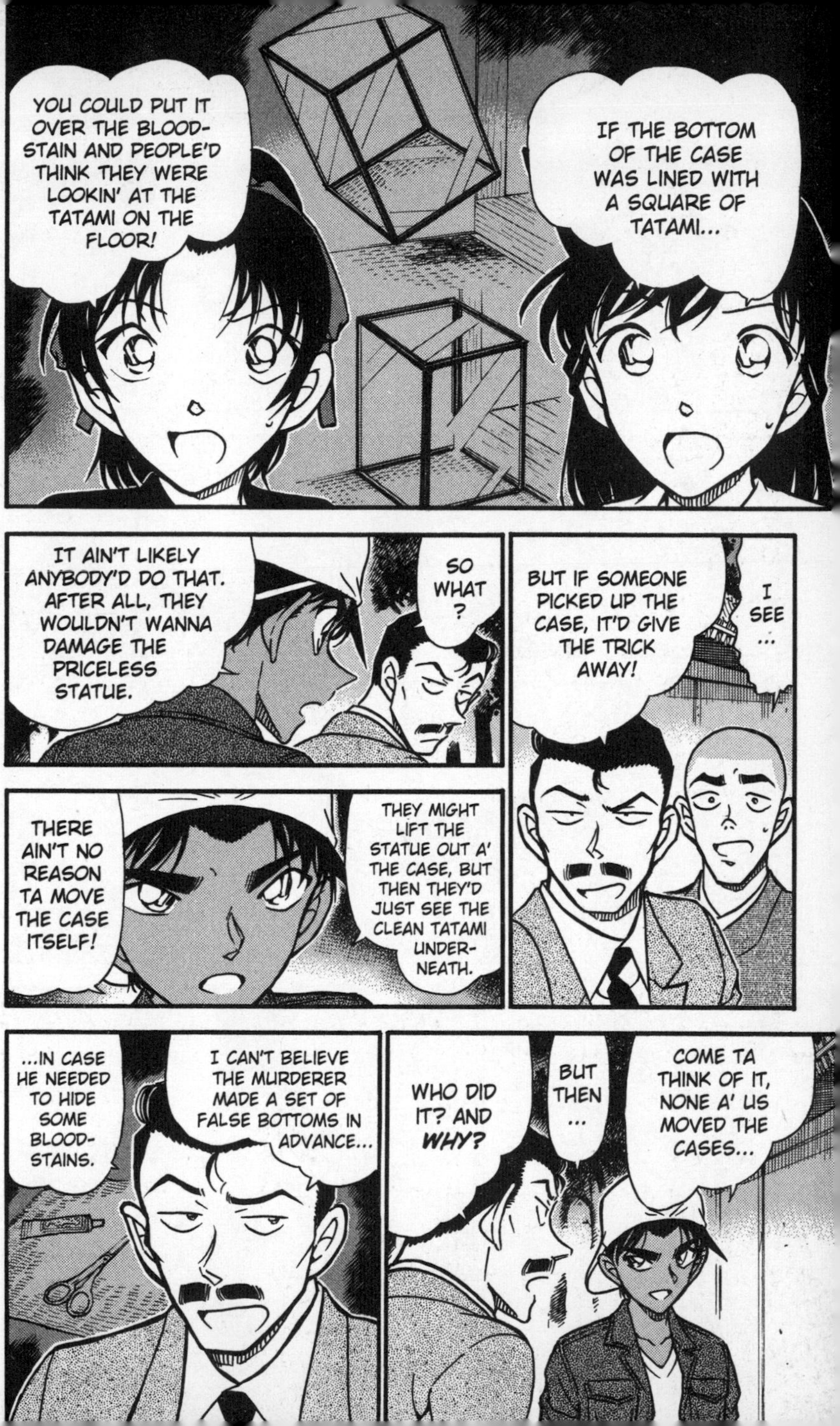
IF THE BOTTOM OF THE CASE WAS LINED WITH A SQUARE OF TATAMI...
YOU COULD PUT IT OVER THE BLOOD-STAIN AND PEOPLE'D THINK THEY WERE LOOKIN' AT THE TATAMI ON THE FLOOR!
I SEE...
BUT IF SOMEONE PICKED UP THE CASE, IT'D GIVE THE TRICK AWAY!
SO WHAT?
IT AIN'T LIKELY ANYBODY'D DO THAT. AFTER ALL, THEY WOULDN'T WANNA DAMAGE THE PRICELESS STATUE.
THEY MIGHT LIFT THE STATUE OUT A' THE CASE, BUT THEN THEY'D JUST SEE THE CLEAN TATAMI UNDER-NEATH.
THERE AIN'T NO REASON TA MOVE THE CASE ITSELF!
COME TA THINK OF IT, NONE A' US MOVED THE CASES...
BUT THEN...
WHO DID IT? AND *WHY?*
I CAN'T BELIEVE THE MURDERER MADE A SET OF FALSE BOTTOMS IN ADVANCE...
...IN CASE HE NEEDED TO HIDE SOME BLOOD-STAINS.

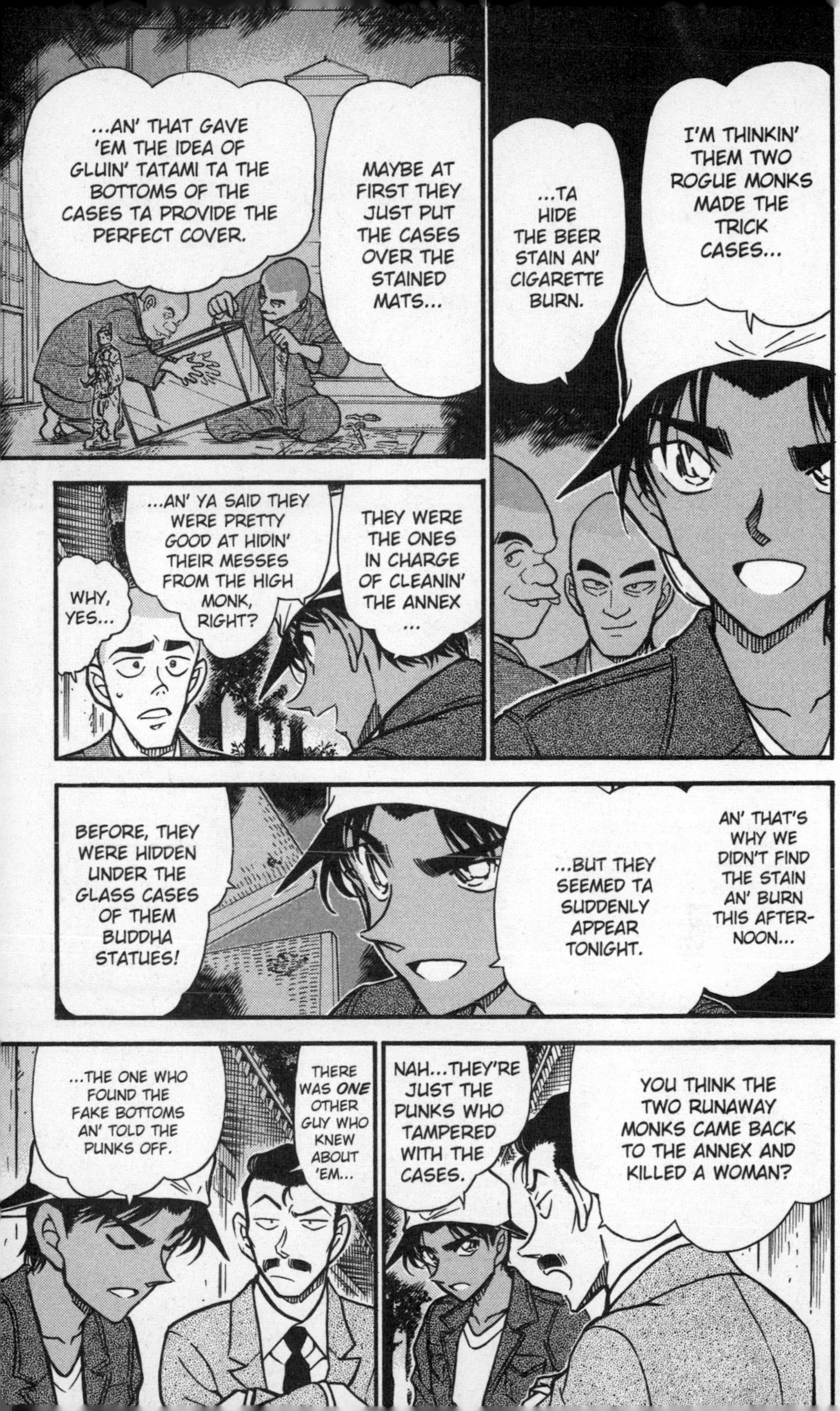
I'M THINKIN' THEM TWO ROGUE MONKS MADE THE TRICK CASES...
...TA HIDE THE BEER STAIN AN' CIGARETTE BURN.
MAYBE AT FIRST THEY JUST PUT THE CASES OVER THE STAINED MATS...
...AN' THAT GAVE 'EM THE IDEA OF GLUIN' TATAMI TA THE BOTTOMS OF THE CASES TA PROVIDE THE PERFECT COVER.
THEY WERE THE ONES IN CHARGE OF CLEANIN' THE ANNEX ...
...AN' YA SAID THEY WERE PRETTY GOOD AT HIDIN' THEIR MESSES FROM THE HIGH MONK, RIGHT?
WHY, YES...
AN' THAT'S WHY WE DIDN'T FIND THE STAIN AN' BURN THIS AFTER-NOON...
...BUT THEY SEEMED TA SUDDENLY APPEAR TONIGHT.
BEFORE, THEY WERE HIDDEN UNDER THE GLASS CASES OF THEM BUDDHA STATUES!
YOU THINK THE TWO RUNAWAY MONKS CAME BACK TO THE ANNEX AND KILLED A WOMAN?
NAH...THEY'RE JUST THE PUNKS WHO TAMPERED WITH THE CASES.
THERE WAS *ONE* OTHER GUY WHO KNEW ABOUT 'EM...
...THE ONE WHO FOUND THE FAKE BOTTOMS AN' TOLD THE PUNKS OFF.

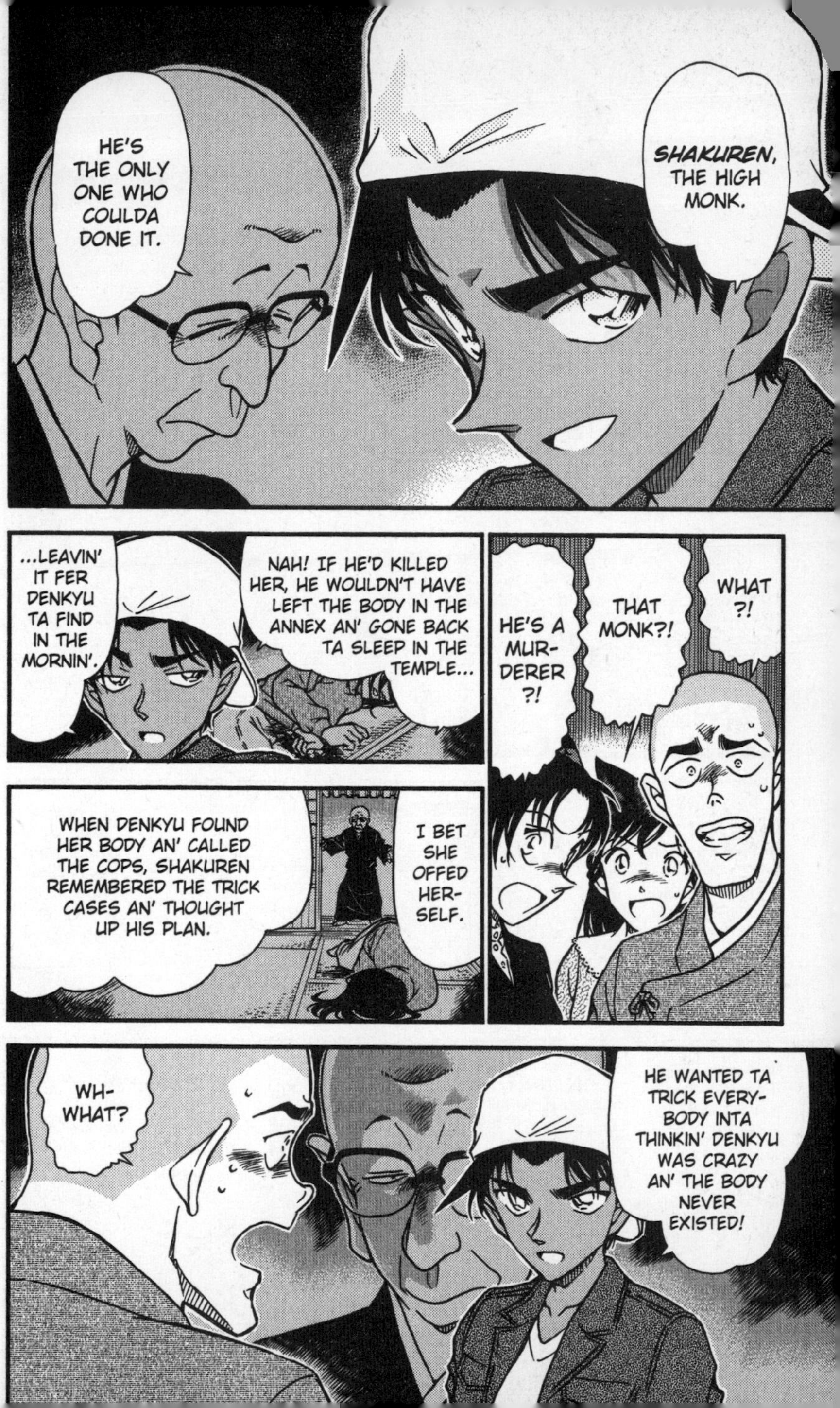
SHAKUREN, THE HIGH MONK.
HE'S THE ONLY ONE WHO COULDA DONE IT.
WHAT?!
THAT MONK?!
HE'S A MURDERER?!
NAH! IF HE'D KILLED HER, HE WOULDN'T HAVE LEFT THE BODY IN THE ANNEX AN' GONE BACK TA SLEEP IN THE TEMPLE...
...LEAVIN' IT FER DENKYU TA FIND IN THE MORNIN'.
I BET SHE OFFED HERSELF.
WHEN DENKYU FOUND HER BODY AN' CALLED THE COPS, SHAKUREN REMEMBERED THE TRICK CASES AN' THOUGHT UP HIS PLAN.
HE WANTED TA TRICK EVERYBODY INTA THINKIN' DENKYU WAS CRAZY AN' THE BODY NEVER EXISTED!
WH-WHAT?

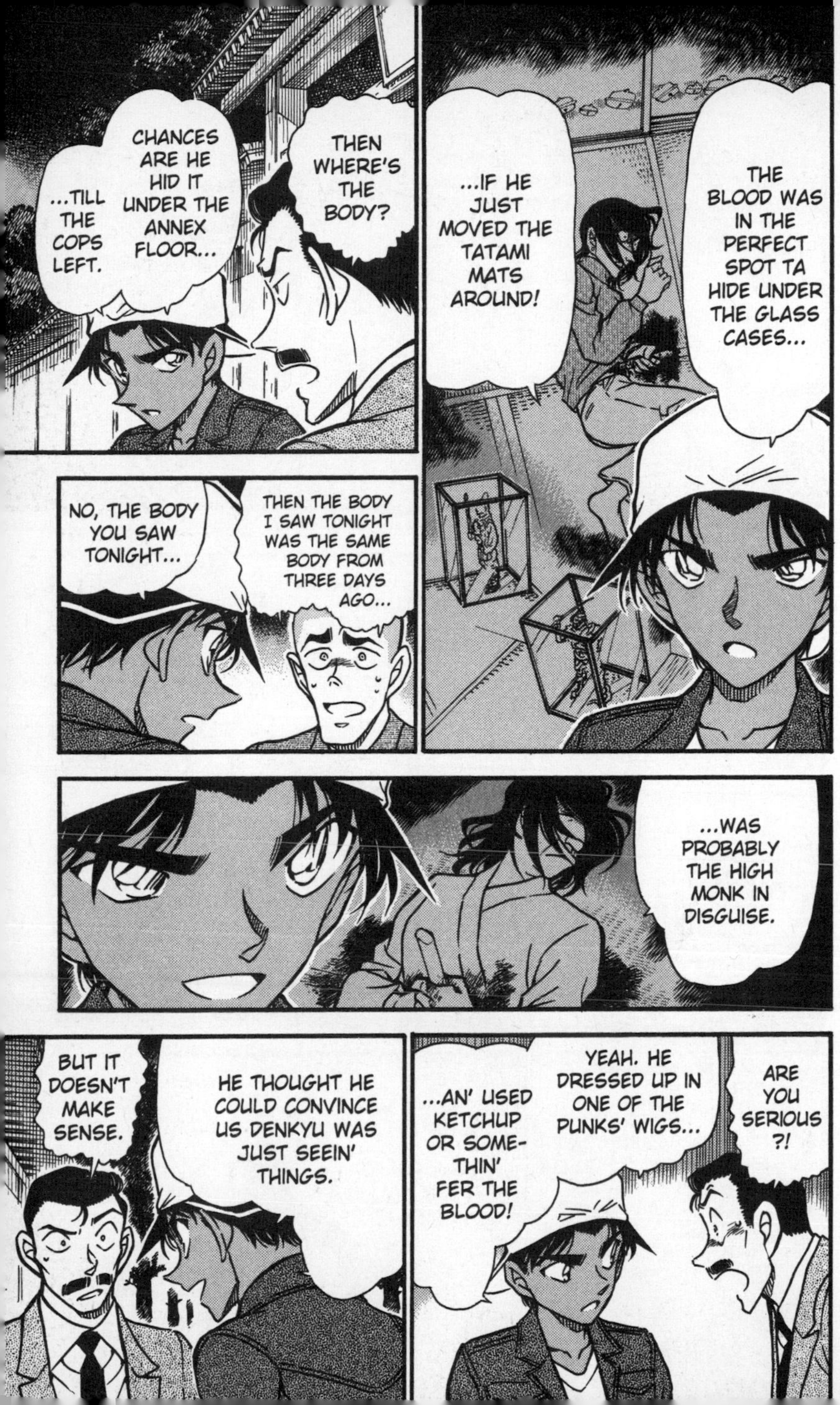
THE BLOOD WAS IN THE PERFECT SPOT TA HIDE UNDER THE GLASS CASES...
...IF HE JUST MOVED THE TATAMI MATS AROUND!
THEN WHERE'S THE BODY?
CHANCES ARE HE HID IT UNDER THE ANNEX FLOOR...
...TILL THE COPS LEFT.
THEN THE BODY I SAW TONIGHT WAS THE SAME BODY FROM THREE DAYS AGO...
NO, THE BODY YOU SAW TONIGHT...
...WAS PROBABLY THE HIGH MONK IN DISGUISE.
ARE YOU SERIOUS?!
YEAH. HE DRESSED UP IN ONE OF THE PUNKS' WIGS...
...AN' USED KETCHUP OR SOME-THIN' FER THE BLOOD!
HE THOUGHT HE COULD CONVINCE US DENKYU WAS JUST SEEIN' THINGS.
BUT IT DOESN'T MAKE SENSE.

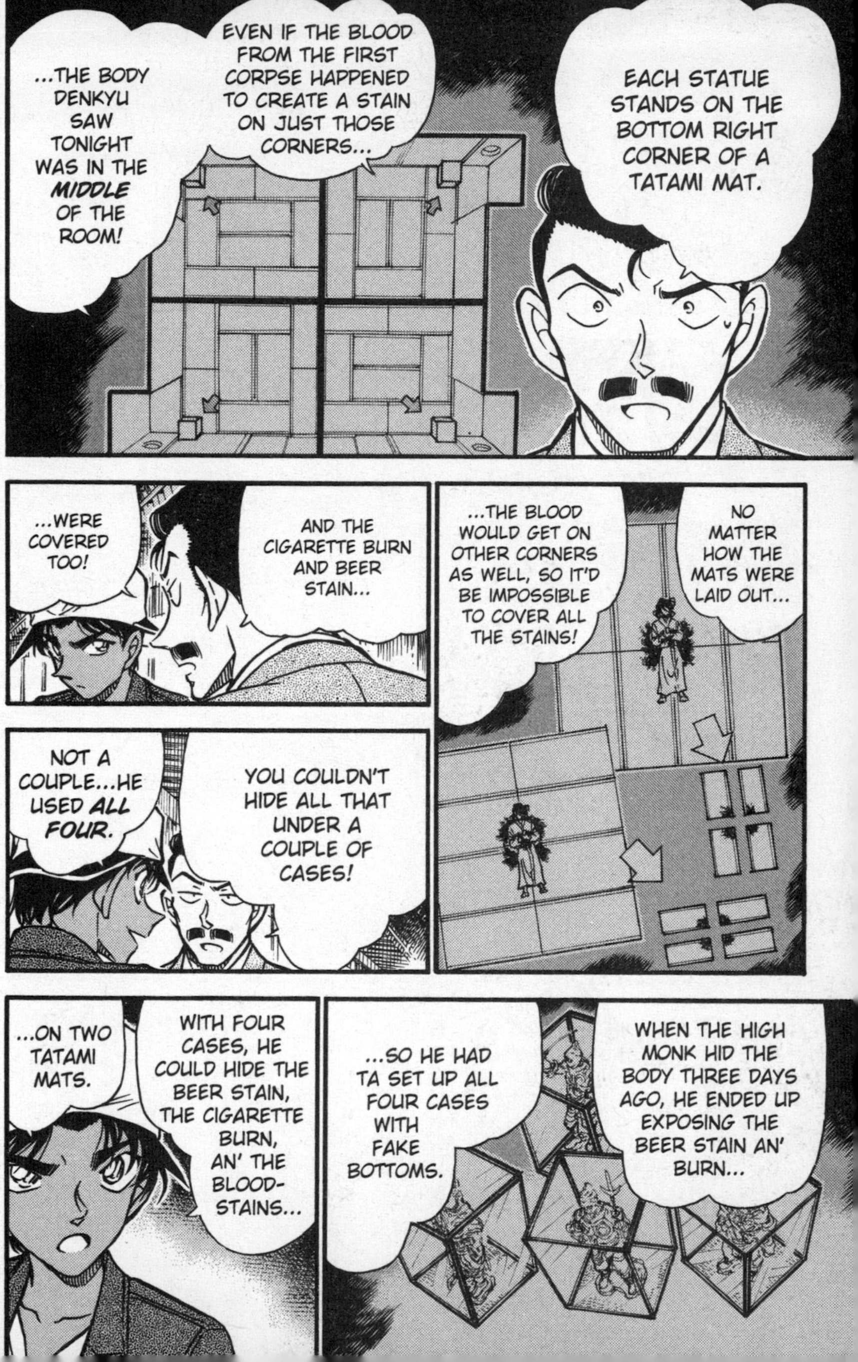
EACH STATUE STANDS ON THE BOTTOM RIGHT CORNER OF A TATAMI MAT.
EVEN IF THE BLOOD FROM THE FIRST CORPSE HAPPENED TO CREATE A STAIN ON JUST THOSE CORNERS...
...THE BODY DENKYU SAW TONIGHT WAS IN THE *MIDDLE* OF THE ROOM!
NO MATTER HOW THE MATS WERE LAID OUT...
...THE BLOOD WOULD GET ON OTHER CORNERS AS WELL, SO IT'D BE IMPOSSIBLE TO COVER ALL THE STAINS!
AND THE CIGARETTE BURN AND BEER STAIN...
...WERE COVERED TOO!
YOU COULDN'T HIDE ALL THAT UNDER A COUPLE OF CASES!
NOT A COUPLE...HE USED ***ALL FOUR.***
WHEN THE HIGH MONK HID THE BODY THREE DAYS AGO, HE ENDED UP EXPOSING THE BEER STAIN AN' BURN...
...SO HE HAD TA SET UP ALL FOUR CASES WITH FAKE BOTTOMS.
WITH FOUR CASES, HE COULD HIDE THE BEER STAIN, THE CIGARETTE BURN, AN' THE BLOOD-STAINS...
...ON TWO TATAMI MATS.

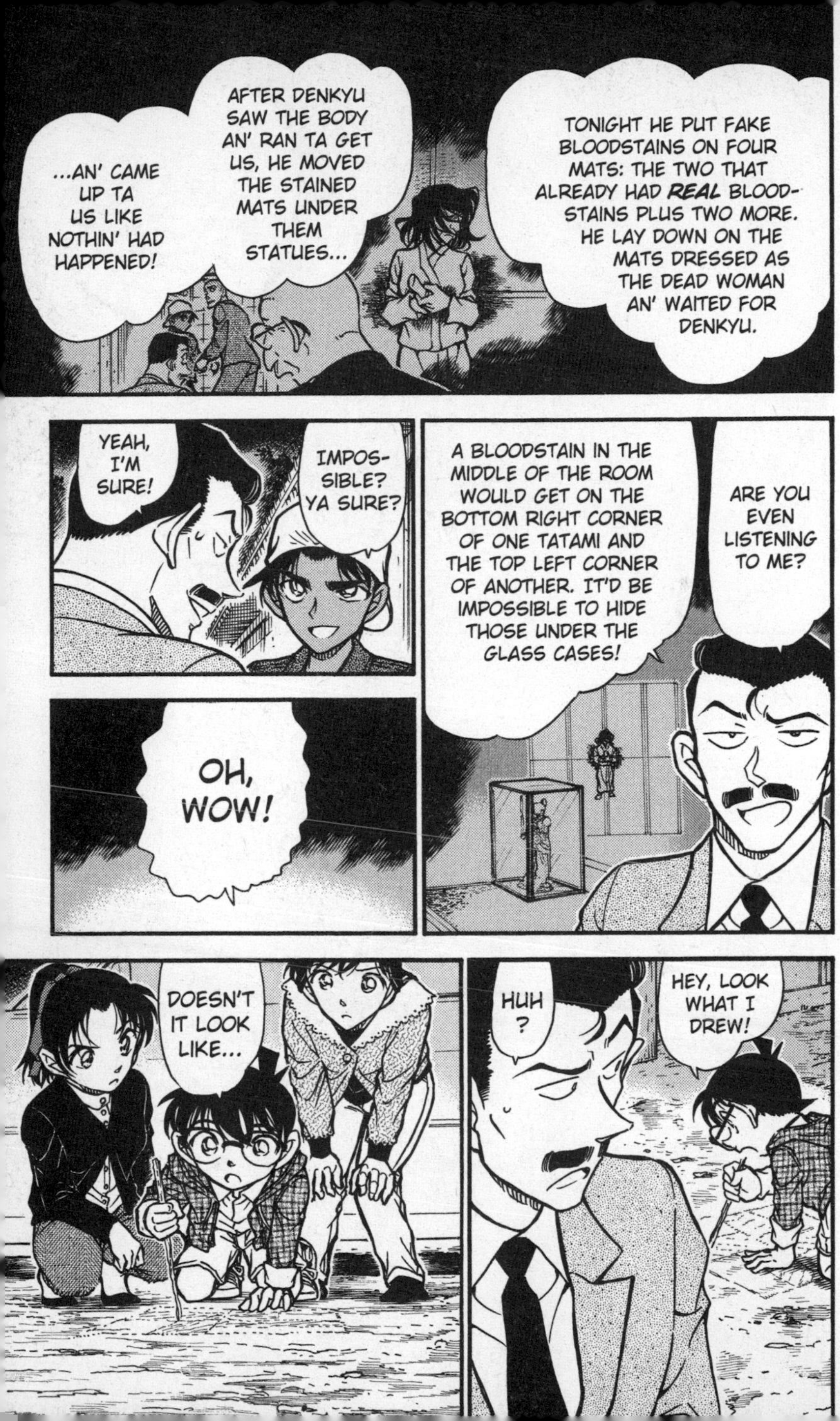
TONIGHT HE PUT FAKE BLOODSTAINS ON FOUR MATS: THE TWO THAT ALREADY HAD *REAL* BLOOD-STAINS PLUS TWO MORE. HE LAY DOWN ON THE MATS DRESSED AS THE DEAD WOMAN AN' WAITED FOR DENKYU.
AFTER DENKYU SAW THE BODY AN' RAN TA GET US, HE MOVED THE STAINED MATS UNDER THEM STATUES...
...AN' CAME UP TA US LIKE NOTHIN' HAD HAPPENED!
ARE YOU EVEN LISTENING TO ME?
A BLOODSTAIN IN THE MIDDLE OF THE ROOM WOULD GET ON THE BOTTOM RIGHT CORNER OF ONE TATAMI AND THE TOP LEFT CORNER OF ANOTHER. IT'D BE IMPOSSIBLE TO HIDE THOSE UNDER THE GLASS CASES!
IMPOS-SIBLE? YA SURE?
YEAH, I'M SURE!
OH, WOW!
HEY, LOOK WHAT I DREW!
HUH?
DOESN'T IT LOOK LIKE...

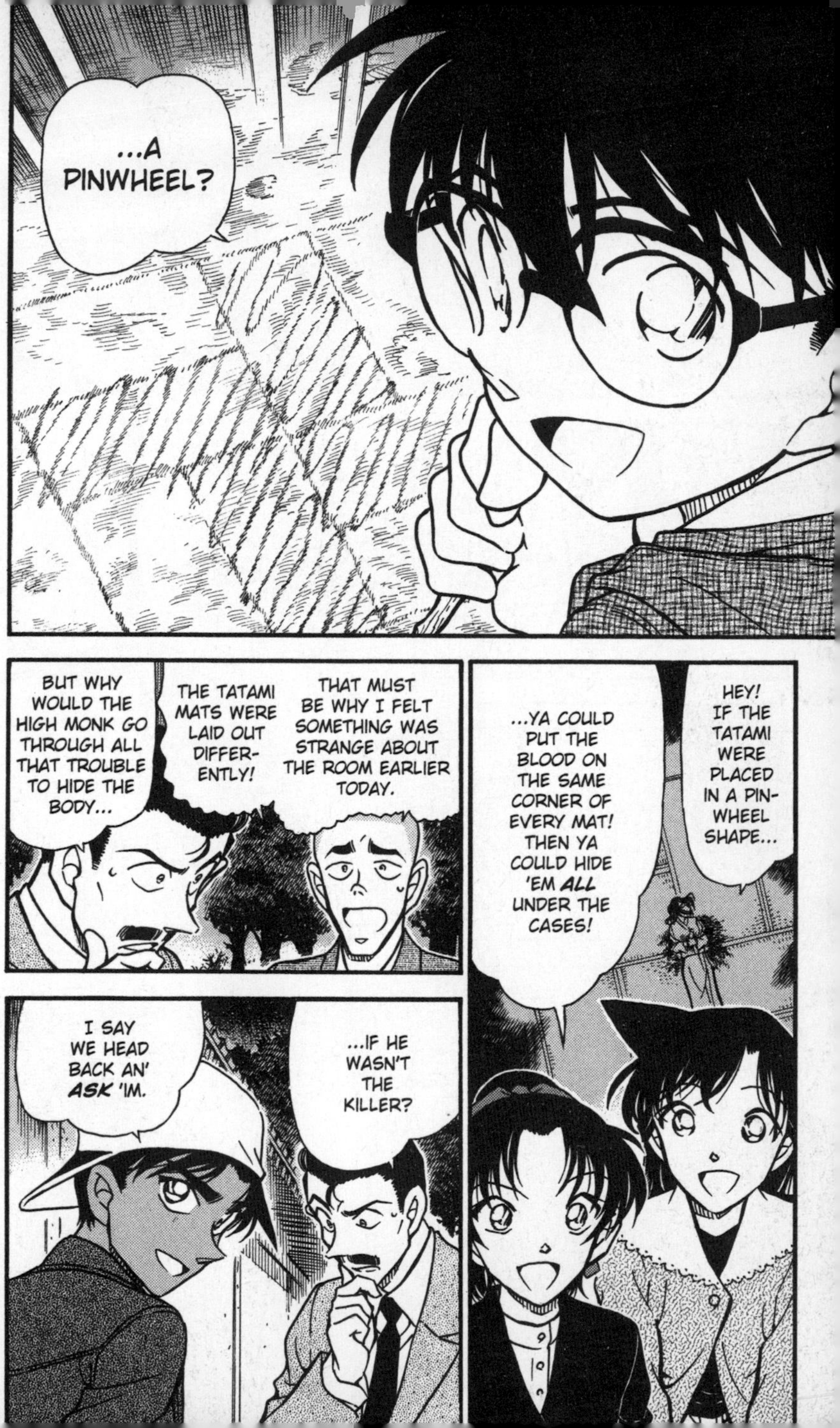
...A PINWHEEL?
HEY! IF THE TATAMI WERE PLACED IN A PIN-WHEEL SHAPE...
...YA COULD PUT THE BLOOD ON THE SAME CORNER OF EVERY MAT! THEN YA COULD HIDE 'EM *ALL* UNDER THE CASES!
THAT MUST BE WHY I FELT SOMETHING WAS STRANGE ABOUT THE ROOM EARLIER TODAY.
THE TATAMI MATS WERE LAID OUT DIFFER-ENTLY!
BUT WHY WOULD THE HIGH MONK GO THROUGH ALL THAT TROUBLE TO HIDE THE BODY...
...IF HE WASN'T THE KILLER?
I SAY WE HEAD BACK AN' *ASK* 'IM.

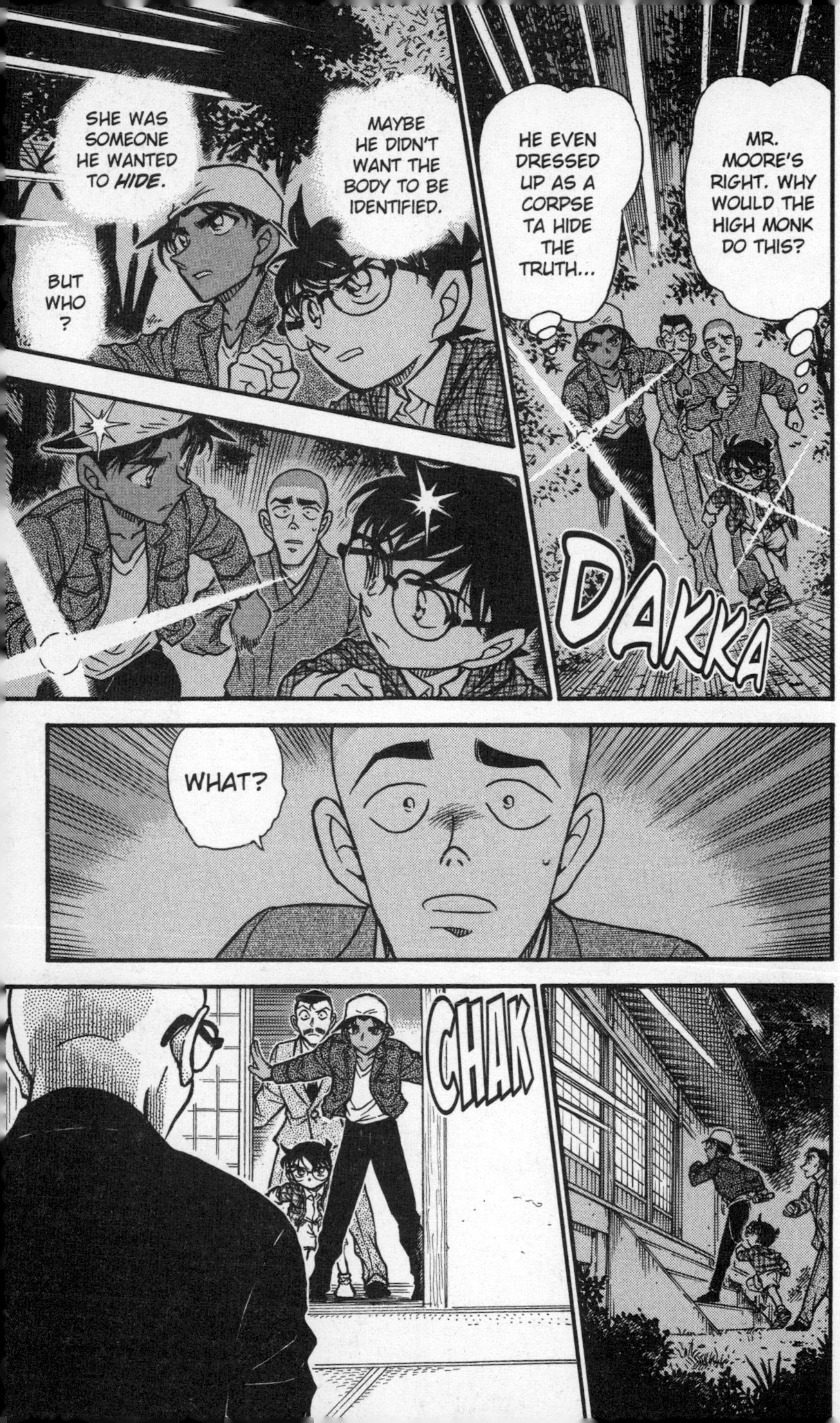
MR. MOORE'S RIGHT. WHY WOULD THE HIGH MONK DO THIS?
HE EVEN DRESSED UP AS A CORPSE TA HIDE THE TRUTH...
DAKKA
MAYBE HE DIDN'T WANT THE BODY TO BE IDENTIFIED.
SHE WAS SOMEONE HE WANTED TO *HIDE*.
BUT WHO?
WHAT?
CHAK

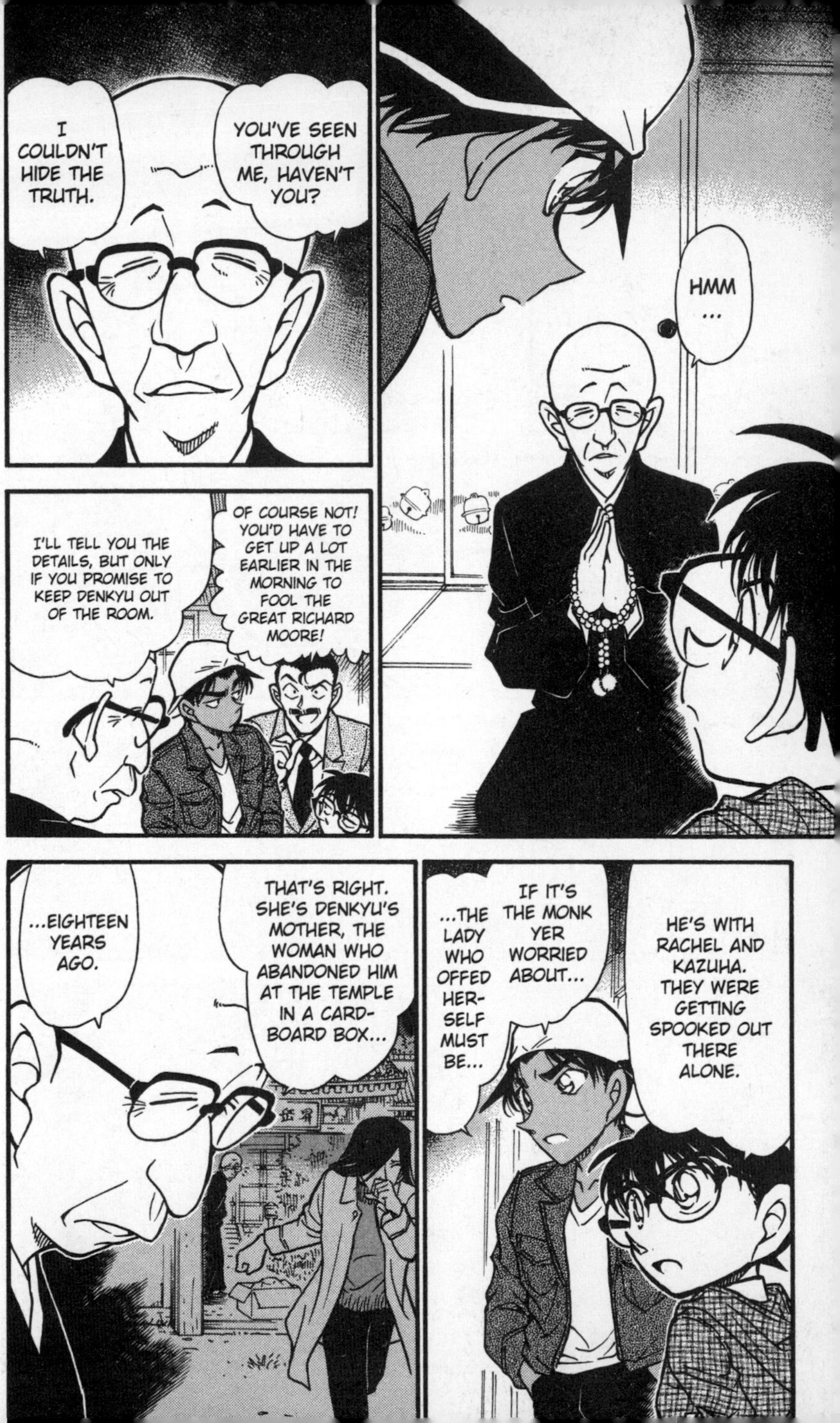
HMM ...
YOU'VE SEEN THROUGH ME, HAVEN'T YOU?
I COULDN'T HIDE THE TRUTH.
OF COURSE NOT! YOU'D HAVE TO GET UP A LOT EARLIER IN THE MORNING TO FOOL THE GREAT RICHARD MOORE!
I'LL TELL YOU THE DETAILS, BUT ONLY IF YOU PROMISE TO KEEP DENKYU OUT OF THE ROOM.
HE'S WITH RACHEL AND KAZUHA. THEY WERE GETTING SPOOKED OUT THERE ALONE.
IF IT'S THE MONK YER WORRIED ABOUT...
...THE LADY WHO OFFED HER-SELF MUST BE...
THAT'S RIGHT. SHE'S DENKYU'S MOTHER, THE WOMAN WHO ABANDONED HIM AT THE TEMPLE IN A CARD-BOARD BOX...
...EIGHTEEN YEARS AGO.

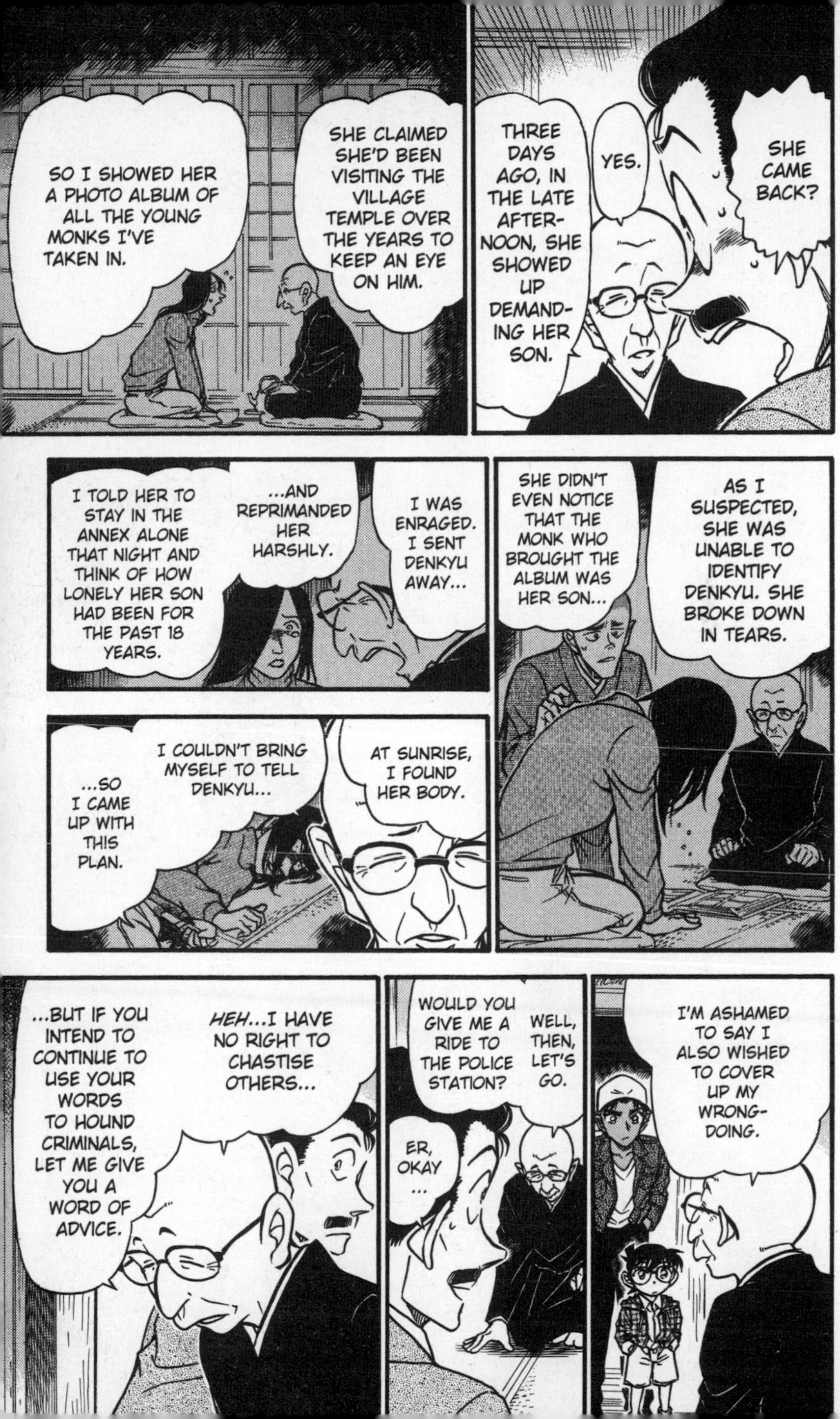
SHE CAME BACK?
YES.
THREE DAYS AGO, IN THE LATE AFTERNOON, SHE SHOWED UP DEMANDING HER SON.
SHE CLAIMED SHE'D BEEN VISITING THE VILLAGE TEMPLE OVER THE YEARS TO KEEP AN EYE ON HIM.
SO I SHOWED HER A PHOTO ALBUM OF ALL THE YOUNG MONKS I'VE TAKEN IN.
AS I SUSPECTED, SHE WAS UNABLE TO IDENTIFY DENKYU. SHE BROKE DOWN IN TEARS.
SHE DIDN'T EVEN NOTICE THAT THE MONK WHO BROUGHT THE ALBUM WAS HER SON...
I WAS ENRAGED. I SENT DENKYU AWAY...
...AND REPRIMANDED HER HARSHLY.
I TOLD HER TO STAY IN THE ANNEX ALONE THAT NIGHT AND THINK OF HOW LONELY HER SON HAD BEEN FOR THE PAST 18 YEARS.
AT SUNRISE, I FOUND HER BODY.
I COULDN'T BRING MYSELF TO TELL DENKYU...
...SO I CAME UP WITH THIS PLAN.
I'M ASHAMED TO SAY I ALSO WISHED TO COVER UP MY WRONG-DOING.
WELL, THEN, LET'S GO.
WOULD YOU GIVE ME A RIDE TO THE POLICE STATION?
ER, OKAY ...
HEH...I HAVE NO RIGHT TO CHASTISE OTHERS...
...BUT IF YOU INTEND TO CONTINUE TO USE YOUR WORDS TO HOUND CRIMINALS, LET ME GIVE YOU A WORD OF ADVICE.

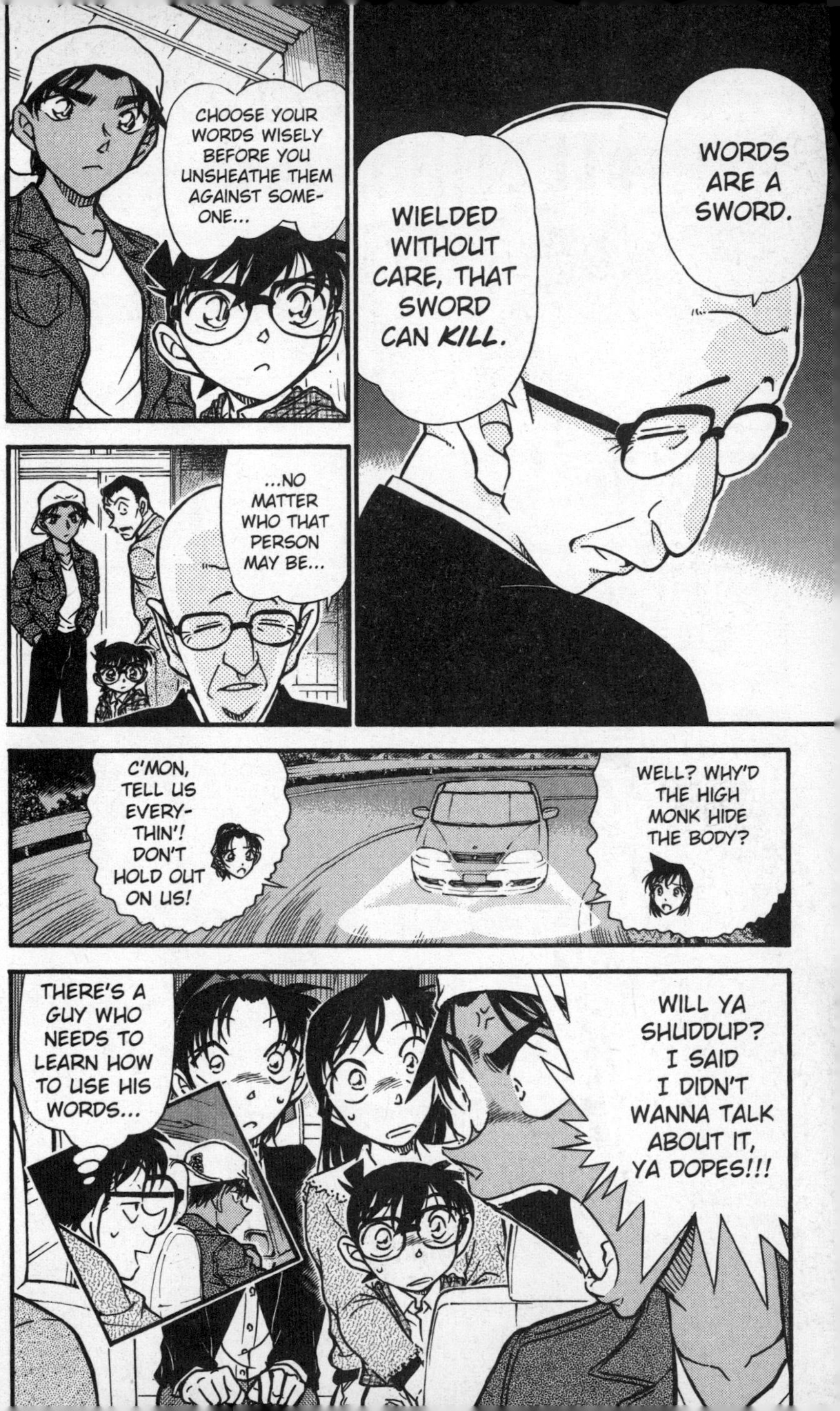
WORDS ARE A SWORD.
WIELDED WITHOUT CARE, THAT SWORD CAN KILL.
CHOOSE YOUR WORDS WISELY BEFORE YOU UNSHEATHE THEM AGAINST SOME-ONE...
...NO MATTER WHO THAT PERSON MAY BE...
WELL? WHY'D THE HIGH MONK HIDE THE BODY?
C'MON, TELL US EVERY-THIN'! DON'T HOLD OUT ON US!
WILL YA SHUDDUP? I SAID I DIDN'T WANNA TALK ABOUT IT, YA DOPES!!!
THERE'S A GUY WHO NEEDS TO LEARN HOW TO USE HIS WORDS...

THE TEEN DETECTIVE OF THE WEST

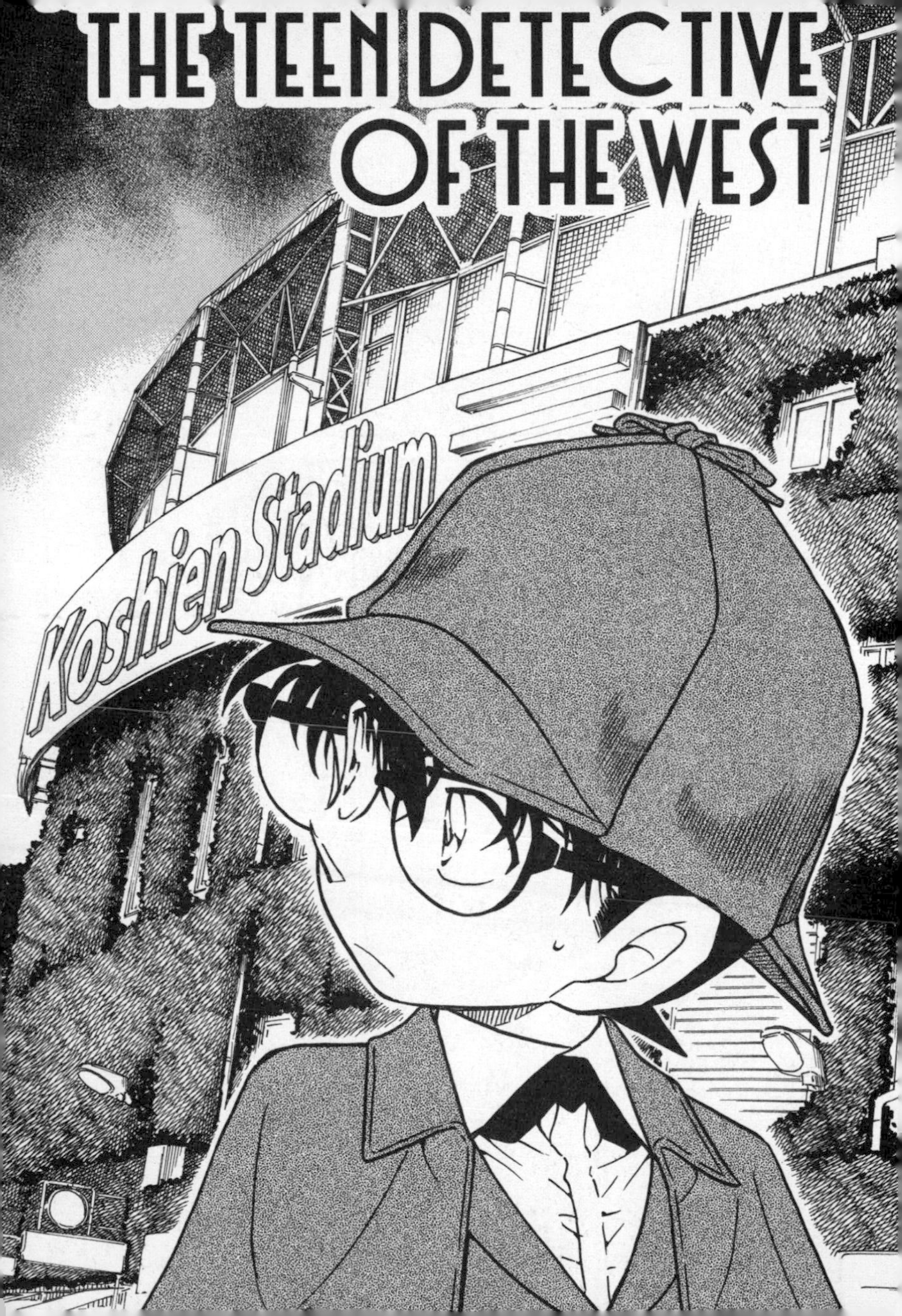
Koshien Stadium

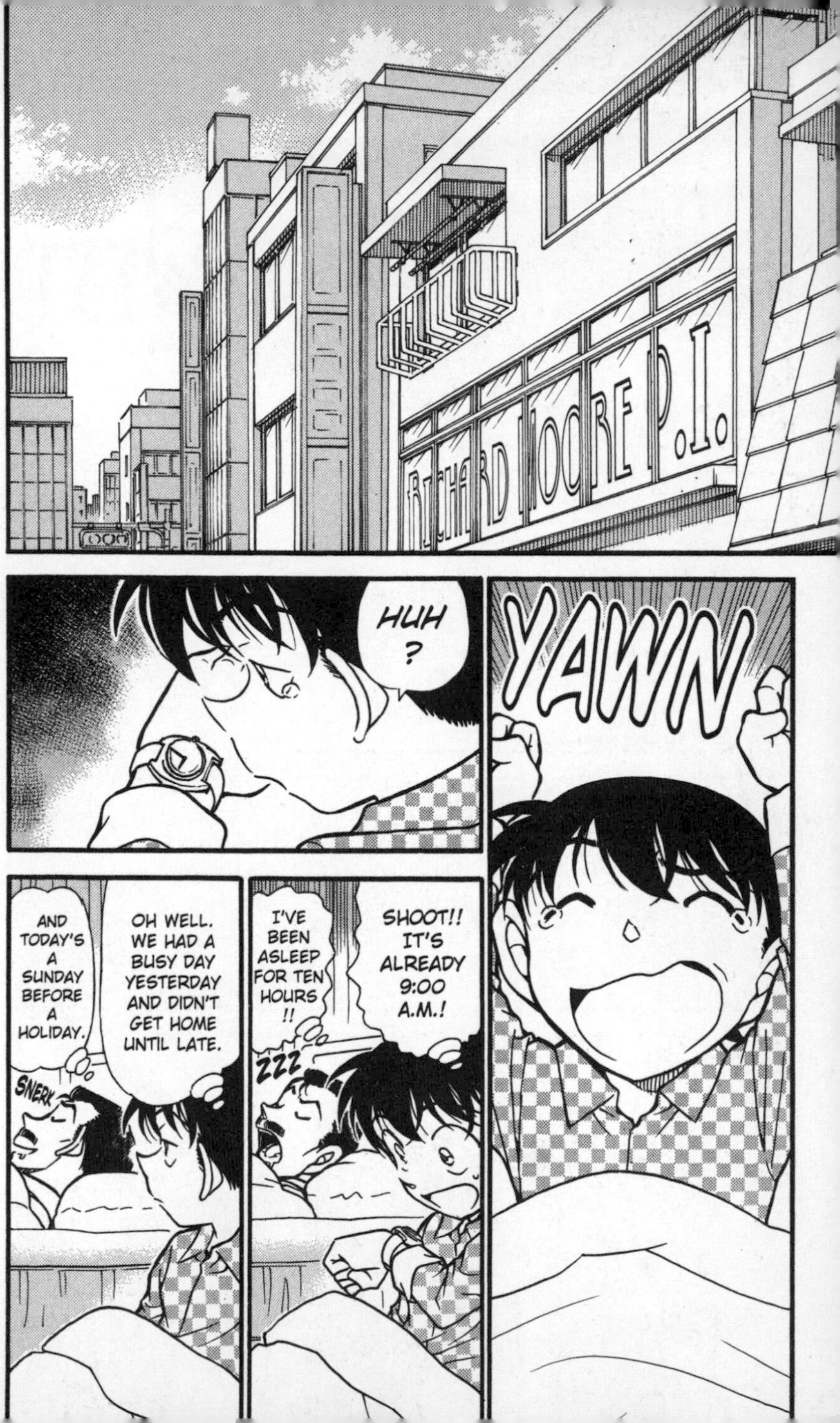
RICHARD MOORE P.I.
YAWN
HUH ?
SHOOT!! IT'S ALREADY 9:00 A.M.!
I'VE BEEN ASLEEP FOR TEN HOURS !!
ZZZ
OH WELL. WE HAD A BUSY DAY YESTERDAY AND DIDN'T GET HOME UNTIL LATE.
AND TODAY'S A SUNDAY BEFORE A HOLIDAY.
SNERK

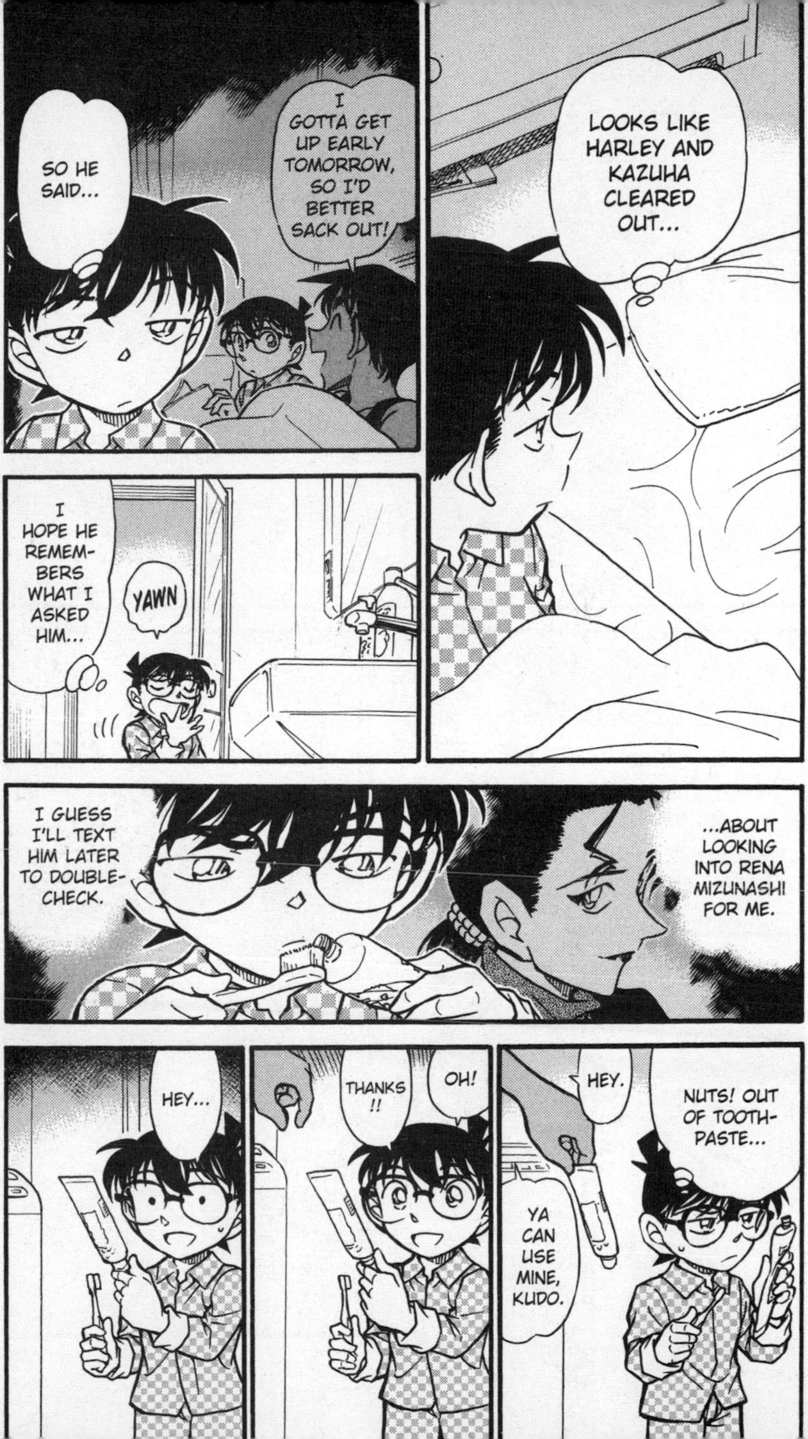

LOOKS LIKE HARLEY AND KAZUHA CLEARED OUT...
I GOTTA GET UP EARLY TOMORROW, SO I'D BETTER SACK OUT!
SO HE SAID...
I HOPE HE REMEMBERS WHAT I ASKED HIM...
YAWN
...ABOUT LOOKING INTO RENA MIZUNASHI FOR ME.
I GUESS I'LL TEXT HIM LATER TO DOUBLE-CHECK.
NUTS! OUT OF TOOTH-PASTE...
HEY.
YA CAN USE MINE, KUDO.
OH!
THANKS !!
HEY...

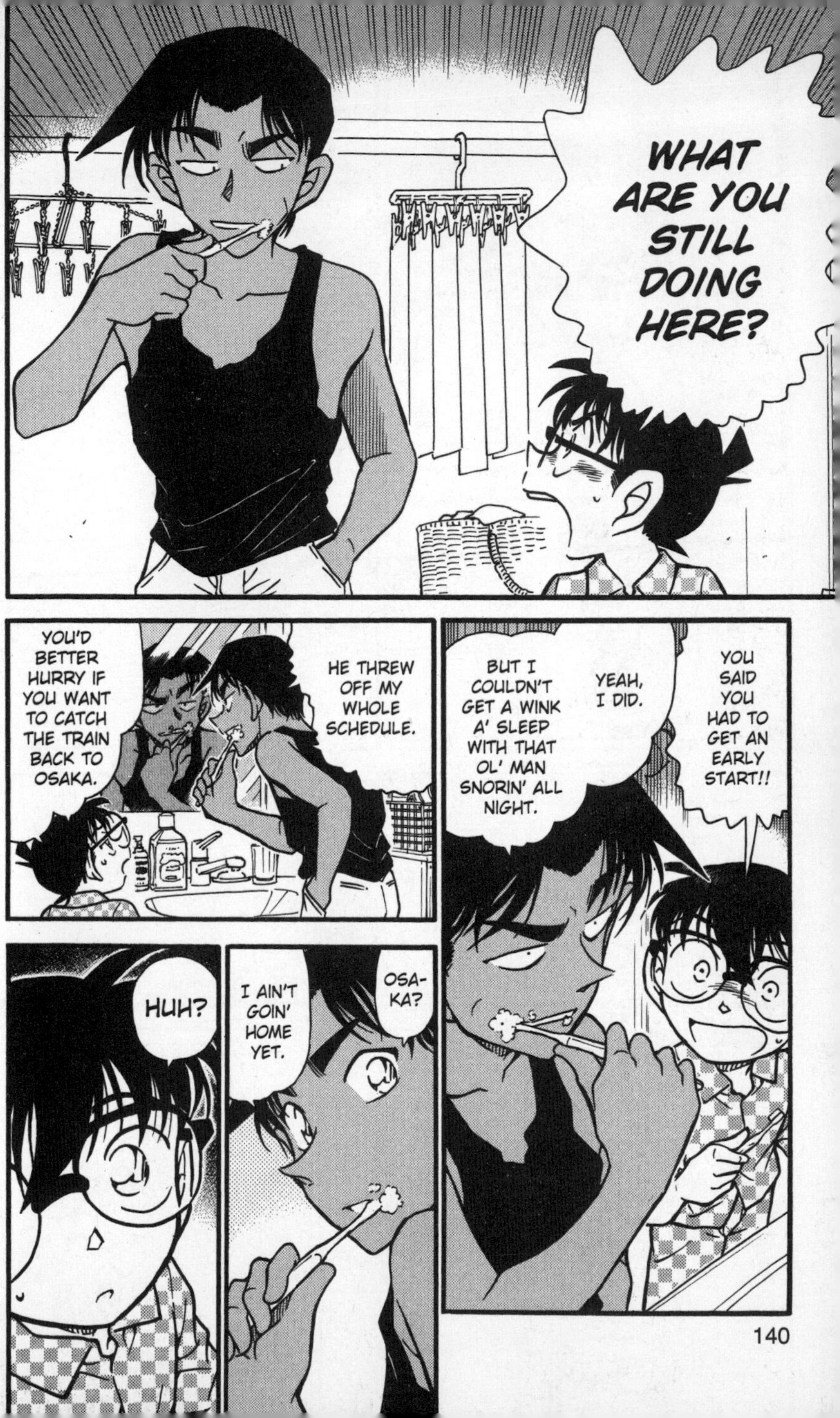
WHAT ARE YOU STILL DOING HERE?
YOU SAID YOU HAD TO GET AN EARLY START!!
YEAH, I DID.
BUT I COULDN'T GET A WINK A' SLEEP WITH THAT OL' MAN SNORIN' ALL NIGHT.
HE THREW OFF MY WHOLE SCHEDULE.
YOU'D BETTER HURRY IF YOU WANT TO CATCH THE TRAIN BACK TO OSAKA.
OSA-KA?
I AIN'T GOIN' HOME YET.
HUH?

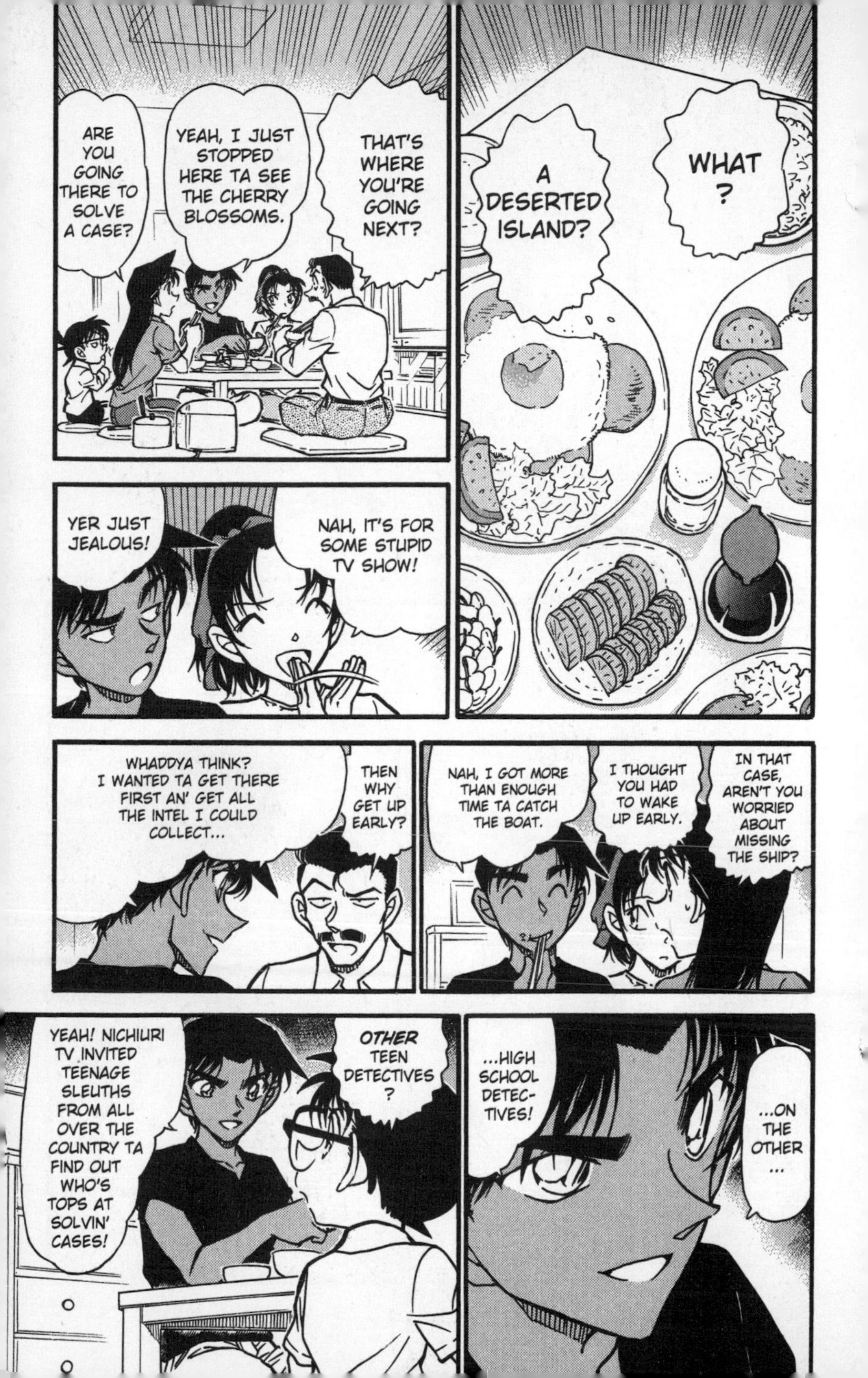
WHAT?
A DESERTED ISLAND?
THAT'S WHERE YOU'RE GOING NEXT?
YEAH, I JUST STOPPED HERE TA SEE THE CHERRY BLOSSOMS.
ARE YOU GOING THERE TO SOLVE A CASE?
NAH, IT'S FOR SOME STUPID TV SHOW!
YER JUST JEALOUS!
IN THAT CASE, AREN'T YOU WORRIED ABOUT MISSING THE SHIP?
I THOUGHT YOU HAD TO WAKE UP EARLY.
NAH, I GOT MORE THAN ENOUGH TIME TA CATCH THE BOAT.
THEN WHY GET UP EARLY?
WHADDYA THINK? I WANTED TA GET THERE FIRST AN' GET ALL THE INTEL I COULD COLLECT...
YEAH! NICHIURI TV INVITED TEENAGE SLEUTHS FROM ALL OVER THE COUNTRY TA FIND OUT WHO'S TOPS AT SOLVIN' CASES!
OTHER TEEN DETECTIVES?
...ON THE OTHER...
...HIGH SCHOOL DETECTIVES!

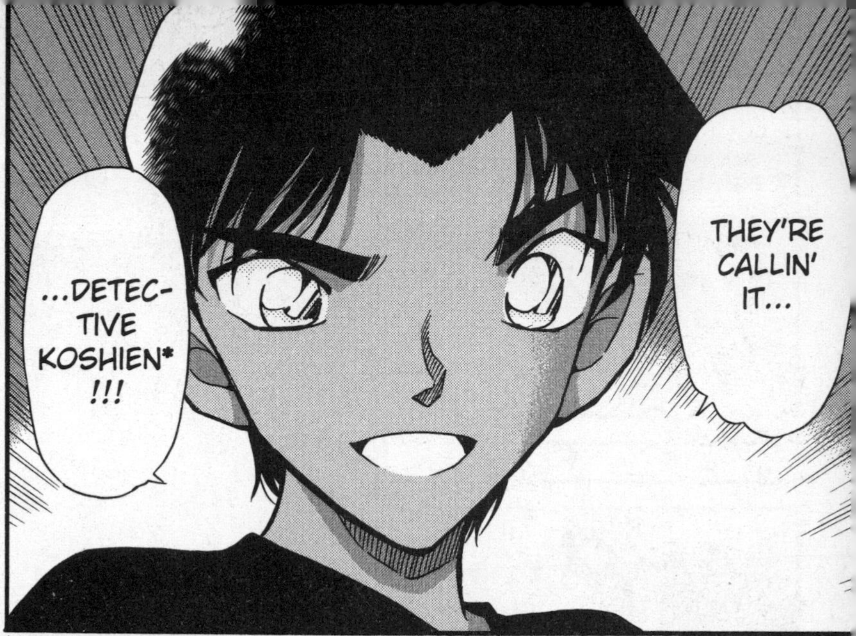
THEY'RE CALLIN' IT...
...DETEC-TIVE KOSHIEN* !!!

*As seen in volumes 43-44, Koshien is Japan's national high school baseball championship.

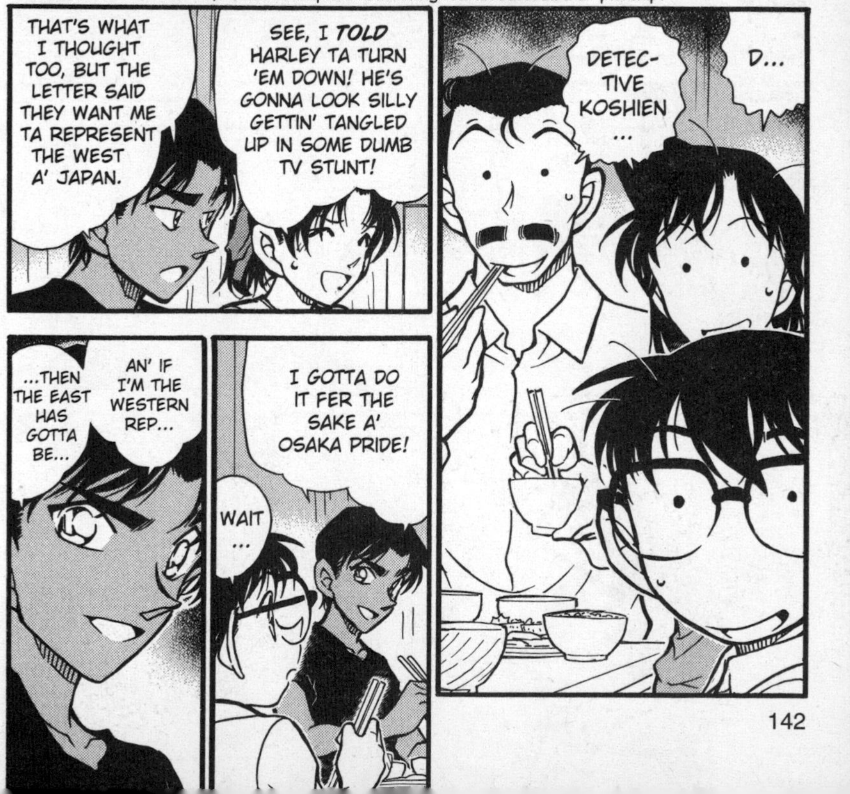
D...
DETEC-TIVE KOSHIEN ...
SEE, I *TOLD* HARLEY TA TURN 'EM DOWN! HE'S GONNA LOOK SILLY GETTIN' TANGLED UP IN SOME DUMB TV STUNT!
THAT'S WHAT I THOUGHT TOO, BUT THE LETTER SAID THEY WANT ME TA REPRESENT THE WEST A' JAPAN.
I GOTTA DO IT FER THE SAKE A' OSAKA PRIDE!
WAIT ...
AN' IF I'M THE WESTERN REP...
...THEN THE EAST HAS GOTTA BE...

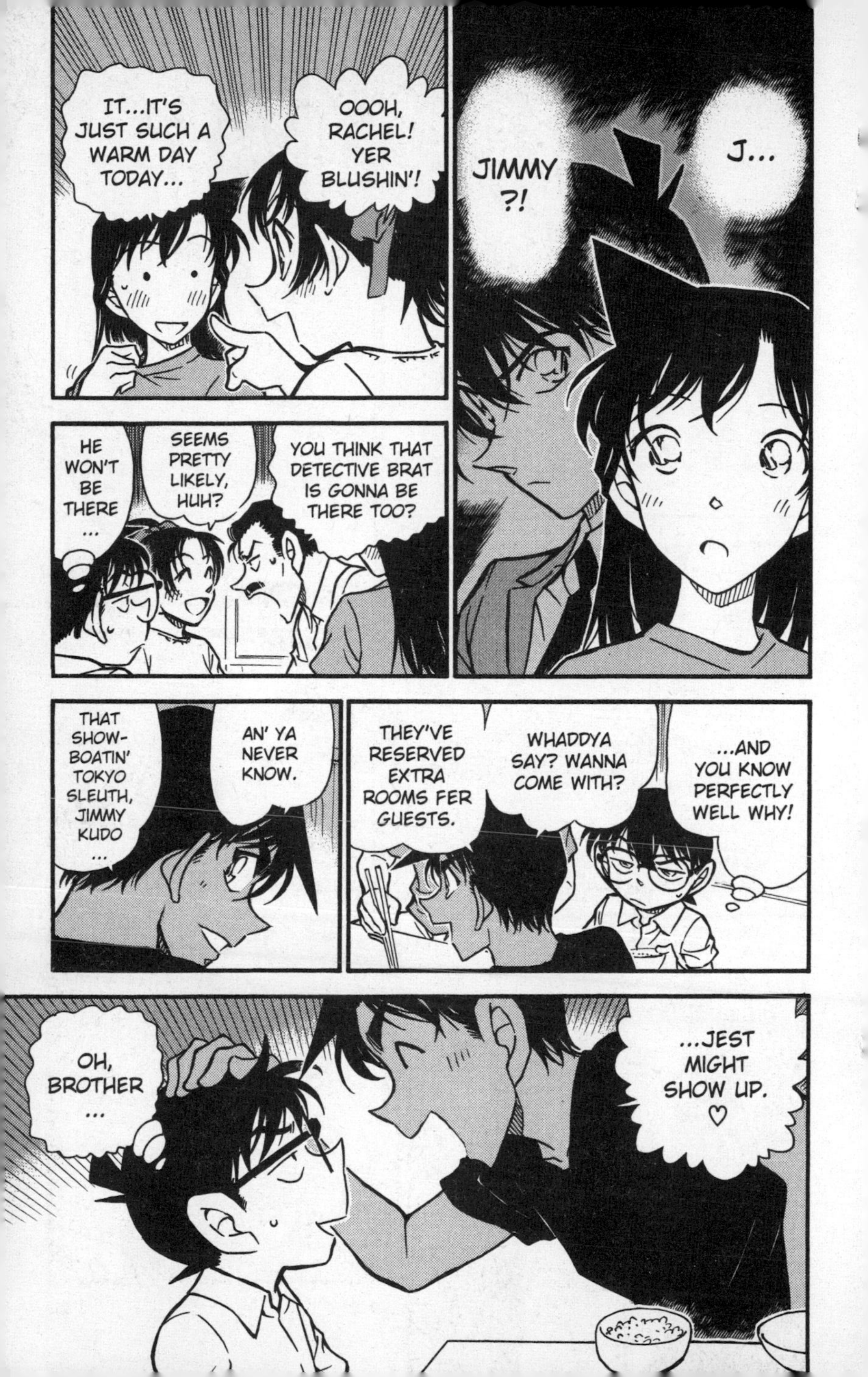
J...
JIMMY ?!
OOOH, RACHEL! YER BLUSHIN'!
IT...IT'S JUST SUCH A WARM DAY TODAY...
YOU THINK THAT DETECTIVE BRAT IS GONNA BE THERE TOO?
SEEMS PRETTY LIKELY, HUH?
HE WON'T BE THERE ...
...AND YOU KNOW PERFECTLY WELL WHY!
WHADDYA SAY? WANNA COME WITH?
THEY'VE RESERVED EXTRA ROOMS FER GUESTS.
AN' YA NEVER KNOW.
THAT SHOW-BOATIN' TOKYO SLEUTH, JIMMY KUDO ...
...JEST MIGHT SHOW UP. ♡
OH, BROTHER ...

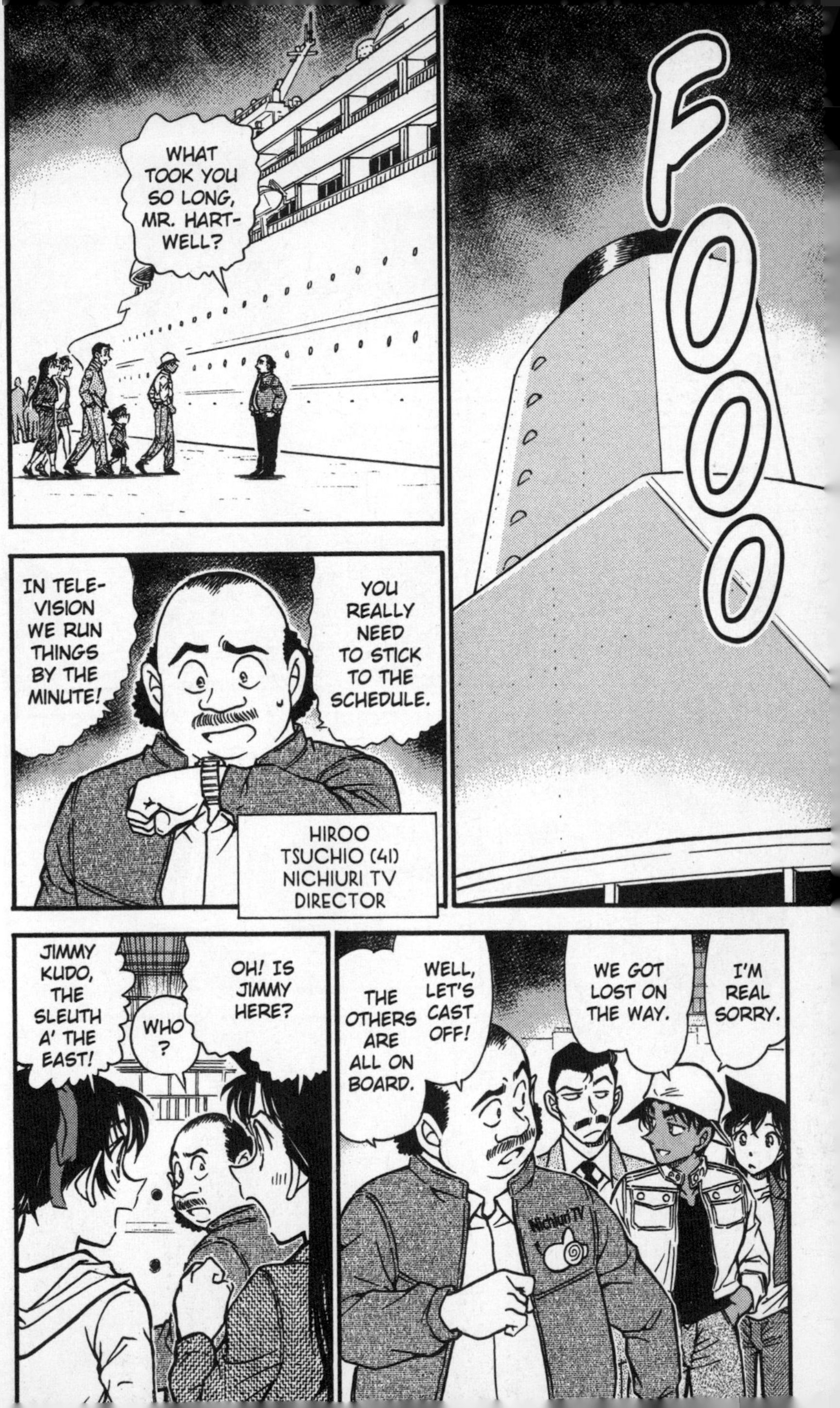
FOOO
WHAT TOOK YOU SO LONG, MR. HART-WELL?
YOU REALLY NEED TO STICK TO THE SCHEDULE.
IN TELE-VISION WE RUN THINGS BY THE MINUTE!
HIROO TSUCHIO (41) NICHIURI TV DIRECTOR
I'M REAL SORRY.
WE GOT LOST ON THE WAY.
WELL, LET'S CAST OFF!
THE OTHERS ARE ALL ON BOARD.
Nichiuri TV
OH! IS JIMMY HERE?
WHO?
JIMMY KUDO, THE SLEUTH A' THE EAST!

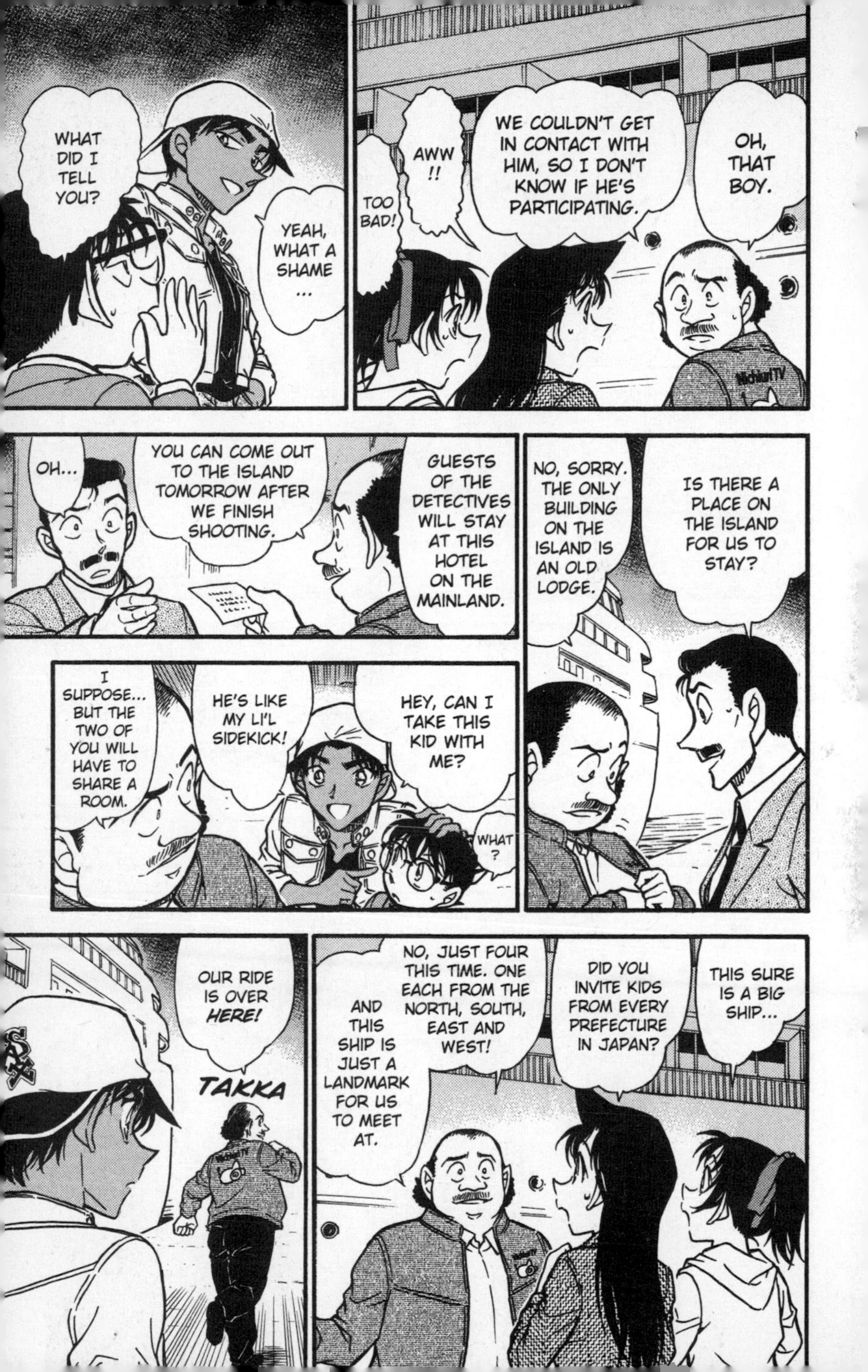
OH, THAT BOY.
WE COULDN'T GET IN CONTACT WITH HIM, SO I DON'T KNOW IF HE'S PARTICIPATING.
AWW !!
TOO BAD!
WHAT DID I TELL YOU?
YEAH, WHAT A SHAME ...
IS THERE A PLACE ON THE ISLAND FOR US TO STAY?
NO, SORRY. THE ONLY BUILDING ON THE ISLAND IS AN OLD LODGE.
GUESTS OF THE DETECTIVES WILL STAY AT THIS HOTEL ON THE MAINLAND.
YOU CAN COME OUT TO THE ISLAND TOMORROW AFTER WE FINISH SHOOTING.
OH...
HEY, CAN I TAKE THIS KID WITH ME?
HE'S LIKE MY LI'L SIDEKICK!
WHAT ?
I SUPPOSE... BUT THE TWO OF YOU WILL HAVE TO SHARE A ROOM.
THIS SURE IS A BIG SHIP...
DID YOU INVITE KIDS FROM EVERY PREFECTURE IN JAPAN?
NO, JUST FOUR THIS TIME. ONE EACH FROM THE NORTH, SOUTH, EAST AND WEST!
AND THIS SHIP IS JUST A LANDMARK FOR US TO MEET AT.
OUR RIDE IS OVER *HERE!*
TAKKA

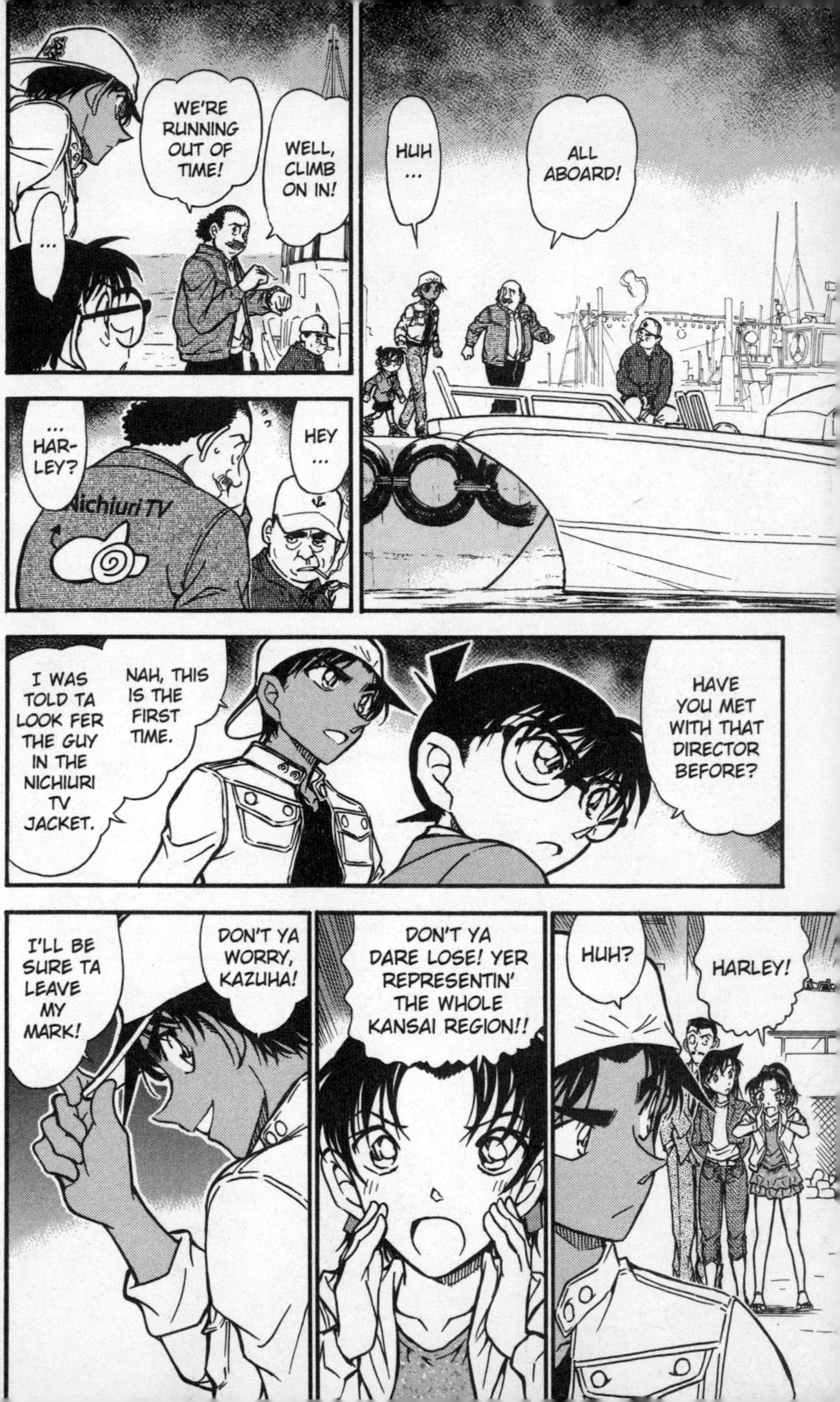
ALL ABOARD!
HUH ...
WELL, CLIMB ON IN!
WE'RE RUNNING OUT OF TIME!
...
HEY ...
... HARLEY?
Nichiuri TV
HAVE YOU MET WITH THAT DIRECTOR BEFORE?
NAH, THIS IS THE FIRST TIME.
I WAS TOLD TA LOOK FER THE GUY IN THE NICHIURI TV JACKET.
HARLEY!
HUH?
DON'T YA DARE LOSE! YER REPRESENTIN' THE WHOLE KANSAI REGION!!
DON'T YA WORRY, KAZUHA!
I'LL BE SURE TA LEAVE MY MARK!

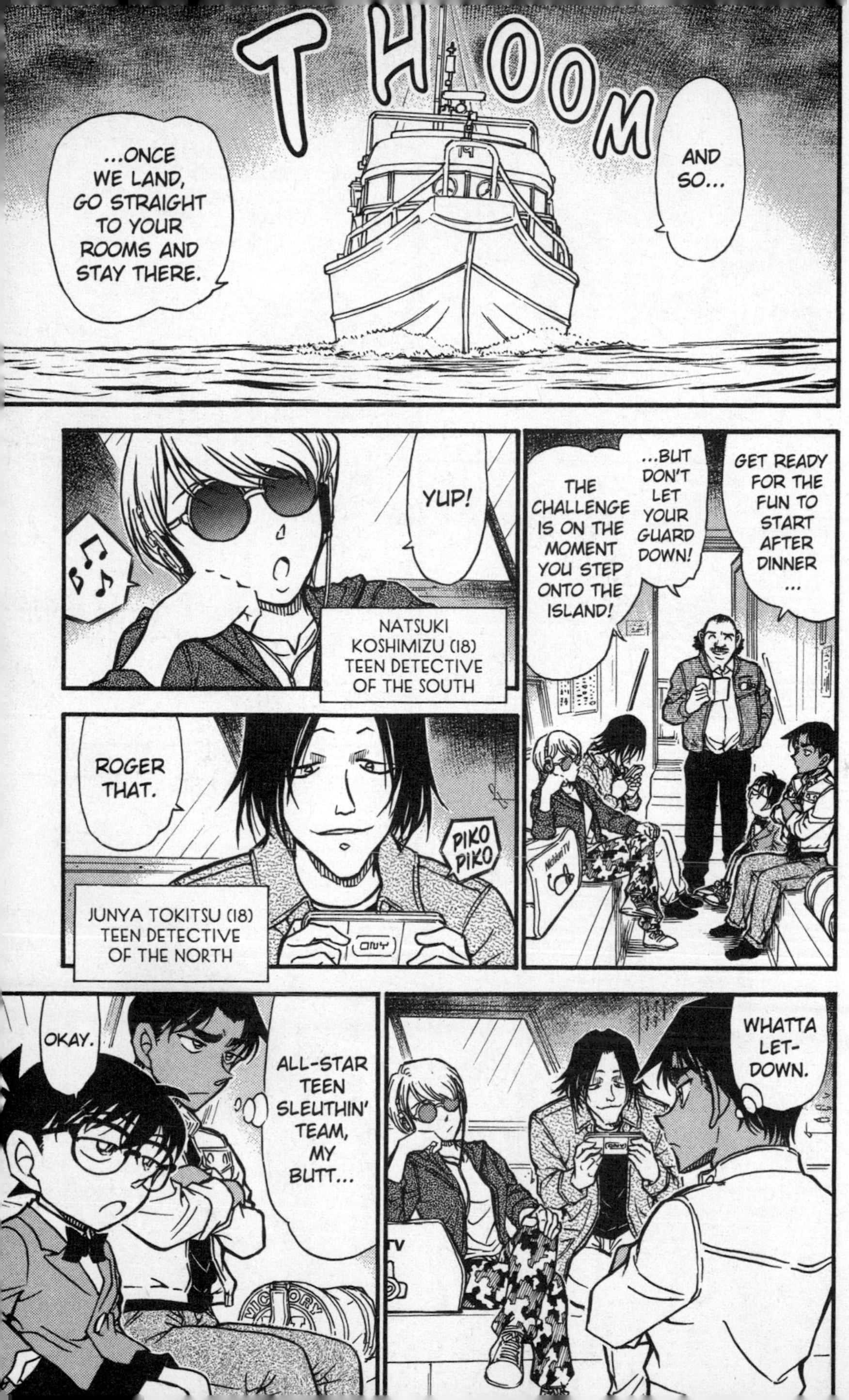
AND SO...
THOOM
...ONCE WE LAND, GO STRAIGHT TO YOUR ROOMS AND STAY THERE.
GET READY FOR THE FUN TO START AFTER DINNER ...
...BUT DON'T LET YOUR GUARD DOWN!
THE CHALLENGE IS ON THE MOMENT YOU STEP ONTO THE ISLAND!
YUP!
NATSUKI KOSHIMIZU (18) TEEN DETECTIVE OF THE SOUTH
PIKO PIKO
ROGER THAT.
JUNYA TOKITSU (18) TEEN DETECTIVE OF THE NORTH
WHATTA LET-DOWN.
ALL-STAR TEEN SLEUTHIN' TEAM, MY BUTT...
OKAY.

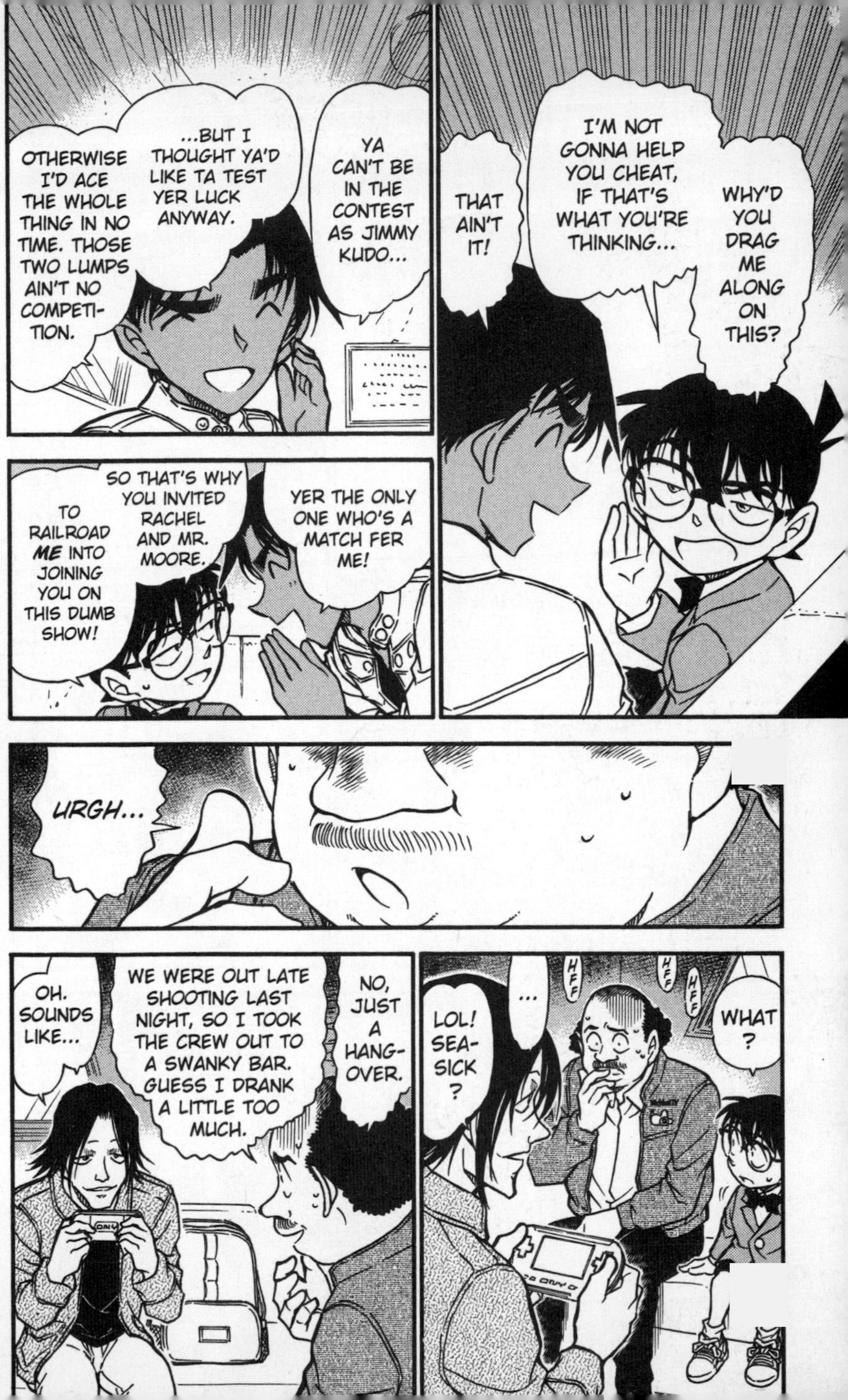
WHY'D YOU DRAG ME ALONG ON THIS?
I'M NOT GONNA HELP YOU CHEAT, IF THAT'S WHAT YOU'RE THINKING...
THAT AIN'T IT!
YA CAN'T BE IN THE CONTEST AS JIMMY KUDO...
...BUT I THOUGHT YA'D LIKE TA TEST YER LUCK ANYWAY.
OTHERWISE I'D ACE THE WHOLE THING IN NO TIME. THOSE TWO LUMPS AIN'T NO COMPETITION.
YER THE ONLY ONE WHO'S A MATCH FER ME!
SO THAT'S WHY YOU INVITED RACHEL AND MR. MOORE.
TO RAILROAD ME INTO JOINING YOU ON THIS DUMB SHOW!
URGH...
WHAT?
HFF
HFF
HFF
...
LOL! SEA-SICK?
NO, JUST A HANG-OVER.
WE WERE OUT LATE SHOOTING LAST NIGHT, SO I TOOK THE CREW OUT TO A SWANKY BAR. GUESS I DRANK A LITTLE TOO MUCH.
OH. SOUNDS LIKE...

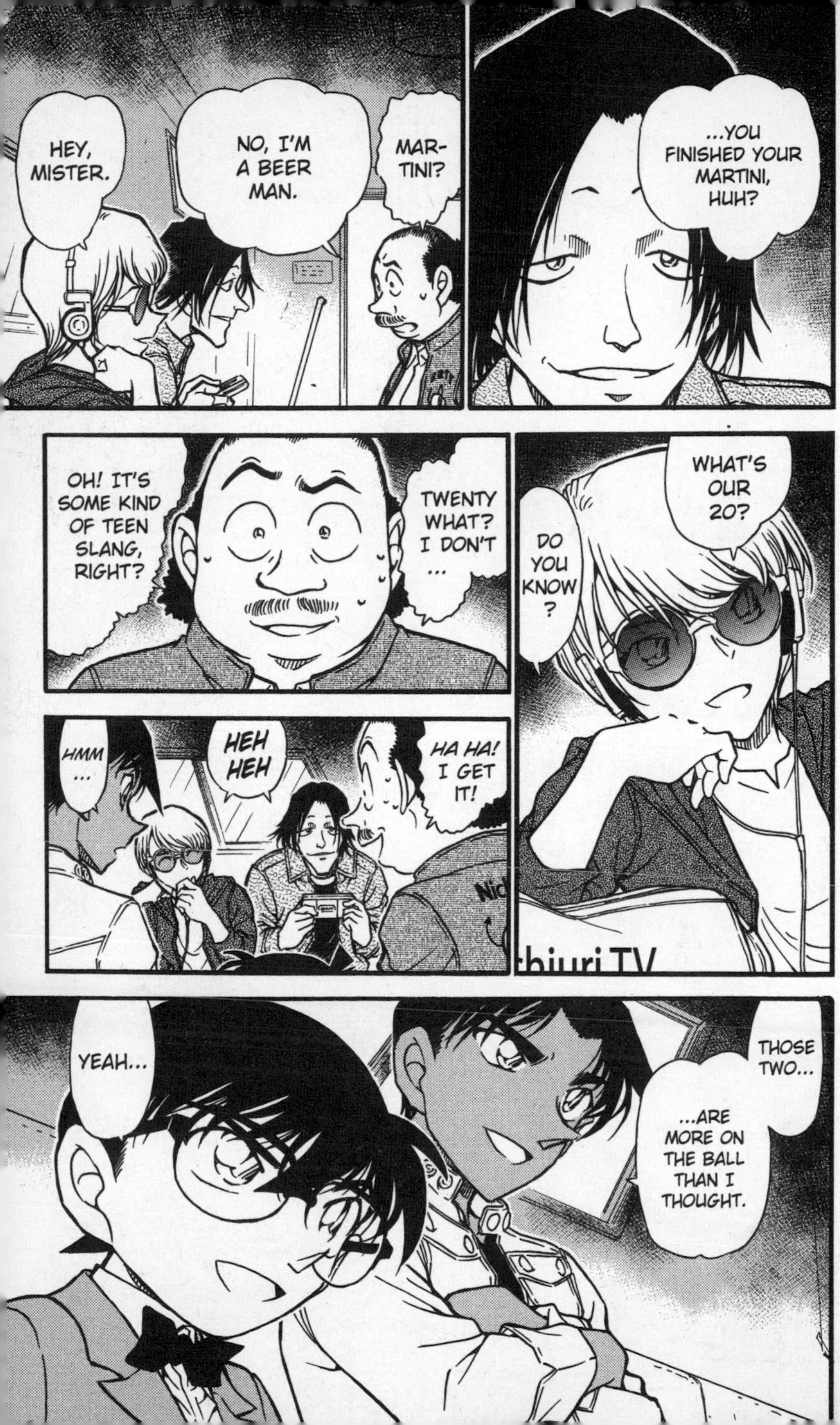
...YOU FINISHED YOUR MARTINI, HUH?
MAR-TINI?
NO, I'M A BEER MAN.
HEY, MISTER.
WHAT'S OUR 20?
DO YOU KNOW ?
TWENTY WHAT? I DON'T ...
OH! IT'S SOME KIND OF TEEN SLANG, RIGHT?
HA HA! I GET IT!
HEH HEH
HMM ...
THOSE TWO...
...ARE MORE ON THE BALL THAN I THOUGHT.
YEAH...

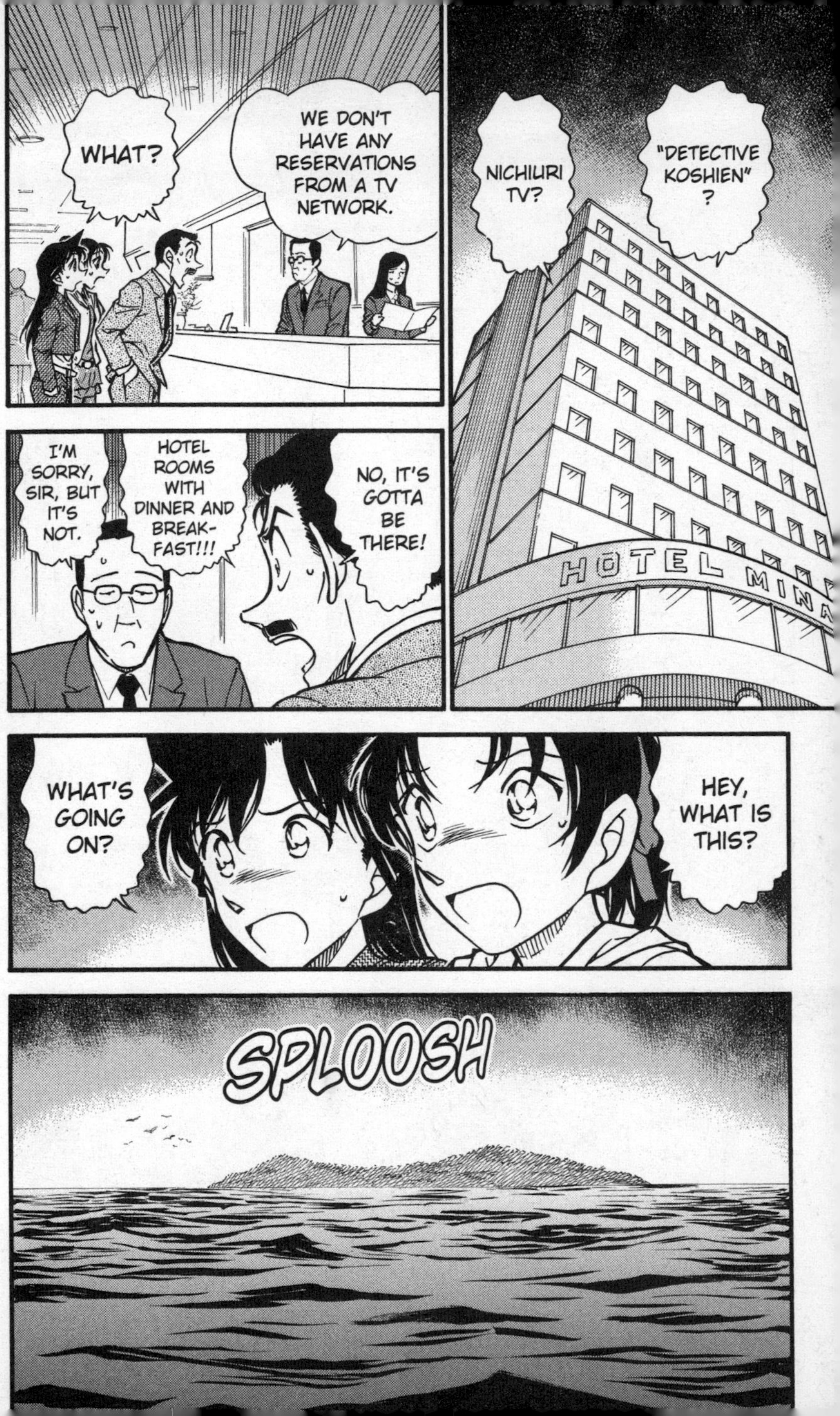
"DETECTIVE KOSHIEN"?
NICHIURI TV?
HOTEL MINA
WE DON'T HAVE ANY RESERVATIONS FROM A TV NETWORK.
WHAT?
NO, IT'S GOTTA BE THERE!
HOTEL ROOMS WITH DINNER AND BREAK-FAST!!!
I'M SORRY, SIR, BUT IT'S NOT.
HEY, WHAT IS THIS?
WHAT'S GOING ON?
SPLOOSH

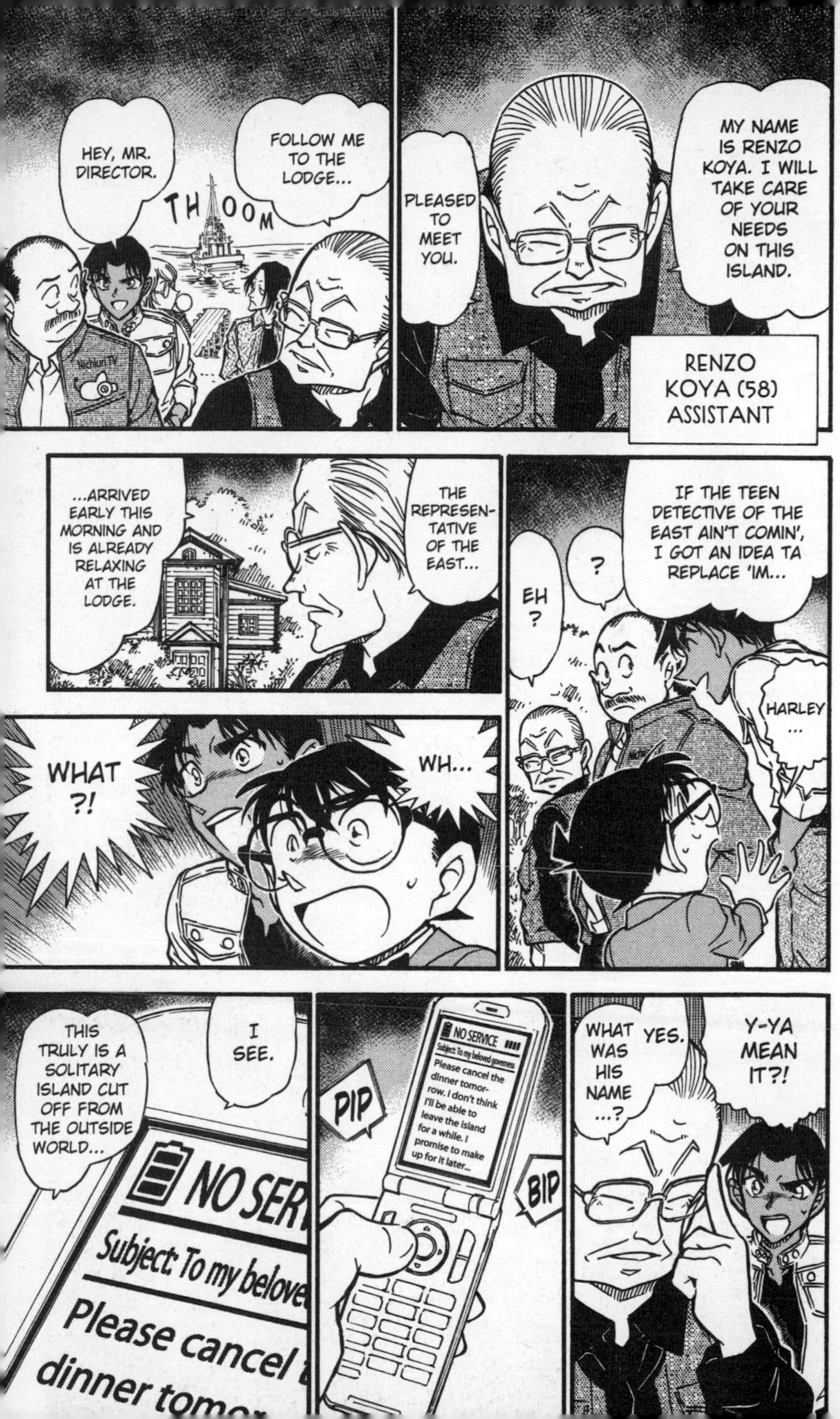

MY NAME IS RENZO KOYA. I WILL TAKE CARE OF YOUR NEEDS ON THIS ISLAND.
PLEASED TO MEET YOU.
RENZO KOYA (58) ASSISTANT
FOLLOW ME TO THE LODGE...
HEY, MR. DIRECTOR.
THOOM
IF THE TEEN DETECTIVE OF THE EAST AIN'T COMIN', I GOT AN IDEA TA REPLACE 'IM...
?
EH ?
HARLEY ...
THE REPRESENTATIVE OF THE EAST...
...ARRIVED EARLY THIS MORNING AND IS ALREADY RELAXING AT THE LODGE.
WH...
WHAT ?!
Y-YA MEAN IT?!
YES.
WHAT WAS HIS NAME ...?
BIP
NO SERVICE
Subject: To my beloved governes
Please cancel the dinner tomorrow. I don't think I'll be able to leave the island for a while. I promise to make up for it later...
PIP
I SEE.
THIS TRULY IS A SOLITARY ISLAND CUT OFF FROM THE OUTSIDE WORLD...
NO SER
Subject: To my belove
Please cancel
dinner tomo

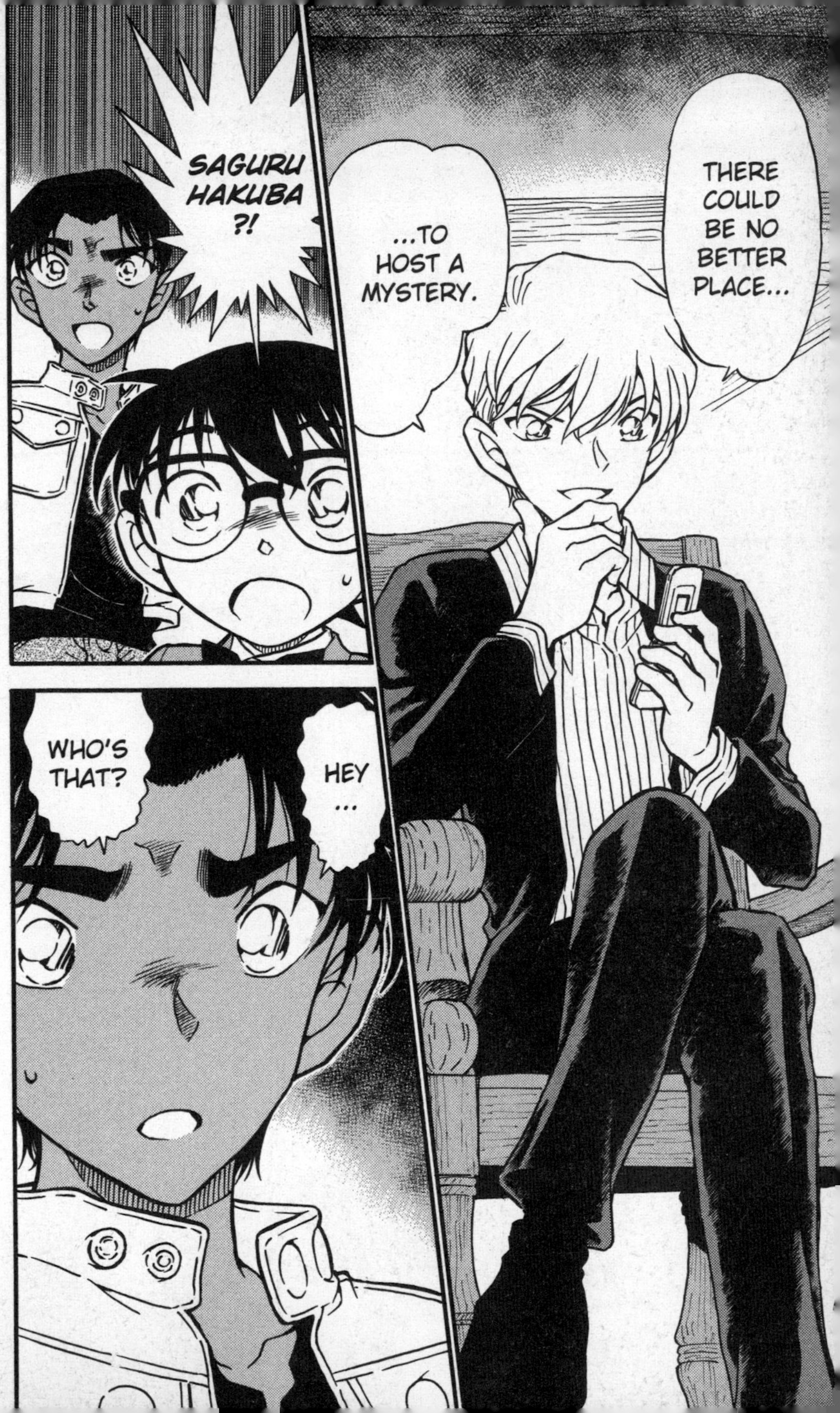
THERE COULD BE NO BETTER PLACE...
...TO HOST A MYSTERY.
SAGURU HAKUBA ?!
HEY ...
WHO'S THAT?

FILE 10: DETECTIVE KOSHIEN

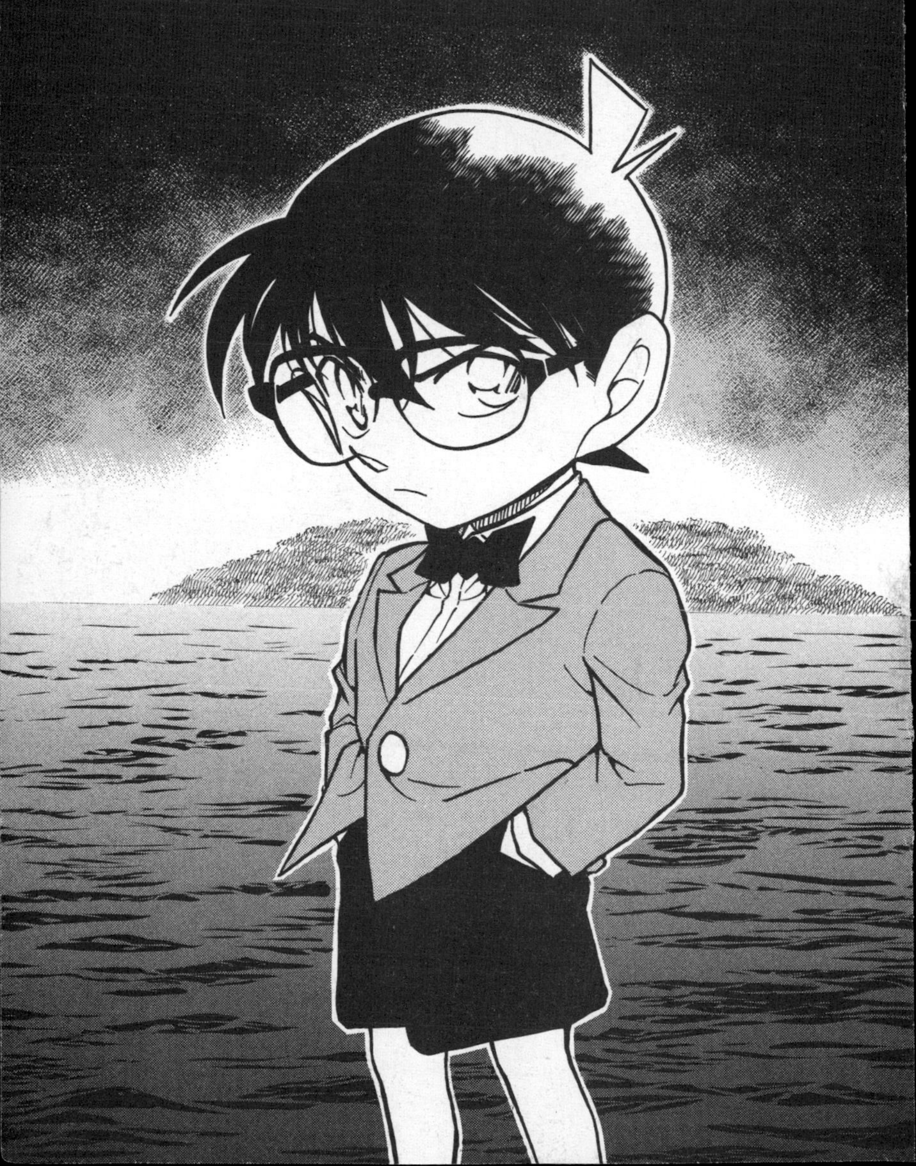

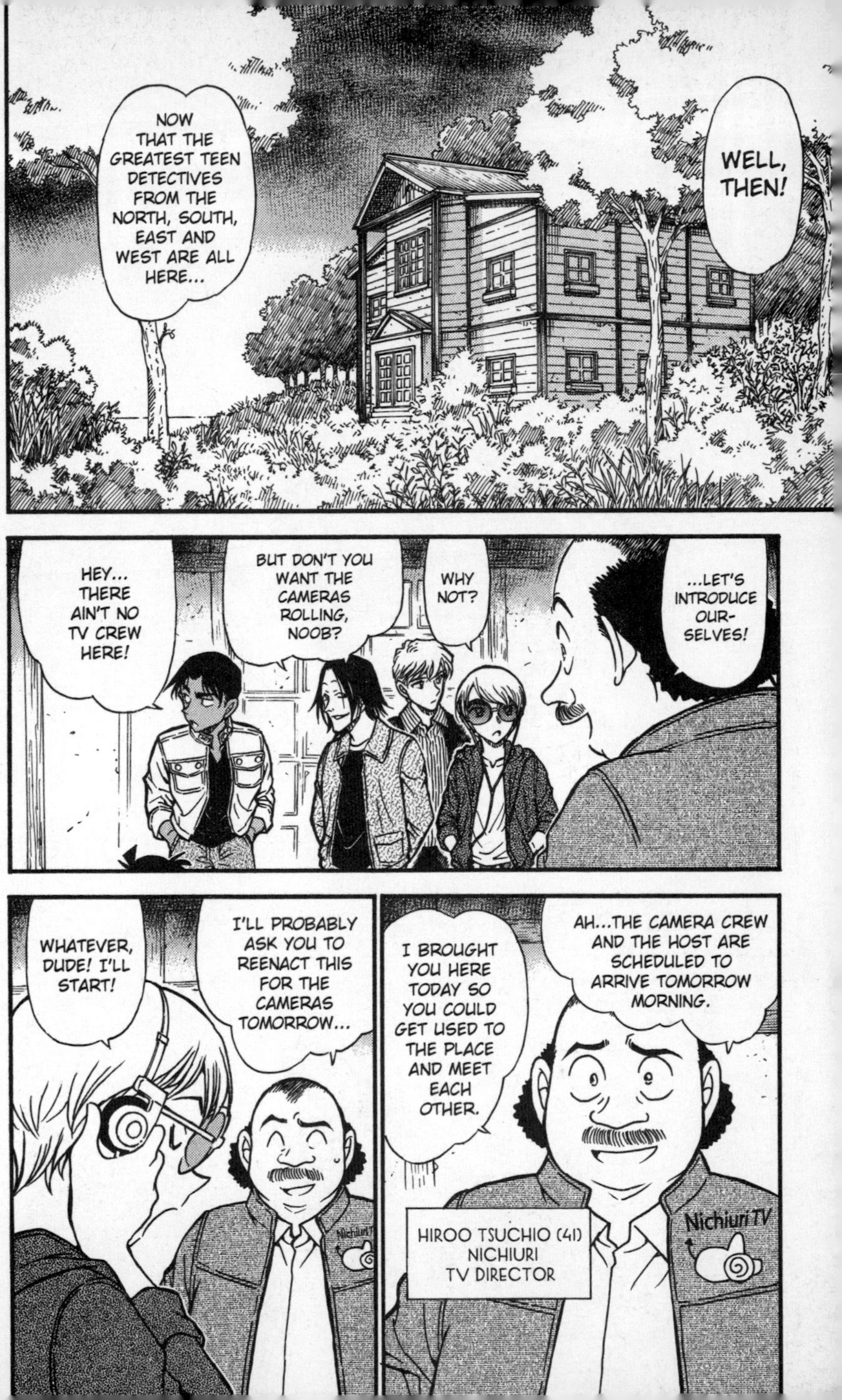
WELL, THEN!
NOW THAT THE GREATEST TEEN DETECTIVES FROM THE NORTH, SOUTH, EAST AND WEST ARE ALL HERE...
...LET'S INTRODUCE OURSELVES!
WHY NOT?
BUT DON'T YOU WANT THE CAMERAS ROLLING, NOOB?
HEY... THERE AIN'T NO TV CREW HERE!
AH...THE CAMERA CREW AND THE HOST ARE SCHEDULED TO ARRIVE TOMORROW MORNING.
I BROUGHT YOU HERE TODAY SO YOU COULD GET USED TO THE PLACE AND MEET EACH OTHER.
Nichiuri TV
HIROO TSUCHIO (41) NICHIURI TV DIRECTOR
I'LL PROBABLY ASK YOU TO REENACT THIS FOR THE CAMERAS TOMORROW...
WHATEVER, DUDE! I'LL START!

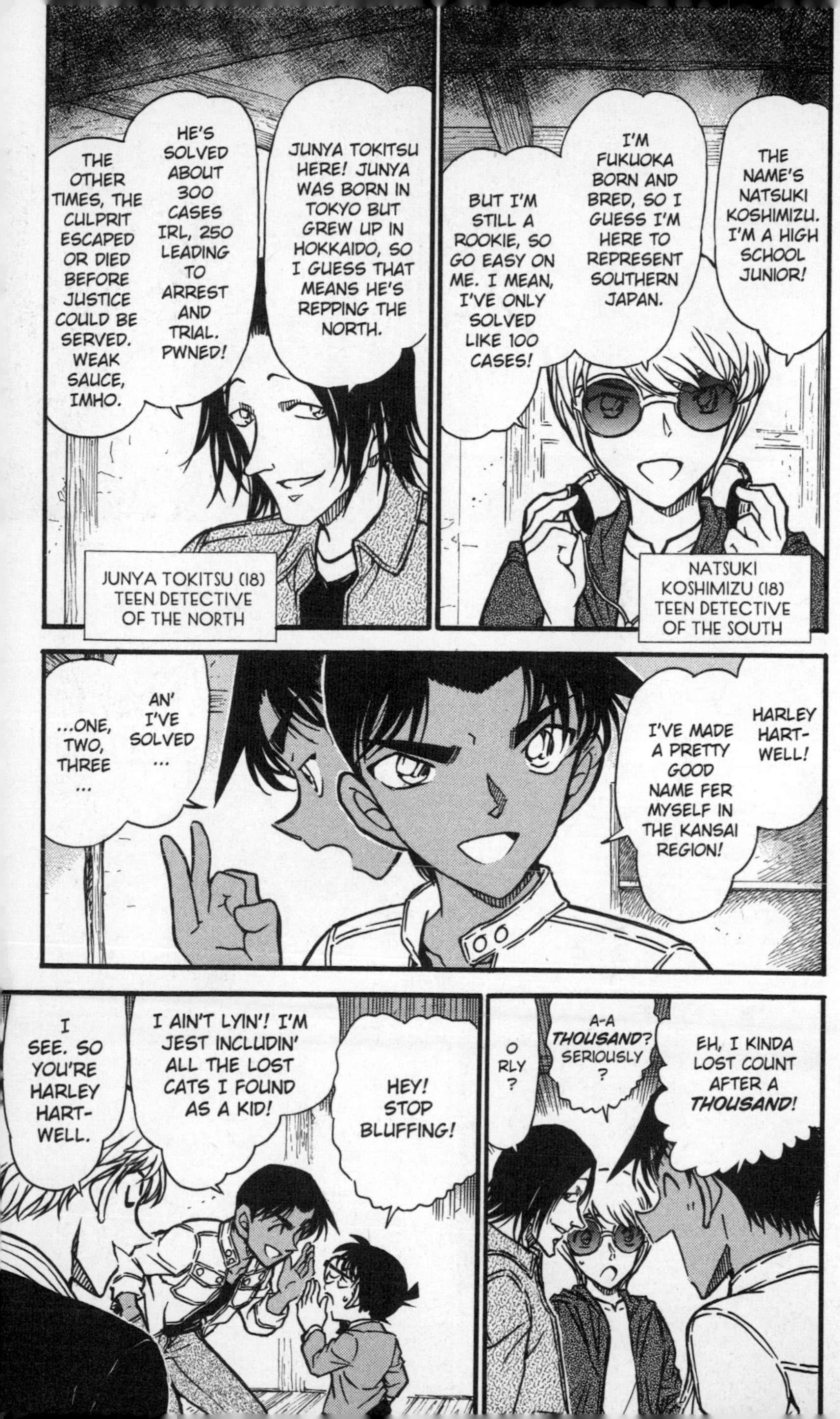
THE NAME'S NATSUKI KOSHIMIZU. I'M A HIGH SCHOOL JUNIOR!
I'M FUKUOKA BORN AND BRED, SO I GUESS I'M HERE TO REPRESENT SOUTHERN JAPAN.
BUT I'M STILL A ROOKIE, SO GO EASY ON ME. I MEAN, I'VE ONLY SOLVED LIKE 100 CASES!
NATSUKI KOSHIMIZU (18) TEEN DETECTIVE OF THE SOUTH
JUNYA TOKITSU HERE! JUNYA WAS BORN IN TOKYO BUT GREW UP IN HOKKAIDO, SO I GUESS THAT MEANS HE'S REPPING THE NORTH.
HE'S SOLVED ABOUT 300 CASES IRL, 250 LEADING TO ARREST AND TRIAL. PWNED!
THE OTHER TIMES, THE CULPRIT ESCAPED OR DIED BEFORE JUSTICE COULD BE SERVED. WEAK SAUCE, IMHO.
JUNYA TOKITSU (18) TEEN DETECTIVE OF THE NORTH
HARLEY HARTWELL!
I'VE MADE A PRETTY GOOD NAME FER MYSELF IN THE KANSAI REGION!
AN' I'VE SOLVED ...
...ONE, TWO, THREE ...
EH, I KINDA LOST COUNT AFTER A *THOUSAND*!
A-A *THOUSAND*? SERIOUSLY?
O RLY?
HEY! STOP BLUFFING!
I AIN'T LYIN'! I'M JEST INCLUDIN' ALL THE LOST CATS I FOUND AS A KID!
I SEE. SO YOU'RE HARLEY HARTWELL.

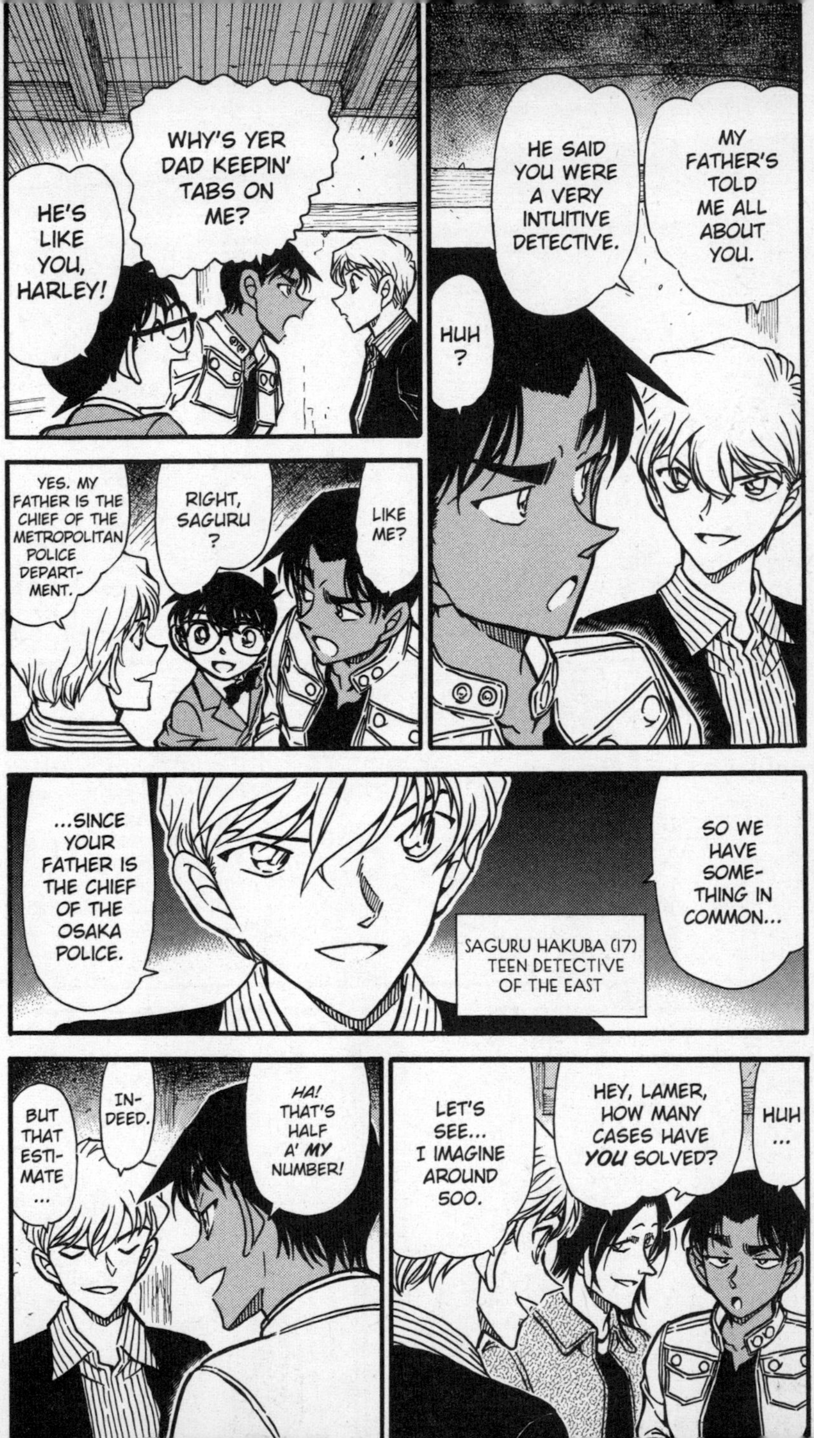
MY FATHER'S TOLD ME ALL ABOUT YOU.
HE SAID YOU WERE A VERY INTUITIVE DETECTIVE.
HUH?
WHY'S YER DAD KEEPIN' TABS ON ME?
HE'S LIKE YOU, HARLEY!
LIKE ME?
RIGHT, SAGURU?
YES. MY FATHER IS THE CHIEF OF THE METROPOLITAN POLICE DEPARTMENT.
SO WE HAVE SOMETHING IN COMMON...
SAGURU HAKUBA (17) TEEN DETECTIVE OF THE EAST
...SINCE YOUR FATHER IS THE CHIEF OF THE OSAKA POLICE.
HUH...
HEY, LAMER, HOW MANY CASES HAVE *YOU* SOLVED?
LET'S SEE... I IMAGINE AROUND 500.
HA! THAT'S HALF A' *MY* NUMBER!
INDEED.
BUT THAT ESTIMATE...

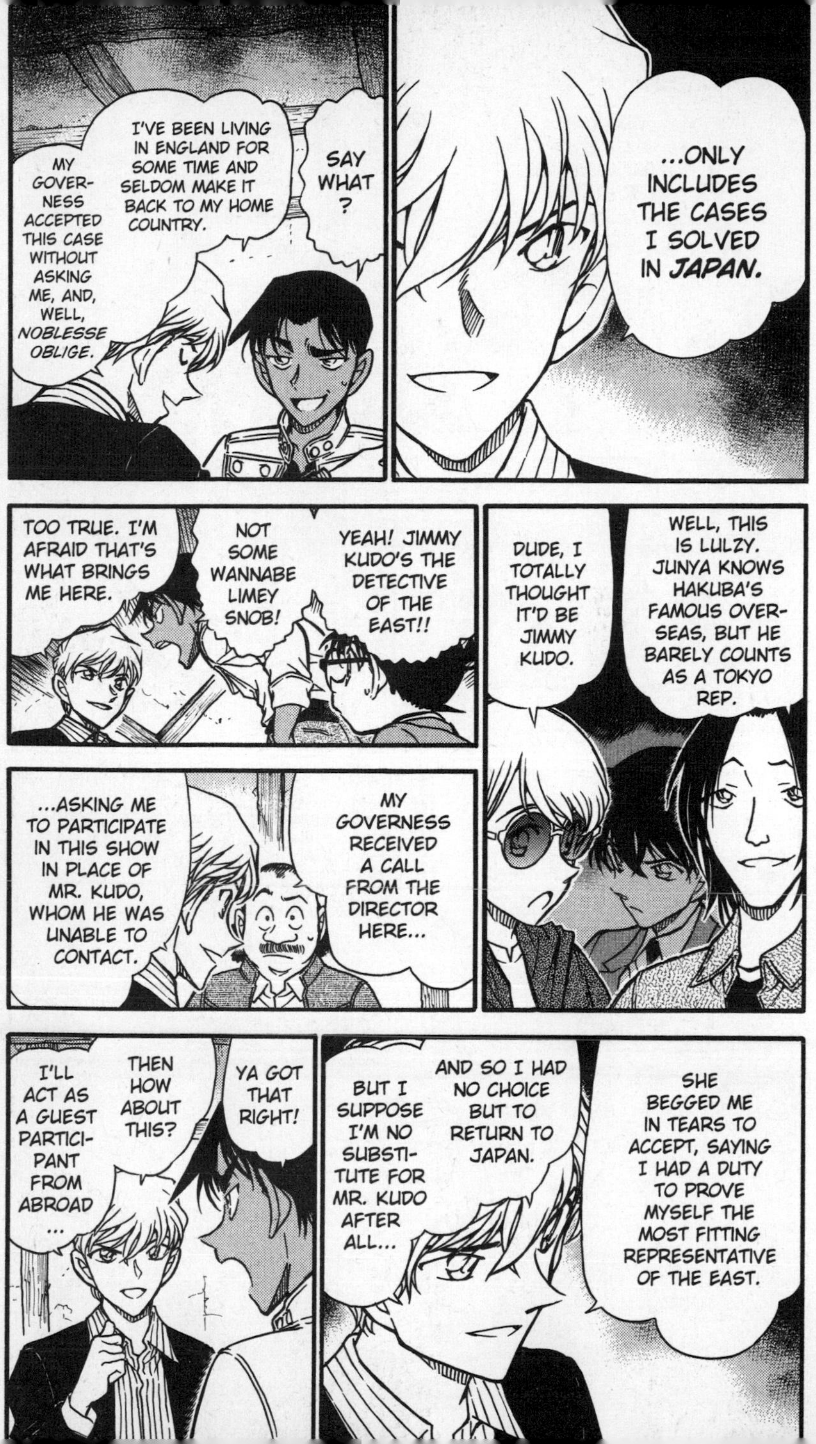

...ONLY INCLUDES THE CASES I SOLVED IN *JAPAN.*
SAY WHAT?
I'VE BEEN LIVING IN ENGLAND FOR SOME TIME AND SELDOM MAKE IT BACK TO MY HOME COUNTRY.
MY GOVERNESS ACCEPTED THIS CASE WITHOUT ASKING ME, AND, WELL, *NOBLESSE OBLIGE.*
WELL, THIS IS LULZY. JUNYA KNOWS HAKUBA'S FAMOUS OVERSEAS, BUT HE BARELY COUNTS AS A TOKYO REP.
DUDE, I TOTALLY THOUGHT IT'D BE JIMMY KUDO.
YEAH! JIMMY KUDO'S THE DETECTIVE OF THE EAST!!
NOT SOME WANNABE LIMEY SNOB!
TOO TRUE. I'M AFRAID THAT'S WHAT BRINGS ME HERE.
MY GOVERNESS RECEIVED A CALL FROM THE DIRECTOR HERE...
...ASKING ME TO PARTICIPATE IN THIS SHOW IN PLACE OF MR. KUDO, WHOM HE WAS UNABLE TO CONTACT.
SHE BEGGED ME IN TEARS TO ACCEPT, SAYING I HAD A DUTY TO PROVE MYSELF THE MOST FITTING REPRESENTATIVE OF THE EAST.
AND SO I HAD NO CHOICE BUT TO RETURN TO JAPAN.
BUT I SUPPOSE I'M NO SUBSTITUTE FOR MR. KUDO AFTER ALL...
YA GOT THAT RIGHT!
THEN HOW ABOUT THIS?
I'LL ACT AS A GUEST PARTICIPANT FROM ABROAD...

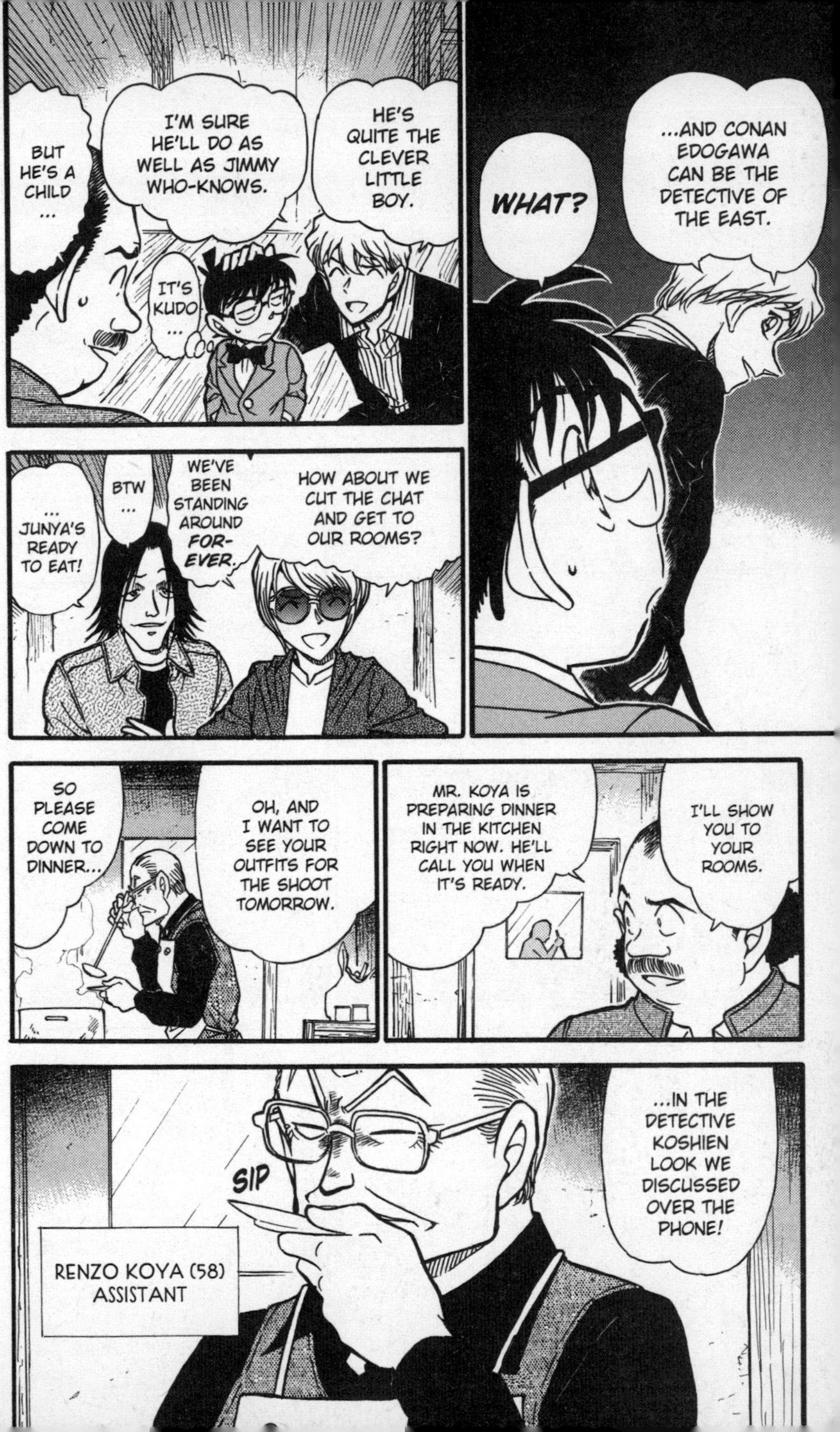
...AND CONAN EDOGAWA CAN BE THE DETECTIVE OF THE EAST.
WHAT?
HE'S QUITE THE CLEVER LITTLE BOY.
I'M SURE HE'LL DO AS WELL AS JIMMY WHO-KNOWS.
BUT HE'S A CHILD ...
IT'S KUDO ...
HOW ABOUT WE CUT THE CHAT AND GET TO OUR ROOMS?
WE'VE BEEN STANDING AROUND FOREVER.
BTW ...
... JUNYA'S READY TO EAT!
I'LL SHOW YOU TO YOUR ROOMS.
MR. KOYA IS PREPARING DINNER IN THE KITCHEN RIGHT NOW. HE'LL CALL YOU WHEN IT'S READY.
OH, AND I WANT TO SEE YOUR OUTFITS FOR THE SHOOT TOMORROW.
SO PLEASE COME DOWN TO DINNER...
...IN THE DETECTIVE KOSHIEN LOOK WE DISCUSSED OVER THE PHONE!
SIP
RENZO KOYA (58) ASSISTANT

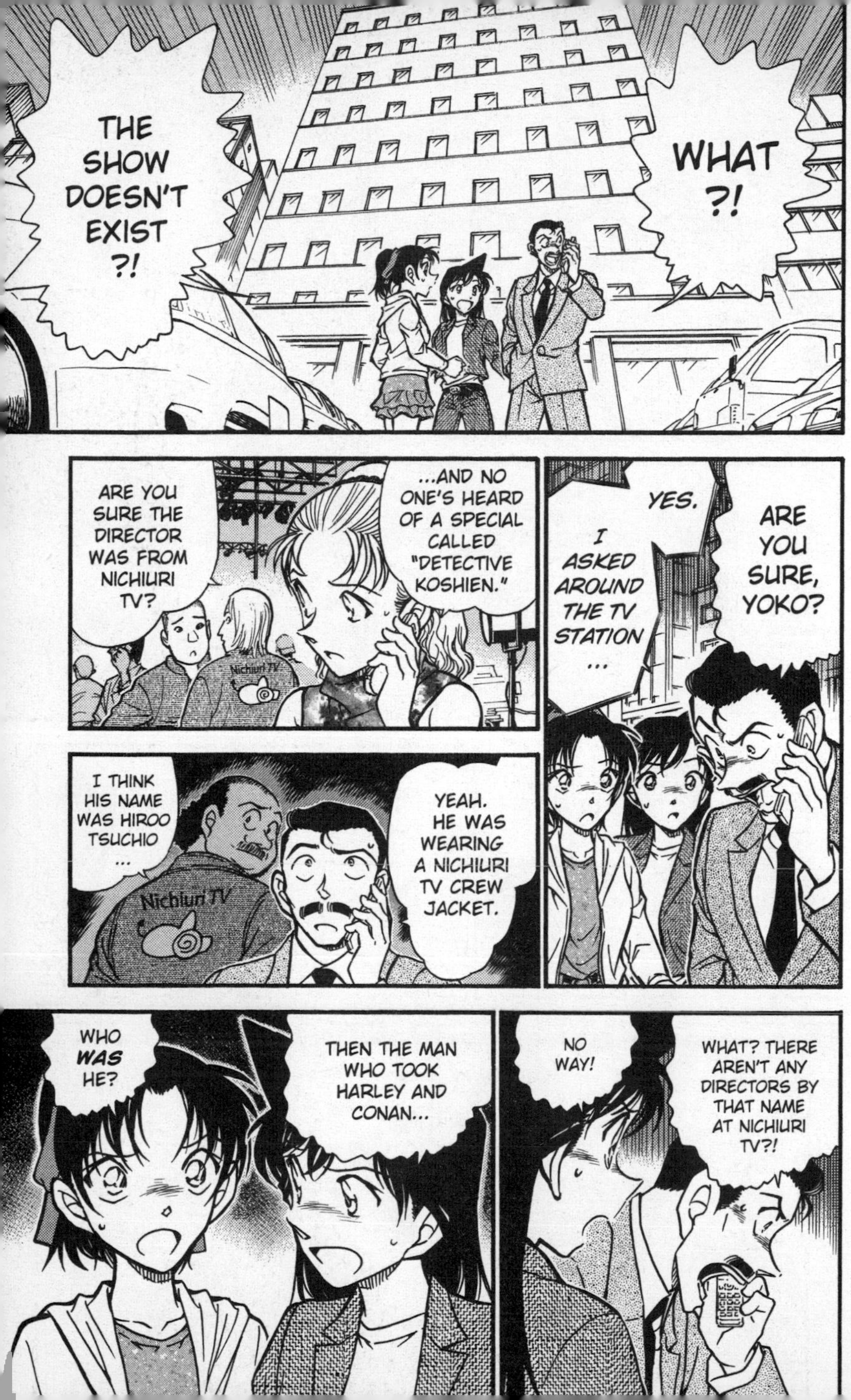
WHAT ?!
THE SHOW DOESN'T EXIST ?!
ARE YOU SURE, YOKO?
YES.
I ASKED AROUND THE TV STATION ...
...AND NO ONE'S HEARD OF A SPECIAL CALLED "DETECTIVE KOSHIEN."
ARE YOU SURE THE DIRECTOR WAS FROM NICHIURI TV?
Nichiuri TV
YEAH. HE WAS WEARING A NICHIURI TV CREW JACKET.
I THINK HIS NAME WAS HIROO TSUCHIO ...
Nichiuri TV
WHAT? THERE AREN'T ANY DIRECTORS BY THAT NAME AT NICHIURI TV?!
NO WAY!
THEN THE MAN WHO TOOK HARLEY AND CONAN...
WHO ***WAS*** HE?

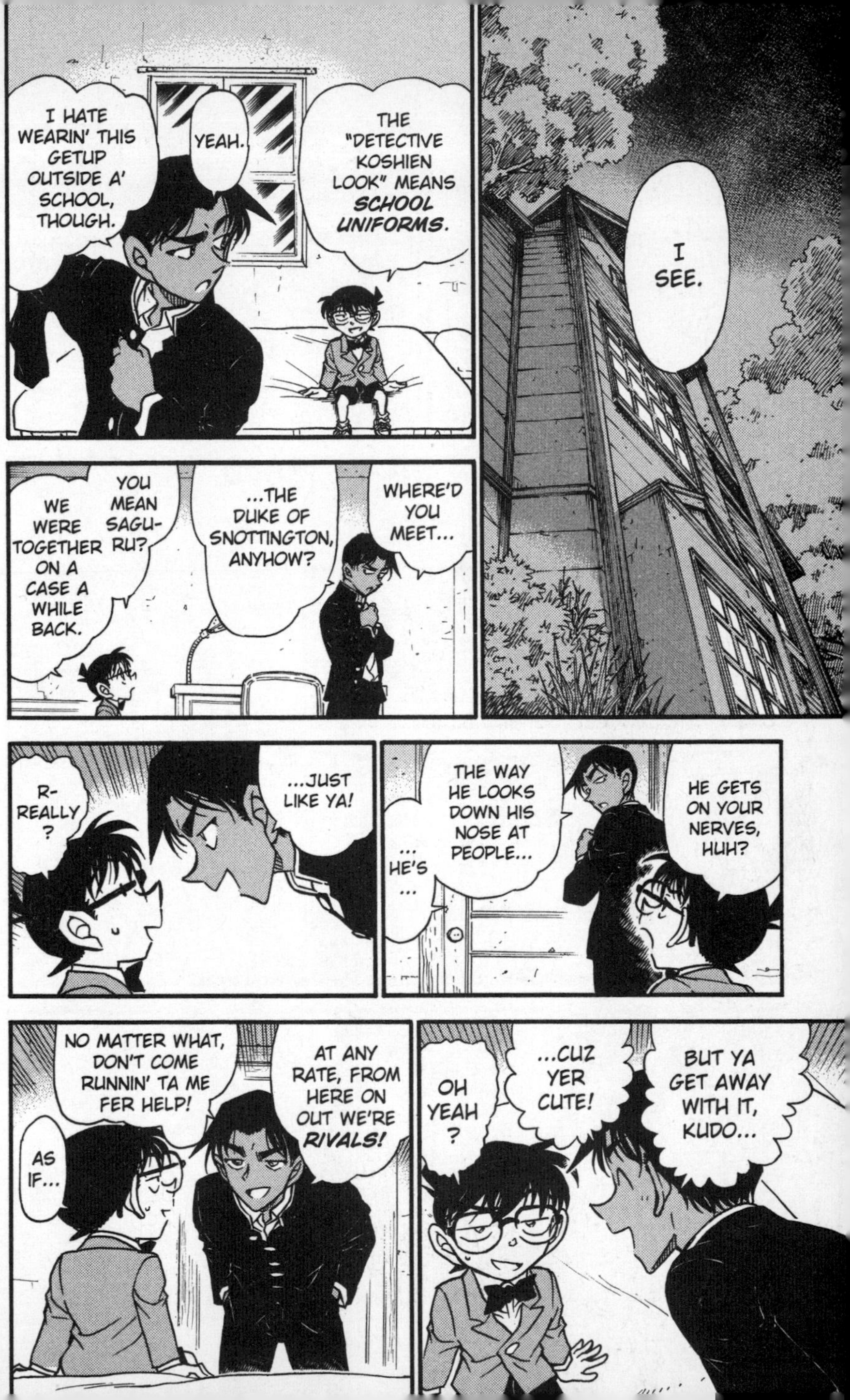
I SEE.
THE "DETECTIVE KOSHIEN LOOK" MEANS *SCHOOL UNIFORMS*.
YEAH.
I HATE WEARIN' THIS GETUP OUTSIDE A' SCHOOL, THOUGH.
WHERE'D YOU MEET...
...THE DUKE OF SNOTTINGTON, ANYHOW?
YOU MEAN SAGU-RU?
WE WERE TOGETHER ON A CASE A WHILE BACK.
HE GETS ON YOUR NERVES, HUH?
THE WAY HE LOOKS DOWN HIS NOSE AT PEOPLE...
... HE'S ...
...JUST LIKE YA!
R-REALLY?
BUT YA GET AWAY WITH IT, KUDO...
...CUZ YER CUTE!
OH YEAH?
AT ANY RATE, FROM HERE ON OUT WE'RE *RIVALS!*
NO MATTER WHAT, DON'T COME RUNNIN' TA ME FER HELP!
AS IF...

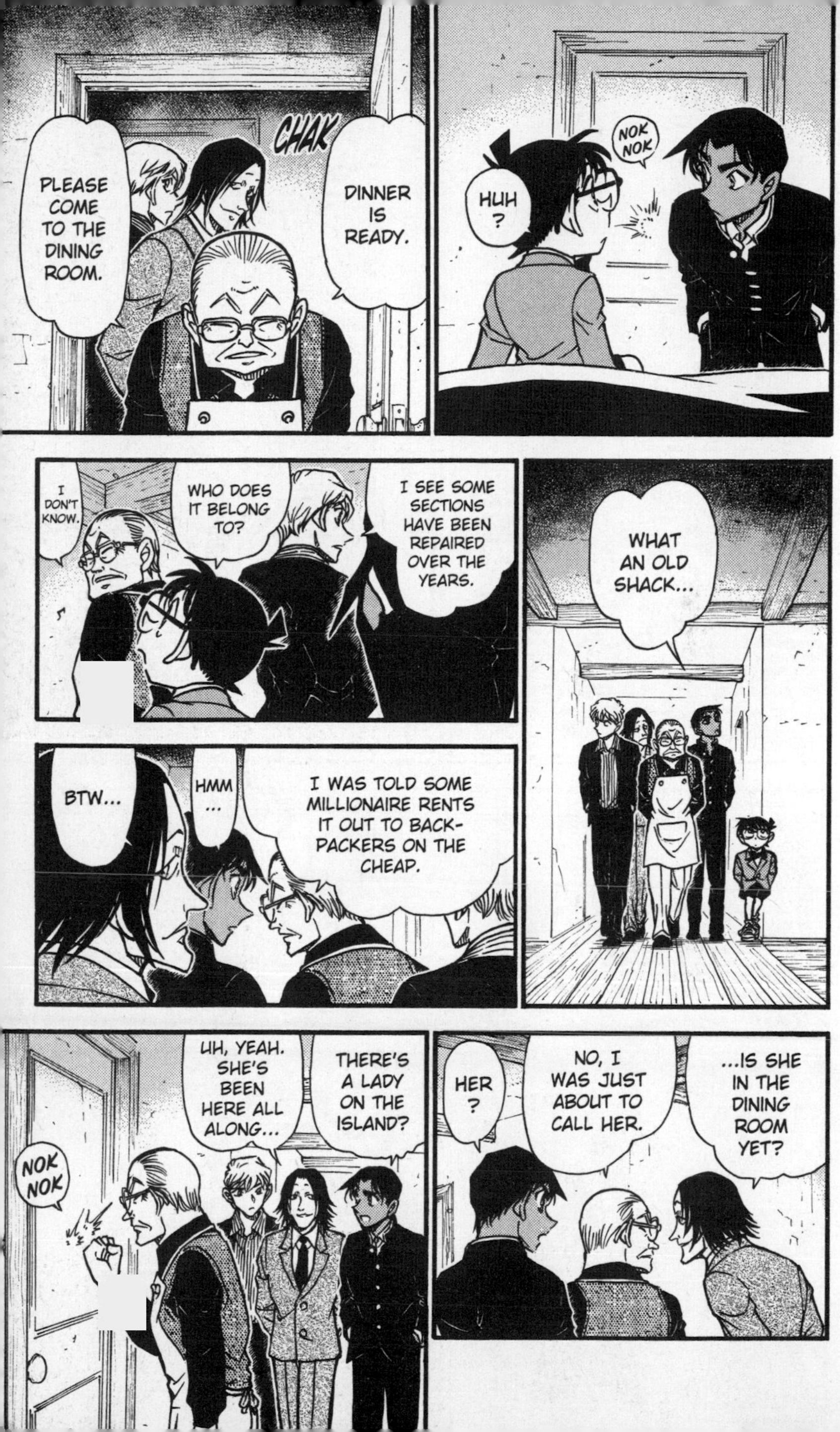
NOK NOK
HUH ?
CHAK
DINNER IS READY.
PLEASE COME TO THE DINING ROOM.
WHAT AN OLD SHACK...
I SEE SOME SECTIONS HAVE BEEN REPAIRED OVER THE YEARS.
WHO DOES IT BELONG TO?
I DON'T KNOW.
I WAS TOLD SOME MILLIONAIRE RENTS IT OUT TO BACK-PACKERS ON THE CHEAP.
HMM ...
BTW...
...IS SHE IN THE DINING ROOM YET?
NO, I WAS JUST ABOUT TO CALL HER.
HER ?
THERE'S A LADY ON THE ISLAND?
UH, YEAH. SHE'S BEEN HERE ALL ALONG...
NOK NOK

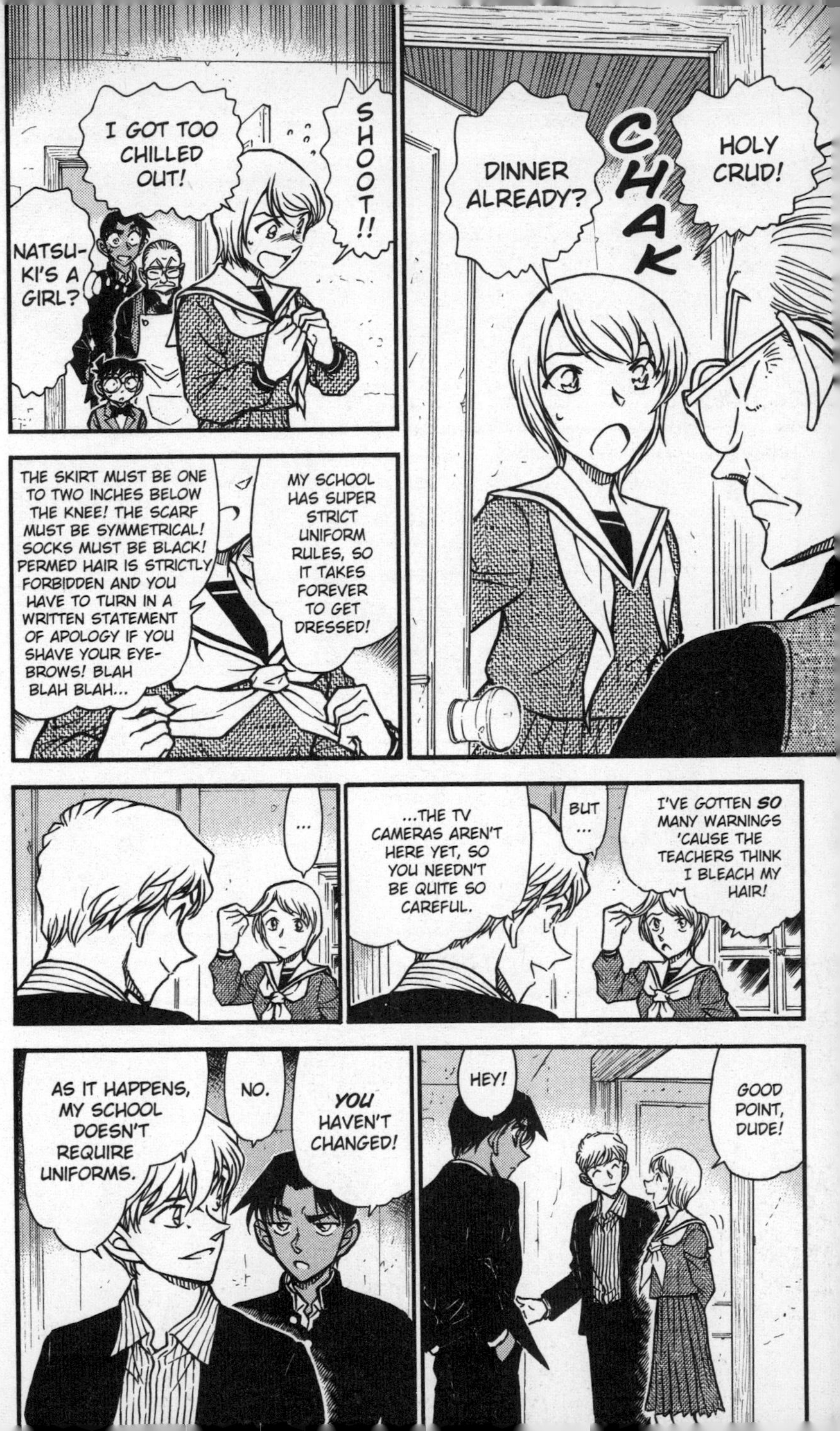
HOLY CRUD!
CHAK
DINNER ALREADY?
SHOOOT!!
I GOT TOO CHILLED OUT!
NATSU-KI'S A GIRL?
MY SCHOOL HAS SUPER STRICT UNIFORM RULES, SO IT TAKES FOREVER TO GET DRESSED!
THE SKIRT MUST BE ONE TO TWO INCHES BELOW THE KNEE! THE SCARF MUST BE SYMMETRICAL! SOCKS MUST BE BLACK! PERMED HAIR IS STRICTLY FORBIDDEN AND YOU HAVE TO TURN IN A WRITTEN STATEMENT OF APOLOGY IF YOU SHAVE YOUR EYE-BROWS! BLAH BLAH BLAH...
I'VE GOTTEN *SO* MANY WARNINGS 'CAUSE THE TEACHERS THINK I BLEACH MY HAIR!
BUT...
...THE TV CAMERAS AREN'T HERE YET, SO YOU NEEDN'T BE QUITE SO CAREFUL.
...
GOOD POINT, DUDE!
HEY!
YOU HAVEN'T CHANGED!
NO.
AS IT HAPPENS, MY SCHOOL DOESN'T REQUIRE UNIFORMS.

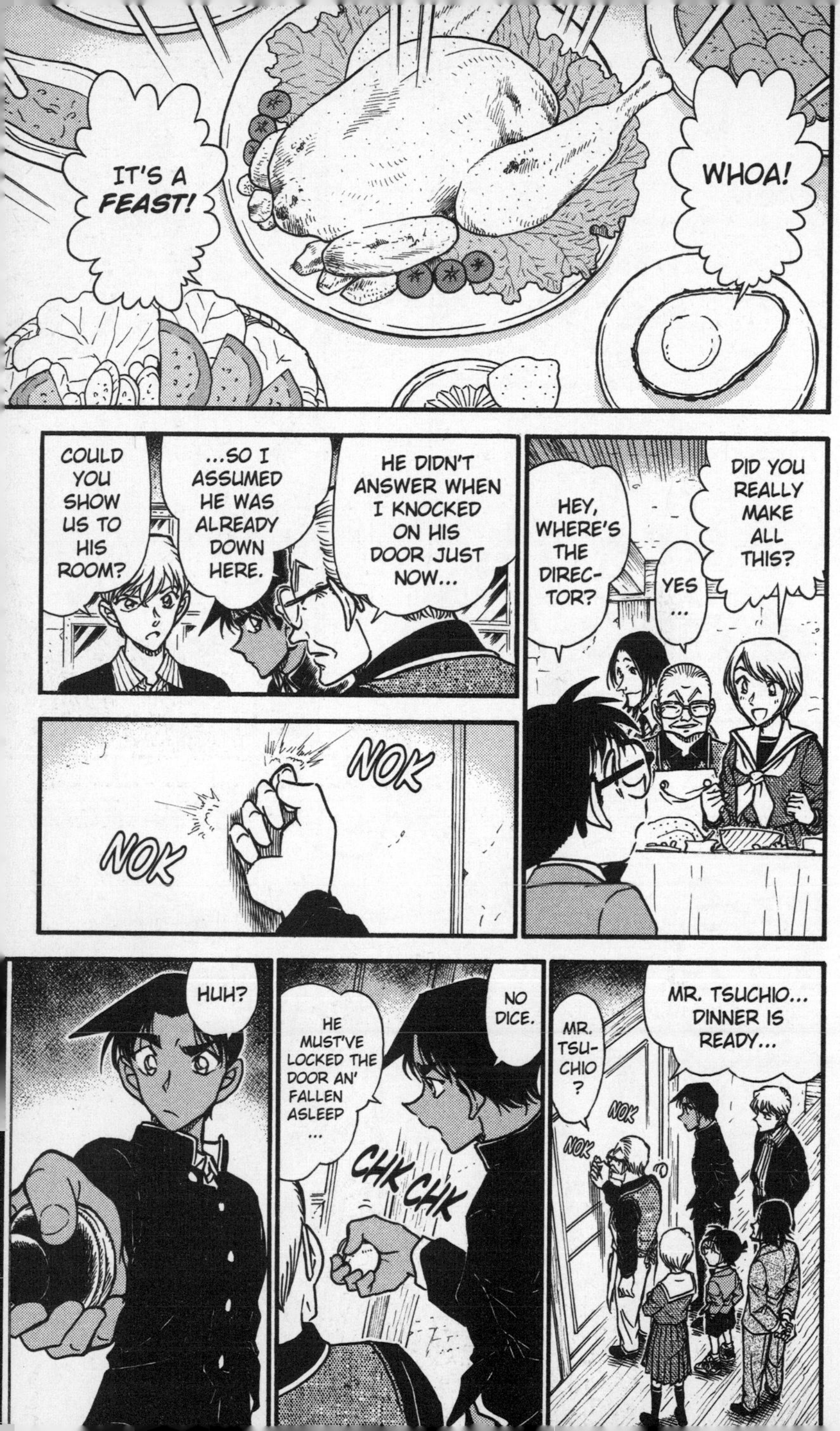
WHOA!
IT'S A FEAST!
DID YOU REALLY MAKE ALL THIS?
YES...
HEY, WHERE'S THE DIRECTOR?
HE DIDN'T ANSWER WHEN I KNOCKED ON HIS DOOR JUST NOW...
...SO I ASSUMED HE WAS ALREADY DOWN HERE.
COULD YOU SHOW US TO HIS ROOM?
NOK
NOK
MR. TSUCHIO... DINNER IS READY...
MR. TSUCHIO?
NOK
NOK
NO DICE.
HE MUST'VE LOCKED THE DOOR AN' FALLEN ASLEEP...
CHK CHK
HUH?

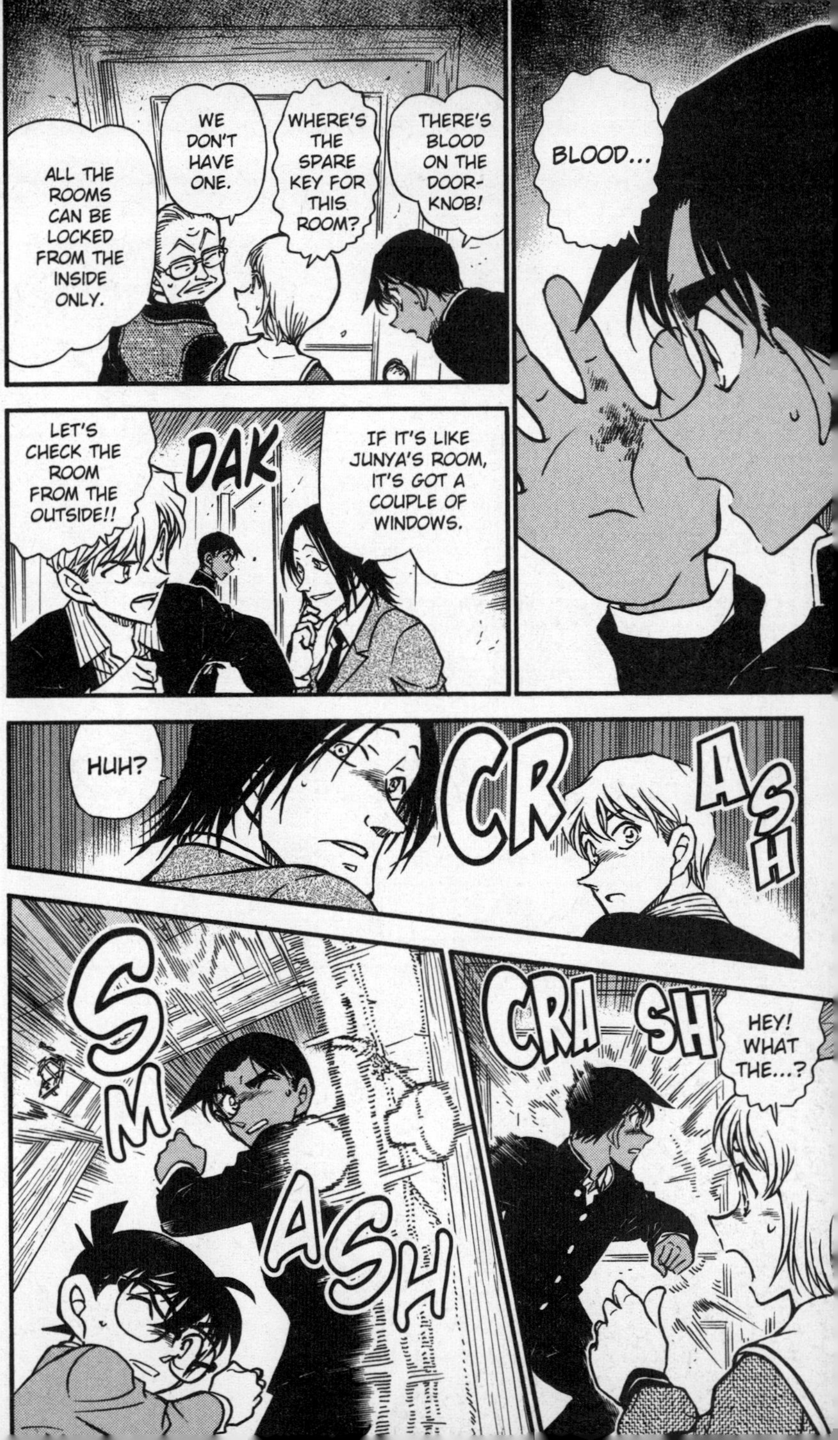
BLOOD...
THERE'S BLOOD ON THE DOOR-KNOB!
WHERE'S THE SPARE KEY FOR THIS ROOM?
WE DON'T HAVE ONE.
ALL THE ROOMS CAN BE LOCKED FROM THE INSIDE ONLY.
IF IT'S LIKE JUNYA'S ROOM, IT'S GOT A COUPLE OF WINDOWS.
DAK
LET'S CHECK THE ROOM FROM THE OUTSIDE!!
CRASH
HUH?
CRASH
HEY! WHAT THE...?
SMASH

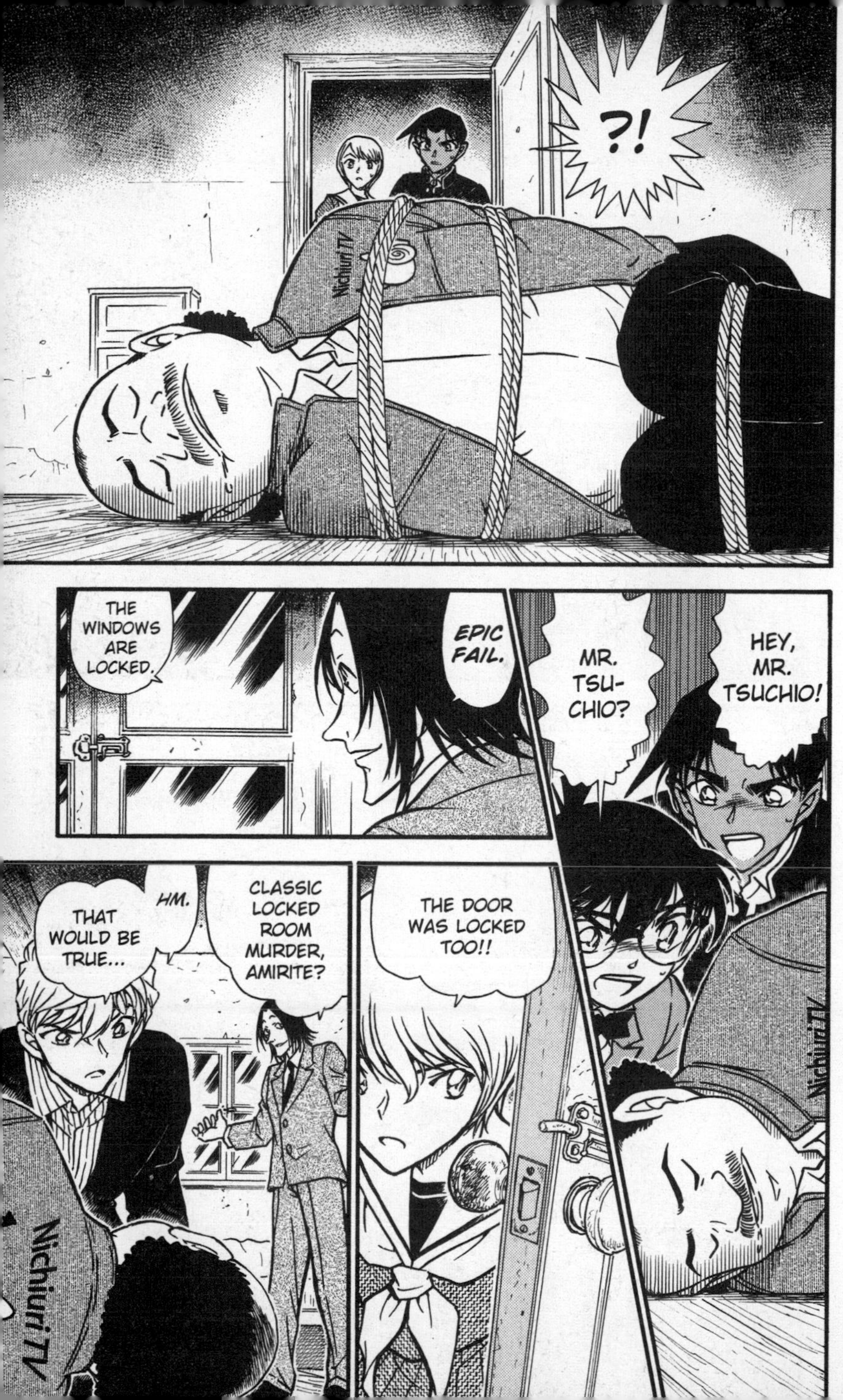
?!
Nichiuri TV
HEY, MR. TSUCHIO!
MR. TSUCHIO?
EPIC FAIL.
THE WINDOWS ARE LOCKED.
THE DOOR WAS LOCKED TOO!!
CLASSIC LOCKED ROOM MURDER, AMIRITE?
HM.
THAT WOULD BE TRUE...

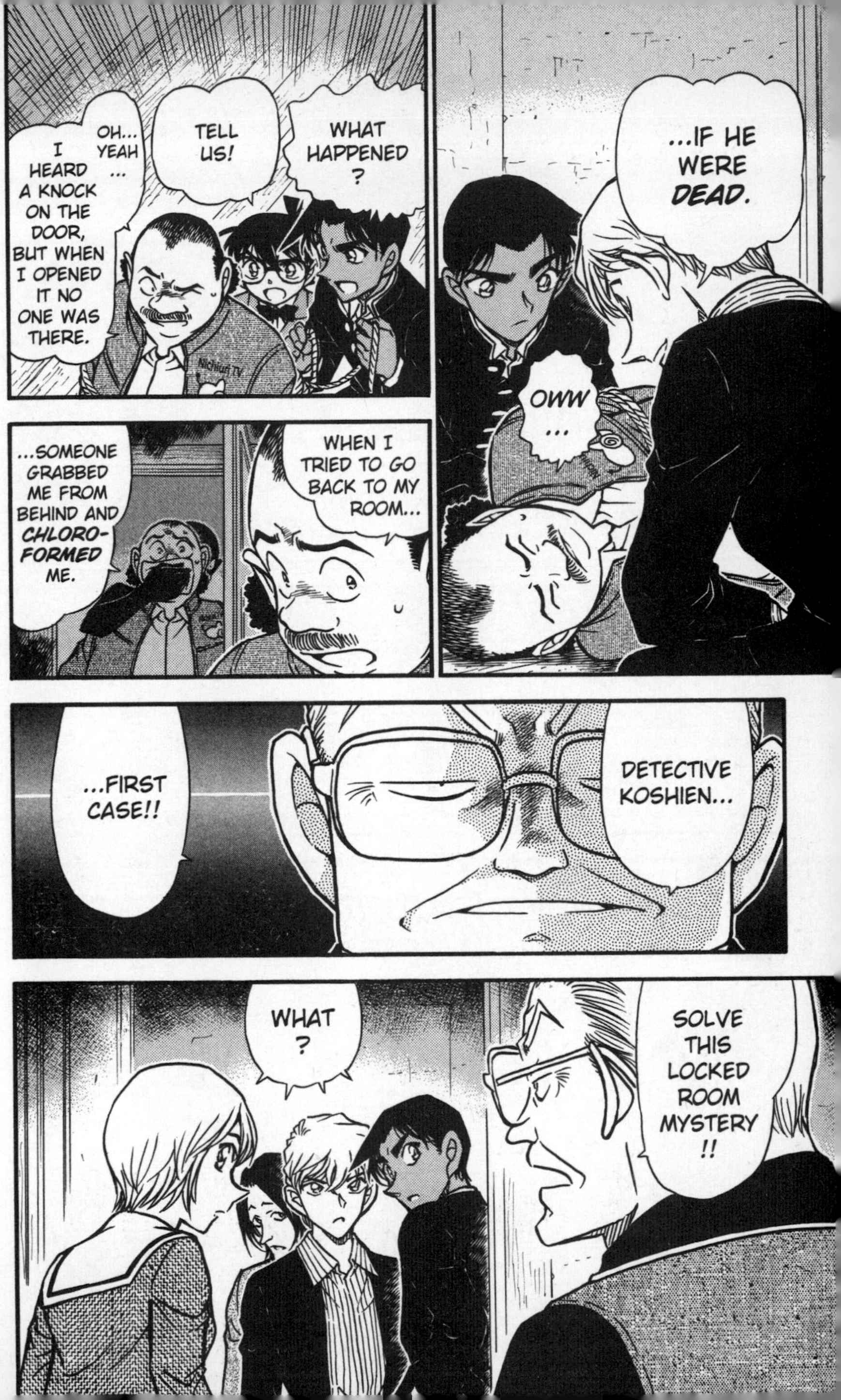
...IF HE WERE DEAD.
OWW...
WHAT HAPPENED?
TELL US!
OH... YEAH...
I HEARD A KNOCK ON THE DOOR, BUT WHEN I OPENED IT NO ONE WAS THERE.
Nichiuri TV
WHEN I TRIED TO GO BACK TO MY ROOM...
...SOMEONE GRABBED ME FROM BEHIND AND CHLOROFORMED ME.
DETECTIVE KOSHIEN...
...FIRST CASE!!
SOLVE THIS LOCKED ROOM MYSTERY!!
WHAT?

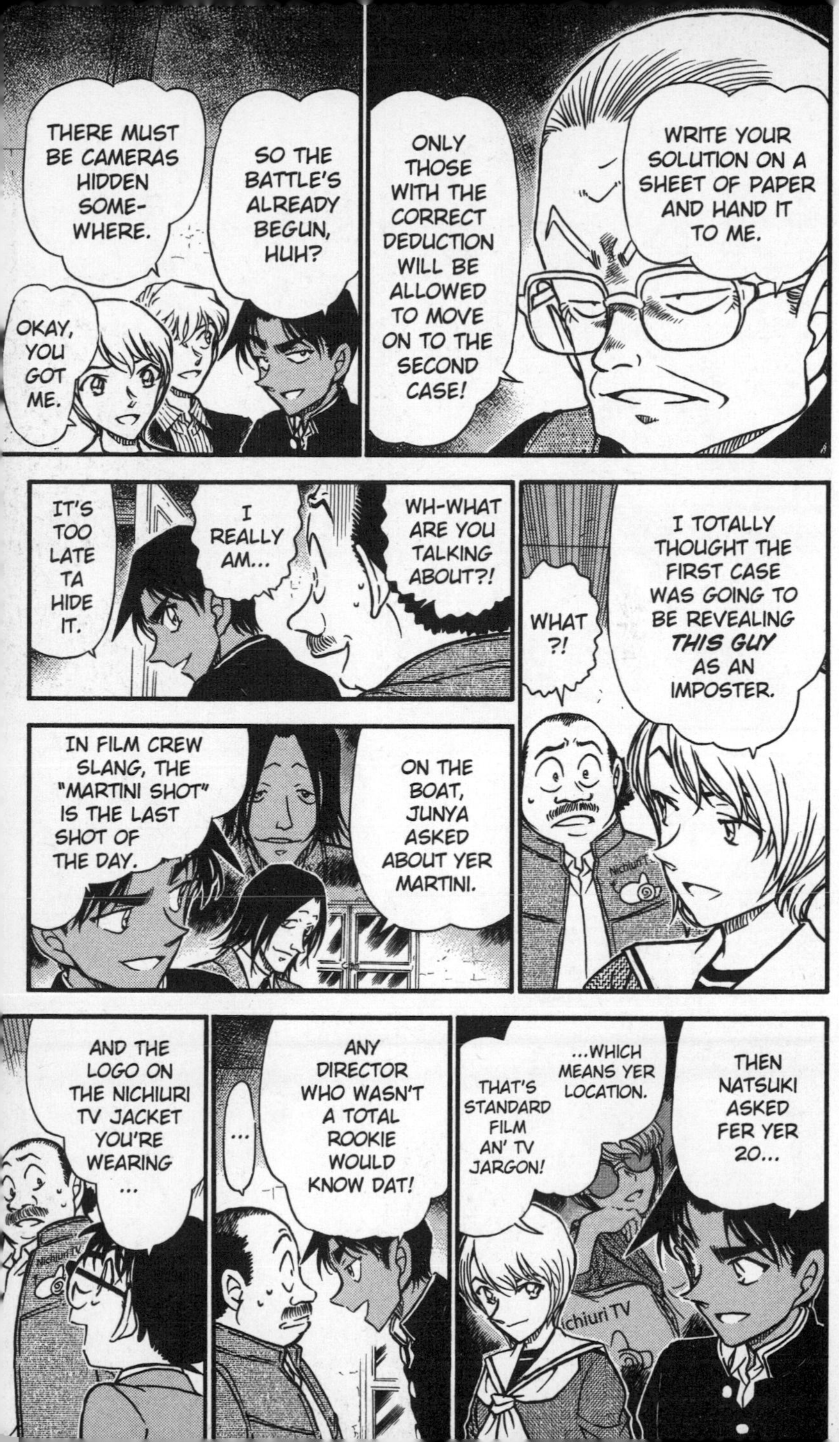
WRITE YOUR SOLUTION ON A SHEET OF PAPER AND HAND IT TO ME.
ONLY THOSE WITH THE CORRECT DEDUCTION WILL BE ALLOWED TO MOVE ON TO THE SECOND CASE!
SO THE BATTLE'S ALREADY BEGUN, HUH?
THERE MUST BE CAMERAS HIDDEN SOME-WHERE.
OKAY, YOU GOT ME.
I TOTALLY THOUGHT THE FIRST CASE WAS GOING TO BE REVEALING *THIS GUY* AS AN IMPOSTER.
WHAT?!
WH-WHAT ARE YOU TALKING ABOUT?!
I REALLY AM...
IT'S TOO LATE TA HIDE IT.
ON THE BOAT, JUNYA ASKED ABOUT YER MARTINI.
IN FILM CREW SLANG, THE "MARTINI SHOT" IS THE LAST SHOT OF THE DAY.
THEN NATSUKI ASKED FER YER 20...
...WHICH MEANS YER LOCATION.
THAT'S STANDARD FILM AN' TV JARGON!
ANY DIRECTOR WHO WASN'T A TOTAL ROOKIE WOULD KNOW DAT!
...
AND THE LOGO ON THE NICHIURI TV JACKET YOU'RE WEARING ...

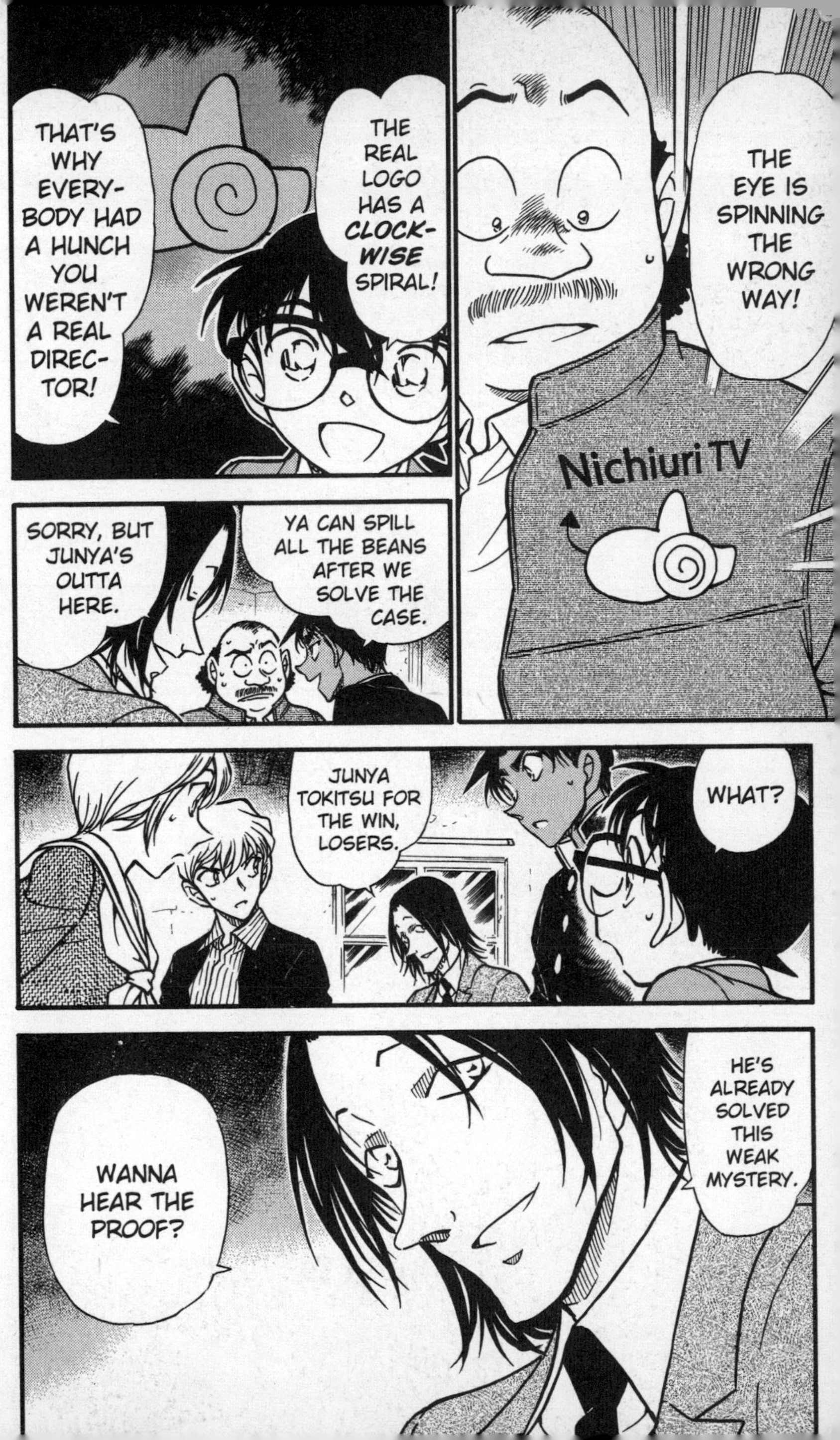
THE EYE IS SPINNING THE WRONG WAY!
Nichiuri TV
THE REAL LOGO HAS A CLOCKWISE SPIRAL!
THAT'S WHY EVERYBODY HAD A HUNCH YOU WEREN'T A REAL DIRECTOR!
YA CAN SPILL ALL THE BEANS AFTER WE SOLVE THE CASE.
SORRY, BUT JUNYA'S OUTTA HERE.
WHAT?
JUNYA TOKITSU FOR THE WIN, LOSERS.
HE'S ALREADY SOLVED THIS WEAK MYSTERY.
WANNA HEAR THE PROOF?

FILE 11: THE LOCKED ROOM SOLUTION

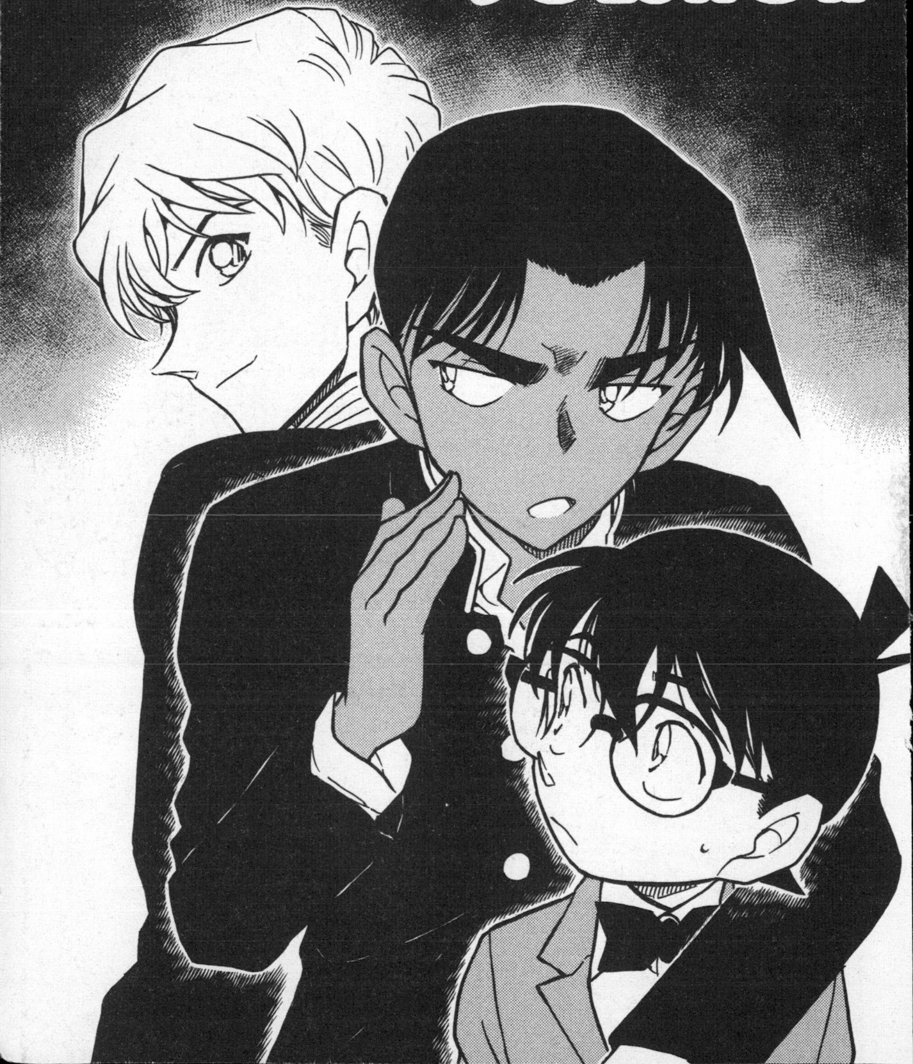

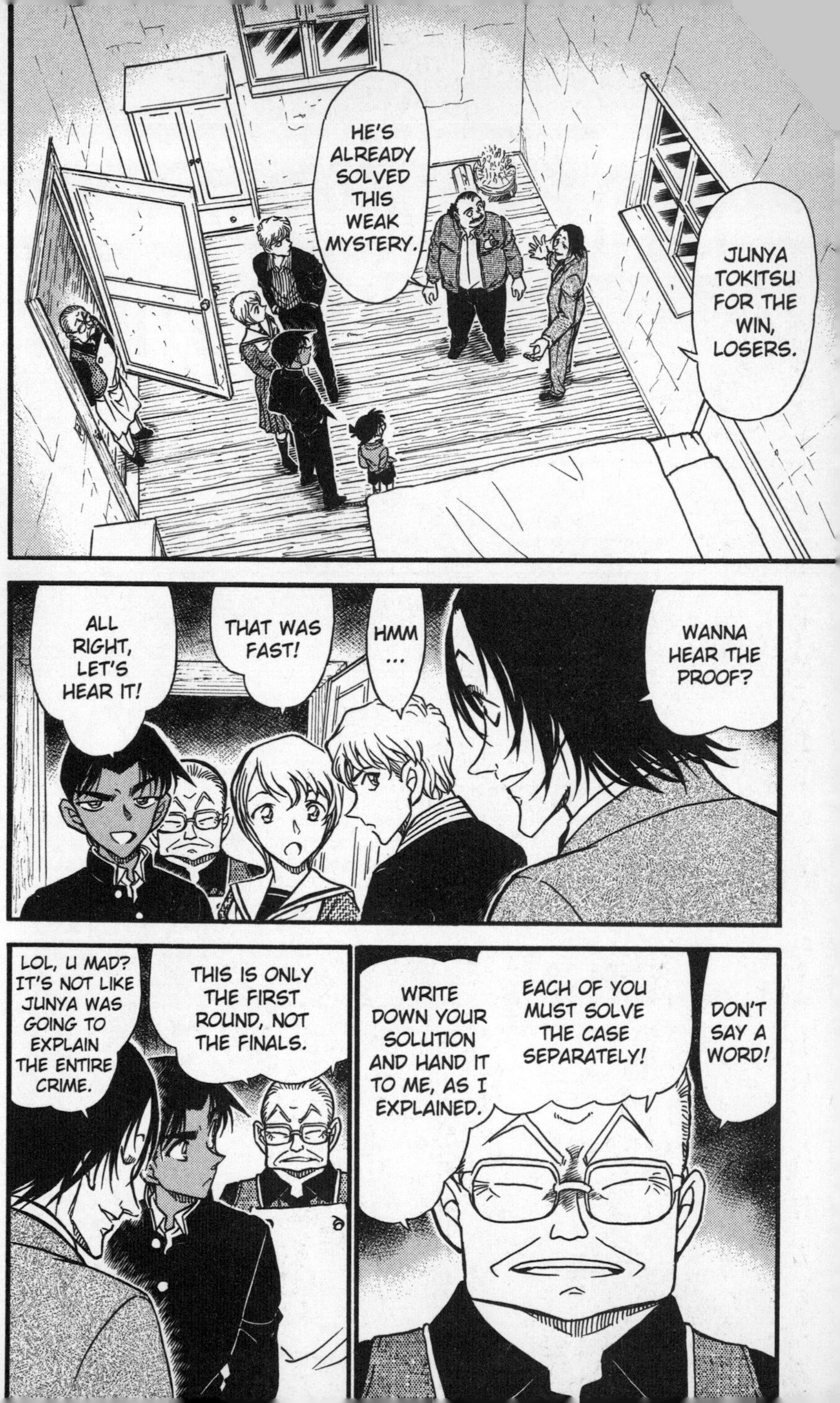
JUNYA TOKITSU FOR THE WIN, LOSERS.
HE'S ALREADY SOLVED THIS WEAK MYSTERY.
WANNA HEAR THE PROOF?
HMM ...
THAT WAS FAST!
ALL RIGHT, LET'S HEAR IT!
DON'T SAY A WORD!
EACH OF YOU MUST SOLVE THE CASE SEPARATELY!
WRITE DOWN YOUR SOLUTION AND HAND IT TO ME, AS I EXPLAINED.
THIS IS ONLY THE FIRST ROUND, NOT THE FINALS.
LOL, U MAD? IT'S NOT LIKE JUNYA WAS GOING TO EXPLAIN THE ENTIRE CRIME.

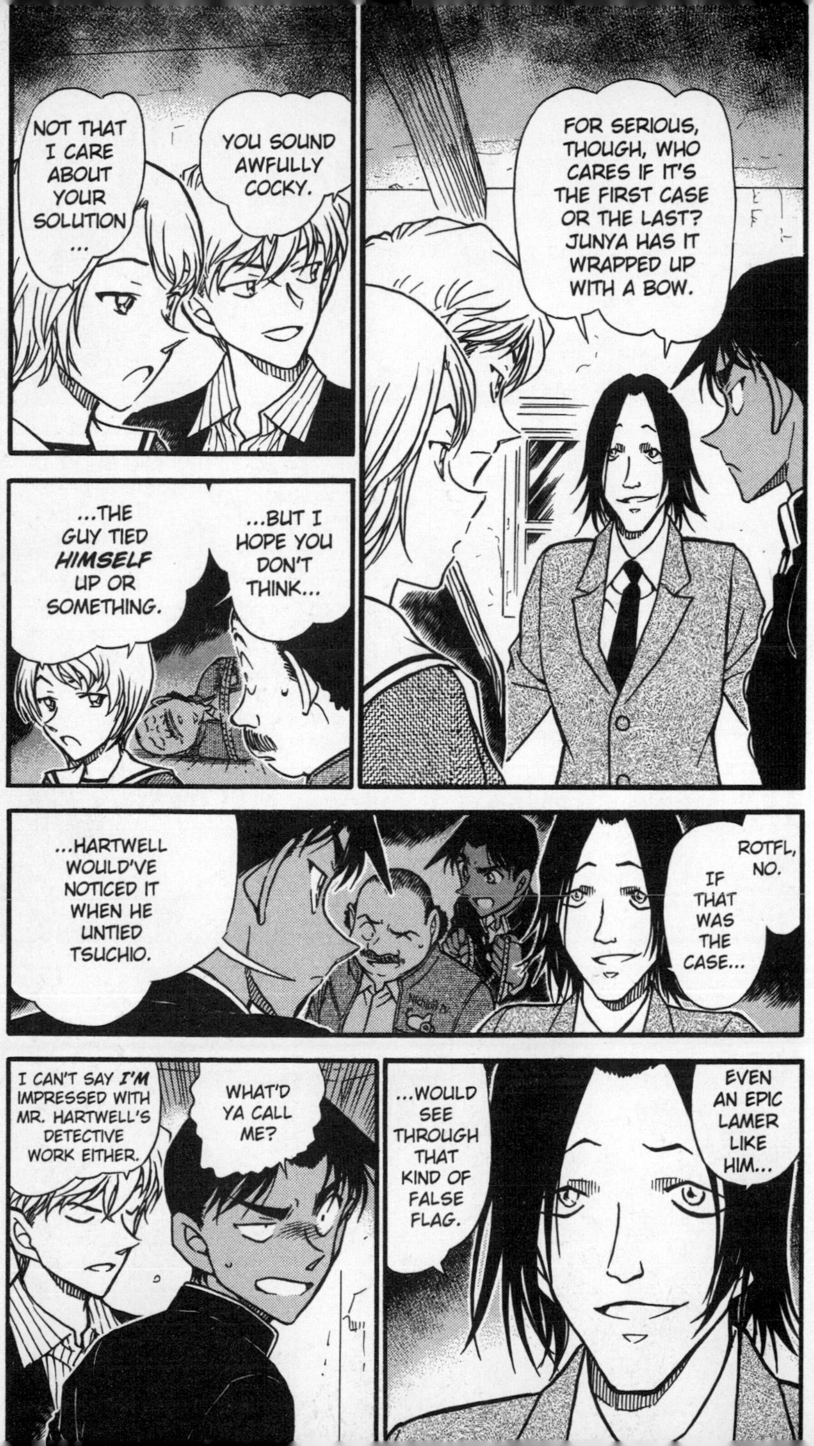
FOR SERIOUS, THOUGH, WHO CARES IF IT'S THE FIRST CASE OR THE LAST? JUNYA HAS IT WRAPPED UP WITH A BOW.
YOU SOUND AWFULLY COCKY.
NOT THAT I CARE ABOUT YOUR SOLUTION ...
...BUT I HOPE YOU DON'T THINK...
...THE GUY TIED *HIMSELF* UP OR SOMETHING.
ROTFL, NO.
IF THAT WAS THE CASE...
...HARTWELL WOULD'VE NOTICED IT WHEN HE UNTIED TSUCHIO.
EVEN AN EPIC LAMER LIKE HIM...
...WOULD SEE THROUGH THAT KIND OF FALSE FLAG.
WHAT'D YA CALL ME?
I CAN'T SAY *I'M* IMPRESSED WITH MR. HARTWELL'S DETECTIVE WORK EITHER.

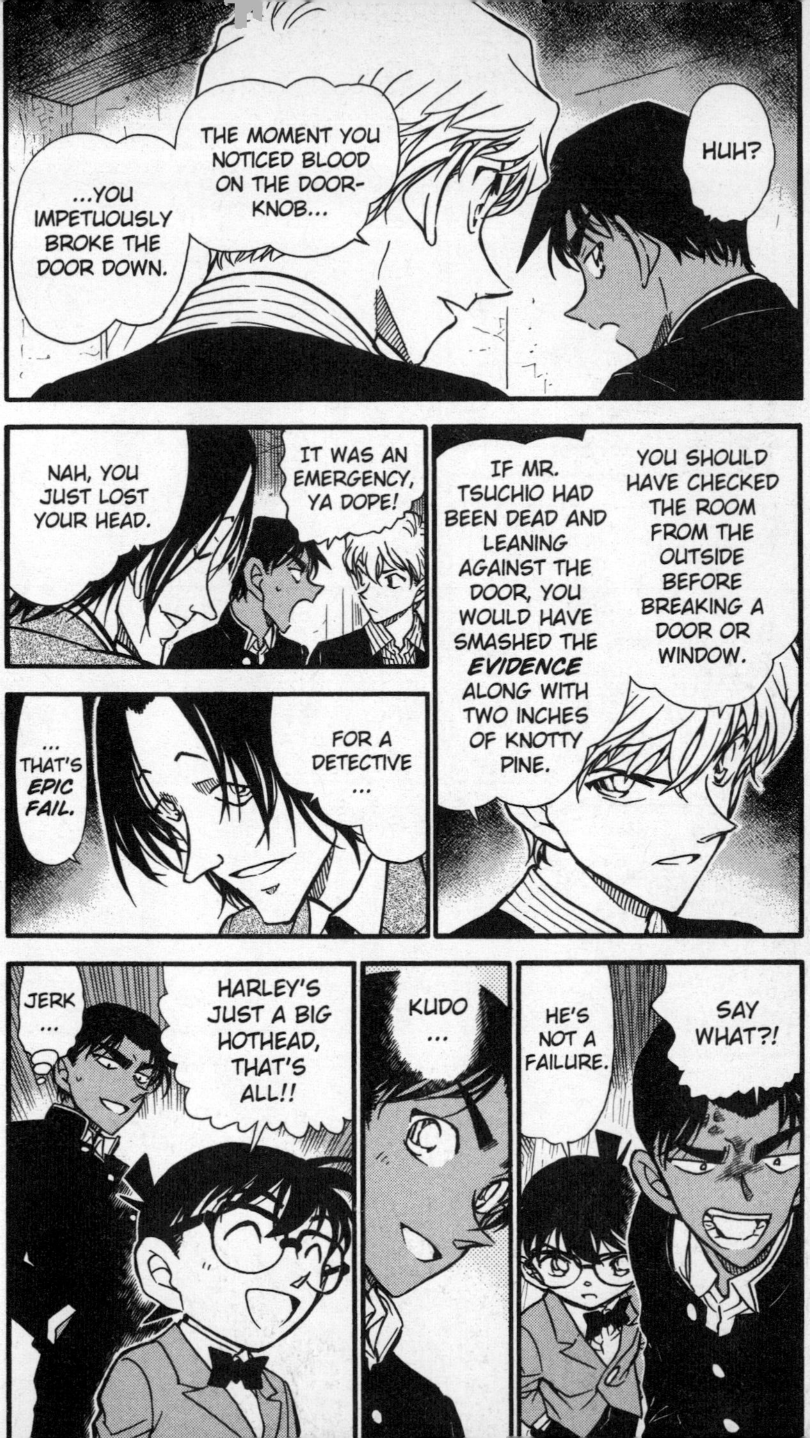
HUH?
THE MOMENT YOU NOTICED BLOOD ON THE DOOR-KNOB...
...YOU IMPETUOUSLY BROKE THE DOOR DOWN.
YOU SHOULD HAVE CHECKED THE ROOM FROM THE OUTSIDE BEFORE BREAKING A DOOR OR WINDOW.
IF MR. TSUCHIO HAD BEEN DEAD AND LEANING AGAINST THE DOOR, YOU WOULD HAVE SMASHED THE EVIDENCE ALONG WITH TWO INCHES OF KNOTTY PINE.
IT WAS AN EMERGENCY, YA DOPE!
NAH, YOU JUST LOST YOUR HEAD.
FOR A DETECTIVE ...
... THAT'S EPIC FAIL.
SAY WHAT?!
HE'S NOT A FAILURE.
KUDO ...
HARLEY'S JUST A BIG HOTHEAD, THAT'S ALL!!
JERK ...

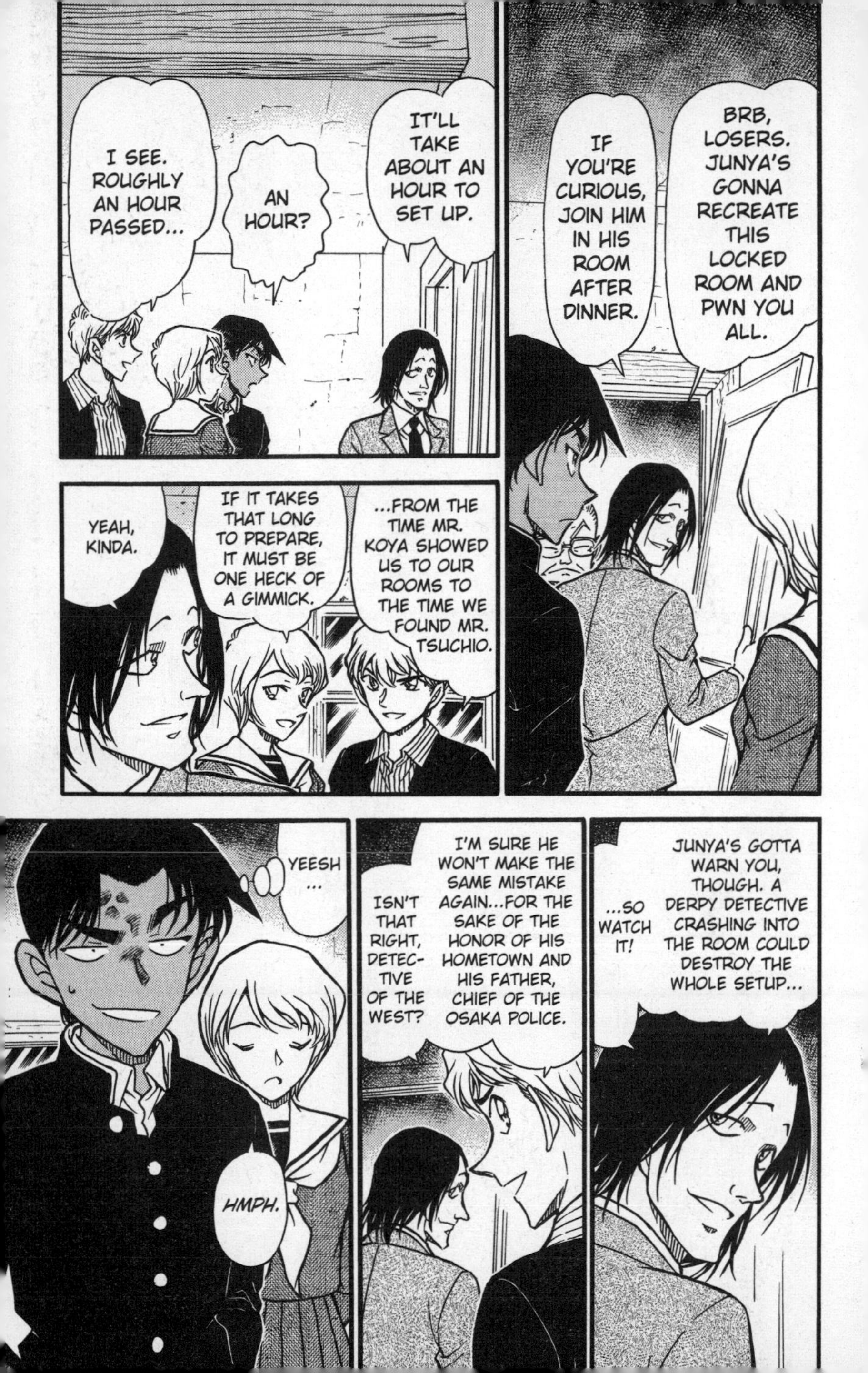
BRB, LOSERS. JUNYA'S GONNA RECREATE THIS LOCKED ROOM AND PWN YOU ALL.
IF YOU'RE CURIOUS, JOIN HIM IN HIS ROOM AFTER DINNER.
IT'LL TAKE ABOUT AN HOUR TO SET UP.
AN HOUR?
I SEE. ROUGHLY AN HOUR PASSED...
...FROM THE TIME MR. KOYA SHOWED US TO OUR ROOMS TO THE TIME WE FOUND MR. TSUCHIO.
IF IT TAKES THAT LONG TO PREPARE, IT MUST BE ONE HECK OF A GIMMICK.
YEAH, KINDA.
JUNYA'S GOTTA WARN YOU, THOUGH. A DERPY DETECTIVE CRASHING INTO THE ROOM COULD DESTROY THE WHOLE SETUP...
...SO WATCH IT!
I'M SURE HE WON'T MAKE THE SAME MISTAKE AGAIN...FOR THE SAKE OF THE HONOR OF HIS HOMETOWN AND HIS FATHER, CHIEF OF THE OSAKA POLICE.
ISN'T THAT RIGHT, DETEC-TIVE OF THE WEST?
YEESH...
HMPH.

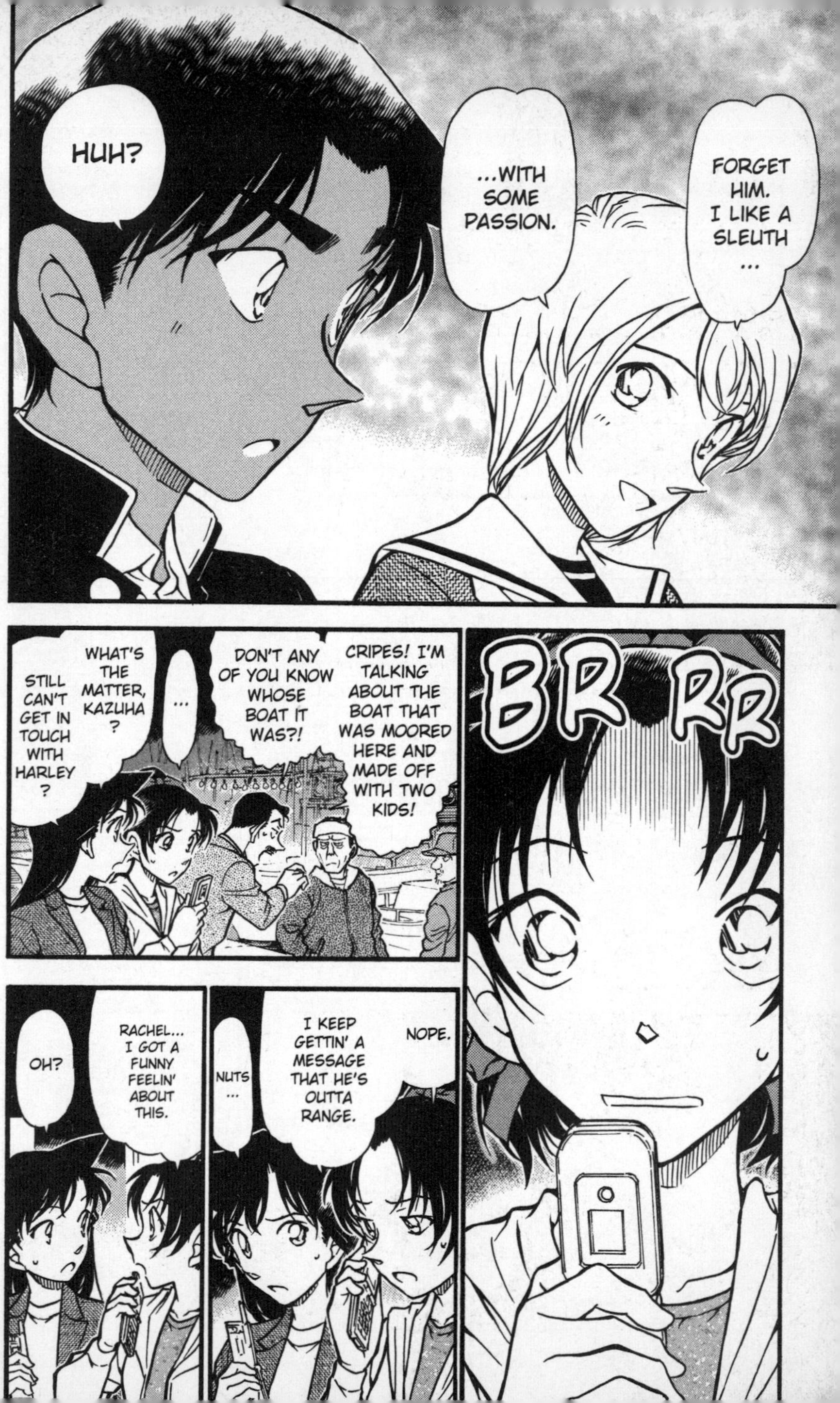
FORGET HIM. I LIKE A SLEUTH ...
...WITH SOME PASSION.
HUH?
BR RR
CRIPES! I'M TALKING ABOUT THE BOAT THAT WAS MOORED HERE AND MADE OFF WITH TWO KIDS!
DON'T ANY OF YOU KNOW WHOSE BOAT IT WAS?!
...
WHAT'S THE MATTER, KAZUHA?
STILL CAN'T GET IN TOUCH WITH HARLEY?
NOPE.
I KEEP GETTIN' A MESSAGE THAT HE'S OUTTA RANGE.
NUTS ...
RACHEL... I GOT A FUNNY FEELIN' ABOUT THIS.
OH?

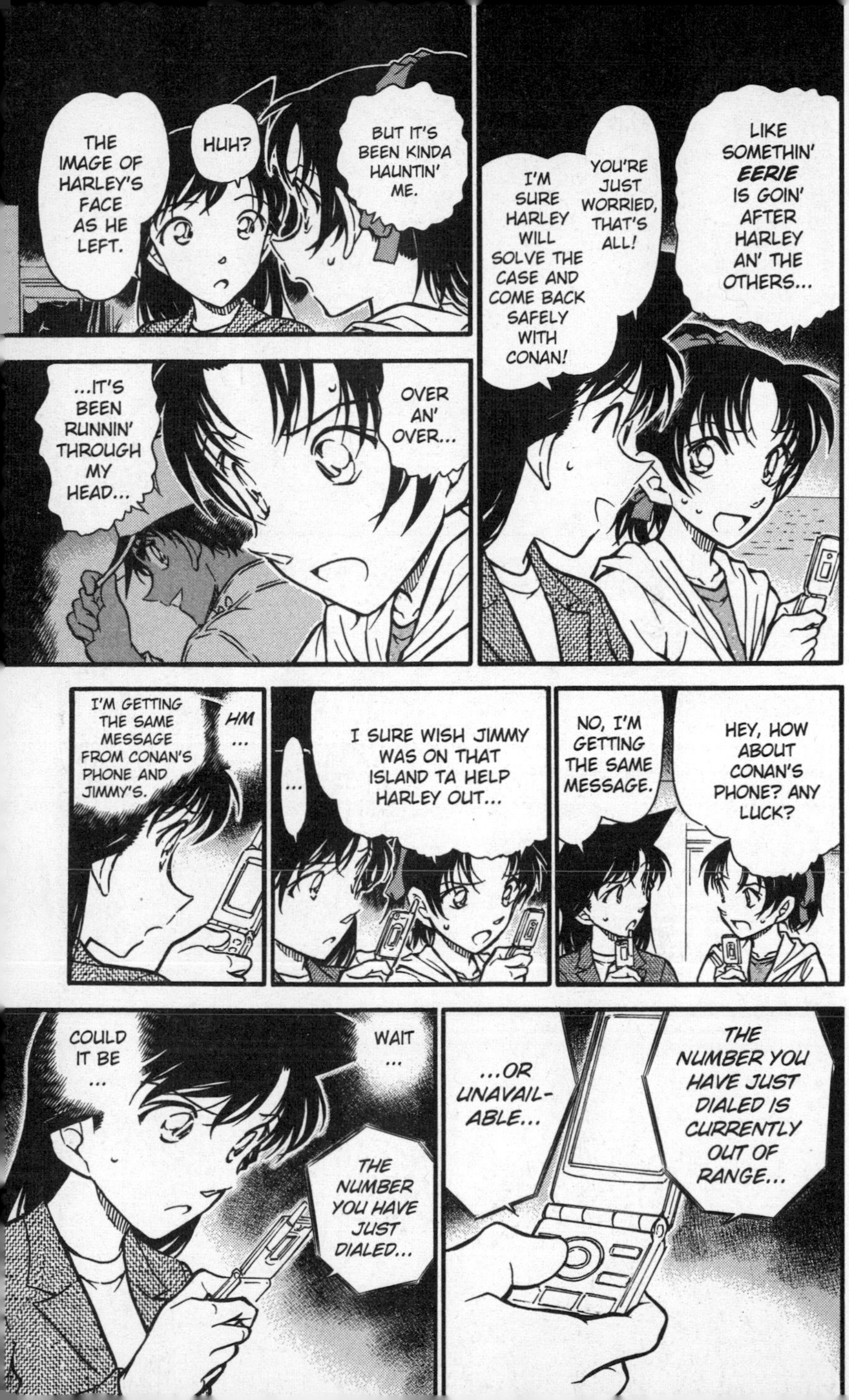
LIKE SOMETHIN' **EERIE** IS GOIN' AFTER HARLEY AN' THE OTHERS...
YOU'RE JUST WORRIED, THAT'S ALL!
I'M SURE HARLEY WILL SOLVE THE CASE AND COME BACK SAFELY WITH CONAN!
BUT IT'S BEEN KINDA HAUNTIN' ME.
HUH?
THE IMAGE OF HARLEY'S FACE AS HE LEFT.
OVER AN' OVER...
...IT'S BEEN RUNNIN' THROUGH MY HEAD...
HEY, HOW ABOUT CONAN'S PHONE? ANY LUCK?
NO, I'M GETTING THE SAME MESSAGE.
I SURE WISH JIMMY WAS ON THAT ISLAND TA HELP HARLEY OUT...
...
HM ...
I'M GETTING THE SAME MESSAGE FROM CONAN'S PHONE AND JIMMY'S.
THE NUMBER YOU HAVE JUST DIALED IS CURRENTLY OUT OF RANGE...
...OR UNAVAIL-ABLE...
WAIT ...
COULD IT BE ...
THE NUMBER YOU HAVE JUST DIALED...

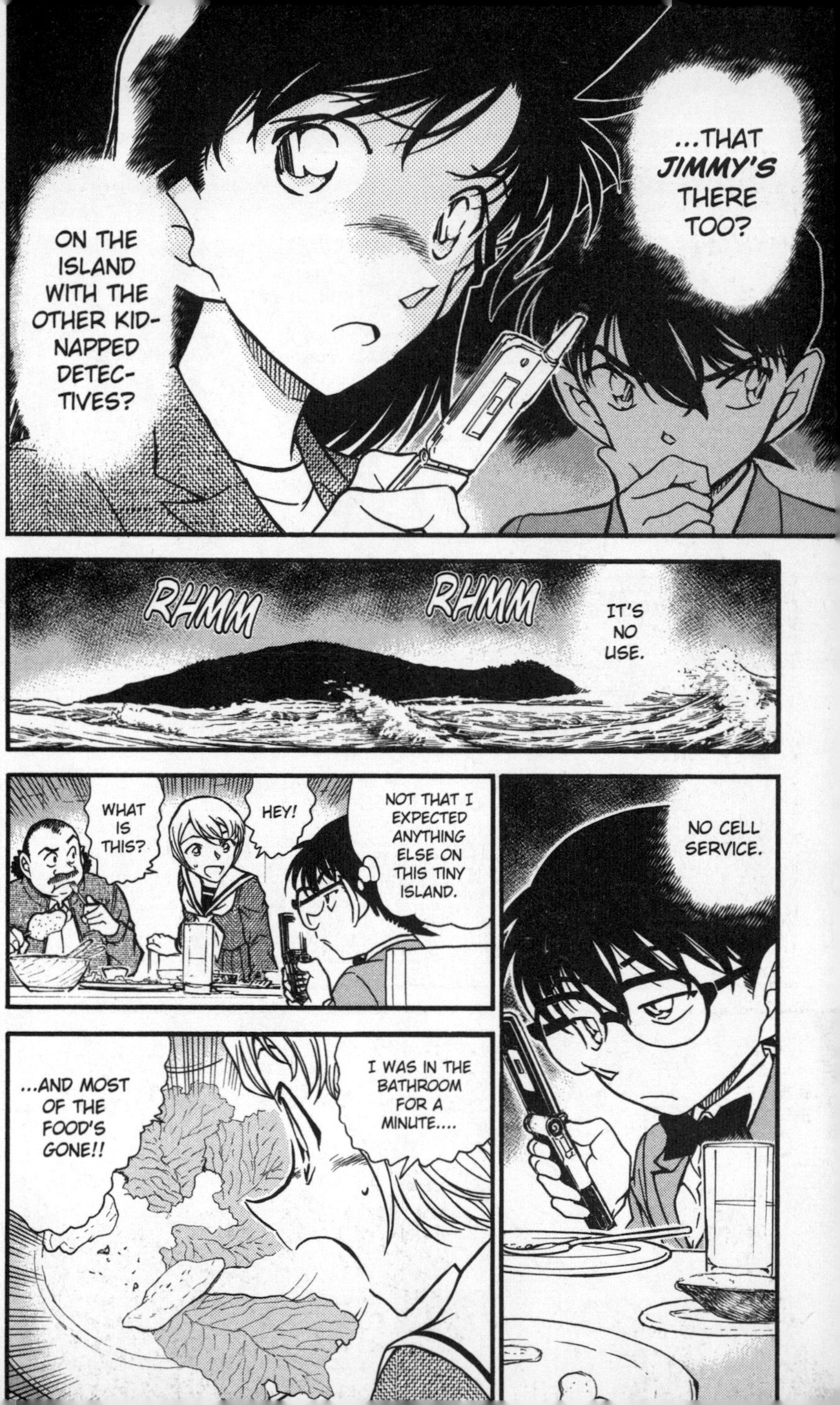
...THAT JIMMY'S THERE TOO?
ON THE ISLAND WITH THE OTHER KID-NAPPED DETECTIVES?
IT'S NO USE.
RHMM
RHMM
NO CELL SERVICE.
NOT THAT I EXPECTED ANYTHING ELSE ON THIS TINY ISLAND.
HEY!
WHAT IS THIS?
I WAS IN THE BATHROOM FOR A MINUTE....
...AND MOST OF THE FOOD'S GONE!!

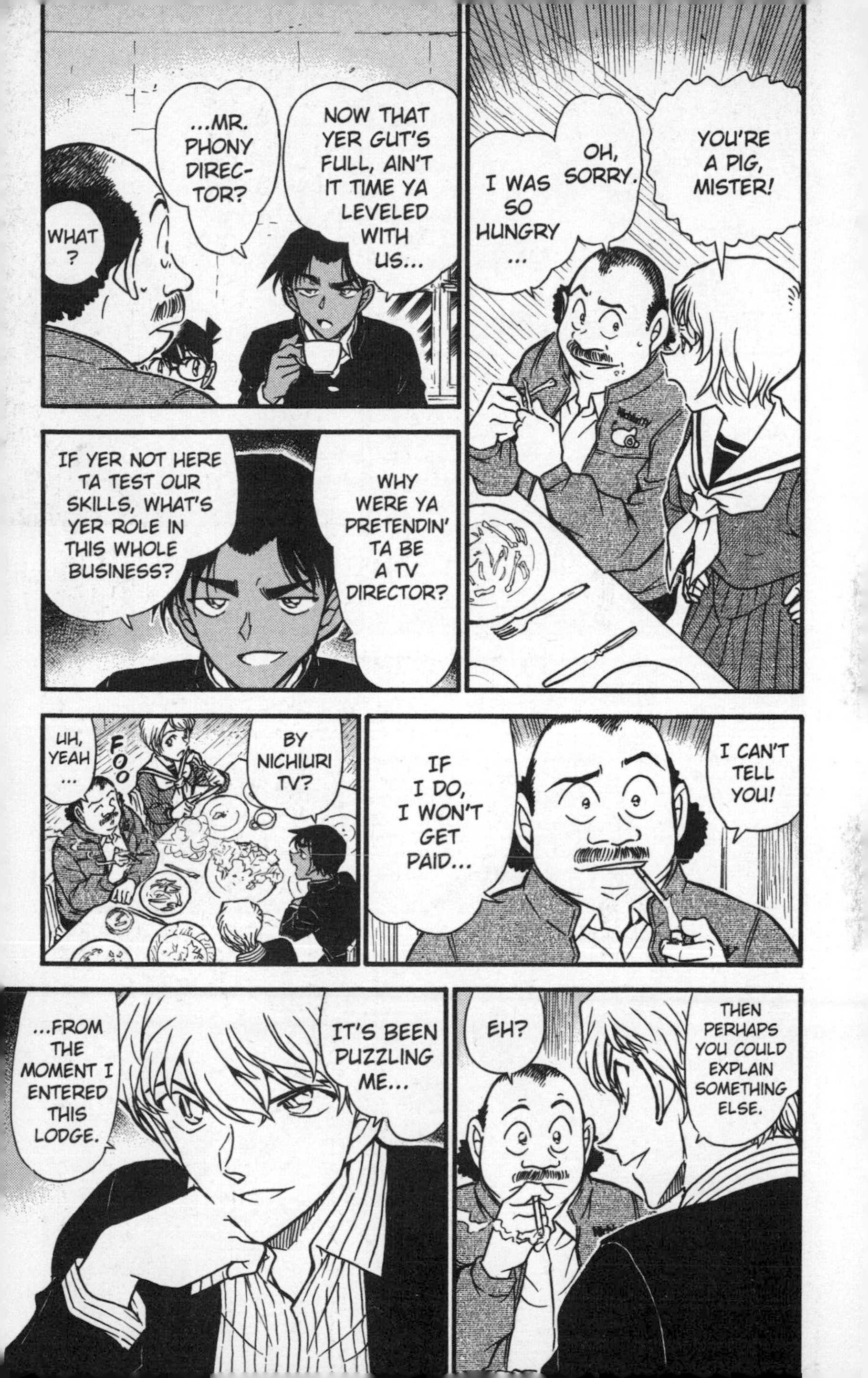
YOU'RE A PIG, MISTER!
OH, SORRY.
I WAS SO HUNGRY...
NOW THAT YER GUT'S FULL, AIN'T IT TIME YA LEVELED WITH US...
...MR. PHONY DIRECTOR?
WHAT?
WHY WERE YA PRETENDIN' TA BE A TV DIRECTOR?
IF YER NOT HERE TA TEST OUR SKILLS, WHAT'S YER ROLE IN THIS WHOLE BUSINESS?
I CAN'T TELL YOU!
IF I DO, I WON'T GET PAID...
BY NICHIURI TV?
FOO
UH, YEAH...
THEN PERHAPS YOU COULD EXPLAIN SOMETHING ELSE.
EH?
IT'S BEEN PUZZLING ME...
...FROM THE MOMENT I ENTERED THIS LODGE.

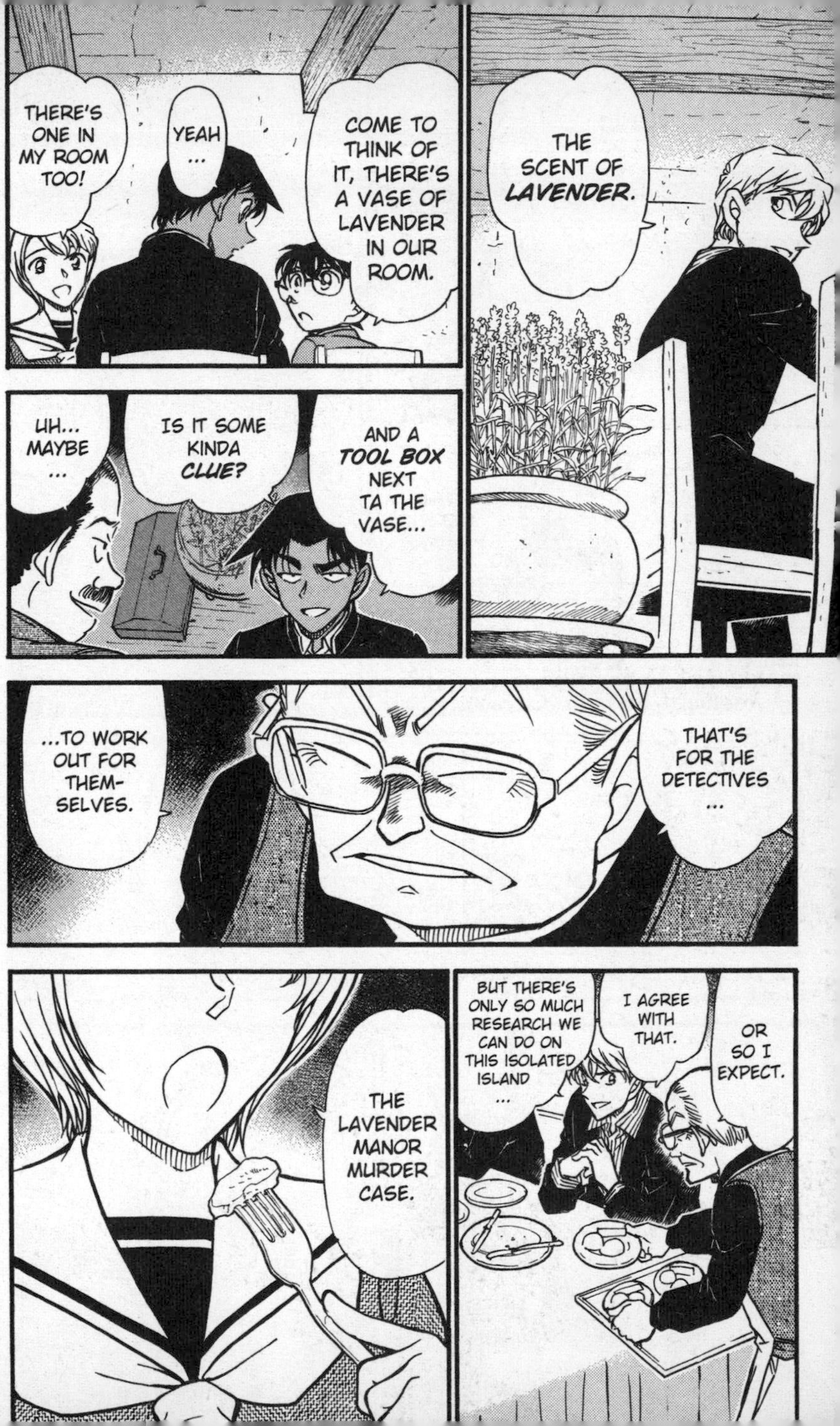
THE SCENT OF LAVENDER.
COME TO THINK OF IT, THERE'S A VASE OF LAVENDER IN OUR ROOM.
YEAH ...
THERE'S ONE IN MY ROOM TOO!
AND A TOOL BOX NEXT TA THE VASE...
IS IT SOME KINDA CLUE?
UH... MAYBE ...
THAT'S FOR THE DETECTIVES ...
...TO WORK OUT FOR THEM-SELVES.
OR SO I EXPECT.
I AGREE WITH THAT.
BUT THERE'S ONLY SO MUCH RESEARCH WE CAN DO ON THIS ISOLATED ISLAND ...
THE LAVENDER MANOR MURDER CASE.

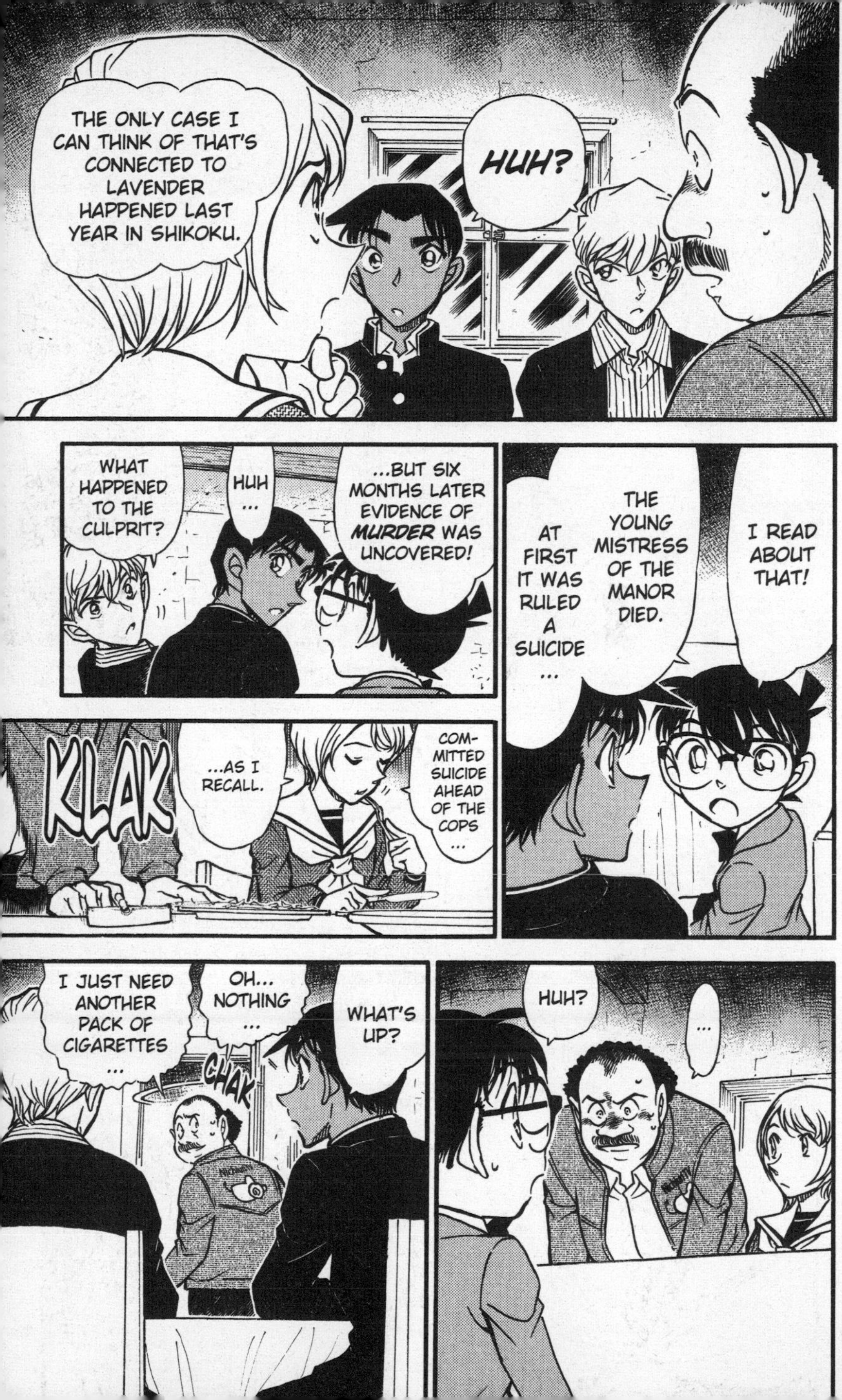
HUH?
THE ONLY CASE I CAN THINK OF THAT'S CONNECTED TO LAVENDER HAPPENED LAST YEAR IN SHIKOKU.
I READ ABOUT THAT!
THE YOUNG MISTRESS OF THE MANOR DIED.
AT FIRST IT WAS RULED A SUICIDE...
...BUT SIX MONTHS LATER EVIDENCE OF MURDER WAS UNCOVERED!
HUH...
WHAT HAPPENED TO THE CULPRIT?
COM-MITTED SUICIDE AHEAD OF THE COPS...
...AS I RECALL.
KLAK
...
HUH?
WHAT'S UP?
OH... NOTHING...
CHAK
I JUST NEED ANOTHER PACK OF CIGARETTES...

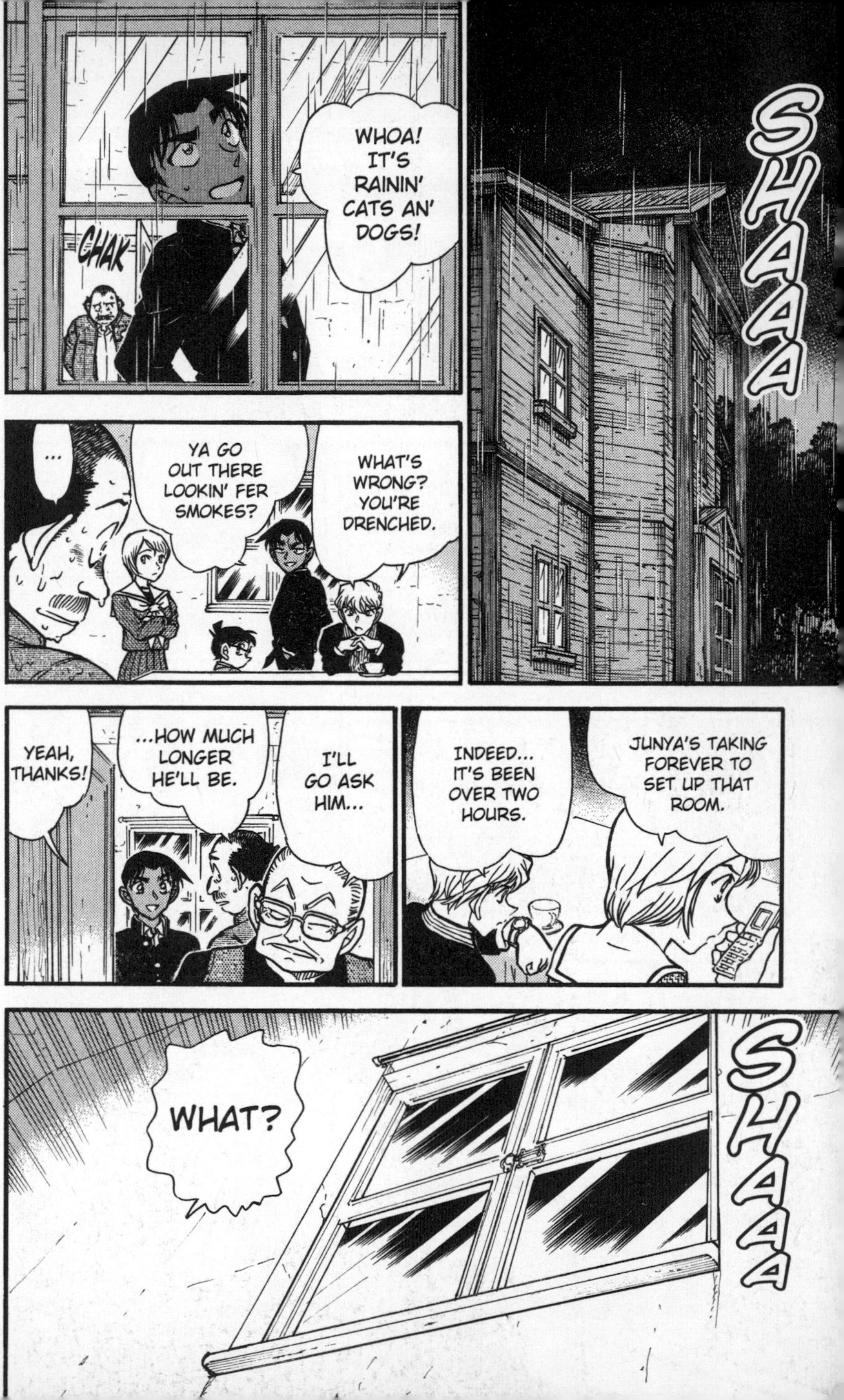
SHAAAA
WHOA! IT'S RAININ' CATS AN' DOGS!
CHAK
WHAT'S WRONG? YOU'RE DRENCHED.
YA GO OUT THERE LOOKIN' FER SMOKES?
...
JUNYA'S TAKING FOREVER TO SET UP THAT ROOM.
INDEED... IT'S BEEN OVER TWO HOURS.
I'LL GO ASK HIM...
...HOW MUCH LONGER HE'LL BE.
YEAH, THANKS!
SHAAAA
WHAT?

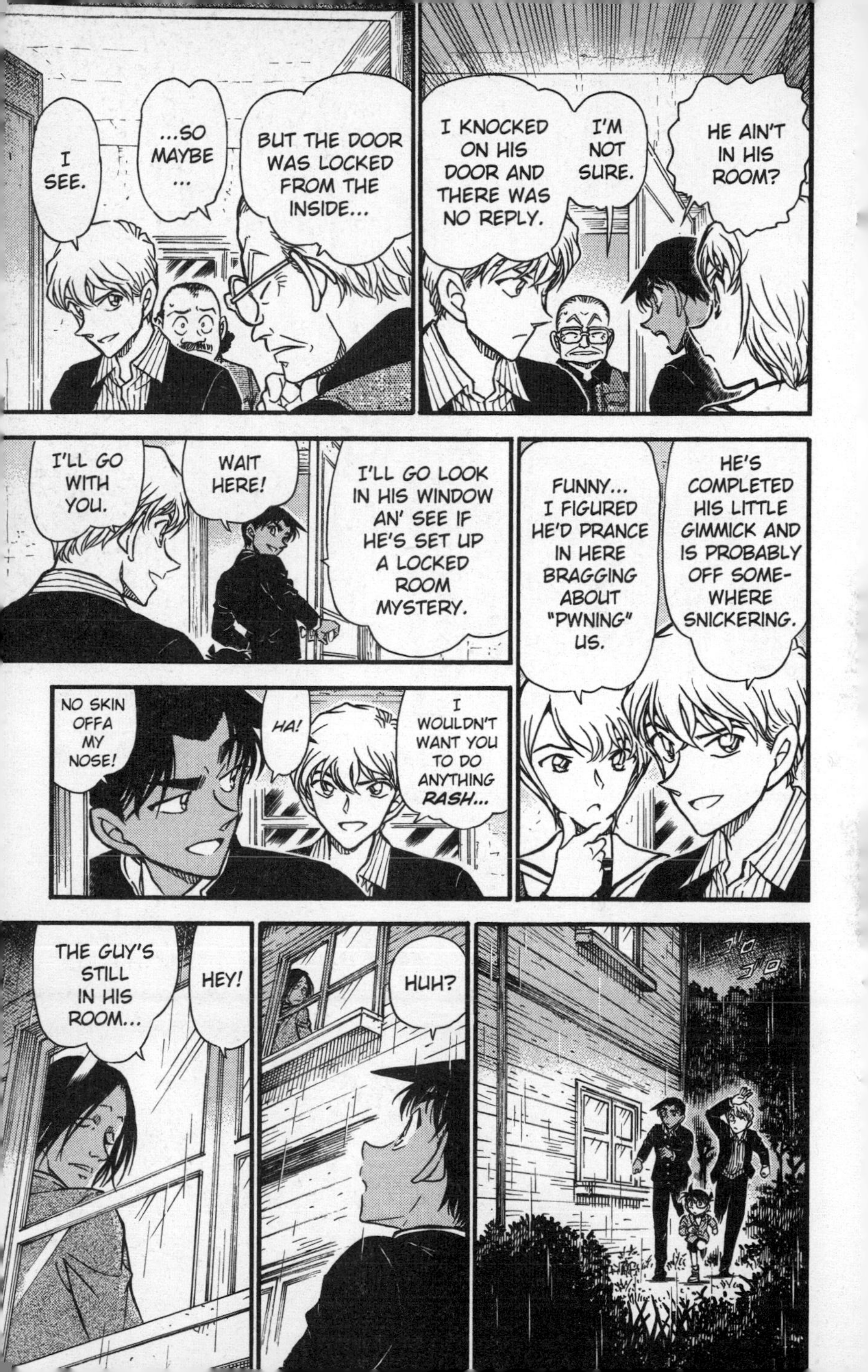
HE AIN'T IN HIS ROOM?
I'M NOT SURE.
I KNOCKED ON HIS DOOR AND THERE WAS NO REPLY.
BUT THE DOOR WAS LOCKED FROM THE INSIDE...
...SO MAYBE ...
I SEE.
HE'S COMPLETED HIS LITTLE GIMMICK AND IS PROBABLY OFF SOME-WHERE SNICKERING.
FUNNY... I FIGURED HE'D PRANCE IN HERE BRAGGING ABOUT "PWNING" US.
I'LL GO LOOK IN HIS WINDOW AN' SEE IF HE'S SET UP A LOCKED ROOM MYSTERY.
WAIT HERE!
I'LL GO WITH YOU.
I WOULDN'T WANT YOU TO DO ANYTHING ***RASH***...
HA!
NO SKIN OFFA MY NOSE!
ゴロゴロ
HUH?
HEY!
THE GUY'S STILL IN HIS ROOM...

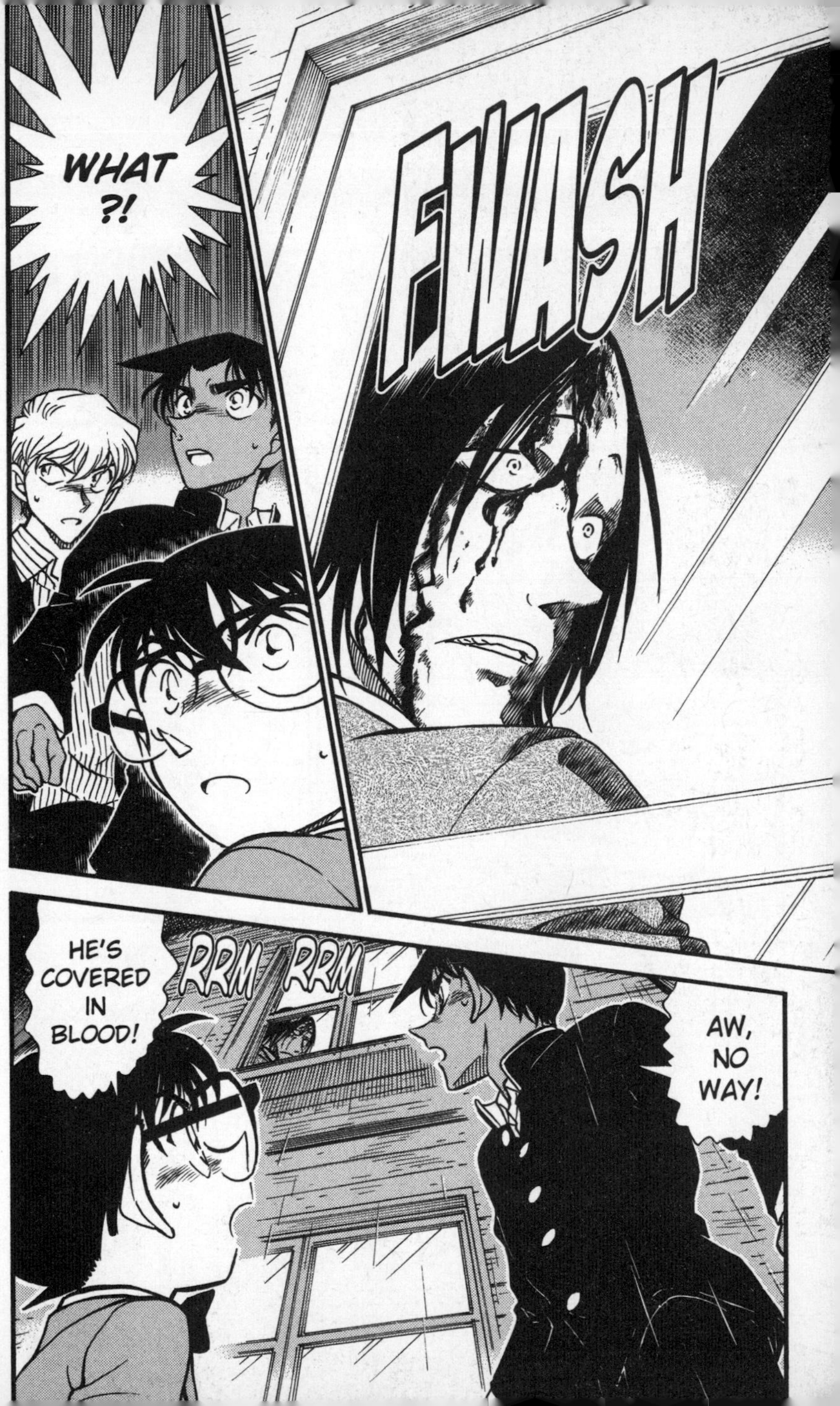
FWASH
WHAT ?!
AW, NO WAY!
RRM RRM
HE'S COVERED IN BLOOD!

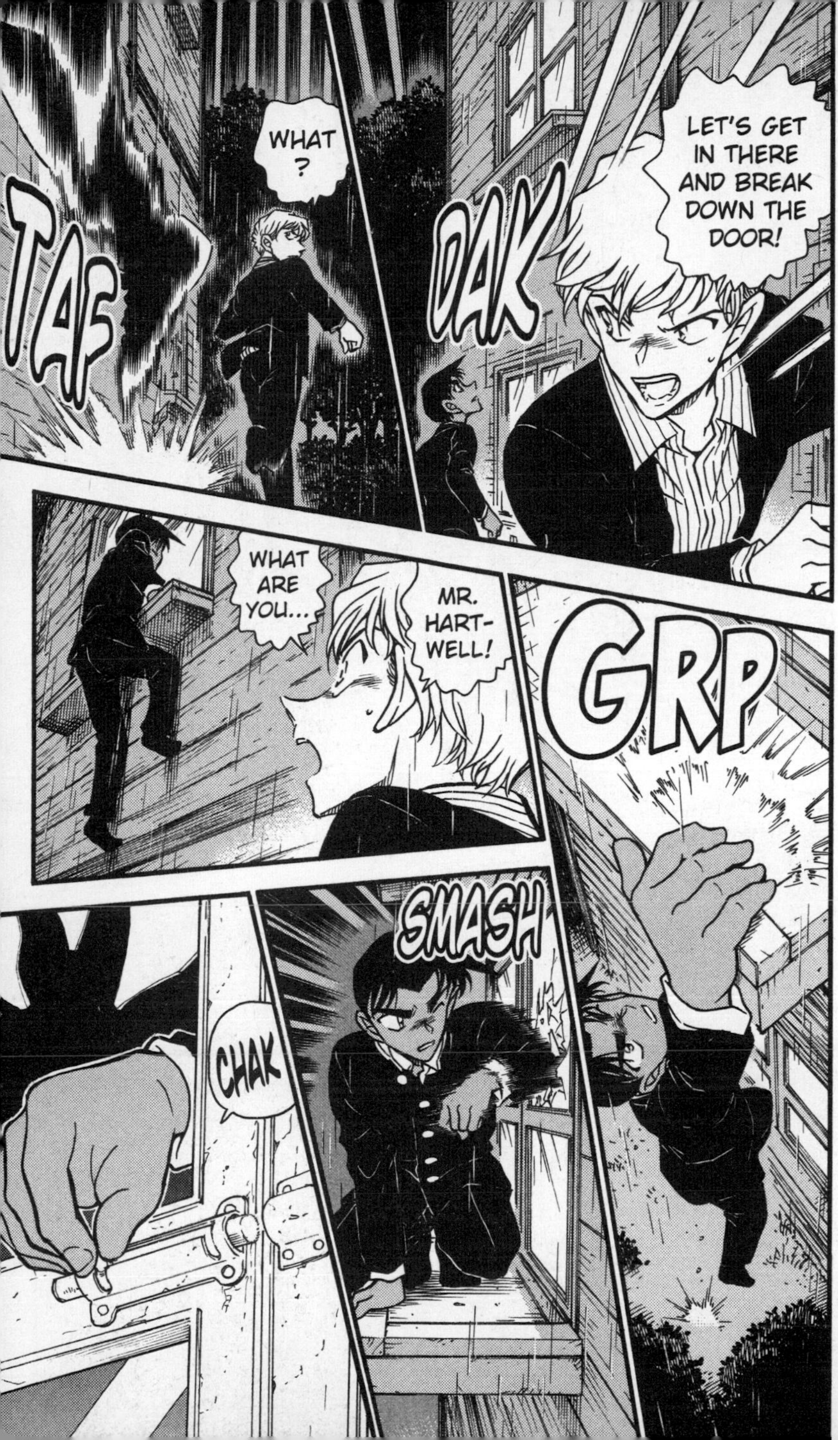
LET'S GET IN THERE AND BREAK DOWN THE DOOR!
DAK
WHAT ?
TAF
GRP
MR. HART-WELL!
WHAT ARE YOU...
SMASH
CHAK

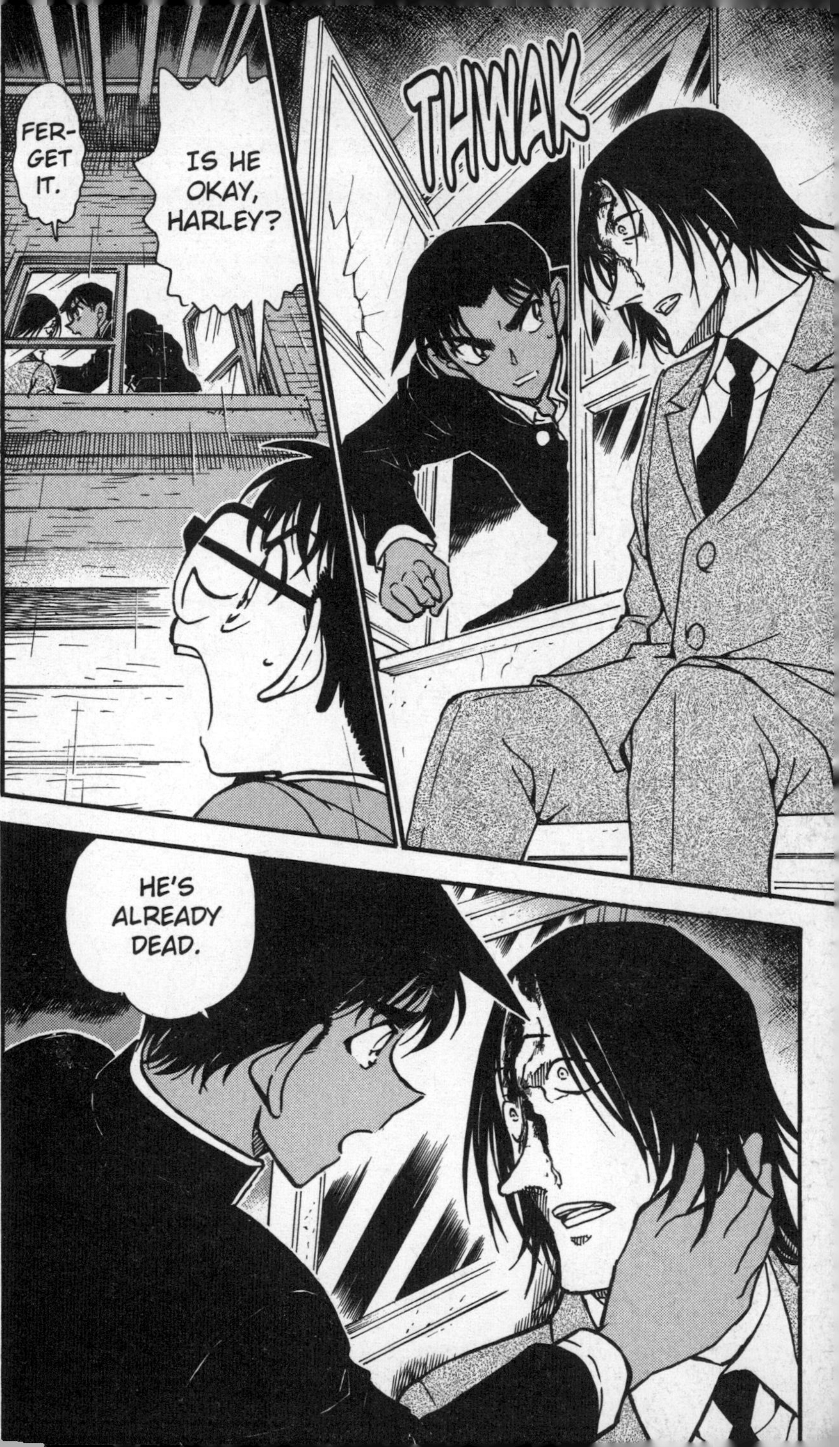
THWAK
IS HE OKAY, HARLEY?
FER-GET IT.
HE'S ALREADY DEAD.

Hello, Aoyama here.

The great detective tournament has finally begun! It's been five years since my assistant Tani muttered, "I wish there was a story arc like that..." (Or has it been longer?) I spent a lot of time creating the idea for this locked room mystery, so please enjoy! ♪ Of course, you'll have to read volume 55 for the solution... Heh.

Gosho Aoyama's Mystery Library

54

KIYOSHI SHIMADA

A murder spree in a mysterious mansion...and the sleuth who takes on the challenge is Kiyoshi Shimada! Shimada is a tall, scraggly man in his late 30s with deep-set eyes staring from beneath shaggy hair. Despite his gloomy appearance, he's polite and friendly when you talk to him. He was once an avid smoker, but ever since he damaged his lungs his pleasure has been "one cigarette per day." He is also a master of origami. His greatest weapon is his wild imagination, which is not bound by common sense. His seemingly over-the-top deductions shine light upon the truth.

Writer Yukito Ayatsuji came up with the name "Kiyoshi Shimada" by combining the names of his mentor, mystery writer Soji Shimada, and Shimada's detective character, Kiyoshi Mitarai. Similarly, Conan Edogawa's name is a combination of the writers Rampo Edogawa and Arthur Conan Doyle...but I haven't met either of them.

I recommend *Murder at the Decagon Mansion*.

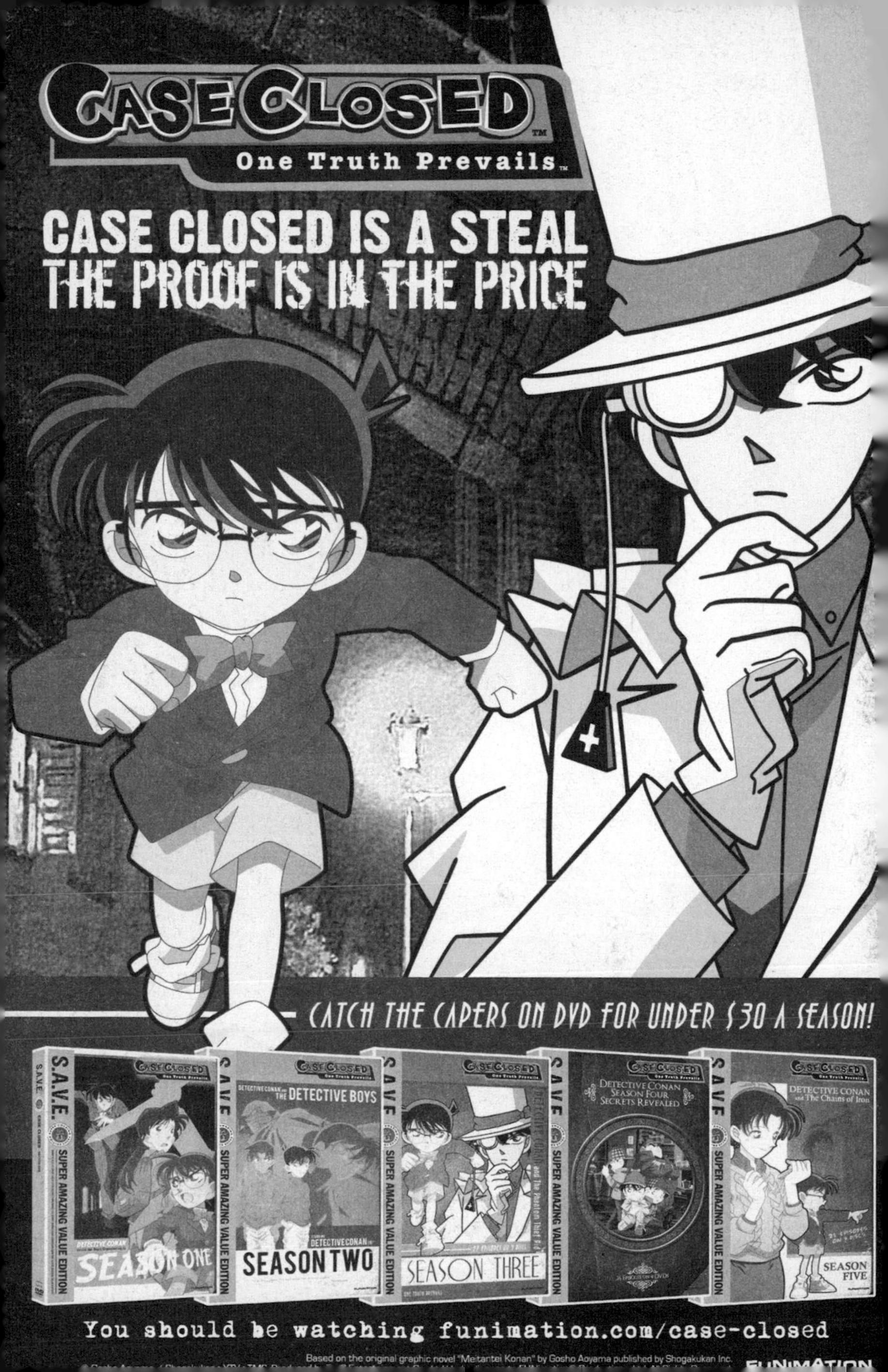

CASE CLOSED
One Truth Prevails
CASE CLOSED IS A STEAL
THE PROOF IS IN THE PRICE
CATCH THE CAPERS ON DVD FOR UNDER $30 A SEASON!
S.A.V.E. SUPER AMAZING VALUE EDITION
SEASON ONE
DETECTIVE CONAN THE DETECTIVE BOYS
SEASON TWO
SEASON THREE
DETECTIVE CONAN SEASON FOUR SECRETS REVEALED
DETECTIVE CONAN and The Chains of Iron
SEASON FIVE
You should be watching funimation.com/case-closed
Based on the original graphic novel "Meitantei Konan" by Gosho Aoyama published by Shogakukan Inc.
FUNIMATION

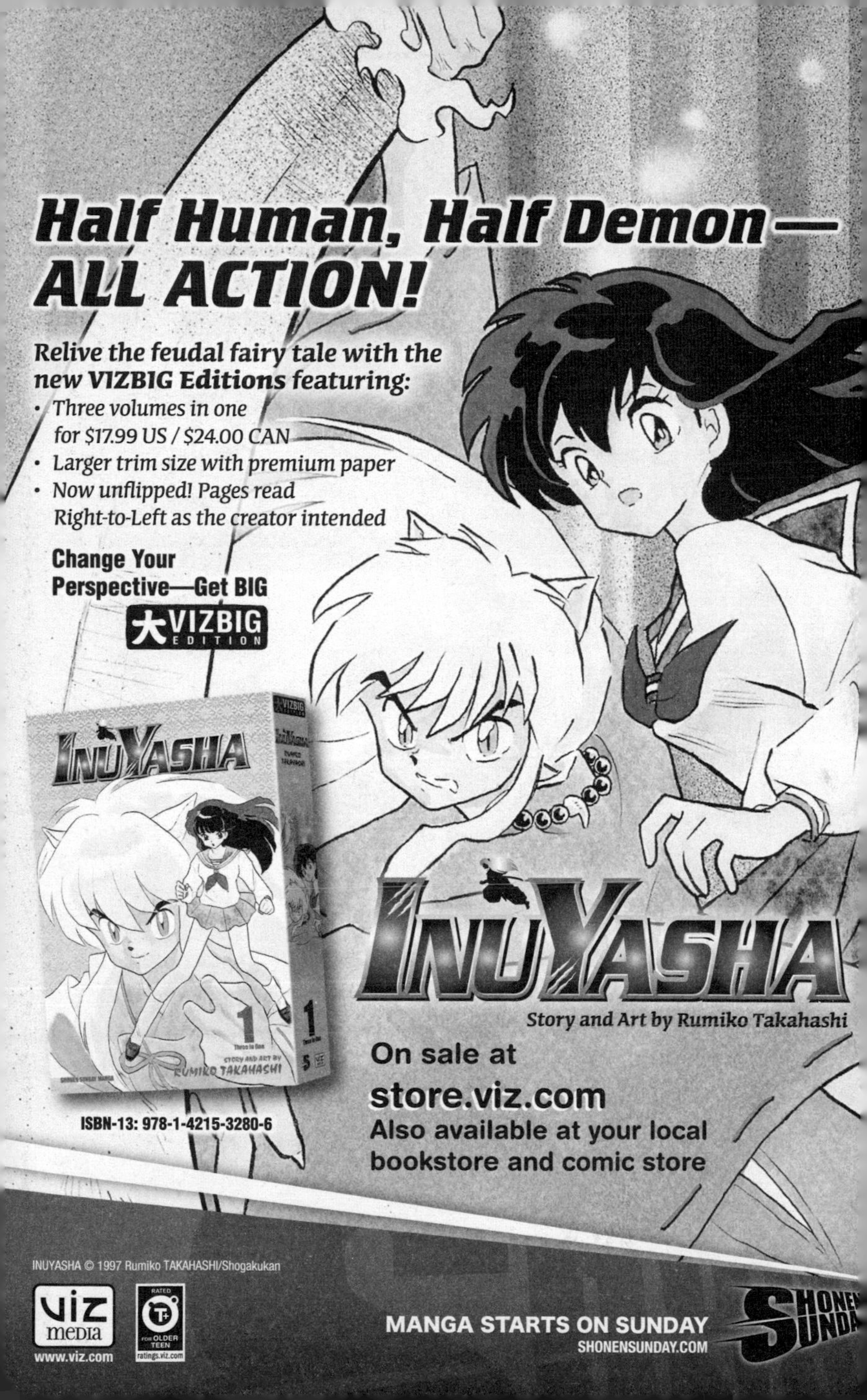
Half Human, Half Demon—
ALL ACTION!
Relive the feudal fairy tale with the new VIZBIG Editions featuring:
• Three volumes in one for $17.99 US / $24.00 CAN
• Larger trim size with premium paper
• Now unflipped! Pages read Right-to-Left as the creator intended
Change Your Perspective—Get BIG
大 VIZBIG EDITION
INUYASHA
Story and Art by Rumiko Takahashi
On sale at
store.viz.com
Also available at your local bookstore and comic store
ISBN-13: 978-1-4215-3280-6
INUYASHA © 1997 Rumiko TAKAHASHI/Shogakukan
viz media
www.viz.com
RATED T+ FOR OLDER TEEN
ratings.viz.com
MANGA STARTS ON SUNDAY
SHONENSUNDAY.COM

Hey! You're Reading in the Wrong Direction!

This is the **end** of this graphic novel!

To properly enjoy this VIZ graphic novel, please turn it around and begin reading from **right to left.** Unlike English, Japanese is read right to left, so Japanese comics are read in reverse order from the way English comics are typically read.

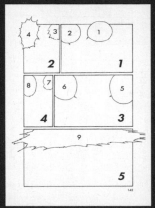

Follow the action this way

This book has been printed in the original Japanese format in order to preserve the orientation of the original artwork. Have fun with it!